Police Forces
in History

Police Forces in History

Edited by *George L. Mosse*

SAGE Readers in 20th Century History   Volume 2

SAGE Publications   London · Beverly Hills

For information address:

SAGE Publications Ltd.
44 Hatton Garden
London EC1N 8ER

SAGE Publications Inc.
275 South Beverly Drive
Beverly Hills, California 90212

International Standard Book Number 0–8039–9928–3 (paper)
0–8039–9934–8 (cloth)

Library of Congress Catalog Card Number 74–84258

First Printing

Printed and Bound in Great Britain by
Burgess & Son (Abingdon) Ltd., Abingdon, Oxfordshire

CONTENTS

NOTES ON CONTRIBUTORS

Tom Bowden is Senior Lecturer in Politics at Manchester Polytechnic,
UK. He has published numerous articles on political science,
and three books: *Community and Change* (1974); *Revolt to Revolution* (1974), and *Beyond the Limits of the Law: The Police in Crisis
Politics* (forthcoming Penguin special).

George C. Browder completed his Ph.D. at the University of Wisconsin at Madison, and is presently Associate Professor at the
State University of New York, Fredonia. He is currently working on the detective forces and security agencies from late Weimar
Germany through their final coordination in the Nazi *Sipo und SD*.

Nathan Douthit received his Ph.D. from the University of Cali-
fornia at Berkeley in 1972, and is presently Assistant Professor of
History and Instructor in Police Science at Southwestern Oregon
Community College in Coos Bay Oregon.

Rayner Heppenstall is a novelist and critic, and the author of four volumes on French criminal history: *A Little Pattern of French Crime, French Crime in the Romantic Age, Bluebeard and After,* and *The Sex War and Others.* He is also the author of *Reflections on the Newgate Calendar* (forthcoming, January 1975).

Peter Hoffmann was born in 1930, and currently holds the Chair of German History at McGill University, Montreal. His writings include *Die diplomatischen Beziehungen zwischen Württemberg und Bayern im Krimkrieg und bis zum Beginn der Italienienischen Krise, 1853–58; Widerstand, Staatsstreich, Attentat: Der Kampf der Opposition gegen Hitler* (English edition to be published early 1975); and a larger work on Hitler's residences, headquarters, and security to be published in Spring 1975. He is currently working on a study dealing with Stauffenberg.

Richard J. Johnson studied at the Russian Institute of Columbia University, and received his Ph.D. from Columbia in 1970. He is presently Associate Professor of Political Science at Glassboro State College, New Jersey.

Eric D. Kohler received his B.A. from Brown University in 1965, his M.A. from Stanford University in 1967, and his Ph.D. from Stanford (where he worked with Professor Gordon A. Craig) in 1971. He is presently Assistant Professor of History at the University of Wyoming at Laramie.

William R. Morrison is Assistant Professor of History at Brandon University, Brandon, Manitoba, Canada.

George L. Mosse is the Bascom Professor of History at the University of Wisconsin at Madison, and a co-editor of the *Journal of Contemporary History.*

James F. Richardson was born in New York City in 1931, and received his Ph.D. from New York University in 1961. He is presently Professor of History and Urban Studies at the University of Akron, Ohio. He is the author of *The New York Police: Colonial Times to 1901* (Oxford University Press: New York, 1970), and *Urban Police in the United States* (Kennikat Press: New York, 1974).

Cyril D. Robinson is Associate Professor of Criminal Justice at the Pennsylvania State University. He is a lawyer, and the author of many articles in law journals dealing with criminal procedure and control of police practices.

Lawrence D. Stokes received his Ph.D. from the Johns Hopkins University, Maryland in 1972, and is presently Associate Professor of History at Dalhousie University, Halifax, Nova Scotia, Canada. He has published articles on Dutch fascism and on German responses to the persecution of Jews under Nazism, as well as a bibliographical pamphlet on medieval and reformation Germany for the Historical Association, London. He is currently researching the political and social history of a town in northern Germany between the wars, and also working on a study of Canadian policy towards European refugees during the 1930s and 1940s.

Glen W. Swanson is Associate Professor and Chairman of the Department of History at Nathaniel Hawthorne College, Antrim, New Hampshire. He has studied at the University of Connecticut, the School of Oriental and African Studies at the University of London, and Indiana University, where he completed his Ph.D. in history in 1970. He has written several articles on the Middle East, and is now completing a book about the Young Turk period.

J. J. Tobias was for fifteen years on the staff of the Police College, Bramshill House, Basingstoke, UK, and toward the end of his work there was Director of Academic Studies of the Special Course. He is the author of *Crime and Industrial Society in the 19th Century* (1968); *Nineteenth-Century Crime Prevention and Punishment* (1972), and *Prince of Fences: The Life and Crimes of Ikey Solomons* (1974).

Police Forces in History: Introduction

George L. Mosse

From Elizabethan rogues and vagabonds to the riots of our cities, accounts of lawlessness and disorder have fascinated many a modern historian. The police, guardians of the peace, have not fared so well. Until fairly recently police history could easily be confused with adventure or detective stories. Yet the history of police forces assumed a special significance in the decade of the nineteen sixties, when, through a multitude of confrontations, the very word 'police' was transformed into a slogan: for some the guardians of the law became the enemies of the people, while for others they represented the last bastion of besieged society. The police force has always been a controversial institution, but today many seem to regard it as endowed with a life of its own and an uncontrollable urge to action.

A study of the history of the police can recall us to reality, for they have always been an integral part of the social and political fabric of the times. As an institution they are wholly dependent upon the values and the social structure of a particular society. Here as elsewhere, history can serve as part of a demystifying process. For example, durings the 1920s the Berlin police possessed all the ingredients American writers on police affairs thought necessary for their own departments: freedom from petty political pressure; a high level of education; and an ingrained distaste for corruption. Police forces in the United States, by contrast, were often corrupt and subject to political manipulation. But it was the 'exemplary' Weimar police who lost control of the streets while the police forces of the United States managed to retain control. Obviously, the strength and weaknesses of the national political structure were decisive. It is possible to experiment with various forms of police organization, as in the Ottoman Empire, but a disintegrating centre of political authority nullifies even the most laudable intention to keep law and order intact.

In our own century the relationship between the police and the state posed a special and ominous problem for parliamentary democracies. What for example, was to be the attitude of the police

POLICE FORCES IN HISTORY

towards political parties which, after all, provide the essential political mechanism and support for the liberal and parliamentary state. The Weimar Republic can serve to illustrate the dilemma: the police was to be the pillar of the state while, at the same time, hopefully, unresponsive to the appeal of all political parties, even those which supported the Republic. Such a contradictory attitude was built into the liberal polity. By being above politics, as it were, the police as individuals could exercise their freedom of choice among all political parties.[1] This was theory, but in practice, as Eric Kohler's chapter shows, the police took such freedom as licence to support parties hostile to that Republic which they were supposed to support. Freedom from petty political pressure was thought to be identical with standing above politics, and here the parallel with the *Reichswehr*, also supposedly 'above party', rightly springs to mind. Such a concept, even if proclaimed with the best of intentions, tended to be counterproductive from the point of view of the parliamentary and liberal state.

The idea of affirming the democratic state even while at liberty to join anti-democratic parties might make sense at a time when the liberal concept of the state was intact, but it was bound to fall victim to the general crisis of liberalism in the first half of the twentieth century. Indeed it is startling how many leading officials of the Nazi security police (SD), passed easily from service to the Republic to service to National Socialism. For example, Gerald Reitlinger tells us that as late at 1938 it was found that all but ten or fifteen out of a hundred Gestapo men in the city of Coblenz had joined the police under the Weimar Republic.[2] Heinrich Müller who became chief of the Gestapo and who played a crucial role in the 'final solution' of the Jewish question, had been praised during his service under the Republic as a 'matter of fact' official who showed great energy. Still more startling, Franz Josef Huber, a colleague of Müller's, had fought the NSDAP as a Republican police official, only to make a highly successful career in the political police of the Third Reich.[3] The motives which led to such easy change and continuity have not yet been investigated, and perhaps it will never be possible to do so. But the fact that the police were urged to be above politics, free from the 'luxury of

[1] Bernard Weiss, *Polizei und Politik* (Berlin 1928), 15, 18, 21.
[2] Gerald Reitlinger, *The SS: Alibi of a Nation* (London 1956), 39.
[3] Shlomo Aronson, *Reinhard Heydrich und die Frühgeschichte von Gestapo und SD* (Stuttgart 1971), 97.

2

political parties'[4] meant in practice that the custodians of law and order tended towards authoritarian groups which promised to sacrifice freedom to order. There is little evidence that men who had served the Republic loyally behaved better in the SD than a 'classical representative of the new SD generation'[5] like Otto Ohlendorf who joined the Nazi party at the age of eighteen, and to whom a chapter of this book is devoted. During the crisis of the democratic and liberal state the police became a centre of dissatisfaction, for they depended upon a strong national structure and instead, more often than not, found themselves surrounded by weakness and civil strife. In England, where the Parliamentary state remained strong in spite of all crises, the loyalty of the police was never in question, and its relationship to the population remained unique in its respect and popularity.

The police can cope with individual crimes and localized disorder, but they are apt to be powerless in a situation of undeclared civil war such as prevailed in Italy before the advent of fascism or in the last years of the Weimar Republic. Not only did they have to face paramilitary mass movements on a national scale, but the legal government had lost the will to take decisive action. Moreover, and equally serious, the judiciary was no longer willing to enforce the law upon those political criminals whom the police had managed to secure. The police can be paralyzed not only during a revolution, but also at a time when an indecisive central government is incapable of grappling with deep social and political divisions. They are subjected to social and political forces which are more often than not, beyond their control. Hence, the history of the police throws an important light upon the general state of society.

However, the police can become an instrument of power in their own right when they are transformed from a peace-keeping force into an instrument of political surveillance. This police function is of ancient origin, but in modern times it became total. Typically enough, for example, Soviet police activity has been greater than that of the notorious Czarist police, and where the Okhrana was an investigative body, however cruel, the Soviet police has both investigative and punitive functions.[6] Within the liberal and parliamentary state the police has the task of upholding the external

[4] The Prussian minister of internal affairs, Severing, quoted in Bernard Weiss, op. cit., 18.

[5] Shlomo Aronson, op. cit., 202.

[6] Ronald Hingley, *The Russian Secret Police* (London 1970), 271.

order and of protecting the individual, but in the anti-liberal state its tasks have no limits. Just as left or right saw in the liberal state an instrument of bourgeois rule and contrasted this with the 'true' rule of the people, so the task of the police opposed to liberalism was not to protect the individual but the community as a whole. The police, as a Nazi publication has it, 'must guard the health of the German Volk' and fight with all possible means the danger of disease and disintegration. This means that police are not merely government officials but must conceive of themselves instead as members of 'a fighting organization'.[7]

The police was here an integral part of a political party, the official party of the one party state. Just as treason was no longer defined by law as an 'overt act' of support for the enemy, but judged in accordance with loyalty to the ideology of the state (however often that might change), so the police had no legal limitations upon their power. The principle of political obligations between governed and governors was discarded on behalf of the state viewed as an instrument of the general will. This concept of democracy which brooked no limitations upon itself is basic to most modern authoritarian states, indeed it is inherent in much of modern mass politics. The police and its functions are always determined by the nature of the state which they serve and the theory upon which such a state is based. Thus in modern communist, fascist and all other authoritarian regimes the police force is apt to become a state within a state, and to serve as one of the principal pillars of a dictatorship, with all legal and traditional limits on its actions removed. This brings with it a fundamental change in police operations as they had developed through the years. The political police now becomes predominant: usually a new institution with cadres selected because of their loyalty to the regime. Thus Heinrich Himmler first founded a political 'security police' and then integrated the ordinary police into this new instrument of power. Violence against individuals was always possible as an abuse under ordinary police procedure, but violence against masses of the population required basic changes in organization and purpose. The history of the police as the agent of totalitarian regimes must be distinguished from its history as the guardian of law and order.

To these problems which concern the police and state, and which

[7] Adolf Liepelt, *Über den Umfang und die Bedeutung der Polizeigewalt im nationalsozialistischen Staat* (Würzburg 1938), 42.

are reflected in the subsequent pages, we must add that of the image of the police in the popular imagination. Such an image was spread by the press in earlier times, according to their political orientation, but it becomes crucial in the age of television. What was the effect of seeing the police in often brutal action during late nineteen sixties upon the popular imagination? Theodore H. White believed that the unfavourable way the police were shown on television at the Democratic National Convention in Chicago in 1968 was influenced by the harassment of television reporters by the Chicago police under the mantle of tight security.[8] Yet the police themselves can break under stress, no matter what the regime, and there have been police riots in recent years in the United States directed against dissidents and students who had harrassed the 'pigs' (as they called them) unmercifully. The image of the police in the popular imagination and in the minds of dissidents or of those who riot is equally dissidents and students who had harassed the 'pigs' (as they called mand or fulfilling a duty, but a force larger than life which is either to be feared or praised.

We need much more investigation into the image of the police in different societies, among different groups and, last but not least, among the individual policemen themselves. Such investigations not only entail an analysis of the state and society, but also of the mass media. Thus, it seems clear from the American experience, that however brutal the image of the police which comes over the screen, the vast majority of the population feels satisfaction in seeing law and order prevail in times of crisis and is not particularly squeamish over the methods used. Such feeling may be a danger to individual rights and liberties in parliamentary states, even if their political fabric is strong and intact.

Police history is as yet in its infancy. The problems raised in this introduction are only a few of the many worth investigation. Historians have analyzed almost every aspect of the men, movements and states which rule over us; it seems high time to examine in greater depth the prime instrument of power of the modern state. It is hoped that this book, however incomplete in its coverage, might stimulate further research in this field.

George L. Mosse

[8] Theodor H. White, *The Making of the President 1968* (New York 1970), 327, 328.

Balzac's Policemen

Rayner Heppenstall

Prostitution and crime greatly preoccupied French novelists in the Romantic age, including those who were also, and whom we may think of as primarily, poets. Théophile Gautier's poem on the mummified 'hand of glory' of the executed murderer Lacenaire is perhaps sufficiently well known; less so the fact that to the nine volumes of *Les Français peints par eux-mêmes* he contributed, in 1841, two years before Dumas's *Filles, Lorettes et Courtisanes*, a pornotypological monograph on *Le Rat*, the juvenile, or, as we might now say, nymphet appurtenance to noblemen's households. Like everything about him, Victor Hugo's concern with the criminal classes, from the Middle Ages to his own protracted time, was vast. He took, indeed, little enough interest in prostitution, more in murder or, rather, in its consequences. For Hugo was an insistent penal reformer, more especially in respect of capital punishment, which he denounced mightily at intervals over a period of 22 years, from the publication of *Le Dernier Jour d'un Condamné* in 1829 to a curious appearance as defending counsel at assizes only a matter of months before his 20 years' exile began.

It was not to be until that exile had already lasted 11 years that, from Guernsey, in 1862, Victor Hugo, with *Les Misérables*, gave the nineteenth century and perhaps all time one of its three or four greatest novels. Apart from Jean Valjean, the unjustly sentenced, heroic, and saintly escaped convict, its two most memorable characters are, to many minds, the street urchin Gavroche and the policeman Javert. This last is not a sympathetic figure. Indeed, in respect of the trouble he causes throughout the whole work, he must be regarded as one of its two principal villains. And yet, as Jean Valjean does, we must respect him, insensitive, hard-hearted and even vindictive as he may be, for his devotion to duty, his dedication to a task we are meant to think misconceived. When Valjean has saved his life and he has let Valjean go, the life

7

saved by a convict no longer makes sense to him, and he jumps into the Seine off the parapet between the Pont Notre-Dame and the Pont au Change, where the current is stiffest. We see his end as at once fitting, noble, and comical, and Hugo gives it a special emphasis by making the chapter in which it is recounted the only one in Part V, Book 4.

The riots to which, in the novel, these episodes form an epilogue were, it may be noted, those of June 1832, directly ensuing upon the funeral of General Lamarque, though no doubt with deeper causes, among them a cholera epidemic of which Alfred de Musset's father was a victim but to which neither Hugo nor Balzac paid literary attention.

Louis Philippe had been king of the French for two years past. Victor Hugo and Alexandre Dumas were men of 30, Honoré de Balzac of 33 years, Théophile Gautier a stripling not yet quite 21. Largely unbought in bookshops lay a novel, *Le Rouge et le Noir*, based on a real-life murder near his home town of Grenoble, by a middle-aged and pseudonymous French consular official in Italy. The prefect of police in Paris was Gisquet. At the Petite Rue Ste Anne, the Brigade de Sûreté was again for the moment headed by Vidocq, whose active part in controlling the riots was to be paid public tribute at the highest level.[1] A younger policeman on duty was, 30 years later, to describe the riots as he had seen them with a vividness approaching Hugo's and with more truth.[2]

It is somewhat by accident that the June days of 1832 have provided us with a first standpoint date, but it will do as well as any. By then, Balzac had published, of the novels in which his policemen appear, only *Les Chouans*, whose action dates back as far as 1799 and in which figures Corentin, most respectable and surviving member of the trio against whom, 20 years later in *Splendeurs et Misères des Courtisanes*, the assiduous Balzac reader would see Vautrin's wits victoriously pitted, in an action whose supposed date was early 1830. For, although to us the fact may rarely be obvious, Balzac's novels are almost invariably historical, in that their action precedes the time of writing by an average of some 20 years. Until the last years of his life, it was very uncommon indeed for him to write about his own time in the sense of the time at which he was writing or a mere year or so

[1] See P. J. Stead, *Vidocq, Picaroon of Crime* (1953), 133-38.
[2] *Mémoires de Canler*, first complete edition 1882, reprinted 1968.

before it.[3] The distancing is much the same as in Proust. The one is as full as the other of *temps perdu*, though Balzac does not dwell on it subjectively as such, far less as *temps retrouvé*, despite a passage towards the end of *Illusions Perdues* which Proust's M. de Charlus, invoking a poem by Victor Hugo, was to recall Swann describing as the *Tristesse d'Olympio* of pederasty. Thus, in the novels and the play which most directly concern us, he is writing in 1827 of 1799, in 1834 of 1819–20, in 1840 of 1816, in 1841 of 1803–16, in 1844–45 of 1809, and in 1847 of 1830. More broadly, we may say that towards the close of the reign of Charles X he wrote about the police of the Consulate, and that under Louis-Philippe, though with major reversions, he recalled police matters from beginning to end of the Restoration.

More broadly still, we may perhaps also say that, in our own terms, his interest was veering from the work of Special Branch to that of plain CID, from spy thriller to murder mystery. For at no time and in no country has the uniformed policeman on his beat received much attention from novelists and their public. It is true that, at need, a detachment of gendarmerie will gallop up to arrest Lucien de Rubempré, and that other gendarmes will be seen loafing about the Law Courts, just as two had waited handily outside the church at Verrières to arrest Julien Sorel the moment he fired his pistol at Mme de Rênal. But Messrs Peyrade, Corentin, and Contenson had known the darkest state secrets before they were involved with fraud, theft, and murder, while convict garb was the only uniform Bibi-Lupin or Jacques Collin, *dit* Vautrin, had ever worn. Similarly, in London, no sooner had we started our own CID than Dickens was introducing Inspector Bucket. This he did, we may note, six years after Balzac had effected in Vautrin a transformation which real life had effected 35 years before in Vidocq. Eight years after *Bleak House*, a year before the completion of *Les Misérables*, but 14 years after *Splendeurs et Misères* and 27 after *Le Père Goriot*, Dickens would be giving us his version of the beneficent escaped convict, similarly distanced historically.

IN *Les Chouans*, by command of the great Fouché, a beautiful spy

---

[3] A critical fact of the highest importance, this is admirably brought home by the table in Félicien Marceau's Preface to his *Balzac et son Monde* (1955). The authority there quoted, M. Pierre Abraham, makes the average time-lag 15 years, but has his own way of working out averages.

is sent out to lure the young leader of the Breton royalists to his doom. They fall in love and meet this doom together. Then a green-eyed young man in his early twenties, dressed in the fashion of the *incroyables*, Corentin, like a commissar with a Russian football team or a shop steward with a delegation of workmen, is of the lady's party. Though she finds him reprehensibly cold, he himself loves or at least desires her. One is led to feel that he is in some way responsible for the fatal outcome, and indeed he forges a letter which has some effect. There is no reason whatever to suppose that, in 1827, Balzac intended to use him as a character again, as indeed he would not do for the next 14 years.

Within a year or so of the publication of *Les Chouans*, he must inevitably have heard a fair amount about Vidocq, the four volumes of whose ghosted memoirs enjoyed a great vogue, though it appears that Balzac himself did not buy them until early 1830.[4] During the revolution of that year and the riots of two years later, he wrote a very great deal but none of it about police matters. In 1833, we meet his first escaped convict in *Ferragus*, a short novel to which, the following year, were added two others, *La Duchesse de Langeais* and *La Fille aux Yeux d'Or*, making up *Histoire des Treize*. In *Ferragus*, Vidocq 'and his sleuth-hounds' (*limiers*) are mentioned briefly and supply useful information by way of 'le chef de la police particulière', an expression to which I can give no real-life meaning. On Saturday, 26 April 1834, Balzac dined with Vidocq at the house of the rich philanthropist, Benjamin Appert, in Neuilly. This dinner party must have been one of the most remarkable occasions in literary or perhaps any other history. Among the other guests were Alexandre Dumas, the public executioner, Sanson the younger, and the English radical Lord Durham, who was greatly interested in the guillotine and in French prisons.[5]

That year, Balzac wrote his best-known novel, *Le Père Goriot*, in which first appeared the figure of Jacques Collin, known as Vautrin, the escaped convict who became a police chief. To what extent this most famous of Balzac's characters was 'based on' the

[4] The date is known from a bookseller's invoice. See the Introduction by P. G. Castex to his Classiques Garnier edition of *Le Père Goriot*, xxvii.

[5] A brief account of the proceedings may be found in the present writer's *French Crime in the Romantic Age* (London 1970), 101. The sources are listed by Castex in his *Père Goriot* Introduction.

world's most widely heard-of and frequently mentioned real-life detective is a matter of frequent debate, in which I have myself joined more than once.[6] I shall say little about either here. Should it be suggested that this article ought therefore to have been called 'Balzac's *Other* Policemen', a sufficient answer might be found in the fact that, among the hundreds of pages in which Vautrin appears in four novels and a play, only twice, for half a page or less at a time,[7] is it as a policeman. In *Le Père Goriot*, the Vidocq of the day is called Gondureau.

The play *Vautrin* ran for one night. This was on 14 March 1840. It is not a good play, but the reason for the shortness of its run was that the heir to the throne was present at the first and last night and that in one scene the great comedian, Frederick Lemaître, had been made up to look like Louis-Philippe.[8]

The action of *Le Père Goriot* takes place in 1819-20, that of *Vautrin* three years earlier, in 1816, at the beginning of the Restoration, while the Allies still had their military police in Paris. There are no legitimate policemen in the cast, apart from those who appear in the last scene to arrest Vautrin-Collin, much as others do, three supposed years later, in *Le Père Goriot*; but one impostor, in Act Two, laments the disbanding of Napoleon's 'magnificent Asiatic police' and says, no doubt with reason, that if Fouché's organization had remained intact, the return from Elba would have been effectively opposed, and Louis XVIII need not have fled to Ghent (so that the French would have been spared their traumatic defeat at Waterloo). He also says that 'you might as well resign', now that 'they're trying to get police work done by respectable people'—a fact more apparent, with its disadvantages, in 1840 than in 1816. We shall find similar laments, on other lips for other great days, in the later novels. For Balzac's policemen, times have always been better.

The action of *Une Ténébreuse Affaire*, written in 1841, begins in 1803, a mere four years after that of *Les Chouans*. The cold Corentin is still a young man. Of the eventual fearsome trio of *Splendeurs et Misères*, the unfortunate Contenson has not yet appeared in Balzac's work, but Corentin is found in the neighbour-

[6] *French Crime in the Romantic Age*, 113–15; Introduction to my translation of *Splendeurs et Misères*, *A Harlot High and Low*, viii–x.

[7] *Splendeurs et Misères*, concluding paragraphs, and *La Cousine Bette*.

[8] See for example Robert Baldick, *The Life and Times of Frédérick Lemaître* (London 1959), 179–81; Stead, op. cit., 175.

hood of Troyes in the company of a man almost twice his age, Peyrade, a Provençal, whose career in the police goes back to the days of the *ancien régime*. He is a *viveur*, whose vices have impeded his advancement in the service. He has a big nose, grog blossoms, no teeth, and small piglike eyes. His clothes are too large for him and infrequently laundered. The two are looking for four young noblemen believed to be involved in a Royalist plot. They 'frame' these four and a local farmer, Michu, on criminal charges of abduction and illegal restraint, which in the transitional code of the day might carry the death penalty. Michu is in fact executed. *Une Ténébreuse Affaire* is, essentially, the account of a grave miscarriage of justice. Its purely juridical side strikes me as wholly admirable, a fact by no means simply to be ascribed to Balzac's own law studies at a time when the Napoleonic codes had been in full operation for seven or eight years. The police side of the matter is perhaps less good, but it is interesting. The gendarmerie of Troyes and Arcis are active, and two officers are even given names. Though Corentin and Peyrade machinate perhaps a little too madly even for Fouché's day, the former performs at least one smart piece of detection in the modern manner (how had the gendarme and his horse so remarkably parted company in mid-canter ?), and much use is made of differing hoof prints both as real and 'planted' evidence. The lawyers and magistrates,[9] it may be said, come out of the matter with reasonable credit.

It is in the spring of 1830 that, in what is now the second of the four parts of *Splendeurs et Misères des Courtisanes*, Contenson is pitched to his death off a roof top by Vautrin, then disguised as a Spanish priest. Of the famous trio, he there appears to be the social inferior not only of Corentin but also of Peyrade. His declumination was recounted to magazine readers before they heard in 1845 of his early life, in *Madame de la Chanterie*, the first half of what three years later would become *L'Envers de l'Histoire Contemporaine*. As Contenson, he, like Corentin and Peyrade, lacks

---

[9] The word 'magistrate' has a closely restricted use with us. In France, the equivalents of our High Court Judges, our Director of Public Prosecutions, our Coroners and, in all criminal actions, prosecuting counsel are *magistrats*. So, during their term of office, are the President of the Republic and the mayors of tiny rural districts. These, we may find excuse for noting here, employ their own *gardes champêtres*, who are nevertheless policemen. There is a *garde champêtre* in *Une Ténébreuse Affaire*, as well as the mayor of a small rural commune.

any Christian name. 'Contenson' was a name he adopted on joining the police. His name till then had been Bernard-Polydore, Baron Bryond des Tours-Minières, in his early manhood a Chouan but unincriminated in the attack on the returning Caen mail which, in 1809, led his abandoned wife to the scaffold and his mother-in-law, the saintly Mme de la Chanterie, to the start of a 20-year prison sentence. This case closely reflects one of 1807–08, a year before that in the novel, from real life,[10] for which the long indictment or *acte d'accusation* upon which it was tried at Rouen is, in the novel, reproduced almost verbatim, though abridged and with the names altered.[11]

After reading *Mme de la Chanterie*, few of Balzac's readers can have felt that Contenson's fate was undeserved. Whatever they may have felt about Peyrade, who dies poisoned shortly before the scene on the roof top, they must have remained unhappy about the treatment of his daughter, abducted and confined in a brothel, where forcible debauch has driven her out of her mind. In *Splendeurs et Misères*, neither Contenson nor Peyrade, for the best of reasons, reappears after those first two parts which, under the title of *La Torpille*, had been published before *Mme de la Chanterie*. As we first met him there, Contenson, already a man in his sixties, engaged by the lovesick Nucingen to look for Esther, had come down to working for a detective agency, mainly on behalf of commercial interests. Peyrade, whom we meet again in the pages which immediately follow and who had at one time risen through the younger Corentin to be general commissioner of police in Antwerp, had also fallen on lean days, but was pinning his hopes on an appointment to set up what would still be urgently needed in Paris until recent times, a clearing office for information available both to the Quai des Orfèvres and to what became first the Sûreté Générale and then the Sûreté Nationale, under the Ministry of the Interior, which seems at last to have gathered even the gendarmerie under its wing. The prudent Corentin, somewhat redeemed by his friendship for old Peyrade

[10] Not the famous attack on the Lyons mail, which, though its reverberations sounded all through Balzac's life, dates back to 1796, but an attack on the returning Alençon mail, planned indeed by a young woman of noble antecedents and incriminating her mother. As in the novel, two members of the gendarmerie were among the accused.

[11] The original is printed in full by Regard in his Classiques Garnier edition of *L'Envers de l'Histoire Contemporaine*.

and subsequent care of his daughter, still flourished and would continue to flourish for at least 10 years more.

La dernière Incarnation de Vautrin, which we now read as the fourth and concluding part of Splendeurs et Misères des Courtisanes, was written in 1847. Its action takes place very shortly before the revolution of 1830. The summation of its numerous peripeteia is that, shattered by the suicide of Lucien de Rubempré, the ex-convict renounces his war against society and is appointed its criminal watchdog. The man he replaces as head of the Brigade de Sûreté is Bibi-Lupin, also an ex-convict and his personal enemy. Bibi-Lupin's comical name inevitably suggests that of Coco-Lacour, more properly Barthélemy ('Coco') Lacour, who in real life had replaced Vidocq in the Petite Rue Ste Anne in 1827 and who, by 1830, had himself been replaced by a respectable divisional superintendent, Hébert. But in the concluding sentence of Splendeurs et Misères, we read that Vautrin exercised his functions as head of the Sûreté 'for some fifteen years' until his retirement 'in about 1845'. Well, indeed, François Vidocq also had exercised his functions for some 15 years, but his main tenure of office had been from 1812 to 1827. At least in respect of his dates, he was not Vautrin.

During the greater part of the latter's supposed tenure of office, the job was in real life held by Pierre Allard, with Louis Canler, for long his chief inspector, replacing him for a while between the revolution of 1848 and the coup d'état of 1851, which befell shortly after Balzac's death and drove Victor Hugo into exile. The most famous cases handled by Allard and Canler were those of Lacenaire and the Fieschi attentat, both in 1835, both very carefully written up by Canler in retirement.[12] Allard appears briefly and ineffectually in the early stages of the case of Marie Lafarge, when a school friend's husband, Viscount Léautaud, who had been putting her up, accused her of theft; but Canler says nothing about this, and the main charges against her were incurred far off their manor. That was in 1840. By 1847, when the Duc de Praslin hacked his wife to death and poisoned himself, Canler and Allard were no longer on speaking terms, the former having in consequence got himself appointed divisional superintendent of the VIth arrondissement, with additional supervision of the theatres in the Boulevard du Temple, where, in 1848 and

[12] Op. cit., 191–208, 211–20.

again in the summer of 1849, after replacing Allard, he came into contact with Dumas in connection with a recalcitrant actor at the first night of *Monte Cristo* and with a theft of jewels from one of the actresses at the Théâtre Historique.[13]

About Lacenaire, Fieschi, and especially the Duc de Praslin, there is a fair amount in those jottings of Victor Hugo's which after his death were to be put together in the volume called *Choses Vues*. Of Lacenaire he also made a symbolic figure, emerging, in a theatrical metaphor, from society's *troisième dessous*, in a much-quoted passage of *Les Misérables*.[14] In *L'Envers de L'Histoire Contemporaine*, the *attentats du parti républicain* upon which Godefroid reflects must have included Fieschi's, while it is a reference of his to the recent execution of Lacenaire, though not by name, which provokes the telling of Mme de la Chanterie's dreadful story. It is known that in *Lamiel*, whose fragments were not to be published till 1889, Stendhal, who died in 1842, had intended to portray a figure resembling Lacenaire, of whose character there may indeed be traces, among those of others, in Vautrin, as there may of men like Allard and Canler in the upright and persistent Javert. But in neither Balzac nor Hugo is there any close fictional or dramatic representation of any of these later matters or of the police work they involved.

In the metropolitan or any large context, until what we may think of as Vautrin's 'conversion' (which was to have no important fictional consequences), Balzac's interest had lain almost exclusively in the dark political side of policemanship. The latent tautology is to this day more apparent in French than in English. To us, 'the police' means simply a collectivity of policemen, whereas '*la police*' could mean an insurance policy and in Balzac hesitates between various meanings, rarely quite distinct from politics, secret and rather sinister politics at that. He does not use the word when he comes to mere gendarmerie, *gardes champêtres* and so on, who abound in the late country novels. There is another ex-convict in *Le Curé de Village*, and in *Les Paysans* most of the local names, as though for the purposes of a private joke, begin with V. The Gondureau or Bibi-Lupin man from Paris,

[13] Ibid., 369–70, 488.
[14] In his *Studies of French Criminals of the Nineteenth Century* (1901), 'third sub-stage' is the translation of *troisième dessous* given by H. B. Irving, who must have known as much about theatres as any man.

15

however, who comes to investigate the murder mystery and retires baffled, is nameless.

IN JULY 1850, A MONTH before Balzac's death, Victor Hugo visited him. They talked a long time and disagreed over politics. Balzac charged Hugo with demagogy. He was himself a legitimist. Yet it was Balzac who had started off liberal and anti-clerical, Hugo who 30 years before had written a powerful lament on the assassination of the Duc de Berri and spoken up for the *ultras* accused of the murder of Fualdès. The later Hugo commonly gives the impression of being on the side of the criminal against the police. This, we may think, is normal with visionary progressives. The odd thing is that the reactionary Balzac sometimes gives the same impression.

Few of us, unfortunately, whether progressive or reactionary, are quite proof against a tendency to judge criminal actions by other standards. Balzac condoned those of Royalist conspirators during his boyhood. In consequence, he could not forgive old hands of Fouché's police who survived in his adult years. The glamour attached for him to Royalist plotters was however almost purely literary. The Chouans, in particular, provided him with a French equivalent of Jacobites in the world of Sir Walter Scott. There are murders in those of his later novels which deal with the world more nearly of the time at which he wrote. His interest in these seems merely that of the ordinary, law-abiding, not particularly well-informed newspaper reader today.

Victor Hugo, on the other hand, was a dedicated penal reformer, a bemused evolutionary optimist. He looked forward to a world in which universal education and the removal of poverty would have put an end to crime, so that there would be no need for prisons or the guillotine or policemen, who could therefore all go and jump in the river. The criminals whom Hugo shows us being punished are therefore not really criminals. All Jean Valjean had done was to steal a loaf of bread when children were hungry. It had been much the same with Claude Gueux, who, once in prison, was intolerably provoked by a sadistic head warder. Just what had been done and under what circumstances by the protagonist of *Le Dernier Jour d'un Condamné* is left vague. He was a good man who had, apparently, killed somebody in justified anger. They were all metaphysically innocent.

Zagranichnaia Agentura: The Tsarist Political Police in Europe

Richard J. Johnson

Anti-tsarist political emigration, of sufficient size to be a recognized problem, dates from the 1870s, when the struggle against the autocracy was being conducted by the Party of the People's Will (Narodnaia Volia) through an active campaign of terror against Russian officials. During the 1870s, however, political emigrés were not given serious attention by the regime, and the Russian police operated abroad only to a very limited extent. Foreign operations were often in the hands of several people, each directly responsible to the Third Section of His Majesty's Personal Chancellery. Their work was generally carried out in secret and consisted mainly of surveillance.

An important turning-point in the development of the Russian political police occurred in 1881, in the wake of the assassination of Tsar Alexander II. The police system was reorganized under a newly created Ministry of Internal Affairs, thus effectively centralizing both regular and political police under a single authority. Police functions were centred in the Department of Police in St Petersburg, and, following the tradition of foreign ministries in Europe, came to be known by its location at 17 Ulitsa Fontanka. In common police parlance, the Department of Police became simply 'Fontanka'. The political police were removed from the Tsar's Personal Chancellery and became known as the Political Section of the Police Department. Later, apparently in an attempt to obscure the role and importance of the political police, its name was changed to Osoby Otdel, or Special Section, but its function remained unchanged. The

Osoby Otdel dealt exclusively with political crimes and coordinated the activities of the provincial political police agencies organized by Zubatov in 1902-03 and called Okhrannye Otdelenii, or Security Divisions.[1] In common police usage, the latter were referred to as 'O.O.s'.

The importance of the reorganization of police functions lay in the fact that it was the first serious recognition of a new direction in anti-regime activity. The old Third Section had been principally concerned with the attitudes and activities of the nobility at the court and the officer corps. Historically, threats to the security of the Tsar had come from these quarters, in a position to engineer the palace coups which were so characteristic of Russian political life. The creation of the Department of Police testified to a new element of political insecurity—the radical intelligentsia, with increasing support from a large part of the Russian population. After the assassination of Alexander II, the police became involved for the first time with the 'all-sided surveillance' of the Russian people. Police reorganization was intended to facilitate such surveillance, with special attention being given to urban workers, students, professors, teachers, artists, writers, and the zemstvo intelligentsia.[2]

The 1880s and 1890s were years of extensive and successful police repression of practically all radical Russian political groups—not just the Narodnaia Volia terrorists. Success could be measured not only by the increase in the number of 'politicals' in Russian prisons, but also by the growing number of political emigrés. Most of these emigrés left Russia in fear of their own security, realizing that conditions at home were not propitious for conspiracy. There were others, however, who made their way to 'free Europe' as a consequence of the relatively liberal practices of the Russian police. The political police exercised the legal right

[1] Zubatov is best known, of course, as the originator of 'police socialism', an attempt by the police to control the Russian trade union movement by sponsoring their own legal unions. It is from the Okhrannye Otdelenii that the term 'Okhrana', as a general reference to the Russian political police, apparently originated.

[2] cf. P. Struve, 'Rossiia pod nadzorom politsii', *Osvobozhdenie*, 19 August 1903, 86.

of administrative exile over 'politicals'. In most cases, the individual was exiled to Siberia or some other remote part of the Empire. It became a rather common practice, however, to offer the best-connected radicals the alternative of expulsion to Europe, on the understanding that their illegal return to Russia would constitute grounds for imprisonment.

The Okhrana clearly hoped that expulsion to Europe would act as a prophylactic. Revolutionary contacts would be broken, and the threat of jail should be sufficient reason not to return. In time they would either assimilate themselves to their European environment and renounce their Russian citizenship, or, in the wisdom that would come with age, they would expiate their political sins and plead to be allowed to return to Russia.

Foreign exile, however, was no greater restraint on radicalism than was Siberian exile. Rather than repenting or simply settling into a more relaxed European life, many of the emigrés used their relative freedom to plan subversion and terror. The same characteristics which impelled them to revolutionary activity rendered them unsuitable for assimilation. Moreover, because of language difficulties and discrimination, many found it difficult to find useful employment in Europe. By inclination and force of circumstance, most were led to continue a bohemian existence on the fringes of European social life. The problem of the Russian radical had not been solved. It had simply been removed to a distance. For the police, the question was how to deal with the emigré who, alas, had not changed his ways. The answer was the extension of the Okhrana abroad through the creation of a Foreign Agency in Paris, with satellite offices in Berlin and the Balkans.

The Foreign Agency set up shop in the Russian embassy in Paris in 1885. For most purposes, it was viewed as simply another 'O.O.', but distinguished from the latter by the fact that it was located outside Russia and therefore required rather special treatment. Organizationally, it was responsible, through its head, directly to Fontanka. Reports to St Petersburg were made frequently, and at least once a month.

Similarly, the Police Department gave broad guidance to the work of the Agency through general operational directives and, on occasion, through more explicit orders to take various kinds of action against the emigré. In practice however, the judgment of one historian that the independence of the Agency's head was almost total, seems to be accurate.[3] Operating conspiratorially, controlling its own agents, distant from the prying eyes of Fontanka, the Agency would have been difficult to control in any case. In fact, its heads tended to view Europe as their private sphere of interest and balked at any actions by Fontanka which might preempt or circumvent their authority. The following communication to the Director of the Police Department is instructive:

> From the letter of our Envoy to the Swiss Republic, I see, among other things, that a code for secret messages has been established between the Department of Police and Hodier [head of the Swiss Federal Police] ... I humbly beg to raise the consideration that in the very interest of investigations abroad, it would be better if direct communications with representatives of police institutions abroad were undertaken by the Department of Police only in cases of extreme necessity, and not in common everyday matters, since such direct relations with Petersburg might be construed by the foreign powers as enabling them to ignore the direct authority of the Head of the Foreign Agency, resulting in the undermining of his relations with these representatives. Thus, for example, in the Berlin [Police] Praesidium, they are surprised that the Department of Police applies directly to them for information, passing over their official representative abroad, and I regret to say that Nikolai Sofronsky was arrested by the Praesidium without my prior agreement, when it was known to me that he was planning to go to Russia soon and that an arms affair planned by him might have taken an unhappy turn.[4]

[3] S.M. LaPorte, *Histoire de l'Okhrana, la police secrète des tsars, 1880-1917* (Paris 1935), 187.

[4] *Okhrana Archives*, 36, Vf, 1. Harting to Department of Police, 12 January 1907. The primary source for this study is the archival collection of Foreign Agency documents housed at the Hoover Institution, Palo Alto, California, and referred to here as 'Okhrana Archives'. The documents in this collection are arranged in boxes, index

While such an outspoken defence of administrative prerogative was rare, communications with Fontanka are rife with the implicit or explicit assertion that the Foreign Agency could fulfill its functions only if interference from Petersburg were minimized.

Given his relative independence, and his responsibility for controlling some of the most dangerous and prominent 'politicals', the job of the head of the Foreign Agency must be regarded as one of the most important in the Russian police hierarchy. Only the Director and Vice-Directors of the Police Department, the head of the Osoby Otdel, and the chief of the Moscow O.O. had equal or greater prestige. The Agency head's salary was commensurate with his bureaucratic rank as Active State Councillor: 24,000 francs per year, plus expenses, in 1914.[5]

During its thirty-two years of existence, there were only four heads of the Agency: Rachkovsky, 1885-1902; Rataev, 1902-05; Harting, 1905-09; and Krassilnikov, 1909-17. This relative stability, contrasting sharply with the much more rapid turnover of the top personnel at Fontanka, was both witness to, and partly responsible for, the relative effectiveness and independence of the Agency. Each of the heads was a police professional upon coming to the Foreign Agency. Rachkovsky and Harting were both former revolutionaries-turned-spies who worked their way up the police hierarchy on the basis of serious provocational work. Harting, in fact, was still wanted by the French police for his part in a terrorist conspiracy at the time he took over as head of the Foreign Agency in 1905. Rataev, on the other hand, was a long-time 'straight' police employee who came to Paris from the headship of the Osoby Otdel. Of the four Agency heads, only Krassilnikov had made his career through the quasi-military Corps of Gendarmes and had held military

---

numbers relating to particular topics, and folders holding collections of documents on a particular subject. The citation above, then, refers to a specific report by Harting to Petersburg, found in Box 36, index Vf, folder 3 of the Archives. Hereafter, all citations of Foreign Agency documents will be by box, index, and folder number only.

[5] 26, IVa lB. Smeta zagranichnoi agentury, 24 March 1914.

rank. All appear to have had the professional respect of their European counterparts.

The head of the Foreign Agency was directly responsible for planning and supervising the execution of all Agency operations. His principal tasks, however, were to maintain liaison with foreign police, evaluate information from both surveillance agents and internal collaborators, and to pass that information on in summary form to Fontanka.

Like the security divisions in Russia, the Foreign Agency consisted of four different groups of individuals. The least important was the clerical-secretarial staff, housed with the head in the Paris Embassy. It dealt with translating, copying, typing, and handling the financial accounts of the Agency. More important were the case officers, Russian police, usually from the Corps of Gendarmes, who maintained liaison with secret collaborators and reported directly to the head. Conspiratorial relations required that case officers should not be seen at the embassy, and they maintained their own apartments and several 'conspiratorial' apartments (konspiratyvnye kvartiry) for the purpose of meeting their agents. There were never more than three case officers working for the Foreign Agency at one time, and each was responsible for at most a dozen agents.

The 'internal agency', i.e. the group of revolutionary collaborators controlled by the case officers, was at the heart of successful information-gathering. Varying in size, but never larger than about thirty at any one time, the internal agency provided the most concrete evidence of criminal conspiracies among the revolutionaries. During most of the Agency's history, there were internals (sometimes called *seksoty*, or secret collaborators) in practically every important revolutionary circle, and, where possible, two in each group in order to provide a check on each other's loyalty. The terrorist Evno Azev, in fact, was controlled through the Foreign Agency until the retirement of Rataev in 1905, when he was transferred for work under General Gerasimov at the Moscow O.O.

Internals were generally well paid. A typical salary in 1912, for instance, was about 500 francs per month. Some received as much as 2000 francs per month—the equivalent of the Agency head's salary.[6] In addition, they were often reimbursed for extraordinary expenses and given bonuses for particularly helpful information. With a few exceptions, they reported to case officers, and had no contact with the Agency head. In fact, they were not supposed to know of the existence of the Foreign Agency or the identity of any other collaborator.

Obviously, internal agents needed very special handling and created special problems. Thus when Rachkovsky described his internals to the Director of the Sûreté Générale as being 'of deep conviction and in stern opposition to the very principles of the revolutionary movement in my country', he was indulging in propaganda. While the description may have accurately depicted some of the internals, many more were, like Rachkovsky himself, attracted into double-agency mainly as a means of avoiding police punishment. Another assessment of internals, made by Zubatov, seems more realistic: 'of weak character, deceived by the party, miserable, or designated for deportation. Those who agree to furnish information will neither renounce their convictions, nor modify in any way their style of life'.[7] Agency files tend to corroborate this judgment. One collaborator killed the case-officer, von Kotten, in Paris; another committed suicide shortly after the head of the Belgian Sûreté had reported to Krassilnikov that the agent appeared to be mentally unbalanced. In general, the reliability of internals was not high. For most of them, loyalty was bought by cash.

The second major group within the Foreign Agency was the so-called 'external agency', comprising investigative and surveillance detectives. Unlike internals, all of whom were Russian, no detectives in the external agency were Russian. They were all native to the country in which they habitually worked—an obvious requirement to avoid attracting suspicion and to facilitate contacts with non-Russians for the purpose of acquiring information. Most of them had prior experience

[6] 11, IIIb, 18. Erhardt's agent accounts for January 1912.
[7] LaPorte, op. cit., 38.

23

either as private detectives or as regular police agents in the countries in which they operated.

Until about 1903, surveillance agents reported to a Russian case-officer who transmitted their written reports to the Agency head. After that date, certain long-time and trusted detectives (notably Maurice Bittard-Monin and Henri Bint) became responsible for assigning surveillance agents and for receiving their reports. It appears, however, that the Agency head received some reports directly from the field throughout the entire period. The system of handling externals, in short, was not clear-cut. Like internals, the ordinary surveillance agents were supposed to be ignorant of the Agency's existence, but the secret was not well kept.

Partly because they were not Russian and had no patriotic sentiments towards either Russia or the Tsarist regime, and perhaps partly because of personality characteristics typical of the individual attracted to such work, surveillance agents, too, could present problems. From all accounts, and from an analysis of actual Agency experience, detectives were motivated by a love of money and the excitement of conspiracy. They were drawn to the Agency by decent salaries, averaging about 300 francs per month, and by a job which offered free travel and the exhilaration of the spy game. Their venality was of considerable concern, as Agency heads frankly admitted. They could not easily be dismissed, nor could they easily be refused salary increases for fear that they might make their experience and information available either to a hostile press or, more frequently, to Vladimir Burtsev, an emigré who spent most of his time after 1905 trying to expose the Okhrana and its police collaborators abroad.[8] Some were dismissed, of course, usually on the grounds that their services were no longer required. They were given substantial severance pay or, in some cases, a pension which it was hoped would secure their continuing goodwill. Interestingly, one agent (the Swiss detective Rigault) was dismissed because his obesity attracted too much public attention.[9]

[8] 36, IIa, 1. Harting to Department of Police, 14 September 1905. See also 8, IId, 11, Durin to Krassilnikov, 17 November 1913.
[9] 36, IIa, 1. Harting to Department of Police, 14 September 1905.

At the height of the Agency's operation in 1914, there were perhaps 40 detectives in all European countries. A precise figure is difficult to pin down because some worked on a part-time basis aiding principal agents in specific tasks. Ordinarily, surveillance agents worked as two-man teams, observing and recording the movements of their targets, their associations and customary haunts. Although generally understaffed, the external agency had the advantage in Paris of dealing with radical emigrés who tended to inhabit restricted neighborhoods. Azev and several other Social Revolutionaries, for instance, all lived at 23 Rue de la Glacière, while another group of S-Rs lived next door at No. 25. Thus a single day's surveillance over one individual was likely to bring at least half a dozen other 'interesting' emigrés under scrutiny. Such surveillance was used to discover revolutionary 'families', to identify any new additions to the Russian colonies, and to provide a secondary check on the accuracy of information emanating from the internal agency. In addition, constant surveillance was kept over radicals attempting to return to Russia.

At any given time, perhaps half of the external agents were in Paris. A handful were in London, two or three in Germany, and after 1912, about six in Italy. Surveillance in Switzerland, Belgium, and the Baltic countries was entrusted to local police or carried out by agency detectives sent out from Paris on special assignment. In short, constant Okhrana surveillance was maintained only over the Russian colonies in Paris, London, and Berlin. In Switzerland, an important centre of emigré activity, the internal agency was depended on heavily for information. In this task it had the support of three Geneva policemen who were on the Agency payroll to pass on whatever information came to them at the Geneva police office, and secondly to provide a check on information sent directly from Geneva police officials to the head of the Foreign Agency.[10] Similar arrangements were found in Berlin.[11]

[10] Ibid. The three were Depassel, Deleamon, and Bocque. In addition, a postal worker, Mercier, provided correspondence for perlustration.

[11] 63, VIIIa, 1. Harting to Department of Police, 12 October 1907.

To the emigré, the Agency was a vast network reaching into every corner. In one article, published in the *Daily Express* (London), the S-R Rubanovich claimed that there were 60 or 70 Russian agents in England in 1905, although in fact there could not have been more than ten. In the same article it was stated that the Okhrana had 200 agents in Paris, and spent three million rubles a year on 'collaborators' within the Foreign Agency alone.[12] Such claims were, of course, gross exaggerations. The Agency never controlled more than about 30 internals and 40 externals at any one time. If it was the case that Fontanka sometimes sent detectives to Europe on special assignment, these were few and infrequent. Agency heads had little use for these Russian detectives, who had neither the mastery of languages nor the general familiarity with the emigrés which were essential for the task. Similarly, there were internal agents in Europe who were controlled from Russia rather than Paris. Given the difficulty of controlling agents at such a distance, however, their number must have been small.[13]

If Rubanovich's assertions regarding the number of agents in Europe are extreme, his budgetary figures are absurd. The largest total Agency budget, in 1916, was 702,000 francs. That budget (which financed everything from paper clips to agents salaries) was affected by war-time inflation, and included a one-time extraordinary outlay of 116,000

Harting writes that he has four Berlin agents, but is dropping one who has not been useful.

[12] 54, VIk, 23C. Farce's report on the *Daily Express*, March 1905. Cf. 35, Vc, 1, 'Russian Political Brigades in Europe', n.d.

[13] Because internals were considered prestigious commodities among officials, they were not easily transferred when an agent changed his area of operation. Most of the *seksoty* controlled from Russia, then, were probably ones who had undertaken emigration rather late and probably as a temporary move. Aside from considerations of prestige, the reluctance to transfer agents was dictated by secrecy: not even senior police officials (except the Director of the Department of Police) were supposed to know any agents other than their own. At times the practice of harbouring agents appears to have been seriously dysfunctional. When Rataev left the Foreign Agency, Harting had to plead that Rataev's internals be transferred to him in order to maintain operational continuity. Andreev, acting head for eight months in 1909, made the same plea regarding Harting's former agents.

francs.[14] Less than half of the budget went to salaries in the internal agency—about 300,000 francs or 750,000 rubles. For the 1905 budget which Rubanovich alluded to, the figures would be less than half that for 1917, or roughly 350,000 rubles for the internal agency. While the Agency grew considerably between 1905 and 1917, it never came near the size attributed to it by Rubanovich.

In general terms, the functions of the Okhrana's Foreign Agency can be described as 'emigré-control'. 'Controlled' emigration, from the police perspective, conjured up the image of people whose activities were strongly influenced by, or contingent upon, the actions of the police. They were controlled if they did what the police wished, avoided doing what the police disapproved, or at least found it difficult to carry out successfully anti-regime activities. Control meant restrictions on action, constraint on choice, the inability to act freely in line with their self-prescribed goals. Rachkovsky had something like that in mind when he told the Director of the French Sûreté: 'I am trying to demoralize [the radical emigré] politically, to inject discord among revolutionary forces, to weaken them, and at the same time to suppress every revolutionary act at its source.'[15] In other words, control of the emigré meant creating a situation in which he could operate only with great insecurity—a situation corresponding as closely as possible to what he would endure in Russia—to make him feel that his activities were neither approved nor safe.

In more specific terms, the Agency's functions may be analysed in terms of an informational/operational dichotomy: informational functions were to provide a basis for operational acts. As much as possible needed to be known about who the emigrés were, what they were doing, where they were located, what sorts of associations they maintained, how they were financed, etc. The collection of data was carried out by surveillance, internal collaborators,

---

[14] 28, IVa, 14. Monthly accounts for 1916. Cf. 26, IVa, 1A. The estimate for 1908 is only 364,800 francs.
[15] 10, IIIa, 7. Rachkovsky to Fragnin, n.d. [1885?]

informers, the perlustration of correspondence, and by seeking information from local police sources.

The general tasks of the internal and external agencies were in most respects complementary. Exposure by internal agents could provide the basis for maintaining surveillance over specific emigrés involved in illegal activities or preparing to return to Russia. Conversely, information from surveillance agents could be used to corroborate internal reports and to raise questions about apparent conspiratorial associations. On the basis of surveillance reports, for instance, a case officer might ask one of his internals to ascertain the meaning of frequent contacts among selected emigrés. Although the secret collaborators were central to control, both agencies were important. Okhrana activities would have been greatly hampered without good surveillance.

Obviously surveillance could not be kept over all Russians in Paris or elsewhere. Some distinctions had to be made, and Harting indicated what these were in defining particular surveillance targets in 1905: (1) emigrants and revolutionary groups; (2) those coming from Russia for revolutionary purposes; (3) centres where revolutionaries met frequently for conspiracies; (4) publishers of revolutionary tracts, illegal passports, etc.; (5) those involved in bomb experiments and construction; (6) those smuggling arms and bombs to Russia; (7) identifying Russians who came to Europe for socialist congresses, or who had ties with socialists; (8) discovering criminal plots of emigrants and anarchists during trips of Important Personages abroad.[16]

After paying lip service to 'all-sided surveillance' (number 1, above), Harting emphasized his fundamental concern with the most dangerous activities of the emigré, those which were clearly illegal, or which might otherwise facilitate operational actions in control of an emigré (numbers 2, 4, 5, 6, and 8). The surveillance over those attending socialist congresses or who had ties with socialists was apparently for the purpose of identifying individuals who might be targets for deeper investigation, in the hope that they might be

[16] 36, IIa, 1. Harting to Police Department, 23 March 1906.

implicated in an actual crime or conspiracy. Although emigrés were the Agency's general subject matter, radical emigrés were obviously their central concern.

As a supplement to information obtained through the internal and external agencies, the Foreign Agency relied heavily on intercepted correspondence among revolutionaries. Much of this came to the Agency from Fontanka, which systematically screened mail from abroad at so-called 'black cabinets' in major Russian post offices.[17] A considerable number of letters were perlustrated in Europe, too, as the emigrés soon discovered. In Geneva and Italy, these were supplied by postal employees on the Agency payroll.[18] A few letters were apparently intercepted in Denmark as well, although there is no indication of the manner in which those were acquired.

By all odds, the largest volume of correspondence, and generally the most useful, was intercepted in Paris. There the technique of acquisition was reasonably simple: the concierge of a radical domicile was approached and offered money in return for her tenants' mail. This procedure was ordinarily undertaken by surveillance agents who paid a standard rate of three francs for a postcard and five francs for a letter or inter-city telegram.[19] After a letter had been obtained, by whatever method, it was immediately copied and returned to the owner, on the same day if possible, to avoid suspicion. In some cases the concierge did the copying herself, by sketching over the unfamiliar Russian words on tracing paper. Most letters, however, were taken to the Russian Embassy for copying. In 1909, when hand-copying was too slow to handle the inflow, a photographic laboratory was set up to expedite the process.[20]

There is no doubt that in Paris perlustration was widely

[17] R. Kantor, 'K istorii chernykh kabinetov', *Katorga i ssylka*, 1927, 94-95. Apparently only seven cities (Petersburg, Moscow, Warsaw, Kiev, Kharkov, Odessa, and Tiflis) had secret censors, employing altogether 49 officials.
[18] 36, IIa, 1. Harting to Department of Police, 14 September 1905; 92 Xc, 3. Protocol 6984/1/56, 12 August 1913.
[19] 92, Xc, 1C. Dépenses du mois d'Avril 1909.
[20] 92, Xc, 3. Harting to Police Department, 25 January 1909.

used and was a fruitful source of information. The agent Bint, for instance, had succeeded in gaining the confidence of the concierges of the important S-Rs Agafonov, Rubanovich, and Natanson, as well as that of the counter-police agent, Burtsev. He received their entire correspondence.[21] In descriptions of other operations, it appears that the Agency had frequent access to the correspondence of most of their important targets in Paris. If an expense statement for April 1909 is at all typical, some 30 to 50 pieces of correspondence were perlustrated monthly in Paris alone.[22] Even Edgar Farce, a detective operating in the more restrictive environment of London, paid tribute to the notorious concierge: 'There are', he said, 'no porters here, as in Paris for example, where with 100 sous you can buy their souls'.[23]

The emigrés were not unaware of the practice, of course, and tried to counter it by using codes, disappearing ink, and other devices. These techniques were sometimes successful. Other emigrés, however, apparently believed that the task of screening letters even in Russian censorship offices, could not deal with more than a small percentage of conspiratorial correspondence. Whether or not that was the case, the following emigré letter, intercepted in Russia and sent to Paris for Harting's amusement, puts their point of view: 'If the administration of the Autocratic State were talented enough to track down every separate conspiratorial letter, it could survive for another century'.[24] Unfortunately for the Tsar, perlustration did not enable the Autocratic State to endure even fifteen years more, much less a hundred. It did enable the Agency to discover close associations, to follow plots, and to know which revolutionaries might be returning to, or coming from, Russia. Moreover, it gave the Agency some solid grounds for judging emigré morale and the relative impact of police operations on emigré circles, all of considerable importance in the work of control.

Another standard source of police information has

[21] 92, Xc, lC. Bint to 'Monsieur' [Andreev], 30 April 1909.
[22] 92, Xc, 1C. Dépenses du mois d'Avril 1909.
[23] 54, VIk, 23C. Farce to Harting, 28 April 1906.
[24] 91, Xc, 1. 'C' to E. Gurvich, 9 November 1905.

traditionally been the permanent or casual informer—an individual who is not an agent, but who is in a position to observe activities or overhear conversations of interest to the police. While these played an important role in Russia, the Foreign Agency did not cultivate informants systematically, probably because their inability to understand Russian would have rendered them almost useless. The few who did act on a more or less continual basis were usually restaurant waiters or hotel clerks working in districts frequented by the Russian colony. These were paid on a piece-rate basis whenever their information seemed important; almost all were in Paris. Sometimes, however, useful information came from informants with no police connections—at least not with the Foreign Agency. Important help in tracking a large revolutionary arms shipment, for instance, came from a French hotel clerk who approached the Russian Embassy directly with his information.[25]

Of far greater importance as a source of information were local police who had numerous informers, and a far more extensive surveillance staff than the Foreign Agency could field. If they were cooperative, local police surveillance could serve the Okhrana as adequately, or nearly so, as their own. Information from local police served the same general purposes as that gathered by the Agency. Sometimes it was the only source the Agency had, and it could always be used, of course, as a check on other sources of information.

The informational function of the Agency occupied most of its time and energies, yet was clearly not sufficient in itself to achieve control of the radical emigré. Knowing about a conspiracy was not the same as quashing it. Establishing a crime was no substitute for an arrest. In general, information could identify problems and suggest solutions. The solutions themselves had to be executed, however, and this is where the operational functions of the Agency were important: in the actual implementation of control when necessary.

Operational actions of the police were those designed to

[25] 64, VIIIa, 4. *Chernoviki donosenii s 25 iunia 1905 g. do 10 avgusta toi zhe goda.*

influence opposition behaviour directly. One technique used extensively in Russia, and to some extent in Europe, to isolate the emigré was to conduct anti-emigré propaganda through the press. In Russia, this was carried out principally by subsidizing right-wing newspapers and journals, including *Russkoe Znamia, Russkoe Delo, Golos Rossii, Russkaia Starina,* and a large part of the provincial press. Payments were made through the Chief Administration for Press Affairs in the Ministry of Internal Affairs, and reached high levels during the first world war—1.7 million rubles in 1916 alone, according to one source.[26]

In Europe, a similar task was undertaken through the Foreign Agency and other Fontanka representatives abroad. The effort to influence opinion abroad took various forms, the most important of which was 'seeding' the press, i.e. inserting police articles and press releases into foreign publications to counter harmful public opinion or to discredit the radical emigré. Before 1902, this job was one of the many for which the Agency head was responsible. So long as it remained in his hands, it was carried on rather haphazardly, sporadically rather than systematically—he had simply too many other responsibilities. In late 1902, however, Fontanka sent a special agent, Manuilov-Mannase-vich, to Paris to systematize the practice, in the expectation that a full-time public relations man would yield better results. The decision to do so was made by the Director of the Police Department, Lopukhin, with the approval of his chief political affairs assistant, Zubatov. The new approach, then, can be seen as part of Zubatov's more active, public, and experimental approach to police problems which, along with police-supported trade unions and student organizations, was supposed to project a new image of the regime at home and abroad.

How the foreign press was approached depended largely on the nature of the material used. Propaganda and semi-official interpretations of Russian problems were dealt with differently from official statements of the government

[26] 'Reptilny Fond, 1914-1916 g.g.', *Krasny Arkhiv,* 1925, 332.

or the Tsar. It was expected that the latter would be published without objection in leading papers like *Figaro*, *Gaullois*, *Matin*, or *L'Eclair*.[27] The question of inserting articles which might be considered propaganda, had to be attacked otherwise: usually by paying newspapers to print them. This was not difficult with the smaller right-wing publications, but when an attempt was made to get a 'respectable' paper, *Le Matin*, to run propaganda at 2 to 6 francs per line, the offer was rejected.[28] Another attempt to capture the allegiance of a newspaper with wide circulation relied on different techniques, but was similarly unsuccessful. Thus, in 1890, as a reward for favourable coverage of the trial of some Russian terrorists in Paris, the editor and two journalists of *L'Eclair* were awarded Russian Imperial Orders.[29] There is no indication, however, that a long-term dependence was created thereby.

The policy of paying for a favourable press reflected the cynicism not only of the police, but of the French press as well. Russophiles like Maurice Paléologue regarded the ethics of the French press with abhorrence. For him, 'the dirtiest and most distasteful feature of the inner workings of the Franco-Russian alliance had been the constant blackmail by our press-lords of the Russian Imperial Treasury, with the alleged object of protecting Russian credit in the French market'.[30] Responsible journalism was nowhere very widespread during this period, of course, and the French press may not have been worse than most. It still posed very difficult problems for the Foreign Agency.

Where it was not possible to seed the press, or as a supplement to that technique, the Agency relied on another method, the establishment of strictly police organs to reflect the Russian government's point of view. Rachkovsky had

[27] 66, IXb, 2A. Lopukhin to Manuilov, 15 February 1904. When Manuilov received a copy of the Tsar's Manifesto of 26 February 1903, he was instructed to arrange for its being given prominence in three leading newspapers.

[28] 66, IXb, 2A. Krassilnikov to Zuev, 6 January 1910.

[29] 34, Vb, 1. Proposal for decorations, August 1890.

[30] M. Paléologue, *Three Critical Years: 1904-05-06* (New York 1957), 193.

founded one such publication, *Revue Russe*, as an enterprise wholly owned by the Police Department.[31] Another 'house organ', *Le Courrier Franco-Russe*, was owned and edited by a French Russophile who considered it a patriotic task, albeit one that was strongly reinforced by a large police subsidy.[32] The only problem with publications like *Revue Russe* and *Le Courrier Franco-Russe* was that they were of practically no significance as opinion leaders. The Tsar may have appreciated reading encomiums on his wisdom and moderation, but he did not need to be convinced. In general, the deliberate use of anti-emigré propaganda as an operational tool does not appear to have been a major weapon in the police arsenal. At the very least, the success of such activities is open to serious question.

Of far greater consequence to the emigré's situation were the typical police and judicial operations meant to deprive him of his independence of movement and action, and to reinforce the psychological insecurity which his conspiratorial life created. Ultimately, the best means of controlling the emigré lay in techniques like deportation and extradition, arrests and searches, imprisonment and expulsion. Each of these methods served a fairly specific purpose. The choice depended, from a purely professional point of view, on the outcome desired. Extradition, with its probable sequel in imprisonment in Russia, might remove a radical from circulation, but the anti-revolutionary struggle was not always best served thereby. Taken together, however, these various methods enabled the police to immobilize the radical emigré, to isolate him, to impede communication with others, to harass him, undermine his personal security, and perhaps even raise doubts about the value of conspiratorial life. Such were the general aims of the Agency's activities.

Not all emigrés would be affected by such techniques, because the police were concerned only with the radicals, and while most of them could not be used against political

[31] 66, IXb, 2A. Sondorff to Manuilov, 20 January 1904. According to Sondorff, *Revue Russe* was sent to the Tsar each week.
[32] 66, IXb, 1C. Krassilnikov to Police Department, 22 February 1911.

criminals as such, the most radical emigrés were likely to be involved in criminal or illegal activity in one way or another. Of particular interest to the Foreign Agency were the smuggling of illicit arms and literature, the printing of forged passports for conspiratorial movement, and terrorism. The Okhrana's operational techniques were ultimately aimed at controlling specific types of activity. If these ceased, or were significantly curtailed, then other emigré activities could be ignored: the emigration would have been tamed.

At this point, one must note that the operational functions of the Foreign Agency depended on an authority which it did not have. What executive power could the Russian police exercise abroad? Obviously the answer is that in a strictly legal sense it had no authority in Europe. With the permission of the local government or with the complicity of foreign police, however, it could carry out surveillance. Moreover, it could attempt to persuade local authorities to carry out the operational acts on which successful control depended. If the Agency were reasonably successful in instigating action, if local police acted in compliance with Russian demands and aims, then the Agency could be said to have demonstrated power over the emigration. It could not make arrests, could not imprison, could not issue extradition orders, could not expel a single emigré. Its power, its ability to carry out operational functions, depended on its success in winning the support of local governments and police forces. To the extent that foreign authorities acted towards the emigré in a manner similar to that in which the Okhrana itself might have acted, to that extent Russian authority could, in effect, be extended beyond its own borders. Without such connivance, the Agency's quest for control would have been fruitless.

Although an examination of the nature and extent of European police cooperation with the Foreign Agency lies outside the scope of this paper, it should be stated that such cooperation was generally forthcoming. In part this was the result of formal arrangements between the Russian government and other governments of Europe. The multilateral obligations imposed by the Anti-Anarchist Pact of 1906 also explain certain kinds of cooperation on the part of some governments. But more often the Foreign Agency relied on informal contacts and arrangements with European security agencies—arrangements which were the outcome of a shared concern with radical activities, a developing sense of professional esprit de corps, various kinds of material and honorific rewards, and even by personal friendships among police officials.

Cooperation with European officials was not, of course, complete. The European political environment was not as a rule cordial towards a Russian regime popularly regarded as starkly reactionary. Liberal and socialist politicians opposed collaboration with the Okhrana on principle, while simultaneously enjoying the benefit of embarrassing their own conservative governments. Moreover, through the protection of politicians like Jaurès, Clemenceau, and Huysmans, many of the best-known radical emigrés were virtually immune to official police harassment.

Whatever his emotional and professional inclinations, a European security chief was aware of the underlying connections of his institution and the national political structure. That awareness, on occasion, imposed restraints on his dealings with the Russians. Sometimes, too, professional and bureaucratic considerations led him, for the welfare of his own agency, to refuse cooperation or to keep it to a minimum. But such considerations were the exception rather than the rule. On the whole, the police acted in an almost fraternal fashion, and shared certain tasks. Indeed, when some specific act of cooperation was refused, the explanation given the Okhrana for refusal was almost invariably the intervention of extra-police authority or influence. In a great many cases, however, the secret nature of security police operations facilitated the avoidance or circumvention of such obstacles to cooperation.

It is understandable, then, that a very significant part of the time of the Agency head should have been given over to creating and maintaining cooperative relations with his professional colleagues at Scotland Yard, the Sûreté, and other security offices. Such informal relationships were crucial to his success, because through them the Agency could often pursue its aims in cooperation with local police even when its activities were being publicly repudiated by the host country's government. On several occasions, the Agency's informal, unofficial, and often secret relations with local police enabled it to function as it could not have done if its activities had been regulated exclusively by formal agreements made through diplomatic channels.

Much of whatever success might be attributed to the Foreign Agency, then, depended on the cooperation of foreign police. The penchant of radicals to exaggerate both the extent of the Okhrana's foreign operations and the size of its European apparatus, may be explained by their inability to grasp the extent and importance of police cooperation. Okhrana agents were not on every street corner in Paris—but there were large numbers of Prefecture and Sûreté agents and informers who acted in concert with the Foreign Agency, and sometimes even under its operational control.

For the younger, less experienced, or less committed revolutionary, police harassment could result in extreme insecurity, dejection, and disillusionment. If for these reasons they dropped out of the movement, police control would have been at least partially effective. That police action could have such results is poignantly portrayed in a letter from a young Russian student, in the aftermath of a round-up of Russian radicals in Switzerland in 1908:

It has been a month since my court appearance; how it ended is history. I thought I'd be released and find a letter from you, but so far I've heard nothing, I am writing now in fearful anxiety . . . Searches and arrests are beginning again among the emigrants. I want to get out of here and go to where there aren't any Russians. There are provocateurs and traitors here at every step. The situation is ridiculous. You sit and wait for them to come to you and ask you whether you knew about such and such. I urgently beg you to send 50 rubles, otherwise danger will again threaten me and I'll have to get out of here even sooner. I can't even write calmly, because even if things were otherwise, I don't have a passport. I am going to Belgium, where there aren't any of these damned Russians, and start to prepare for exams.[33]

There were, perhaps, more serene occupations than revolutionary conspiracy.

This article is based on a paper delivered at the first annual meeting of the Rocky Mountain Association for Slavic Studies in May 1971.

[33] 36, Vf, 1 (Swiss). Intercepted letter from 'Pyotr' to unidentified recipient in Russia, 21 May 1908.

The Ottoman Police

Glen W. Swanson

Abdülhamid II, ruler of the Ottoman empire from 1876 to 1909, received an alarming report one day from police agents who had observed students from the school for the deaf communicating with each other by means of hand signals. The spies thought they saw political danger in this practice, and warned the sultan of the difficulty in eavesdropping on citizens who used such methods of communication. The accommodating sultan reacted by closing down the school for the deaf.[1] Once again an Ottoman ruler had been aided by special agents, members of the larger police network whose history is the topic of this paper.

Historically, the Ottoman police system reflected in several ways the heritage and growth of a powerful and durable empire. The origins of this Muslim political unit go back to the early fourteenth century, when a group of Turkish warriors and settlers established a Muslim border state on the Byzantine frontier in northwest Anatolia. Under the leadership of Osman (from whose name comes the dynastic label Ottoman) and his successors, the Ottoman Muslim forces advanced into the Balkans and dealt Byzantium a lethal blow with the conquest of Constantinople in 1453. The Ottoman rulers now shed their former identity as march warriors and assumed the tasks of managing an expanding empire. Ottoman penetration into the Arab lands and seizure of Mamluke Egypt in the early sixteenth century served to expand the new identity and to reinforce the Islamic traditions of empire and state to which the Ottomans fell heir. Manifesting a profound sense of duty to their Islamic mission, the Ottoman dynasty paid particular attention to a

---

[1] I wish to express my appreciation to Professor Ilhan Basgöz for bringing this account to my attention.

39

concept of justice that emphasized balance and stability in society. Each individual and class was to have their proper place. To maintain this proper order it was necessary to respect the Holy Law that emanated from God and to prevent the transgression of that law, known as the *sharia*.

To execute this religio-political mission, the Ottoman sultans worked through an intricate power apparatus led by a managerial elite whose duties included the policing of the empire. At first, this elite consisted largely of frontier warriors for Islam. Then, in the fifteenth century and after, theologians and administrators from the Muslim east assumed greater importance. To prevent the formation of a potentially dangerous entrenched governing class, the Ottomans adopted one feature of the classical Islamic state, the slave household, whose members had no roots outside the sultan's service. It was from this group that most of the leading Ottoman police officials were to come.

The organization and effectiveness of the police force was directly related to the nature of the empire. Born under the shadow of Byzantium, the Ottoman state developed as a Balkan power before it became an Asiatic one. Reaching out into vast territories and encompassing communities of different religious, ethnic, and cultural origins, the empire lacked the coherence and compactness that make a centralized administration, in the normal sense, possible. This governmental system was neither that of the Arab world nor that of Europe; Muslim models, when they did exist, had passed to the Ottomans through the medium of earlier regimes; and Byzantine practices were adopted only piecemeal. The Ottoman rulers, however, adapted to the situation without losing sight of their Islamic and dynastic mission. Instead of decentralizing authority by giving it to local units, the Ottoman sultans delegated authority to field administrators whose power was neither their own nor that presented them by the local population. In principle, the power remained with the sultan through a system of land tenure and leases. In practice, this system had so deteriorated by the seventeenth century that power was divided between the sultan and the local notabilities. Although reform-minded sultans and administrators arrested further decentralization in the nineteenth century, the problem of how to share responsibility continued to trouble the police and other divisions of imperial administration. Complicating the issue was the traditional Muslim approach to corporate units of society.

Neither in the Muslim world nor in the Byzantine empire did towns have the autonomy that they had in classical times or in the medieval West. For one thing, Muslim law recognized no corporate bodies or collective organizations standing between the state and the individual. This does not mean that towns possessed no corporate spirit; it is merely that towns, serving as centres of culture and administration, were considered as integral parts of the state structure. Without civic institutions and without citizenship, the town was governed through two groups of men, the civic-military and the religious. The civil and military officers exercised an authority deriving from the sultan's power, and were mainly responsible for general public security, fire fighting, and police duties. The members of the religious learned group were concerned with matters of Islamic law, which also included such police obligations as watching over public morality.

The lack of autonomy of the Ottoman town served to enhance the position of the Ottoman capital. The city was divided for administrative purposes into four units—the ancient Constantinople, or Istanbul proper; Galata, lying on the opposite shore of the Golden Horn; Eyyub, situated at the northern end of the Golden Horn; and Üsküdar, nestled on the Asiatic shore of the Bosporus. In Istanbul, the centre of power was the complex of Topkapi, which served as palace, court, household, and residence of the Ottoman sultans from about 1478 to the nineteenth century. Among the officials serving at Topkapi were several officers who had important police duties.

At the top of the managerial structure was the grand vizier, who was generally responsible for all security and police matters along with his many other obligations. No fewer than five palace officers served under him to supervise the policing of the four areas of the capital—the supreme admiral (Kapudan Pasha), the chief of the armourers (Jebeji Bashi), the chief of the gunners (Topchu Bashi), the leader of the elite fighting unit, known as the Aga of the Janissaries, and the head gardener (Bostanji Bashi), whose title was not completely indicative of his real influence in the empire.

The Aga of the Janissaries controlled the most powerful military force in the Ottoman empire and served as chief of police for most of the capital. He was a member of the council of state and held a position over all other generals and all ministers below the rank of vizier. His responsibilities included the protection of property and the maintenance of order in most of Istanbul. Twice a week he inspected the capital to see personally that everything was in order. The Sekban Bashi, or Segmen Bashi, was the Janissary officer who substituted for the Aga when the latter left the capital. In time of peace, when the Aga would be present in the city, the Sekban Bashi was responsible for the defence of the capital. Another Janissary officer, the Muhdir Aga, provided protection for the grand vizier and acted as intermediary between the grand vizier and the Aga of the Janissaries. He, with the grand vizier, ruled over judicial questions concerning the Janissaries and was responsible for punishing Janissaries found guilty of infractions.

The Janissary influence in police matters was evident at the non-officer level as well. Janissary units stationed at the capital performed many police duties, with each district having a unit stationed there for one year. Patrols went from the district posts into all the streets and markets of that district, preventing or punishing crimes, and executing the decisions of the religious authorities on matters relating to the laws of Islam and the rulings of the sultan. When these Janissary units were outside the capital on campaigns, other military units filled in for them.

Other officers, too, participated in the police system. The commander of the gunners had jurisdiction over Beyoglu or Pera, and the area adjoining the arsenal. The chief of armourers had similar responsibility for Aya Sofya, Hoja

Pasha, and the Stable Gate. The admiral of the fleet was responsible for maintaining public order at the naval base and arsenal at Kasim Pasha, the district of Galata, and other districts situated on the bank north of the Golden Horn. The intermediary between the government and police officers was the court official known as the Chavush-Bashi, who introduced ambassadors to the presence of the sultan and served as an administrator of justice and as envoy. When a man was convicted, a chavush was sent with a commission to the nearest official having the power to execute the sentence. He sometimes waited for tangible proof, often the head of the condemned man, that the mission was accomplished.

A highly influential official was the sultan's chief gardener, the Bostanji-Bashi, who was the only person permitted to wear a beard in the interior of the palace. He was responsible for the surveillance of all the residences of the sovereign and the lands where they were situated, particularly the banks of the Bosporus. Over two thousand men were under his command, and it was he who directed the questioning or execution of delinquent officials. Although some bostanjis actually did gardening work, most served as guards at the sultan's palaces or as watchmen on the palace grounds. Jurisdiction extended from the Dardanelles to the mouth of the Black Sea as well as over many towns on the coast. In the ports located on the Sea of Marmara, the Bosporus, and the Golden Horn, the bostanjis controlled the shipping and served as local police. Another group of bostanjis served as bodyguards to the sultan and had the honour to row his private boat. A description of what occurred when the Bostanji-Bashi made his evening rounds on the Bosporus is contained in an edited account of an eighteenth-century traveller:

All the parties on its shores disperse, and the women, in particular, retire precipitately to their homes. One evening . . . the bostanji-bashi appeared in his barge, manned by twenty-four rowers; he had inflicted punishment on some drunken persons, and ordered some females who were rather too merry to be secured; he then ran, without noise, alongside the kiosk of a Greek lady, and after listening for a few minutes to the conversation that was passing, he climbed over the balustrade with several of his men.

The lady and her paramour were quit with the sacrifice of all the
diamonds, jewels, and money they had about them: and they durst
not hesitate a moment; for the bostanji-bashi, who had surprised
them, would have apprehended them, carried them on board his
barge, and conveyed them to prison, had not his avarice at length
rendered him tractable.

In the matter of punishment, the same writer describes how
the Bostanji-Bashi listened to complaints entered against his
agents and rendered strict justice to both the errant bostanjis
and any inhabitants whom he caught in a wrongful act:

If this officer hears a noise in any house, or sees a light in it at
unseasonable hours, he orders stones to be thrown at the windows;
on the slightest suspicion, he breaks open the door, searches it all
over, and frequently punishes the master with a fine and the
bastinado. He tries in a summary manner the offenders seized by
his people, whatever may be their crimes; and in cases of robbery,
if those who have lost anything recover it by his means, he charges
them ten percent. He is likewise ... superintendent of the
fountains and water conducted into the seraglio or distributed over
the city. If his people catch persons sporting and can secure them,
they take away their arms and bring them before him to be
punished.[2]

Special tasks of surveillance and detective work were given to
two groups known as the Böjek Bashis and the Salma Tebdil
Chokadaris. The Böjek Bashis were responsible for the
punishment of thieves and the prevention of robbery. Their
agents—some of whom were women—possibly acted as
plainclothes detectives and were recruited from the ranks of
repentant thieves and criminals. The Chokadaris, numbering
between twenty to forty men, were concerned with the
neglect of religious duties, such as children who were making
a noise in the mosques during the Muslim month of fasting,
the prevention of gambling that might cause a public
disturbance, and the improper behaviour of Janissaries in
public places. The chief of the Chokadaris had agents, also
disguised, to frequent the markets, bazaars, cafés, taverns,
and public baths, watching that the Janissaries caused no

[2] Frederic Shoberl, ed., *The World in Miniature: Turkey. Being a
description of the manners, customs, dresses, and other peculiarities
characteristic of the inhabitants of the Turkish Empire* (London
[1821?]), III, 250-54.

scandal and prohibiting the prostitutes from plying their trade in public places or in cemeteries. Each day the chief reported to his superiors on the state of popular feeling in the city.

The two police officers closest to the civil population of the capital were the Asas Bashi and the Subashi. They went on rounds of inspection, arresting persons apprehended in the act of committing a crime, and inflicting punishments as decreed by the authorities. The main prison, named after the patron saint of prisoners, was under their joint control. The Asas Bashi was a Janissary officer in charge of the public jails and supervisor of all public executions. Because of these two jobs it was his duty to appear at all meetings in the Saray as well as at the Porte. He was also responsible for clearing crowds from the streets during ceremonial occasions.

Another hat worn by the Asas Bashi was that of chief of the night patrol. During the hours of darkness it was permitted for persons to be out of doors only if they had a lantern. The Asas Bashi seized the violators of this and other regulations and applied a punishment which could consist not only of imprisonment or application of the bastinado but also work tasks such as carrying wood for the public bathhouse furnaces. As part of his remuneration the Asas Bashi received one tenth of the fines imposed for drunkenness and similar offences committed at night.

The general responsibility for policing the city during the daytime was shared by a chief of the local Janissaries, known as the Subashi, and by the market superintendent, the Muhtesib. In the sixteenth century the Subashi of Istanbul brought the persons summoned before the judge and carried out the sentences he handed down. As the police magistrate affiliated with the Chavushes, the Subashi had jurisdiction over everyone except Janissaries. He apparently had a terrible reputation for his harsh treatment of wrongdoers as he went about keeping order during the day and working with the Muhtesib to see that the regulations concerning merchants and artisans were respected.

Although municipal institutions were lacking in the strict sense, corporations or guilds did exist in the capital and did require special attention. The seven hundred or more guilds were divided into sections. The second section, under the supervision of the police provost, contained a strange mixture of guilds: watchmen, horse-jobbers, hangmen, grooms, press-gang men, lictors, thieves and footpads, and policemen. Responsibility for normal surveillance of guild affairs in matters of measures, weights, and prices theoretically rested with the religious judge, but was in fact shared by the grand vizier, who was responsible for all governmental affairs, the Aga of the Janissaries, who was in charge of the general policing of Istanbul, and the Muhtesib. They made periodical rounds to check that the shopkeepers were acting properly in commercial transactions. Accompanied by intendants and soldiers, the Muhtesibs inspected the markets and patrolled the streets. If the law had been broken, they punished the wrongdoer at once, either physically or financially. The Muhtesib specialized in the repression of fraud committed by merchants and artisans, and saw that the laws on commerce were applied correctly, that merchandise imported into the capital was equally distributed, and that the fixed prices for goods were maintained. He inspected the premises, controlled weights and measures, and collected special taxes from the members of the corporations.

The Muhtesib, the Aga of the Janissaries, the Bostanji-Bashi, and the other police officers apparently accomplished their task well because what scant evidence there is indicates that serious crimes were rare in Istanbul and that public tranquillity usually prevailed. Murders were few, possibly because of the code of responsibility for such a crime. If the perpetrator was not found, the inhabitants of the quarter where the crime was committed would have to pay blood-money. As for unrest in the city, although there were Janissary and guild rebellions, the civil population remained quiet. It seemed to recognize the risks it would incur if it acted against the power of the sultan, especially when that power was protected by a well-established police force.

Outside Istanbul, the Ottoman police system retained at least two characteristics already seen in the capital: the importance of the Janissaries, and the sultan's attempt to govern through agents dependent on him. Subashis, for example, carried out police duties in urban and rural areas. One type of Subashi was charged with financial, administrative, and police functions in the provinces. Another, the Subashi of the treasury, was stationed in the towns, where he worked in liaison with the Muhtesib, made day and night rounds, and performed general police work.

Since it is impossible within the limits of a single paper to deal with all the regions and periods that the Ottoman empire embraced, consideration is given to a few selected examples. The region with a developed police system was Egypt, an Ottoman province of great value to the sultan. To administer and exploit his possession, the sultan distributed portions of it in leases (Muqataat), one of which was the urban police function. It was a lucrative lease because the right to keep order and security, to imprison, punish, and fine, produced valuable revenue in each Egyptian port at the close of the seventeenth century.

In Egypt, as in Istanbul, the Janissary corps dominated the scene. Its leader was chiefly responsible for the maintenance of order and security in Cairo. He fulfilled his duties by establishing at major points in the city and its environs police posts manned by Janissaries and his personal slaves. He entrusted the policing of Old Cairo, Bulaq, and Cairo to three officials who were empowered to administer punishment for certain crimes and to charge persons who received their services. Additional income came from urban corporations and holders of urban leases who had to pay protection taxes for police protection.

The policing of greater Cairo involved several problems. After the Ottoman conqueror, Sultan Selim, left Egypt early in the sixteenth century, clashes occurred between the Janissaries and another corps left to patrol the city itself. To halt the fighting the Janissaries were ordered to stay out of Cairo and to restrict their services to the guarding of the citadel and to special expeditions. In 1523-24 the Janissaries reassumed the principal military position in Egypt, with the chief of the corps being placed in charge of the police of Cairo and its environs.

Police administration in the Egyptian countryside was carried out by the holders of the imperial lease, their agents, and local officers. In the sixteenth century a single lease usually had only one holder, known as a Multezim. Thereafter, these holdings were gradually broken up until, by the end of the eighteenth century, each lease was usually held by several Multezims. Since each Multezim had a local director, or shaykh, as his representative, the shaykh of the most powerful Multezim was known as the chief shaykh. He directed the police of the village, punished cultivators who violated local custom or law, settled disputes among the villagers, and enforced court decisions. By this time, however, external events and pressures were gradually having their effect on Egypt and the rest of the Ottoman empire.

At the end of the eighteenth century Egypt was invaded by Napoleon. The French were later ejected, but the incident heralded a distinct change for the Middle East. Egypt gradually separated itself from the influence of Istanbul and initiated its own methods of government under independent-minded rulers, who effected reforms of both positive and negative value. The message that change was necessary had an audience in Istanbul as well; within a few decades the entire structure of Ottoman administration was bent or pounded into new shapes.

At least three aspects of this change had important repercussions on the Ottoman police. The first was the suppression of the Janissaries in 1826 by the reforming sultan, Mahmud II. Secondly, the greater centralization and heightened autocracy ran counter to historical practice. Thirdly, the Ottoman rulers were no longer free agents, for now the great powers and dissident minority groups intensified their demands for reform and representation.

The destruction of the Janissaries in 1826 meant not only the end of a traditional political-military elite but also the elimination of the major source supplying police officers. Sultan Mahmud II and his successors proceeded to fill this gap with a series of reforms which, in place of the Aga of the Janissaries, created the office of Serasker, who had the duties of commander-in-chief and minister of war. Together with inheriting the Aga's responsibility for fire-fighting, police duties, and public security in Istanbul, the Serasker received jurisdiction over some of the police formerly under the command of various Janissary officers. As the police function became more important in the period of growing centralization, the police organization underwent administrative change. In 1846 the police were removed from the jurisdiction of the Serasker and placed under the police directory known as the Zabtiye Mushiriyeti; this, in turn, became a separate ministry of police in 1870. A system of police inspectors under the jurisdiction of the arsenal director also came into being in the 1840s, and in 1880 another step in police reorganization was taken with the formation of police stations (karakols). There were eight companies of police in Istanbul in 1880; by 1901 the number had grown to thirty-nine, with a total of 1,638 policemen, and a regular civil police establishment had been formed.[3]

While the Istanbul police were slowly becoming a non-military security force during the nineteenth century, other units retained an army association. This was especially true of the gendarmerie which increasingly figured in the new methods and problems of empire management and reform.

The results of the Ottoman reform movement from the 1830s to the 1860s were not always favourable, as may be seen in the example of security measures in greater Syria. To carry out new administrative policies in Palestine and Syria, the government had to employ both regular army troops and irregulars who acted as a rudimentary gendarmerie. While the regular army was used to maintain order in towns and countryside, the irregulars were posted as auxiliaries to help the regulars perform duties in the country. Composed of the dregs of society, Bedouin and Turkoman nomads, Albanian mercenaries, and local Arabs, their assistance was more of a liability than an asset in Syria.

The irregulars stationed in the cities served as municipal police. Their responsibilities were to guard city gates and

[3] Dervis Okcabol, *Meslek Tarihi* (Ankara 1939), 77-9.

public buildings, maintain order, carry messages, imprison and punish criminals. They fulfilled their tasks in Beirut and Aleppo, but in Jerusalem and Damascus the corrupt and inefficient police force failed to carry out their duties effectively. The irregulars employed in the countryside were usually known as bashibozuks (empty heads). Their duties were to garrison guard houses and forts, collect taxes in the villages, escort caravans, and protect the countryside from Bedouin raids. These ill-fed, badly-armed, and under-paid soldiers were usually hired by the leader of a group of mercenaries who offered his services to the government. Turkish authorities tried to reform the system in the 1850s by introducing a force of auxiliaries largely composed of local Arabs. The new group not only was just as unreliable, oppressive, and corrupt, but was one of the major participants in the massacre of Christians in Damascus and Lebanon in the 1860s. The Ottoman government again revised the system and placed the auxiliaries under military discipline and within the framework of the regular army.

The period of reform in Syria and Palestine failed to improve the conditions in the countryside, where the lack of security continued to be the dominant factor determining the degree of prosperity. The inefficiency of the police and the apathy and weakness of local authorities permitted the aggression of the outlaws and nomads to continue. As a result, population declined, commerce and agriculture suffered. In the towns the Ottoman authorities were more successful in checking the bloody feuds between urban military organizations. Robbery, murder, and other crime did not cease, however, possibly because of the lack of adequate punishment for criminals or because of the insufficient power of the local governor to punish criminals.

The situation in Syria underlined the complexity of the Ottoman power structure and its police function. Although the empire still lacked homogeneity and compactness, the rulers believed the policy of centralization was feasible. In 1864 the grand vizier introduced the new law of vilayets (provinces), which grouped the old provinces into larger units and placed them under the supervision of able men. With

THE OTTOMAN POLICE

minor amendments it remained the basic Ottoman provincial law for several decades. The governor's administration was divided into political, legal, civil, financial, and police affairs, with subordinate officers serving the governor in each of these fields. The topographical, ethnic, and religious differences within the empire, however, rendered any blanket provincial law difficult to execute. When the brewing unrest in the Balkans exploded in the 1870s, whatever control the Ottomans had of the situation passed from their hands. They now had to share the security mission with agents of the great powers who were loudly demanding protection of Christians in Rumelia and eastern Anatolia.

A semblance of reform was made with the abolition of the Zabtiye Mushirliyi in 1879 and the establishment of a gendarmerie department known as the Jandarma Daire-i Merkeziyesi, but it failed to satisfy the European statesmen. In 1904 the great powers forced on Turkey the reformed Macedonian gendarmerie. Organized by a commission of French, British, Russian, Italian, and Austrian officers, it was modelled on lines suggested by the commission. Twenty-five European officers, under the direction of the Italian general Degiorgis, were given responsibility for the reorganization of the gendarmerie with headquarters in Salonika. Since the greatest obstacle was the Ottoman refusal to supply an adequate number of recruits, the Porte was pressed and finally persuaded to provide a regular supply of recruits in conformity with the demands of Degiorgis. A remaining obstacle was the obstruction of local authorities to the presence of foreign gendarmerie officers. Although hardly visible, underneath the show of Ottoman politeness lurked an intense dislike of foreign interference in internal matters.

The major purpose of this reorganized Macedonian gendarmerie was to combat the Balkan fighters, known as comitadjis, who had formed bands to fight the Ottoman authorities or other comitadji groups. The officers of the international advisory body were charged with surveillance of the comitadji actions and with reform of the Turkish gendarmerie along European lines. A positive beginning was made with the creation of a school of gendarmerie in

Salonika, and the establishment of schools of *chefs de poste* in Salonika, Monastir, and Uskub. Ottoman gendarmes were relocated in posts consisting of five men, dispersed in guard stations in all the important villages to enable them to watch comitadji activities more closely. Little progress was made, however, because of financial difficulties and the want of good will on the part of Turkish authorities. Regular courses could not be held at the school and, as a result, the insufficient number of gendarmes sent out to the provinces were only partially trained.

The difficulties in effecting reform were described in 1907 by a British adviser to the Macedonian gendarmerie. Although the population in most districts was pleased with the gendarmerie, the latter group had insufficient influence with the Muslim population in areas where locally influential people controlled the countryside. Sometimes the reasons for dissatisfaction were financial. Gendarmerie posts were being constructed at a slow pace to be sure, but the arrangement under which the district had to pay for the posts constructed in its area was often unfair and unpopular. Cases also were known of violent assaults by Ottoman army officers on individual gendarmes. As for the foreign sectors, the Italian area was considered to be well run even though the gendarmerie was making little progress; the Russian officers were very unpopular in their sector; the French were industrious; the Austrian advisers appeared to be incapable of working effectively with the material they had at hand; the British sector, according to the British officer, was the best run.[4]

The interval between the departure of General Degiorgis in November 1907 and the arrival of his successor General di Robilant in May 1908 gave the Ottoman inspector-general of Rumelia time and opportunity to act against the gendarmerie reform. Di Robilant's aloofness towards the Turks only made the situation worse. The entire arrangement took a sudden turn with the Young Turk revolution of 1908.

While the major purpose of the Young Turk revolution was

[4] Public Record Office (London), F.O. 195/2363, 'Turkey. Annual Report for 1907', 42-43.

restoration of the 1876 constitution, the movement—like most such revolutions—was characterized by a confusion of ideas, coincidences, and secondary goals. The Ottoman gendarmerie and police had their place in this confusion. Nothing angered many educated military officers more than the sultan's ubiquitous spy system, which reached into the military academy and followed the modernized lieutenant or captain as he proceeded from school to duty station. Abdülhamid's mania for spies knew no bounds, and it benefited many persons to submit reports on any strange activity to the ruler. The sultan's personal police system was not infallible, however, because in early 1907 the German ambassador to Turkey won his laurels among the diplomatic corps by forcing the removal of the master spy, Fehim, from his post. But such incidents were rare, and the Young Turks realized that the spy network was difficult to bring down. Of greater danger to the country was the continuing encroachment of the foreign powers through such channels as the gendarmerie.

When the constitution was declared in effect in 1908, foreign control of the Macedonian gendarmerie ceased. The Young Turks, taking complete authority into their hands, transferred the reorganizing mission in July 1909 to the capital, where a directory of gendarmerie was created. The government retained the services of several French, British, and Italian officers but gave to the foreigners only the role of inspector and adviser without executive powers.

The gendarmerie organization was revised and expanded so that the Macedonian system extended to other parts of the empire except the Hijaz and Yemen. Working under a special section of the ministry of war, the gendarmerie was divided into regiments, battalions, and companies, assigned to each province and then to districts. Led by practically uneducated officers, the men had completed in some cases an initial period of service in the army. While the gendarmerie worked in the villages and countryside, police were used in the large towns and centres of government. They served under the same authorities and were organized in the manner of the gendarmerie.

The requirements and training for gendarmes were more

stringent under the Young Turks. The men had to be unmarried, and for preference able to read and write. While any Ottoman subject was theoretically eligible, he had to know Turkish and was not permitted to serve permanently in his home district. On enlistment, the gendarme received five months training at one of the eight recruit schools located, in 1911, in Istanbul, Salonika, Izmir, Beirut, Trebizond, Adana, Baghdad, and Tripoli in Africa. For promotion to noncommissioned officer he underwent another five months' course at one of the eleven *chef de poste* schools at Istanbul, Salonika, Uskub, Monastir, Yanina, Izmir, Adana, Beirut, Trebizond, Baghdad, and Erzerum.

In addition to the reformed gendarmerie there were many constables from pre-reform days who formed the bulk of the gendarmerie units in Mesopotamia and Kurdistan. Both officers and men were usually of local origin and served their entire lives in the gendarmerie. Such a background proved valuable because their knowledge of the area made them highly useful as guides.

Even the Turkish-directed reorganization had its critics. Legislators spoke out during Ottoman parliamentary hearings on the budget in April 1911. They argued that the ministry of the interior, not the ministry of war, should be in charge, that the only reforms were the new uniforms, that abuses by the gendarmes went unpunished, that the gendarmes were not active in arresting criminals, and that the highest civil authorities in the provinces had no control over the gendarmerie.[5] The arguments eventually had their intended effect, and in April 1912 the government transferred the control of the gendarmerie to the ministry of interior, and placed provincial gendarme posts under the control of the governors. This was followed by major changes in the entire system of provincial administration as provided in the law of 26 March 1913. Its significance was great, because centuries-old traditions of government had been put aside legally, and there was now room in the security system for specified national and local levels of governance.

[5] *The Orient* (Istanbul), 5 April 1911.

Plans were made in 1913 and 1914 for further use of foreign advisers in the Ottoman gendarmerie. The British and Russian governments followed the matter closely, and a scheme was drafted for foreign officers to come as inspectors-general, but the outbreak of war brought a halt to the entire plan.

While the gendarmerie worked mainly in the countryside and villages, the police were still active in the large towns and centres of government. They, too, were affected by the Young Turk revolution. From 17 July 1909, the police came under the public security department of the ministry of interior. The principal police official in each town was a director (mudir), the mudir of Stamboul being the general-director for most of the capital. The directors had no administrative duties however, and functioned only as heads of the detective service. Police officers, from the rank of commissioner upwards, were chosen from among civilian officials who had passed the final examination of the law school and had experience in the ministry of justice. The police force, reorganized on the Austrian model, numbered about 6,500 men in 1912, of whom 2,500 were in the capital. Recruits passed through one of the new police schools, the first school having been opened in 1907 in Salonika, followed shortly by schools in Istanbul, Beirut, Erzerum, Baghdad, Adana, Trebizond, and towns in a few other provinces.

Although many changes were made in the police system after the fall of Abdülhamid II, the spy system continued in various ways, usually under the direction of the political group known as the Committee of Union and Progress. Plot and counter-plot continued to haunt the last days of the Ottoman empire, and police were kept busy, especially in 1913, trying to maintain order and stability in society.

A few years later, the last great Muslim empire collapsed. No longer was there any chance for the reappearance of police officials who for centuries had helped to maintain the integrity of a powerful religio-political structure. In fact, by the beginning of the twentieth century most of them, like the Aga of the Janissaries, the Muhtesib, and the Bostanji-Bashi, had disappeared or had so changed their outer garments and functions that they were no longer recognizable. In their place were new men performing the police function in different ways, men of a contemporary mould whose successors continue to use a similar organization and approach to their responsibilities.

The Irish Underground and the War of Independence 1919–21

Tom Bowden

Our subject, the evolution of revolutionary warfare in Ireland, is not solely concerned with the military sphere. It is in fact part of the wider field of politics—the subrosa politics of assassination and reprisal in the guerrilla war of 1919–21 between the British security forces and the Irish Volunteers or IRA, who were the military arm of an underground Irish government. There was, in the period between the end of the 1916 Easter Rising and the onset of the revolutionary war in 1919, a gradual change of political allegiance on the part of the Irish. The legitimacy of the incumbent British administration dwindled in almost inverse proportion to the growing support in favour of the underground government of the Irish Republic proclaimed on the steps of the Dublin General Post Office, Easter 1916, and endorsed through a series of elections culminating in the Dail Eireann elections of 1918. Primarily, however, this paper is concerned with the fighting arm of the revolutionary government—its nature, operations, and tactics, and in noting some of the antecedents of the revolutionary war which provided the politico-military womb in which the embryo alternative government grew.

On 20 November 1920, in the quiet of a Dublin Sunday, six groups of IRA gunmen began the systematic assassination of a group of specially trained and recruited secret servicemen, mostly MI5 and SIS specialists.[1] This unit had been recruited in the summer of 1920 in London and placed in charge of a Major C. A. Cameron. In all sixty agents were trained and despatched to

[1] See my 'Bloody Sunday—a Reappraisal', *European Studies Review*, 1972, for a detailed account of this episode.

Ireland.[2] It now seems certain that the majority of the men assassinated were members of this group. The attack, coming as it did when the British forces felt they had the IRA breaking,[3] was a momentous act of reassertion. Its timing was also crucial, since it had become apparent to the police, and certainly to the IRA leader Michael Collins, that the IRA boycott of police was crumbling, and general allegiance to the Republican cause weakening. Hence Bloody Sunday not only removed a major threat to the IRA but simultaneously gave a warning to the Irish people that no weakening of their resolve to continue the struggle and support the guerrillas would be tolerated.

Several questions arise out of the incident. How had such a large-scale exercise in liquidation and intimidation come about? Why were so many Irishmen prepared to kill for a cause? What was that cause and how had they been mobilized, inspired, and trained? Above all, what had reduced the British in Ireland to dependence on a coterie of spies, informers, policemen, and some 30,000 troops? Only a decade earlier King George V had been so moved by the reception he and his Queen had received in Dublin that he wrote to the Irish people: 'I cannot leave Ireland without at once giving expression to the feelings of joy and affection inspired by the wonderful reception which the people of Dublin have just given to the Queen and myself.'[4]

The seeds of a revolutionary situation were in fact already present in Ireland, if dormant, at the time of the King's visit. The Special Branch of the RIC (Royal Irish Constabulary) had given warning of coming trouble.[5] However, Augustine Birrell, Chief Secretary for Ireland, a romantic litterateur, and his staff at Dublin Castle chose to ignore them. Castle society, the company of Irish Establishment 'Castle Catholics', and the foyer of the Abbey Theatre were their milieux. They were not at home with the hard-headed reality of police reports.[6]

[2] Ormonde Winter, *Winter's Tale* (London 1955), 296.
[3] 'Lloyd George had confidently asserted that the IRA were defeated with the exception of a small murder gang'. *The Times*, 10 November 1920.
[4] Miscellaneous papers on the police. Public Record Office (PRO) London. C.O. 906/18/1, 12 July 1911.
[5] PRO, C.O. 900/89 to 904/107. See also Cd 8279, *Royal Commission of Inquiry into the Easter Rising*, 13: 'The Government had abundant material on which they could have acted many months before the leaders ... contemplated any actual rising.'
[6] Birrell wrote in 1915: 'I am only waiting for an opportunity to bid the world

Reinforcing the laxity and unsuitability of the chief administrators in Ireland, was the general decay of the administrative infrastructure from the 1880s onward. By 1914, when the Home Rule Bill was passed, the Irish administration had become a 'lame duck' even though the application of the Act was deferred until after the end of the war. As a consequence of the Act, the policy of economy in all departments of state was applied in Ireland with particular rigour. Governing Ireland became a mere holding operation. The sole object was to keep the country quiet. Successive British administrations had refused to take a stand on Irish issues. What few teeth the police still possessed were effectively drawn by political expediency. Ireland was not merely to be kept quiet but kept quiet at all costs. The law, if vigorously enforced, would be provocative. The solution was simple—the law was not enforced. Sir Neville Macready, later to have command of the security forces in Ireland, wrote of the RIC:

> This once magnificent body of men had undoubtedly deteriorated into what was almost a state of supine lethargy, and had lost even the semblance of energy or initiative when a crisis demanded vigorous and resolute action. The immediate reason was not far to seek. If an officer of whatever rank took it upon himself to enforce the law, . . . this action would as often as not be disavowed by the authorities at Dublin on complaint being made to them by the Irish politicians by whose favour the Government held office. This is no idle assertion on my part.[7]

The treatment of the police, and particularly of the Special Branch of the RIC, was in itself indicative of the loss of political will to hold on to Ireland. Special Branch activities were reduced even after the lesson, given by the 1916 Rising, that a government cannot safely ignore the warnings of its police and intelligence officers. In 1919 the extra allowance for the RIC Special Branch

---

of politics goodnight—but the opportunity never comes.' Letter to T. P LeFanu, 21 February 1915. Birrell Papers, Liverpool University, Ms 8.3 (3). Major Price, head of Military Intelligence in 1916, illustrated the lack of rapport between his service and the civil administration when he stated to the Commission of Inquiry into the Easter Rising: 'I liken myself to John the Baptist preaching in the wilderness. As to taking steps on the subject, the civil authorities didn't think it desirable to take steps.'

[7] Neville Macready, *Annals of an Active Life*, I (London 1924), 179.

was cut altogether.[8] It is hardly surprising that the Commission of Inquiry into the 1916 revolt should report that 'the main cause of the rebellion appears to be that lawlessness was allowed to grow up unchecked and that Ireland for several years had been administered on the principle that it was safer and more expedient to leave the law in abeyance if collision with any faction of the Irish people could thereby be avoided'.[9]

Equally important, while the administration's will to govern was declining, the forces of opposition were developing. Largely as a result of political expediency an Irish underground was allowed to form. Frustrated, the police could only watch.

This was part of the malaise within the British administration in Ireland. By directing its blows at the weak points of that structure, the IRA hastened its collapse. So effective was their campaign of terror and intimidation upon the courts, the police, the magistracy, and the local authorities, that all in time abandoned their responsibilities and saw them assumed by the local officers and leading politicians of the underground government represented by Dail Eireann.

The records of the Dublin Brigade IRA reveal, especially by the summer of 1920, the increasing demands placed on them for policing 'owing to the destruction of the alleged "police" force of the enemy and the rapid development of the civil side of Republican government'. The General Executive of the IRA in fact agreed to place at the service of the Dail, under officers specially appointed for the purpose, a police force voluntarily recruited from the ranks of the IRA.[10] The RIC was virtually helpless and useless. A plea from the Ballinasloe police to the de facto Chief Secretary, Sir John Anderson, on 30 August 1920 illustrates their plight:

> We consider it is almost an impossibility to carry out our functions as a civil police force under the present circumstances. The strain on the force is so great, by the daily assassination of our comrades who are ruthlessly butchered and murdered by the roadside . . . and the boycotting and threats arraigned [sic] against us, against our

[8] Winter, op. cit., 290.
[9] Cd 8279, 12.
[10] General Order, New Series No. 9, 19 June 1920. IRA GHQ brigade orders 1919 to 1921. National Library, Dublin. The papers are contained in series Ms 900.

families, our relations and our homes, that the agonies of a suffering force cannot be much further prolonged . . . The men are resigning in large numbers . . . we are now useless as a civil police force . . . We as a body are not able to restore law and order in this country today nor is there any hope on the horizon for a changed order of things when we could do so—we consider the best thing to be done is to wind up the force.[11]

The administration in Ireland thus failed to provide for a modicum of internal law and order. Once a government can no longer guarantee public security it has abdicated its mandate. By 1919, with the result of the Dail elections known, the administration was thus doubly illegitimate.

Of overriding importance in ensuring the efficiency of state controls are the Intelligence services which give warning of and locate threats to the system. Without detailed information as to the organization, personnel, aims and strategies of militant subversive groups, the government has to act blind. Lacking insight into the paths clandestine events are taking, and knowledge of the extent of public support for the rebels, it can only react; it cannot take the initiative. By infiltration and the use of informers it is possible to know where, when, and by what means the insurgents are acting. Where this technique is perfected it is possible not only to slow down the pace of the insurgent movement but also to divert it from its path by controlling it. The English in Ireland had previously demonstrated great skill in such intelligence operations. An Irish police magistrate noted: 'I have repeatedly heard it asserted that all informers should be shot. I can truly and deliberately declare it to be my own firm conviction that if all the informers of 1848 were so disposed of Dublin would have been decimated. There were in one great commercial establishment forty confederates of whom ten were in communication with the police.'[12]

This degree of access to subversive and revolutionary groups diminished sharply, particularly after 1916 when Michael Collins began to remove all informers in his own force as well as zealous Special Branch officers of both the Dublin Metropolitan Police

[11] PRO, C.O. 904/188/97, Sir John Anderson's Papers.
[12] F. T. Porter, *Twenty Years Recollections of an Irish Police Magistrate* (London 1880), 182.

(DMP) and the RIC. In addition to this the police suffered from the economies in the Irish administration, but, above all, from the effects of subjecting all police action to the test of political expediency. They were briefed to observe. At no cost must they disturb the peace. This irony bit deeply into the morale of both police forces.

IN THE FIRST INSTANCE it was the failure of the control apparatus which allowed the revolutionary zealots to muster unhampered and then to mobilize. The revolt of 1916 should have been an adequate warning that events and forces in Irish society were moving out of the grasp of the Castle administration and its police. However, within a year the underground forces, shattered in the aftermath of 1916, had been allowed to regroup. Committed and dedicated men already planning 'the next time' were released from internment in August 1917.[13] These developments may well have come to nothing had they not coincided with a major tactical reorientation in the methods of Irish protest, beginning at some point in the 1880s and reaching maturity by 1919. The tactical factor was of central importance, since it implied the existence of an organized force in opposition to the state with the ability to exploit favourable circumstances to the full. Easter 1916, the failed rising, demonstrated what was wrong with the thinking and practice of Irish revolutionaries. Their goal was the once-and-for-all major success; an all out engagement committing their forces totally in a static battle for a well defended position against enemy forces known to be far superior. The Irish risings of 1798, 1803, 1848, 1867, and finally 1916, revealed a revolutionary *idée fixe* at work in Irish revolutionary thought. In the revolutionary mainstream no practical or theoretical initiatives were taken to develop the techniques of protracted war, but outside that mainstream a group of men, the Irish Nationalist Invincibles,[14] a radical offshoot of Fenianism, took the first practical step towards a tactical reorientation. It was their example of systematic targeted assassination which was later taken up by the guerrilla leader Michael Collins.

[13] PRO, C.O. 904/106.
[14] See P. J. P. Tynan, *The History of the Irish Nationalist Invincibles and Their Times* (London 1894), and T. Corfe, *The Phoenix Park Murders* (London 1968). The former was written by an active member of the movement; the latter gives the most detailed account of the assassinations.

The Invincibles were responsible for the assassination of the Chief Secretary, Lord Frederick Cavendish, and his Under Secretary, Thomas Burke, in Phoenix Park, Dublin, on 6 May 1882. This act marked a crucial tactical and strategic change; its goal was the same as that behind Collins' advocacy of selective assassinations, namely, to provoke a war with England, in Ireland, so as to bring the struggle for Irish independence on to the international scene. Assassination for the Invincibles as for Collins, was to form the core of a war of attrition, a positive alternative to the restrictions imposed by the belief in the need to wait for the right time. Through such tactics the Invincibles sought to determine the timing and scale of the conflict, an example on which Collins was later to improve.

Coupled with this reorientation was a change in the location of revolutionary protest. Previously rural, it became urban-centred. Dublin, Cork, and Belfast became the foci of activity,[15] and this helped to change the class composition of the militantly active groups. From the 1880s onward there was a rapid decline in the conservative middle-class leadership of Irish politics and the rise of a far more radical lower middle class, epitomized by Padraig Pearse,[16] and presenting a curious amalgam of nationalist, cultural, revolutionary spirituality—a form of Gaelic messianism. The revival or creation of this spiritual movement was a major conditioning factor of the revolutionary war of independence.

Militant nationalism combined with the willingness to sacrifice oneself for the cause provided the dynamo for the revolutionary movement. In brief, there was a deep and pervasive cultural regeneration in Ireland fostered by organizations such as the Gaelic Athletic Association, the Gaelic League, various sections of the priesthood, and the quasi-monastic teaching order, the Christian Brothers, in particular.[17] There was also a spontaneous

[15] *Judicial Statistics, Ireland*, Cd 3112, 1905, 42; Cd 5866, 1910, 30, 34.
[16] Patrick Lynch, 'The Social Revolution That Never Was', in T. Desmond Williams, *The Irish Struggle* (London 1968), 42.
[17] Of the priests a police report noted: 'They exercise an immense influence over the youth in their parishes and unless some means can be used to make them abstain from interference in politics I fear that disaffection will be dangerously spread'. C.O. 904/102, January 1917. 'To the making of the new Ireland that we know today no one body has contributed more than the Christian Brothers. It could well be said that the insurrection of 1916 was a Christian Brothers Easter Week. Almost all the leaders of that heroic uprising and the glorious years that followed, had been pupils of the Christian Brothers ...

renaissance of all manner of Gaelic literature. In sum, there was a revival of Irishness and the assertion of a distinct national identity through which the Irish political will was regenerated. There was now an alternative to the ideas and allegiances imposed in schools and other institutions by the British administration. One vital revolutionary lesson the Irish learned in the process of this cultural renaissance was that a nation which is to succeed in modern war has to convince its people that the cause is worthy of martyrdom. It was a lesson the Irish took to heart, so that by 15 August 1920 *An t'Oglach* (the official newspaper of the IRA) could advise its readers that 'we realize it is far more profitable to kill for Ireland than to die for her'. It was this type of idealism which Michael Collins was able to canalize and direct against the ailing British administration. It also sanctified the violence which was to ensue during the War of Independence. Padraig Pearse had written: 'we must accustom ourselves to the thought of arms, to the sight of arms, to the use of arms. We may make mistakes in the beginning and shoot the wrong people; but bloodshed is a cleansing and sanctifying thing, and the nation which regards it as the final horror has lost its manhood. There are many things more horrible than bloodshed and slavery is one of them.'[18] Many Irishmen died in the years 1919 to 1921 in the belief expressed by Liam Mellows, a prominent IRA tactician and fighter, in his last letter to his mother: 'I believe that those who die for Ireland have no need for prayer.'[19]

These then were the major antecedents of the War of Independence; an increasingly inefficient administration faced by men fired with revolutionary zeal and convinced they could attain their ends by war. A set of contingent events was to provide the final catalyst.

First there was the example of the failed 1916 Rising and the canonization of its leaders, executed during General Maxwell's brief reign of terror when martial law was declared in the aftermath of the revolt. In a letter to Bryce, Chief Secretary for Ireland

---

from the Brothers the 1916 leaders learned their love of freedom, their desire for nationhood and the Gaelic way of life.' William Myles, 'The Irish Christian Brothers', in *St Mary's Centenary Record* 1860–1960.

[18] Padraig Pearse, 'The Coming Revolution', in *Political Writings and Speeches* (Dublin 1962), 98–99.

[19] T. P. Coogan, *The IRA* (London 1970), 53–54.

from December 1905 to January 1907, a witness of the Rising wrote: 'Of course this is not Ireland's rebellion—only a Sinn Fein rising.' Later she wrote that 'the Sinn Fein leaders were such good men. They died like saints. Oh! the pity of it! And Ireland wanted them so much. They were men of such beautiful character, such high literary power and attainments—mystics who kept the light burning . . . But as sure as God's sun rises in the east, if England does not get things right . . . if there's not immediately conciliation and love and mercy poured out on Ireland—all the Sinn Fein leaders will be canonized . . . Already the tone is changing.'[20]

The Rising was to prove superb propaganda for the Republican cause. It showed the Irish (or at least made Irishmen feel that they knew) where their true allegiance lay. What remained of the administration's legitimacy perished with this act. Majority opinion now lay with those seeking an end, most probably a violent end, to Dublin Castle and all it stood for.

Second, the death of the prominent Republican Thomas Ashe from being forcibly fed while on hunger strike, aroused tremendous passion. His funeral led to massive defiance of the orders against uniformed marches. Volunteers from all over Ireland gathered in Dublin to pay their last respects. Michael Collins' funeral oration gave some hint of things to come when he said that 'the volley we have just heard is the only speech it is proper to make above the grave of a dead Fenian'.[21]

Finally, the campaign for conscription of Irishmen to serve in the war jolted those groups who still stood with the British in Ireland into reconsidering their position. The attempt to enlist Irishmen to fight in a war ostensibly for the independence of small nations proved too harsh an irony. Priests, policemen, and people united at first against the conscription campaign[22] and later against the British. A letter to the *Manchester Guardian* (11 May 1918) from G. W. Russell (AE) poet, painter, and editor of the *Irish Homestead*, reported the events and indicated their likely outcome: 'if they [the British Government] persist in enforcing military service upon Ireland, if they insist on breaking the Irish

[20] Ms 11,016, Bryce Papers 1915/16 (1). Letter from Margaret Ashton, 16 July 1916, National Library, Dublin.

[21] F. O'Donoghue, 'The Reorganisation of the Volunteers', *Capuchin Annual*, 1967, 384.

[22] PRO, Report from the Midland and Connaught Region. Military Intelligence Report 523/G1/E.

will, there will not be a parish here where blood will not be spilt. There will grow up A HATE WHICH WILL NOT BE EXTINGUISHABLE lasting from generation to generation. It will be fed by tradition everywhere and our people live by tradition.'

THE WAR OF INDEPENDENCE, 1919 to 1921, was waged by the Irish from the outset with strong reliance on Intelligence, propaganda, politics, and guerrilla tactics, coordinated to make up a fully orchestrated plan of campaign. British forces, on the other hand, at no time fought their campaign in all these arenas. Their approach was piecemeal. There was no overall strategy and no conception of a coordinated counter-insurgency. During the summer and autumn of 1920 they did reorganize and develop in the Intelligence, political, and military arenas,[23] but by this time it was perhaps too late to put down the revolt. The battle for the minds of the Irish people had already been won by the IRA.

The IRA or Volunteers was the fighting arm of an underground, alternative government. It was made up entirely of volunteers. At the time of the 1916 Rising its strength, according to police estimates, was some 15,000 men, but in fact little more than 1,800 participated in the revolt.[24] The Volunteers had a long pedigree. A volunteer organization had been formed in 1778 but lapsed several years later. Its delayed successor was formed at the famous Rotunda Rink meeting on 25 November 1913, largely as a response to the Carsonite Volunteers in Ulster. Throughout the War of Independence the Army of the Republic called itself the Volunteers; it never officially adopted the name IRA.

At the heart of the organization was a far more clandestine and important group known as the Irish Republican Brotherhood (IRB). It was this organization which was later to use the Volunteers, the Gaelic Athletic Association and the Gaelic League as its 'front'. Michael Collins, as Director of Organization of the Army and President of the IRB was, in terms of control of the Irish underground, a far more significant man than the often absent De Valera. His intelligence network, based on the IRB, was

[23] See my 'Bloody Sunday', loc. cit., for a detailed analysis of this reorganization.
[24] CSO Registered Papers. Calendar of papers relating to the 1916 Rising in the State Papers Office, Dublin Castle. See F. X. Martin, O.S.A., 'Eoin MacNeill and the 1916 Rising', *Irish Historical Studies*, 1961, for a detailed account.

very much his personal apparatus. The IRB had been formed in Dublin in 1858 'as an oath-bound secret society with the uncompromising intention of overthrowing English government in Ireland by force of arms and of establishing an Irish Republic'.[25] Its members were picked men. As an organization it had a far more rigorous structure than the many amorphous conspiratorial groups that had emerged periodically throughout Irish history. As the one organized anti-government group within the state from the 1880s, it was able to canalize and direct the emergent revolutionary movement. The IRB was the vanguard of the forces of opposition, and it is of interest to examine its organizational structure—a structure which on paper at least remained the same from the 1880s down to 1921.

The main unit of organization was the 'circle'. This was the basis of the IRB in each locality. Members of the circle elected as their chief an officer who was known as 'the centre'. Each circle also had a sub-centre, a secretary, and a treasurer. All were elected officials. For operational purposes each circle was divided into sections of not more than ten men commanded by a section leader. Next in the ascending hierarchical structure was the district level. Each county in Ireland was divided into two or more districts. 'Centres', the leaders of the circle in each district, formed a board for directing the organization of IRB affairs in the district. Each district elected a chairman, vice-chairman, secretary, and treasurer. The chairman was known as the 'district centre' and was responsible to the county centre for the efficiency and discipline of his IRB unit. For the purposes of organization, operations, and recruitment, each city was considered a district.

Underground democracy also operated at the next level, the county. Here, periodically, local IRB centres held a convention to elect the county centre, county sub-centre, county secretary and treasurer. The county centre was in turn responsible to the divisional centre of the IRB for IRB affairs within the county. At divisional level the IRB was divided into eleven divisions covering the whole country and in addition Southern England, Northern England, and Scotland. The claim to have IRB organizations in the last three areas was certainly no idle boast, especially in the later period under Michael Collins.

[25] F. X. Martin, *The Irish Volunteers 1912-1915* (Dublin 1963), who treats this theme fully.

At the head of the IRB underground was the Supreme Council. This was the governing body of the organization, made up of one member from each of the eleven divisions and four additional co-opted members whose names were known only to the Council. The Council alone had power to inflict a sentence of death and give it effect. Indeed, from its inception it had regarded itself as the government of the Irish Republic with the power to levy taxes, raise loans, and carry out all the functions of a legitimate government.[26]

It was the Council which decided upon and engineered the Easter Rising, and the execution of its leaders also meant that (with the exception of the discredited MacNeill and the moderate Bulmar Hobson, who survived), the Volunteer executive was removed, since the personnel coincided. This interlocking directorate command structure was maintained throughout the War of Independence, with the Volunteers or IRA acting only on instructions from the IRB Executive, dominated by Michael Collins.

The failure of the Rising and the execution or internment of so many of the senior personnel of both the Volunteers and the IRB made it appear, on the surface at least, as if the Irish underground had been virtually destroyed. However, the work of two men in particular, Michael Collins operating amongst his IRB contacts, and Cathal Brugha, working through the Volunteers, began quickly and effectively to reconstitute the Irish underground. Brugha, seriously wounded in the 1916 fighting, escaped execution and when discharged immediately began recruiting for the Volunteers. He made contact with senior Volunteer officers still in Ireland and a group of some fifty men assembled under his chairmanship at Flemings Hotel in Dublin in November or December 1916. It was either at this or at a meeting held in the spring of 1917, that a provisional executive of the Volunteers was formed.[27].

Collins, like Brugha a member of both Volunteers and IRB, similarly began to reconstitute the Supreme Council of the IRB upon his release from internment in North Wales. He had joined the IRB in November 1909 and the Volunteers on 25 April 1914.

---

[26] PRO, W.O. 32/4308, 1920.
[27] F. O'Donoghue, op. cit., 381. Charles Burgess (Cathal Brugha) was later IRA Chief of Staff for a short time.

His first allegiance was to the IRB of which he later became President.[28]

The outcome of these efforts was that contact between the Dublin centre and the localities was restored and a degree of organizational unity within and between the two underground structures was re-established, so that when the internees were released they could rejoin a still intact underground which reflected the fusion between the old structure and the new methods evolved in the internment camps.

Theoretically, according to plans made after 1916, the Republican Army was to be a national force organized on the lines of the British Army and using its training manuals. (Its guerrilla content was marginal until Collins and Richard Mulcahy, later Chief of Staff of the IRA, intervened.) At first it was decided that the Army structure was to be based upon squads of eight men, sections of sixteen, and companies of four sections. With a full complement of officers and some special service personnel, each local unit should have numbered eighty-seven in all.[29] But this proved impractical, and the force was given a territorial basis, which meant that a great deal depended upon the local leadership. There was little or no uniformity of unit numbers. For example, company strength could vary between twenty-five and one hundred, while a battalion might be composed of three or ten companies, depending upon local conditions.

In 1917, following its annual convention in October, national coordination of the IRA began in earnest. The convention elected a National Executive with Brugha as its chairman, Collins as director of army organization, Mulcahy in charge of training, Rory O'Connor in charge of engineering, Diarmuid Lynch supervising communications, and Michael Staines in charge of supply. Although the National Executive functioned in name at least down to 1920, real power over the Army had passed by March 1918 to the GHQ Staff and then to the Ministry of Defence when Dail Eireann, the Republican underground government, was proclaimed in January 1919. Nevertheless, Collins and Mulcahy remained in command of the Army as well as Intelligence throughout the war.[30]

---

[28] Margery Forester, *The Lost Leader* (London 1971), Chapter 5.
[29] PRO, W.O. 32/4308.
[30] F. O'Donoghue, op. cit., 380–84.

Training and organization were most thorough. The whole of Ireland was divided into brigade areas. Sometimes these corresponded to the counties of Ireland but this was not a rule. Often the extent of a particular brigade depended solely upon where the writ of the local commander was enforceable. In most cases brigades consisted of four battalions, their nominal strength 4,000 men. Army Staff headquarters was at 6 Harcourt Street, Dublin, with some of the GHQ members also seeing active service as commanders of the Dublin Brigade IRA. Sinn Fein and its myriad clubs, the political arm of the IRA, often supplemented the work of the Army training staff by lecturing on military subjects. The clubs were also a most important source of recruitment and funds.

The chief staff officer in the IRA was a Brigade Adjutant, while an IRA Brigade Quartermaster had the same functions as staff captain in the British Army, except that he was also responsible for Intelligence. The better organized brigades also possessed a signals engineer, and scout, cycle, and medical officers, all holding the rank of captain. The subjects laid down for training were uniform throughout the Army and covered drill, cycling, scouting, engineering, and first aid. In addition, in each section two men were detailed for special services: engineering, scouting and despatch riding, signalling, transport and supply, first aid and musketry. In regard to all these a great deal of information was gleaned from demobilized soldiers. General Headquarters of the IRA in fact issued a memorandum to all units of the Army instructing them to make every effort to enlist ex-soldiers.[31]

UNIFIED, COHESIVE, AND READY for action by the middle of 1919, the IRA concentrated its activities on the British administration and the League of Nations, through which it hoped to reach international opinion. Intelligence was its strongest point. Indeed, it was largely because of the efficiency of the IRA's intelligence arm that their plan of campaign proved so effective. This was Michael Collins' own empire. Almost single-handed he established the intelligence network and this was in fact its major weakness.

[31] PRO, W.O. 32/4308. Sinn Fein was the political arm of the Volunteer army. A police report noted: 'The Irish Volunteers, though a distinct body under separate control, are recruited from the Sinn Fein clubs, each club being supposed to contain a company.' PRO, C.O. 904/105, March 1918.

Collins recognized at an early stage that his twin enemies were the spy and the informer,[32] the parasites of any revolutionary movement, and he systematically removed both. Once this internal sanction had been institutionalized the weapon was turned, with great effect, on the special branches of both DMP and RIC. The impact of the terror campaign was summed up by an observer of the Dublin scene writing in 1920: 'a man might have been murdered in broad daylight (and many were) in the Dublin streets, and not one policeman have lifted a finger. The uniformed men on point duty would have gone on waving traffic this way and that . . . the attitude of the police was reasonable—while they stayed neutral they were safe; as soon as they interfered they became marked men.'[33]

Thus the removal of informers and spies became built into IRA tactics. As late as the spring of 1921 they were still being shot. Between January and April 1921 seventy-three bodies, with placards round their necks announcing the removal of an informer, were taken from the Irish streets.[34] The secrecy of IRA operations was rigorously maintained and Collins' intelligence agency could act with a considerable feeling of security.

The intelligence network was organized on two distinct levels— the civil and the military. The military side, by far the more important, operated mainly through the underground cells of the IRB which Collins commanded. Formally, it was organized on British military lines. Each company and battalion had an intelligence officer whose reports were passed through a Brigade intelligence officer to the central office in Dublin. However, this was an adjunct to Collins' own network of IRB spies operating in most Irish communities.

On the civil side Collins had men and women in post offices, on the railways, on channel ferries, in every prison in Ireland and many in England. Similarly, dockers in all parts of Europe and the USA served in what Collins referred to as his 'Q' Division.

[32] Collins told Hayden Talbot: 'Every man had been tested thoroughly. First I did it myself and thus satisfied myself regarding the trustworthiness of my chief aides. Then gradually the finding of the true measure of each new man became automatic and in turn the clearing out of the ranks of the IRA of undesirables became easier and faster.' H. Talbot, *Michael Collins' Own Story* (London 1923), 79.

[33] J. M. Nankivell & S. Loch, *Ireland in Travail* (London 1922).

[34] J. Bowyer Bell, *The Secret Army* (London 1970), 4.

But by far the most important amongst his agents were the men working for him in the Special Branch of the DMP, men at the heart of the British administration, with access to restricted information, all codes and the like. In particular four Dublin policemen—Broy, Neligan, Kavanagh, and MacNamara, helped to turn what had been Britain's greatest security asset in Ireland against itself. On the night of 7 April 1919 Broy arranged for Collins to have access to all the files at Special Branch GHQ. From 12.30 to 4.30 a.m. Collins buried himself in the documents.[35] It is hardly surprising that every move of the Special Branch was from this point onwards known in advance to the IRA. Detectives in plain clothes were not immune since their identities were known. As they were systematically shot the Special Branch ceased to provide information. Like the senior Castle administrators, they became cloistered men not allowed out of barracks without a strong armed escort.

IRA propaganda, like its Intelligence, was highly efficient. It reached and was planned to reach all the major European capitals and the USA. The department had been established in April 1918 under Robert Brennan. Its functions had first been to supply Sinn Fein leaders with data on which to base their movements, but it soon dropped this information work and became an aggressive arm of the campaign. The *Irish Bulletin* was its main organ and was distributed free to press correspondents and liberal minded men of political influence in England. By 27 April 1921 £4,000 a year was being spent for the 'general routine work' of the London office alone.[36]

However, it was in the military arena that the IRA had its most visible successes. The effect of its operations were such that even in Dublin senior policemen, administrators, and military officers were forced to live a monastic existence within the walls of Dublin Castle. There were so many IRA ambushes in one particular complex of streets that the British forces termed the area 'the Dardanelles'.

Major IRA activities were typical of a guerrilla force—attacks on police barracks, on army and police patrols and convoys;

[35] Forester, op. cit., 114–15.
[36] PRO, C.O. 904/162/1. Sinn Fein Propaganda, and DE 2/10, Correspondence with Publicity Department 14 February 1920 with a report on the department dated April 1922. Dail Eireann Reports, National Library, Dublin.

assassination of individuals; destruction of government property; robbery and highway robbery; the disarming of guards and police for the capture of weapons. The aim of the attacks on police barracks was twofold: to break the hold of the police on the local communities and to capture much needed arms and ammunition. Normally the attacks were carried out by fairly large companies of the IRA, generally one or two companies of a battalion which were either local or had been sent from a neighbouring county. The assembly of such large groups of men was often effected by holding a sports meeting in the neighbourhood. The crowds gathered for such meetings were supposed to disarm suspicion. Bloody Sunday, November 1920, was an excellent example of this tactic in operation. Here some 120 IRA men travelled to Dublin under cover of attending the final of the All Ireland Hurling Championship at Croke Park.

Arms for IRA raids were usually brought in by car and attacks carried out after dark. The thoroughness of so many of these raids is indicated by a British War Office assessment noting in 1920 that 'at a given time the attackers congregate and all roads but one are blocked with obstacles for a radius of anything up to five miles of the point to be attacked (a case has occurred where an area up to twenty miles has been blocked) in order to delay any relieving force'. In the attacks upon patrols and convoys IRA units of varying strength were employed. Normally there were not more than fifty to sixty men or fewer than six to eight waiting behind a wall or a ditch; where a small attacking force was engaging a patrol, as was often the case, it operated from the midst of an apparently innocuous crowd who shielded the attackers afterwards.[37]

The leading edge of the IRA terror campaign was selective assassination, involving groups of three to ten men. Police, magistrates, informers, and men prominent in public life were shot. There were even plans (vetoed at the last minute by Collins and Arthur Griffith) to assassinate the whole of the British Cabinet by machine-gunning the Government front benches from the spectators' gallery in the House of Commons. Assassinations in fact ran the whole gamut from vengeance killings (such as that of a former officer in the British Army, Captain Lee Wilson, who had severely mistreated Collins and other combatants of the

[37] PRO, W.O. 32/4308.

1916 Rising in front of their own men and British soldiers), to expediency.[38] Redmond, Chief Inspector of the DMP, had to be removed because he was pressing Collins too hard; similarly, the magistrate Allen Bell, taken in daylight from a Dublin tram and shot without anyone interfering, was assassinated because he was carrying on a most successful investigation into the origin and whereabouts of the Dail Loan deposits.[39] Assassinations such as these, and particularly the removal of spies, Collins regarded as essential to the success of the IRA campaign. As he wrote: 'England could always reinforce her Army. She could replace every soldier that she lost . . . But there were others indispensable for her purposes which were not so easily replaced. To paralyse the British machine it was necessary to strike at individuals.' Collins had in 1919 drawn around him an elite group of full time assassins known as 'The Squad' or the 'Twelve Apostles'. Police intelligence reported in 1919 that 'according to information received from various sources the Irish Volunteer HQ has directed all county commanders to hold a certain number of men armed and in readiness to execute orders to attack barracks and assassinate police'.[40]

AS AN ARMY THE IRA was thus tactically and organizationally sound. It knew its military limitations and fought within them. It was also highly mobile. By the autumn of 1920 flying columns had been organized in several of the most active brigade areas. Towards the end of 1920 all brigades were instructed to create such units.[41] Militarily the success of the IRA was due to its speed, mobility, and Intelligence—all of which depended in one way or another upon the support of the Irish people. As T. E. Lawrence noted, the insurgent force 'must have a friendly population, not actively friendly but sympathetic to the point of not betraying rebel movements to the enemy. Rebellions can be made by two per cent

[38] Forester, op. cit., 296.
[39] PRO, C.O. 904/177/1.
[40] Michael Collins, *The Path to Freedom* (Cork 1968), 69–70. At first the squad numbered only four, but was later expanded to include some twenty men. Throughout the war it was commanded by Paddy O'Dalaigh. See Donal O'Kelly, 'The Dublin Scene', in *With the IRA in the Fight for Freedom*, ed. D. Nolan (Tralee 1946). PRO, C.O. 904/109 (3), Inspector General's Monthly Report, September 1919.
[41] F. O'Donoghue, 'Guerrilla Warfare in Ireland', *An Cosantoir*, May 1963, 299.

active in a striking force, and ninety-eight passively sympathetic'.[42] The majority of the Irish were not passive but committed to the fighting men and their creed, which made it possible to carry out swift concentrated attacks on selected objectives with the utmost secrecy.

The policies and actions of the British forces were limited to reaction against the moves of their opponents. Rarely did they take the initiative. Neither was there recognition of the need to wage a counter-insurgency campaign in the major arenas of the war. The British response was piecemeal when coordination was called for; it was heavy-handed when there was a need for finesse. The lesson learnt in the Irish War of Independence that, to quote Lawrence again 'guerrilla war is far more intellectual than a bayonet charge', was later forgotten in Palestine, Cyprus, Aden, and Northern Ireland.

The whole British campaign suffered from the lack of strategic and tactical reflection and a clear command structure; security operations were not placed under one man. Sir Mark Sturgis, a senior administrator in the Castle during the struggle, noted 'the more I see of it [the war] the more convinced I am that if it is war we must have a virtual dictator to be obeyed by everybody, military, police, civil service etc. As it is we are a great sprawling hydra-headed monster spending much of its time using one of its heads to abuse one or other of the others, by minute, letter, telegram and good hard word of mouth'. He cavilled at the half measures advocated by the British politicians. 'If we aren't to treat', he wrote, 'we must hit and if we must hit then we must hit damned hard. Why does some hideous fate make all politicians love half measures which of all so-called policies is the only surely fatal one.'[43]

In the vital area of Intelligence the British lack of coordination was all too apparent. Army, Navy, Police, and Secret Service all operated separately, jealously preserving contacts and information from each other. This state of affairs had existed before the War of Independence. H. E. Duke, who became Chief Secretary on 11 August 1916, after Birrell's dismissal, had attempted, without

---

[42] T. E. Lawrence, 'The Science of Guerrilla Warfare', in *Encyclopaedia Brittanica* (1948), 953.

[43] Sir Mark Sturgis' Diary, August 1920, PRO, 30/59.

success, to systematize the disparate intelligence groups. In a memo submitted to the British Cabinet he wrote:

> the General Officer Commanding in Chief and the two Chiefs of Police argue, and the heads of the Administration concur in the view, that there is urgent necessity for better organization and some development of the branch of police investigation which deals with criminal conspiracies and other classes of organized crime and especially with the plotting of revolutionary movements and disorder akin thereto ... I am satisfied that the present organization of the CID in Ireland is entirely inadequate ... Scotland Yard, MI5, the censorship, and the CID of the Irish police forces require to be associated for the purpose of intelligent mutual action.[44]

There were too many organizations and all were inadequate until the counter-insurgency effort of autumn 1920 went some way towards coordinating British actions. For three and a half months from August to mid-November, when the specially trained group of secret servicemen were operating, the IRA and Collins were on the run. IRA leaders and prominent Republicans were systematically assassinated by these British agents. Collins himself was in danger of being captured or killed. Then, on 20 November 1920, he assassinated the core of this group in one operation. There was little chance from that point on that the British would win. Collins and his guerrilla army had grasped the principle enunciated by the narodniks that 'the terrorists cannot overthrow the government, cannot drive it from St Petersburg and Russia; but having compelled it for so many years running to do nothing but struggle with them, by forcing it to do so still for years and years, they will render its position untenable'.[45]

Thus Ireland's future was to lie with the underground government and its fighting arm, the IRA. They had built up an infrastructure of opposition government and their cause was popular. The War of Independence was fought to institute in Ireland a native government deriving its authority from the Irish people. Only when the national consciousness was awakened, when international opinion was to their advantage, and when a sophisticated, violent opposition had matured, were the Irish able

[44] PRO, CAB 37/154, 7-8.
[45] Stepniak, *Underground Russia* (New York 1892), 32.

to defeat what they had come to regard as a foreign power. Collins captured the essence of the struggle when he wrote:

> Ireland's story from 1918 to 1921 may be summed up as the story of a struggle between our determination to govern ourselves and to get rid of British government and the British determination to prevent us from doing either. It was a struggle between two rival Governments, the one an Irish Government resting on the will of the people and the other an alien Government depending for its existence upon military force—the one gathering more and more authority, the other steadily losing ground.[46]

[46] Collins, op. cit., 65.

Berlin Police in the Weimar Republic: A Comparison with Police Forces in Cities of the United States

James F. Richardson

Professor Liang has written an interesting study of Berlin's police during the years from 1919 to 1933.* He contends 'that well-selected topics in the history of one city can lay the basis for a fresh look at the social history of modern Germany', an assertion with which all urban historians would agree. He has examined the surviving police documents (although unfortunately he was not allowed to look at those located in East Berlin), and has read widely in the historical literature and the novels reflecting life in Berlin during the period. He also interviewed a number of veteran policemen who had served in Berlin before 1933. By agreement he did not raise any questions about their activities after the Nazis came to power in 1933.

Professor Liang's choice of subject is an eminently justifiable one, in that the police played an extraordinary role in Berlin during the period as Germany's major problems shifted from war and foreign relations to the maintenance of internal security. The massive police presence on Berlin's streets astounded foreigners and irritated many of the residents, and the historian who would understand the city during the Weimar years must pay attention to the police,

* Hsi-huey Liang, *The Berlin Police Force in the Weimar Republic* (University of California Press 1970).

their perception of their function, and their ability to perform it.

Like American police departments, the Berlin force looked to its history and traditions for guidance. These traditions reinforced a basic conservatism among the police, who conceived of their role as an order-maintaining and indeed a civilizing one. They saw themselves as protecting society's basic values against the unruly, the criminal, and the disorderly. Their traditions were anti-army, especially after the army expanded its internal functions during the first world war, and in so doing constituted a threat to the sphere of the police. They were also traditionally anti-democratic, as democracy seemed synonymous with disorder, and somewhat anti-government, as the politicians might do things which would make the role of the police more difficult. The reader familiar with the speeches of William Parker, Los Angeles Chief of Police in the 1950s and early 1960s, finds many echoes in Liang's comments about Berlin in the 1920s. Parker viewed the police as a thin blue line separating civilization from barbarism, and warned Americans that if they did not support the police in their work American cities would become little better than jungles.[1]

What is perhaps more interesting to the historian of urban America and its police are the fundamental differences between the Berlin force of the 1920s and the early 1930s and American departments of the same period.

During the 1920s, the Berlin police possessed all the ingredients that American writers on police affairs thought necessary for their own departments. Although Liang does not address himself directly to the appointment and tenure of senior administrators, his account does indicate that men remained in high administrative posts for long periods, and seemingly were free from the petty political pressures so common in American cities of the time. American writers like Raymond Fosdick, Bruce Smith, and August Vollmer cherished the hope that 'politics' could be removed from police work, and that well qualified and secure administrators

[1] William H. Parker, *Parker on Police*, ed. O. W. Wilson (Springfield, Ill. 1957).

and commanders could mould their forces in a desired image of efficiency and incorruptibility. They lamented the fact that in some large American cities the average police head lasted about two years in office and found himself constantly pressed and harassed by ward politicians seeking desirable assignments for their favourites and exile for their enemies within departments, and police toleration of illegal activities carried on by people with the right connections. The American proponents of police professionalism wanted administrators to come from the ranks of the well educated and the respectable, from outside a department if necessary to secure an able man, and perhaps from outside police work entirely.[2]

Berlin's administrators met these qualifications. The Deputy Police President, Dr Bernhard Weiss, had a degree in law and served creditably in the judiciary before the war. After the war he joined the police, although apparently always serving in a civilian capacity, and was appointed Deputy Police President in 1927. He held this position until purged in 1932 because he was a Jew.

American reformers pressed for higher qualifications for officer ranks, which the Berlin police apparently achieved. Liang indicates that the officers were more inclined to reactionary monarchism than the rank and file, which implies separate recruitment from higher social levels. American

[2] Raymond B. Fosdick, *European Police Systems* (Montclair, N.J. 1969 [originally published 1915]), 149-80, 369-85; idem, *American Police Systems* (Montclair, N.J. 1969 [originally published 1920]), 217-67; idem, 'Police Administration', *Cleveland: Reports of the Cleveland Foundation Survey of the Administration of Criminal Justice in Cleveland, Ohio* (Montclair, N.J. 1968 [originally published 1922]), 3-82; Bruce Smith, *Police Systems in the United States*, revised and enlarged ed. (New York 1949), 5-9; Citizens' Police Committee, *Chicago Police Problems* (Montclair, N.J. 1969 [originally published 1931]). Bruce Smith served as Staff Director for this study; see especially the chapter on 'Police Leadership and Control'; August Vollmer, 'The Police (in Chicago)', in Illinois Association for Criminal Justice, *The Illinois Crime Survey* (Montclair, N.J. 1968 [originally published 1929]), 357-72. See also Vollmer's remarks in the National Commission on Law Enforcement and Observance (Wickersham Commission), Report No. 14 (Montclair, N.J. 1968 [originally published 1931]), 26-35; Raymond Moley, 'Politics and Crime', *Annals of the American Academy of Political and Social Science*, May 1926.

observers on the other hand criticized the low quality of senior officers. In the aftermath of the war, when intelligence tests achieved more widespread prestige as a result of the army's mass testing programme, the experts were shocked to discover that policemen in general scored badly on the tests, and that the officers sometimes had lower ratings than the patrolmen. One hypothesis advanced to account for this was that the more intelligent men became disillusioned with police work and left it before they had enough service to be promoted.

Raymond Fosdick thought little of the Cleveland Police Department as a whole when he surveyed it in the early 1920s. He had particular scorn for the detectives who had the lowest average I.Q. scores of any group in the department. The bureau was administered in such haphazard fashion that Fosdick wondered how the detectives ever solved any crimes, especially with such a low quality of personnel.[3] In contrast the Berlin *Kriminalpolizei*, the Kripo, demanded at least a secondary school education for its applicants, and many of the men had at least some university training. The Kripo recruited directly from civilian life; its officers did not have to begin as patrolmen as was the case in American police forces. Moreover many American detectives achieved their rank because of their political connections, not their capacity. The upper levels of the Kripo came from the upper levels of society. Twenty-two of its agents possessed doctorates, a situation inconceivable in an American police department, where many of the detectives could barely write literate reports. The Berlin Kripo solved 39 of the 40 homicides committed in the city in 1928. Cleveland, a much smaller city, had 79 homicides in that year, of which 63 were solved.[4] Fosdick also questioned the initial recruiting process in American cities. The tradition of local boys for local jobs limited many departments to residents of their own cities. In some cases out-of-towners could apply, if they lived in the same state, but they would have to establish residence in the

[3] *Criminal Justice in Cleveland*, 64-74.
[4] Cleveland, Ohio, Department of Public Safety, Division of Police, *Annual Report*, 1928.

city before appointment. The Berlin police, on the other hand, recruited from the countryside. Young peasant lads and village craftsmen were more likely to pass the rigid physical examination than city workers. The author interviewed twenty-one men who had served as patrolmen in the 1920s; only three were native Berliners and none was working class in origin. In contrast to the years before 1914, when the Berlin police were old soldiers, the men appointed in the twenties were young, between twenty and twenty-two, and they were scheduled to leave the service after twelve years, at about thirty-two, either with severance pay or a preferred position for a civil service opening. Many American police departments accepted applicants up to the age of thirty-five and in some cases even older, and made no provision for a pensioned retirement until after twenty or twenty-five years of service. Thus a department could easily have much of its patrol force in the forties and fifties, which Fosdick and others considered too old for active service.

The Berlin rookie spent his first year in the police school, which was demanding physically and often stressed preparation for combat. In many American cities the new man got his uniform, club, and gun, and then was sent out on the streets to learn by doing. Even the most elaborate American training programmes lasted only a few months, and whenever cities faced budgetary pinches, one of the first economy measures was to eliminate the police training school. After his year in training the Berlin policeman served in a riot brigade for three or four years, and only after further schooling was he assigned to regular precinct street patrol.

One feature of Berlin's police that American experts would not want transferred to the United States was the existence of police unions. These covered most members of the force, and administrators had to concern themselves with grievance committees as well as parliamentary supervision. In the United States the memory of the Boston police strike of 1919 remained a vivid one. Calvin Coolidge may well have gone to the White House because of his public stand against that strike while governor of Massachusetts. Police organizations in the United States usually had 'benevolent' or 'fraternal' somewhere in the title to disarm public criticism even when their primary activity was legislative lobbying or other forms of political pressure. The last thing Fosdick, Smith, and Vollmer wanted was any further limitation on the police chief or commissioner's freedom of action. To them the basic problem of the American police was not tyranny at the top but impotence.

The American police bureaucracy wanted administrators to come from within their own department. Policemen stressed the value of career service and promotion from within in the selection of heads to ensure that administrators were thoroughly indoctrinated in the traditions and practices of a particular department. Moreover, organized police groups often succeeded in getting legislation framed to protect themselves against unwanted innovation. In New York, for example, the three platoon law passed before the first world war stipulated three eight-hour shifts with the same number of men assigned to each. An administrator then could not decide to put more men on duty during the high crime periods. American cities provided elaborate review procedures so that any man in danger of removal had one or more possible appeals to agencies outside the police department. In many cases the courts or civil service commissions reversed decisions of police chiefs or commissioners. Over the years groups like New York's Patrolmen's Benevolent Association and the Fraternal Order of Police, which has chapters in a number of cities, have come to function more like labour unions, although the word is still avoided and there does not seem to be any inclination to affiliate with organized labour. Indeed, American police departments had a long record of hostility towards unions and unionization. Chicago is a classic example. The Memorial Day massacre of 1937 was only the most outstanding of a long series of incidents of police hostility to strikes, strikers, and labour demonstrators.[5]

[5] Wallace S. Sayre and Herbert Kaufman, *Governing New York City: Politics in the Metropolis* (New York 1960), 75, 428-80; Melvyn Dubofsky, *When Workers Organize: New York City in the Progressive Era* (University of Massachusetts Press 1968), 53, 64, 78, 107, 117-18,

To outside observers and reformers, two of the most troubling aspects of American police concerned corruption and brutality. Corruption in regard to vice laws was ingrained in many American departments and the enactment of prohibition simply intensified a long-standing condition. The underworld had flourished for years with appropriate police payoffs in making available prostitution and gambling; now prohibition opened a new and very profitable area of operations. Again Chicago in the era of Al Capone and Mayor Big Bill Thompson provides the most spectacular example.[6] Corruption was rare in the Berlin police, partly because an appointment as a policeman provided material security for twelve years and the men were not willing to endanger that security. What also seems plausible is that Germany and Berlin did not enact the kind of morals legislation, creating crimes without victims, which made corruption among American policemen so attractive and in a way defensible. Certainly Berlin in the twenties had a flourishing Bohemia and a distinctly unconventional night life. Those who were upset by the immorality of the city crusaded not for improved police performance but rather for a change of regime, for the return of the monarchy or for a nationalist government that would curb vice, restore order, and bring Germany to greatness again.

Although the Berlin police could be heavy handed in dealing with street demonstrations, it was a serious breach of police ethics to employ violence against a criminal suspect. One police detective was reported by his superiors and punished for beating a murder suspect during interrogation. The Wickersham Commission appointed by President Hoover showed a very different pattern in such cities as Chicago, Cleveland, and Buffalo, where third degree practices were commonplace.[7] American police forces developed a code of

---

on police activity against strikers in New York before the war; Irving Bernstein, *Turbulent Years: A History of the American Worker, 1933-1941* (Boston 1970), 485-90 on the Memorial Day violence.

[6] Humbert S. Nelli, *Italians in Chicago, 1880-1930* (Oxford University Press 1970), 125-55, 211-22; John Landesco, 'Organized Crime in Chicago', *Illinois Crime Survey*.

[7] Wickersham Commission Report No. 11, *Lawlessness in Law Enforcement*, 102-04, 118-27.

violence and secrecy. As the sociologist William Westley has demonstrated, policemen had these norms drilled into them during their socialization as rookies. In puting on the uniform, a man not only took up a job but embarked on a way of life. As an occupational and social group, policemen accepted the use of violence to advance their ends. Thus they justified the use of force to impose respect for the police among a cop-hating population, or to make an arrest and secure a confession in a criminal case. The 'good pinch,' the arrest which did not entail negative political consequences, brought prestige to the individual and satisfied the public that the police department was doing a good job. Beating a confession out of a suspect saved police manpower, and if the man escaped punishment in court, he still had his bruises to remind him of his transgression. The police also justified the use of violence in sex cases, where the victim might be reluctant to press a complaint or where the legal machinery seemed inadequate to cope with the offender.

The habit of secrecy came from the policeman's sense of public pressure and hostility, which required solidarity among the police to protect themselves. Therefore men were not to talk about department business to outsiders, and above all, they were not to inform on a fellow officer. In the department Westley surveyed many policemen were willing to commit perjury to avoid informing on colleagues guilty of a felony. Any man suspected of being a 'stoolie' was shunned by his fellows and deprived of any information at all. In this way he would not be 'in the know,' and his ignorance would not only protect his fellows but also harm him if he did not know for example that the chief intended to crack down on smoking on duty.[8] The Berlin police seemed ready to expose corruption if it appeared within their ranks and to punish individual acts of brutality. What they did not seem ready to do was challenge or disclose illegal or disloyal political activities and opinions among themselves. Many of them, especially among the officer ranks, were hostile to the

[8] William A. Westley, *Violence and the Police* (MIT Press 1970), *passim.* This excellent book is based on a study made in the late 1940s, but there is every reason to suppose that the patterns it delineates were also present in the 1920s.

republic, longed for the return of the monarchy, or looked to some right-wing saviour. It was the political climate which made the work of the Berlin police so much more difficult, indeed impossible after 1930, compared to that of American cities.

Berlin did have one major political advantage over the American cities of the Northeast and Middle West, where it was apparent that the outward movement of people and industry had developed to the point where the suburbs of cities like Boston, New York, Cleveland, and St. Louis were growing more rapidly than the cities themselves, and that there was a serious need to integrate the work of local authorities. Police observers lamented the political fragmentation of metropolitan areas where there were scores if not hundreds of separate municipalities, each one of which maintained its own police force. Many of these departments were small, poor in the quality of their people and facilities, and unable to provide effective law enforcement. When the heat was on in Chicago, John Torrio and Al Capone found friendly suburbs like Cicero from which to conduct their operations. Similarly, Berlin found much of its elite moving to the western suburbs after the war, just as wealthy Clevelanders moved to Shaker Heights. The difference was that Berlin and its police could grow to encompass these new areas. In 1920 the jurisdiction of the Berlin police was expanded to 552 square miles as 8 municipalities, 55 suburban districts, and 23 estates were combined into one Greater Berlin. American cities had fought for years to get 'home rule', freedom from legislative interference by their respective states; now they found that the suburbs could chant the same slogan to resist annexation by the central city, and good talent and good taxpayers increasingly moved outside the city's political boundaries.[9]

Greater Berlin had 14,000 to 16,000 men to provide police protection for its 4,000,000 citizens. This was a far larger force than was available to American cities. New York, with a 1920 population of 5,600,000, had only 12,000 policemen,

[9] Blake McKelvey, *The Emergence of Metropolitan America: 1915-1966* (Rutgers University Press 1968), 9-14.

and most other American cities had even smaller departments in relation to their population. Simply put, the German authorities were prepared to pay for a larger force than American cities, whose police authorities often attributed their crime and disorder problems to inadequate staffing, although there is no evidence that increasing the size of a police force has any effect on the crime rate. But if the sight of uniformed men on the streets reassured the citizens, the good burghers of Berlin should have slept soundly at night.

In the most fundamental sense, however, Berlin's political problems far surpassed anything to be found in the United States. To be sure, American society suffered from the dislocations attending the aftermath of the war; 1919 was not a good year. A pessimistic observer, John Dos Passos, for example, could easily believe that the fabric of American society was unravelling as strikes, race riots, and anti-radical and anti-foreign hysteria gripped the land.[10] Five years later, however, the bulk of the population seemed content to 'keep cool with Coolidge' and devote itself to making money and enjoying the new consumer goods like the automobile and the radio pouring out of the nation's increasingly productive plants. The social strains of the twenties manifested themselves in farm bloc interest group politics, the Ku Klux Klan, and in campaigns to restrict immigration and hound radicals, not in attacks on the fundamental economic and political bases of the society. The alienated expressed their discontent in expatriation or art, not in radical politics. The massive impact of the depression that deepened steadily from 1929 to 1932 resulted in shock and apathy, and although there were signs that the mood of the American people was turning ugly in the summer of 1932, still elections proceeded according to schedule and most people retained their faith in the values of the culture and the validity of the system.[11]

How different Germany's experience proved in the same years! The German revolution of 1918-19 was superficial in that many of the institutions and values of the old monarchy survived the rather casual and fortuitous creation of the

[10] John Dos Passos, *1919* (New York 1937).
[11] William E. Leuchtenburg, *Franklin D. Roosevelt and the New Deal* (New York 1963), 23-29.

Weimar Republic. During the 1920s the Republic had numerous enemies both on the right and the left, although as long as the German economy functioned effectively the supporters of the Republic could count on at least the tacit approval of the majority of the voters. Berlin in the decade attained the status of a world city, not only the hub of German life, but a leader in the cultural revolution attendant upon the collapse of the old order and a mecca for 'advanced' young men and women throughout the world. For most Berliners, however, the period was marked by anxiety and a sense of discontinuity. The physical artefacts of the monarchical past remained without providing the people with a sense of the essential continuity of past and present, or a feeling of rootedness and belonging. As Liang puts it, the city 'had lost its former bearings'. The Paris peace settlement, the reparations issue, the war guilt clause, and the great inflation weakened the legitimacy of the Republic and obviously had a great impact on the police force responsible for the security and good order of the nation's capital. The police controlled the streets until 1925, but thereafter new techniques of political agitation and the increasing incidence of violence overwhelmed the force. The police had lost control of the streets by the summer of 1932 and were ripe for a political takeover.

As the depression of 1930-32 shattered the German economy, the political centre began to crumble as sentiment swung towards the extremes of the Communist and Nazi parties. What was lost in Germany after 1930 was the sense of comity, the belief that political conflicts must be fought with some civility and concern for the basic humanity of the opposition, and that all members of the society have to continue to live together no matter what the outcome of an issue or an election. Comity can most easily be maintained when the bulk of the people agree on the fundamentals. As has often been said, government by discussion works best when there is nothing very important to talk about. Germany in the early 1930s did not meet these conditions; the extremist parties denied the legitimacy of the opposition and of the Republic itself.

How could any police agency maintain order and stability

in a time of increasing conflict between political groups bent on each other's extermination unless it was prepared to use the most totalitarian and repressive measures? The Berlin department may have been only imperfectly democratized during the Weimar period, but it was not ready simply to gun down any extremist political group that took to the streets. The maintenance of order in any society rests ultimately on a shared system of values and a willingness to live together without undue violence if not necessarily in full peace and harmony. No police force, no matter how large or technically efficient or politically committed, can act as a substitute for at least a minimal sense of moral community. The police may supplement the social consensus, may enforce its dictates against those who deviate, provided the deviants are only a small proportion of the population; they cannot replace the informal controls inherent in comity.

While the Weimar Republic was undergoing its final illness as Communist and Nazi strength grew, the United States maintained its basic comity. One does not have to be a 'consensus' historian to note the importance of the contrast.[1][2] Indeed, the men most responsible for consensus interpretations of American history written in the 1950s, Louis Hartz and Daniel Boorstin, both made much of the contrast between Europe and America, between the bitter divisiveness of European class and political struggles and the narrow range of disagreement characteristic of American politics. Europeans were ideologues while Americans were either all Lockeans or political pragmatists who concentrated on maximizing their gains within the system rather than seeking its overthrow.[1][3] In recent years historians, not all of whom can be classified as members of the New Left, have been more impressed by the extent to which the vaunted American consensus rested on the exclusion of substantial

[1][2] These comments on comity and consensus owe much to Richard Hofstadter, *The Progressive Historians: Turner, Beard, Parrington* (New York 1968). The final chapter is a valuable discussion of recent trends in American historiography.

[1][3] Louis Hartz, *The Liberal Tradition in America* (New York 1955); Daniel J. Boorstin, *The Genius of American Politics* (University of Chicago Press 1953).

segments of the population. In the 1920s, neither blacks nor working class whites fully participated in the political process. In a system where numbers counted less than organizational strength, men and women of the wrong colour and economic class found their interests sacrificed to those with greater economic and political resources. People committed to a fundamental transformation of the system constituted a small, easily isolated, and easily suppressed minority. Even after the onset of the depression, Americans to a surprising degree retained their faith in the values of enhancing status through the acquisition of material goods, and the unemployed often blamed themselves for their plight. Despite the fact that the rate of unemployment reached 25 per cent at the depth of the depression, and never dropped below 14 per cent until the unintended Keynesianism of the second world war, millions of Americans both with and without jobs believed that any man who really wanted a job could find one. American voters rejected even the mild socialism of Norman Thomas in favour of the essentially conservative policies of Franklin Roosevelt.

In this political context, American police more often had to contend with individuals seeking to enhance their economic status in socially disapproved ways than with political demonstrations and violence. If communists did parade in New York and other cities, the police had no compunction about cracking heads. The majority of the population was more anti-radical and anti-communist than it was pro-civil liberties. Interestingly enough, Liang says that crime in Berlin may even have declined in the 1920s had it not been for the rising levels of political violence. Perhaps much of the energy that might have gone into individual acts against the penal code may have found an outlet in political demonstrations. In American cities, on the other hand, where organized political street activity was noticeably absent, individual crimes were apparently much more frequent. American criminal statistics are unreliable for the present day and infinitely worse for the 1920s. No matter what the reality may have been, Americans certainly thought themselves engulfed in a rising tide of crime and therefore devoted considerable attention to the police and criminal justice systems in an attempt to stem that tide. Scholars and publicists blamed 'politics' for increasing crime and weakening the effectiveness of law enforcement and the court machinery. They rarely asked whether the ideology of the individual pursuit of wealth and the systematic exclusion of substantial elements of the population from the legitimate achievement of this end made crime a reasonable way to attain the goal the culture sanctioned—money—even though the means were formally against the law. Accepted American spokesmen stressed the way to wealth and the road to riches as the American way of life, while at the same time upper and middle class institutions maintained roadblocks against blacks and new immigrants. In these conditions crime might not always represent alienation from the values of the culture, but an attempt to reach its goals by alternative means. During prohibition, the criminal bootlegger could even be considered something of a culture hero, and Al Capone thought of himself as a businessman and social benefactor performing a public service by meeting a public demand.[14]

American cities did have much higher rates of crimes against property and violent crimes than did European cities. Burglary, robbery, and homicide occurred more frequently in New York, Chicago, and Cleveland than they did in London, Liverpool, and Berlin. Fosdick and other contemporary observers concentrated on the poor quality of American police departments and the chaotic conditions of urban criminal courts in accounting for these differences. Fosdick did recognize the greater heterogeneity of American cities with their large foreign-born and Negro populations and its possible implications for crime and public order. He and those of his generation rarely asked, however, whether American individualism and materialism, with the consequent lack of support for many basic human needs, did not also influence men and women to flout the legal code and engage in individual acts of theft and aggression. In short, it seems to

[14] Daniel Bell, 'Crime as an American Way of Life', in *The End of Ideology* (Glencoe, Ill. 1960), 115-36.

me that the history of crime and disorder must be related to the values and the social structure of a particular society, and that a myopic approach to the study of police history will pay only limited dividends.

Police and Public in the United Kingdom

J. J. Tobias

In 1962 the Royal Commission on the Police declared its belief that

> there is a peculiar quality in the relationship between the police and the public of this country . . . It is attested by the foreign visitor whose favourable comments on our police are well known, and it is demonstrated in the common every-day instances in which people instinctively consult a policeman when in difficulty or perplexity even of a minor kind . . . It is not generally disputed that there is a kind of relationship between the policeman and the man in the street in this country which is of the greatest value.

This passage has been criticised by Professor Michael Banton, who mentions the high quality and reputation of the Swedish (and probably other Scandinavian) police and the Royal Canadian Mounted Police, and adds 'There are police departments in the United States and probably in many other industrial countries with standards little different from those in Britain'.[1]

Since these passages were written, however, changing fashions of public demonstrations of political dissent have provided additional opportunities for comparing police forces. Some participants in such activities, contrasting their treatment in Great Britain with that received in some places on the continent of Europe or in the United States of America, have made, albeit somewhat reluctantly, remarks which support the traditional comment of visiting film stars—'I think your policemen are wonderful'. At least one foreign observer agrees with the Royal Commission. Professor A. Beristain, saying that 'in many nations (not in all) the

---

[1] Parliamentary Publications, 1962, para. 327; M. Banton, *The Policeman in the Community* (London 1964), 10.

relations between police and society in general are few, weak, impersonal, and more negative than positive', hastens to add, 'we are not speaking here, for example, of England'.[2] He does not indicate, however, which other nations he thinks fall into the same category. The British police are no doubt not unique; but it seems reasonable to suggest that there are few countries of the world where police forces of a comparable nature cover the whole of the territory or have had so long an existence. It thus seems worth while enquiring into the special nature of British policing.

For Charles Reith, an invaluable if somewhat naive and uncritical historian of the Metropolitan Police, the explanation of the special nature of the police of Great Britain lies in the fact that it springs from common-law roots and represents 'the community policing itself'; while the police of, say, France is the heir of 'the police of the prince' of the Roman Empire, tracing its descent through feudal times and standing armies to the gendarmeries of continental despots. This explanation (derived in part from a mistaken view of the nature of policing in Ireland under British rule) is inadequate. In what sense does a Metropolitan constable of 1829 or 1972 represent 'the community policing itself', while a Parisian *agent* is a member of 'the police of the prince'? Policemen in London and Paris are alike salaried, full-time officials of the state, under the orders of hierarchical superiors who are ultimately responsible to a minister and to an elected assembly; they are alike bound to obey the law of the land and to prevent the overthrow of the government by unconstitutional means. Historical traditions indeed account for many of the differences between the police of London and of Paris, but Reith did not present the whole picture.[3]

Charles Reith was not alone in drawing a distinction between common-law countries and others. Professor Brian Chapman has refined the contrast that Reith made and has

[2] A. Beristain, 'Relations between Police and Society Today', *Abstracts on Criminology and Penology*, May 1971, 295.

[3] cf. Charles Reith, *Police Principles and the Problem of War* (London 1940), 32-33, 77-78; *The Blind Eye of History* (London 1942), 20-21, 147, 242; *British Police and the Democratic Ideal* (London 1943), 14-16, 264-65.

shown how the Roman-law tradition was developed into the 'police state' by a combination of French, Prussian, and Austrian thought. Ideas originating in the Roman law and in administrative practice in Paris under Louis XIV were blended with German efficiency to make Prussia under Frederick William and Frederick II the first police state, on a model later developed by Joseph II of Austria and by Fouché, Napoleon's minister of police. Though the police state itself eventually adopted the totalitarian forms which have given the term its evil connotations in English, the better traditions of the earlier models are clearly still strong in France and elsewhere.[4] Professor Chapman contrasts the states within this tradition with the common-law countries, which had, *inter alia*, a much narrower view of the functions of government and a long tradition of opposition to the very idea of a strong central government. In the climate of opinion which prevailed in England, from the Restoration at any rate, the idea that a main function of the police was the gathering of information about public opinion—the function that makes the *Renseignements Généraux* an important part of the French police—was anathema.

In the light of these distinctions one can attempt to explain the different developments in policing in London and Paris, despite a superficial similarity of starting points. In Paris as in London, there had survived from the Middle Ages a night watch made up of inhabitants of the city or their deputies and under the control of the local authorities. In both cities this watch fell into disrepute and had to be replaced by a centrally organised body under the control of the national government. Yet in London, though its Commissioners have always been directly responsible to the Home Secretary, the Metropolitan Police has never become an arm of the government in the way that enables modern French writers on the police to devote attention to its relations with '*le Pouvoir*'. Resistance to the idea of a strong and well informed

---

[4] B. Chapman, *Police State* (London 1970), 14-32. It would be possible to argue that nineteenth-century Ireland was a traditional police state (as Chapman defines the term) despite its common-law background.

97

government delayed for a long time the improving of London's police. Attempts to reform the police were rebuffed in 1785, in 1818, and in 1822, on these grounds. The makers of opinion did not want a strong government, and this demonstrated a self-confidence which their French contemporaries could not feel: they did not believe that the government needed internal strength to maintain the regime. The House of Commons which passed the Six Acts in 1819 contained many of the men who had the year before accepted the view of a Select Committee that

> Though your committee could imagine a system of police that might arrive at the object sought for [an improvement in the policing of London and a reduction of its crimes], yet, in a free country, or even in one where any unrestrained intercourse of society is admitted, such a system would of necessity be odious and repulsive ... It would be a plan which would make every servant of every house a spy on the actions of his master, and all classes of society spies on each other.

Much the same group of men was told by another Select Committee in 1822 that

> It is difficult to reconcile an effective system of police with that perfect freedom of action and exemption from interference which are the great privileges and blessings of society in this country; and your committee think that the forfeiture or curtailment of such advantages would be too great a sacrifice for improvement in police or facilities in detection of crime.[5]

Thus, though there is contemporary evidence of alarm among the upper classes at popular unrest, it should not be overstated. Alan Silver writes: 'In the London ... of the late eighteenth and the early nineteenth centuries, people often saw themselves as threatened by agglomerations of the criminal, vicious and violent ... The social order itself was threatened.' However, though some members of the ruling classes held these views, their fears of the criminals were not strong enough to overcome their fears of tyranny. It is consistent with this view that, when Parliament finally took its courage in its hand in 1829 and greatly strengthened the police force under the direct control of the government by substituting the Metropolitan Police for the Bow Street

[5] Parliamentary Papers, 1818, viii, 32; 1822, iv, 107.

Patrols, it was the level of crime and not the fear of revolt which led it to do so.[6]

There were other differences between Roman law and common law. One aspect of the greater power of central government in France is the doctrine of 'la tutelle' or 'le contrôle administratif', which enables it to give orders to local authorities in certain circumstances, or even at times to act in their stead. This, coupled with the fact that a *maire* is from certain viewpoints an officer of the central administration, forms a contrast with the limited powers of supervision available to English governments even today; in the early nineteenth century the only weapon with which the central government could force local authorities to do their duty was the cumbrous and uncertain machinery of the law courts, which could be used only when a clear statutory duty was being neglected. Parishes could escape with a very perfunctory performance of duties entrusted to them.

A further difference between the two legal traditions is relevant. The common law differed from the Roman law in that it placed more emphasis on the rights of individuals, and put public officers in a less favourable position. The liberty of an Englishman could be interfered with only by due process of law, and even when arrest or other restraint was justified, it remained lawful only so long as the officer enforcing the law adhered strictly to all the forms of the law, and above all used force only when and only so far as it was strictly necessary to accomplish his duty. Nor was this all: not merely were there these restraints on the actions of law-enforcement officers, but there were remedies readily available[7] should they err. Unlike their fellows in other lands,

[6] cf. J. Hamburger, *James Mill and the Art of Revolution* (London 1963); A. Silver, 'The Demand for Order in Civil Society', in D. J. Bordua, ed., *The Police: Six Sociological Essays* (New York 1967), 3,15n.

[7] 'Readily available' may seem something of an exaggeration, for the nineteenth-century phrase, 'Justice is open to all, like the London Tavern', represents a long-standing truth. But Saunders Welch warned eighteenth-century constables of solicitors 'for ever watching their conduct, and ever preying upon either their ignorance or rashness' (*Observations on the Office of Constable with cautions for the more safe execution of that duty drawn from experience* (London 1754),v),

public officials in England were liable in their personal capacity for acts done in their public capacity which offended in some way the elaborate code of controls. An action for damages, or prosecution for murder, could await an unlucky peace officer. It is hardly surprising that the unpaid officers upon whom so much of the burden of law enforcement rested were not over-zealous in doing their duty, that they developed the style of action that lawyers and police officers call 'minimum force' and sociologists 'a low-profile response'. The early professional forces of Britain grew up in this atmosphere, and certainly the Metropolitan Police itself was born into a suspicious world full of people looking sharply for signs of a threat to liberty, and certainly its first leaders were constantly alert to suppress or prevent conduct likely to put the force in bad odour with the public. The habits the force acquired in its formative days were shaped by the fear of seeming a threat to liberty. 'I want to teach people' wrote Robert Peel 'that liberty does not consist in having your house robbed by organised gangs of thieves, and in leaving the principal streets of London in the nightly possession of drunken women and vagabonds';[8] and Richard Mayne and Charles Rowan, the men whom he had appointed to head the new force, were anxious to prove his point and show that they could combat the thieves, drunken women, and vagabonds without affecting the liberties of ordinary men.

Allied to this fear of being haled before a court of law as defendant in a civil action or prisoner in a criminal action, there was the constant fact of appearance in court as a witness, with its exposure to hostile questioning. It is in the nature of a police officer's duty that he has to appear in the witness box to give a public account in minute detail of many of his activities and to face cross-examination thereon. In former times, moreover, the only authority to which English constables were subject was a court. In country areas the

---

and the legal profession had not then developed its embargoes on taking speculative cases with payment dependent upon a successful outcome.

[8] Peel to Wellington, 5 November 1829, in C. S. Parker, *Sir Robert Peel from his Private Papers* (London 1899), II, 115.

justices of the peace were the only administrative body above parish level, and the only threat the authorities of a borough or urban parish could make to an errant constable was to prosecute him before the justices—an unwilling and unpaid servant cannot be sacked or have his pay docked. These facts help to explain the excessive formalism and adherence to detailed records which is only just disappearing from the police tradition, and they may have played their part too in shaping the distinctive attitude to the public which still survives. The police forces of Roman-law countries, of course, also had to give evidence in court, but the absence of the full adversary system as known to English law would spare them the rigours of hostile cross-examination.

The matters so far discussed clearly cannot provide an explanation for the differences between the police forces of Britain and America, for the United States too is a common-law country, and the sheriff and his posse (both terms, be it noted, coming unchanged from the Middle Ages) represented 'the community policing itself' even more directly than did a parish constable and his paid watchmen.[9] The differences seem to stem in part from the different nature of political life in the two countries. In New York as in London, the growth of the city beyond its original boundaries and the problems presented by the level of crime led to the establishment by the legislature of a metropolitan police for a wider area and a number of local authorities, with commissioners to exercise control over it. Yet in London the force remained remote from politics and the commissioners were soon seen as part of the force, while the New York Metropolitan Police, during its short period of life, was intimately bound up with politics and its commissioners remained very definitely politicians. Mr Richardson's fine study of the New York police in the nineteenth century and before is largely an examination of the political connections of the force. The commissioners controlled from outside an

[9] cf. C. Reith, *Police Principles*, 82 ff.; *British Police*, 204-06. In his *Blind Eye of History* he suggests (80-81) that if there had existed in Boston in 1775 a force like the Metropolitan Police of 1829, the American War of Independence would not have taken place.

organisation which was important both for the patronage it provided—and each commissioner sought to make sure that his own party had its fair share of the plums—and for its role in elections; from 1865 until the end of the century the conduct of elections was part of the responsibility of the police commissioners, and from 1872 the police were actually responsible for counting the votes and declaring the results.[10]

Political control led to undesirable consequences. The power in the force was in the hands of the precinct captains rather than the superintendent at headquarters—always provided that the captains respected the requirements of local politics. Political involvement of police and courts (the justices too were political appointees) meant that conviction and punishment were politically determined, thus weakening policemen's respect for the law and increasing the chance that they would impose summary punishment. Provided they were selective when taking the law into their own hands and did not oppress anyone with political support, they were likely to find the courts and public opinion disinclined to intervene to correct brutality. The lack of homogeneity in the population played its part here—certain minority groups were specially liable to rough handling. Moreover, not all inhabitants of the cosmopolitan city were ready to accept the laws controlling personal conduct passed by the New York State legislature, in which the City had only a minority voice. This difficulty was most acute in relation to the regulation of the drink trade, and the police and courts of the City for much of the nineteenth century were merely making a show of enforcing laws which could probably not have been put fully into operation by the most efficient law enforcement agency conceivable. This situation encouraged the growth of bribery, which eventually became part of the way of life of the force and a prominent feature of the informal organisation. Things had moved a long way from anything found in London.

[10] J. F. Richardson, *The New York Police: Colonial Times to 1901* (New York 1970), 228-29 and *passim*.

Mr Lane's study of the Boston police in the nineteenth century displays some of the same features. Boston in the 1830s modelled its policing on that of London, but it was the pattern London was about to abandon that it copied—the detectives were similar to the Bow Street Runners in status, and the day police and the night watch remained separate forces. It was not until the 1850s that a force on the new police model was established. Boston's police did not have the political involvement of the New York force, but it was, like the remainder of the municipality's services, under the control of the mayor, who had all the power conferred by the American 'strong-mayor system'. Minority groups existed as in New York, and the drink problem was similar: Mr. Lane records a gradual descent into violence by police, tolerated by those in control as long as the victims were carefully chosen. Though the force had not at first been armed otherwise than with clubs, the men eventually began to carry their own firearms, with official connivance. There was not the strict control of the police that existed in London, and again a very different state of affairs was reached by the end of the nineteenth century.[11]

Professor J. Q. Wilson has described three styles of policing in the United States today, the watchman style, the legalistic style, and the service style. Without claiming that this typology can be applied to the past, it can be said that the London police was more akin to the legalistic or service style. while the New York or Boston forces came nearer to the watchman style. This is important, for Wilson notes that the political culture of a community acts as a constraint on the style of law enforcement which is adopted, and he associates the watchman style with cities where party politics permeate the police and other departments of municipal government.[12]

Some writers have called attention to more general factors

[11] R. Lane, *Policing the City: Boston 1822-1885* (Cambridge Mass. 1967), *passim*.
[12] J. Q. Wilson, *Varieties of Police Behaviour* (Cambridge Mass. 1968), 140-45, 172-73, 200-01, 271-77.

which were at work. D. J. Bordua points out that the English police benefit from 'long-standing patterns of deference to the symbols of legitimate authority, coupled with a long-established cultural homogeneity and crowned symbolically by the monarchy'; the performance of public duty, whether paid or unpaid, is more highly valued in Britain than in the USA. Michael Banton mentions the 'producer ideology' that led to a devaluation of the service occupations in the developing United States. Alan Silver adds that the British police 'embody moral consensus in the eyes of the general community, their "clientele" and themselves' more thoroughly than do the American police—and though this is a description of the present situation and is therefore the effect which is to be explained, the contrast may still have been valid in the formative years a century or two ago.[13]

It cannot be claimed that a definite explanation can yet be given why policing in Great Britain is conducted in so gentle a manner, why the Metropolitan Police and the other forces, despite all their trials and tribulations and despite occasional heart-searchings about lost goodwill, have so calm a relationship with the public they serve. Yet our ignorance could be very dangerous. Much of the economic and social change of our modern world affects the task that the police has to perform, and the cumulative result could well be great. Moreover, the police service is itself changing—the structure of forces has been drastically reorganised, foot patrol has largely given way to the panda car, and personal radio has eliminated the isolation that formerly engulfed police officers as soon as they left the station. As T. A. Critchley observes, 'the rapport established for years between a predominantly working-class police, organised for the most part in small local units, and the mass of the population, will not necessarily survive the present changes in police organisation (the grouping of forces into larger units, changes in

[13] D. J. Bordua, 'Police', *International Encyclopedia of the Social Sciences* (London 1968), XIV, 177-78; S. M. Lipset, 'Anglo-American Society', ibid. I, 298-99; M. Banton, op. cit. 87; Silver, op. cit. 22n.

recruitment policies, and growing professional skills) and the accompanying changes in the class structure in Britain'.[14]

The force of this comment is enhanced by its author's personal knowledge of the changes taking place (Mr Critchley was Secretary to the Willink Royal Commission on the Police, 1960-62, and was later an Assistant Secretary in charge of one of the police divisions of the Home Office). It would be a bold man who affirmed that Britain's present advantage in policing will of necessity persist for the foreseeable future, and thus the search for an explanation of that advantage is not just a matter of historical interest.

There is a conventional version of the history of the British model of policing, which was encouraged by Melville Lee, Charles Reith, and other early writers in a not too well cultivated field. This is based on the idea that a new-model police force devised by Robert Peel, perhaps as a result of his Irish experience, was put into operation in 1829, sweeping away a corrupt and inefficient system of parish watches which had in essence changed little from the Middle Ages. The beat system of policing, even the very idea of a regular preventive patrol, is ascribed to Peel or to the first Commissioners, Charles Rowan and Richard Mayne. This picture is based in part on too ready an acceptance of the description of the parochial watches given in 1829 by those who wished to abolish them, and too ready an acquiesence in the view that if the parochial watch system was inadequate in 1829 then it had never served a useful purpose.

In fact, the development of London's policing was continuous. One great milestone is indeed 1829, but the Metropolitan Police did not represent a complete break with the past. It was concerned both with night and with day policing, by contrast with the night watch; it covered a district much larger than that of most other forces in London; its personnel was of a higher class than that of the forces it replaced. But much of the method used by the Metropolitan Police had been developed by the better parochial watches before it, and we have here, in part at any rate, the familiar story of the generalisation over a wide area

[14] T. A. Critchley, *The Conquest of Violence* (London 1970), 204.

of reforms earlier tried out in piecemeal development within a smaller compass. The reforms of 1829 were, of course, fundamental, but concentration on them has led to the neglect of 1735, a year which deserves equal prominence in police history as the one in which the principle of a rate-supported force was established.

The parish constable of the 1820s, on the eve of his replacement by the Metropolitan Police, held an office which had in essence changed little from medieval times. However, it was the watchman's task, rather than the parish constable's, that was performed by the rank-and-file members of the Metropolitan Police, and the watchman superseded in 1829 was a very different creature from the watchman of the Middle Ages. The system of policing which post-Reformation England inherited from the Middle Ages rested on the principle of unpaid performance of duty by members of the community as their turn came round. Householders were liable to be called upon to do duty as constable of their parish for the year, or as watchman of their street for a night. In either case a money payment could relieve one of the burden, but whilst personal performance of duty as parish constable was still common in the early nineteenth century, personal performance of duty as watchman had died out in the metropolis long before. It seems probable that by the end of the seventeenth century the normal, and perhaps the invariable, practice was instead to pay a small sum of money to a parish officer, purely as a private arrangement; the money thus collected, or some of it, would be used to hire paid watchmen. Unofficial practice in time became statute law. A century before the paid professional constable took over from the unpaid amateur, the legal obligation to do personal service as a watchman was ended in much of the metropolis. In 1735 two Westminster parishes obtained parliamentary sanction for the substitution of a new system of watching, based upon a permanent body of watchmen financed from money collected by means of a rate (to Americans a 'local tax') on the inhabitants. The citizen now—without choice—paid a tax for his nightly protection, the money to be used by the parish authorities and not by a parish officer acting privately, to pay watchmen who were now part of the parish's staff of paid public officials and subject to the controls that that status entailed. The system soon spread to much of the rest of the capital, so that for a century there was a mixed system—watchmen paid from the rates were supervised by constables serving either in person or as deputy paid by an inhabitant who did not wish himself to do the duty. One aspect of the reform of 1829 was to extend the principle of 1735 and eliminate the obligation of personal service as constable, substituting an increased burden on the rates. Thus 1735 deserves some of the prominence hitherto given to 1829.

However, the present argument is not that one climacteric should be recognised instead of or as well as another. It is rather that there is a continuous process at work, giving rise to major discontinuities from time to time but effecting great, if more gradual, transformations even when the pattern seems unchanged on the surface. As a society grows richer, its standards rise. A level of crime which is tolerable at one time is too great in a subsequent period; a system of policing which is accepted in one generation seems glaringly inadequate in the next. As time goes by society takes more and more of its higher income in the form of improved policing. 1735 and 1829 were years of major organisational reform, and one consequence of the reforms was an increase in the expenditure on policing caused by an increase in numbers employed and improved methods of working and of supervision, adding up to epoch-making change. But there were less dramatic changes in organisation, less sudden increases in numbers, less marked improvements in technique in other years, which over a period added up to an impressive total. The parochial watches in 1829, on the eve of their supersession by the Metropolitan Police, were more numerous and more highly organised than those of the 1730s, and followed very different methods. It is easier to identify and to describe the years of great change, but this should not lead us to neglect the pattern of constant development.

In Ireland developments followed a different course. John Stuart Mill observed that one cause of the mis-handling of

Ireland's affairs by English politicians was that the same terms were used on both sides of the Irish Sea, but with different meanings in the two countries. No-one, he pointed out, would assume that an Indian zemindar had the same rights and duties as an English landlord, but people thought the relationship between tenant and landlord in Ireland to be the same as in England—which was far from being the case. He could have made his point by referring to the police, for much discussion of the affairs of Ireland turned on the assumption that the word 'police' meant the same there as in the remainder of the United Kingdom. This was not the case.

The system adopted in 1829 for the Metropolitan Police spread subsequently to the remainder of Great Britain. It is this tradition of unarmed civil police which was the model for the recent reshaping of the Royal Ulster Constabulary. However, that force is the lineal descendant of the Irish Constabulary established in 1836 and given the title 'Royal Irish Constabulary' in 1867. Although the latter force was not popular with either the Catholic majority or the Protestant minority, it was accorded a grudging respect even by the opponents of the regime it supported so well and for so long. The Metropolitan Police and the Royal Irish Constabulary had much in common in their standards of adherence to the law and of impartiality in enforcing it—they both, after all, originated in common-law countries. However, in many respects the two concepts of policing were markedly different. The RIC was a semi-militarised force, a *gendarmerie*, and always had in the forefront of its mind the maintenance of law and order amongst a population large elements of which were often actively or passively opposed to the whole system of law which the force sought to uphold. It was indeed explicitly designed to provide a means of suppressing disorder without the use of the military. 'The frequent use of soldiers in that manner', said Robert Peel in the House of Commons on 23 June 1814, 'made the people look upon them as their adversaries rather than as their protectors'.

From the outset the Irish Constabulary had a character very different from that of the London Metropolitan Police and the corresponding forces of the other countries of the United Kingdom.[15] One important aspect of this lay in the different nature of the officer corps. In the London Metropolitan Police, men of the 'officer class' were deliberately restricted to the highest ranks—in the original establishment, indeed, only the two Commissioners were from this class. In the boroughs of England and Wales, save at times in the very largest, even chief constables were not usually drawn from the officer class. In the counties the chief constables were very often retired military or naval officers, but such men were seldom if ever found in ranks below the command posts. In the Irish Constabulary, and in its predecessors (the Peace Preservation Forces formed in 1814 and the provincial Constabularies formed in 1822), there was a gulf between the officers and the men as broad as that which existed in the Army. Some of the first officers were drawn from the armed services, but fairly soon a system of cadetships was established: 'except in extraordinary cases, no gentleman shall be appointed to the office of Sub-Inspector who shall not have undergone a course of training as a cadet'.[16] An indication of the class from which the future officers were drawn is given by the regulation that no-one could be accepted as a cadet unless the guarantee was given that he would receive £50 a year in addition to his pay. It was argued that an officer class was necessary, as the inspectors were 'brought into contact with the local gentry and magistrates. In many cases they could get information by knowing the local gentry that they would not get if they did not associate with them'.[17] It was not, it is true, impossible for a man from the ranks to become an officer: a number of the vacancies in the officer ranks were open to head

[15] The Royal Irish Constabulary had a numerous progeny, for it was the model for the Indian Police Service and many colonial police forces. Much of this material on Ireland appeared in an article by the present writer published in *The Criminologist*, November 1970.

[16] Regulations dated 17 November 1842, cited in P. J. Carroll, *Notes for a History of Police in Ireland* (typescript, Police College Library) ch. 21, 14.

[17] Civil Service (Ireland) Enquiry Commission, Parliamentary Papers, 1873, XXII, 208.

constables, the senior non-commissioned rank, but the proportion was only one in six in the early days of the force, though it rose to one in two towards the end of its life.

The existence of an officer class was only one way in which the police of Ireland had a military character quite foreign to the police forces of Great Britain. Robert Peel himself had used the expression *'gendarmerie'* when in 1814 he was seeking to outline the sort of force that he had in mind for the Peace Preservation Forces. Circumstances gave the Irish Constabulary a different role from that performed by the other forces of the United Kingdom: it was constantly called upon to deal with 'disturbances' which had no counterpart on the other side of the Irish Sea. The men were often summoned by telegram for special duty outside their own area—to help at an eviction, to prevent an illegal meeting, to keep the peace between rival factions, to maintain order during trials for agrarian offences or similar crimes, to provide special armed protection to threatened persons. Someone writing in 1886 about the work of the RIC spoke of Ulster having to be 'invaded annually'—the reference is to the way in which men of the force from other parts of the country were summoned to go to the assistance of those in the northern province at times of sectarian conflict. The writer pointed to the contrast between Dublin, 'where no jarring elements exist' (and where there was a Metropolitan Police like that in London), and Belfast, 'the social volcano of the Empire'.[18]

For these reasons, the RIC was an armed force. Its men, save when performing beat duty in the towns, went armed and in couples. It was organised in larger units than was common in England. Even in the quiet districts, a country village which in England might have had one constable living on his own, was in Ireland policed by three or four constables and a sergeant. The police were housed in barracks which determined the minimum size of the unit. There was a rule that each man in turn must be barrack orderly for a 24-hour stretch, not leaving the barracks during that period.

[18] M. Brophy, *Sketches of the Royal Irish Constabulary* (London 1886), 25.

Another difference between the two systems of policing was that the Irish Constabulary was a national force under the control of the government, whereas Britain was policed by local forces under the control of the local authorities. The capital cities formed exceptions in each case; the law-enforcement body of each was a Metropolitan Police, paid partly from local funds but under the control of the executive government. In the other cities and towns of Ireland the constabulary shared the duties of law enforcement with a local nightwatch force which was a legacy from medieval responsibilities. Most of these night-watches were quietly abandoned, their duties passing to the RIC; but the cases of Belfast and Londonderry were different. Here the town forces were markedly Protestant in their composition, and in each case—in Belfast in 1865 and in Londonderry in 1870—an Act of Parliament deprived the town of the right to its own police force after a riot which gave rise to suspicions of partiality. In each case, the policing of the town was entrusted to the Irish Constabulary.

Another difference lay in the use of firearms. For normal duty in Belfast, the men carried batons, like their colleagues in London and elsewhere. But every man had in his barracks his own rifle and bayonet, and in the particular circumstances of Belfast they had of course frequent occasion to resort to their use. It was only after 20 years of experience that the revolver was substituted for the rifle. Another feature which differentiated the RIC from the normal urban police force was the fact that the men—certainly the single men, and some of the married men as well—were congregated in barracks. It was of course common enough in other urban forces for the single men to be gathered in one officially-provided residence (the section-house), and even in large towns it has at various times been policy to provide quarters for the married men. But there is a world of difference between these means of providing the men with the necessary living accommodation and the RIC's use of barracks. Indeed, the very word 'barracks' in itself conveys the difference. The barracks of a Constabulary unit, in Belfast or elsewhere, was, and was designed to be, a secure place, the defence of which was a

111

prime consideration in the organisation. (This was what lay behind the rule that one of the men must always be detailed as barrack orderly.) Belfast was the only major city of the United Kingdom whose police lived in barracks rather than in houses and section-houses, which were merely places for the men to live and sleep in.

The Belfast section of the RIC became something of a separate entity within the larger force. The men regarded themselves as something of a *corps d'élite*; after 1886 it was not the custom to send men from other parts of Ireland into the city as reinforcement in time of trouble. The use of what were known as 'country men' in Belfast was anathema to the officers of the force after that year, for it was alleged that these men, strangers to town policing and to the particular problems of Belfast, and of course mostly Catholic, had been over-ready to use firearms against the (Protestant) rioters. Even though the charges had been dismissed by the inevitable Commission of Enquiry, there were official fears in 1912 that people would recollect, and tell their children of the shooting of their relatives in 1886 by the country police, who, it was thought, were badly handled and awkwardly situated. Indeed, in the latter years of the nineteenth century and the early years of the twentieth, the RIC was so unpopular with the Protestants of Belfast that in times of acute unrest the patrolling of their areas was left to the soldiers. When the Falls Road area had to be cordoned off from the Shankhill Road, the RIC faced the Catholics while the soldiers faced the Protestants.

In sum, the RIC cannot be regarded as having been successful in its task of policing Belfast. Its failure was conditioned by the circumstances of the force—it was organized and controlled and trained for the task which it had to perform in the country districts but not for the task which it had to perform in Belfast. While to the Catholics it was, in Belfast as elsewhere, the instrument of English rule (though on the whole a not unpopular one), to the Protestants of Belfast and the rest of Ulster it was the instrument by which Westminster and Dublin Castle threatened to force Catholic rule upon them. Insofar as we can ever judge of such things, it had the confidence neither of the majority of Ulster's population nor of the minority. It was, in Reith's terms, a 'police of the prince'; nineteenth-century Ireland can perhaps be regarded as, in Chapman's terms, a 'police state' of the traditional, non-totalitarian variety; but the common law ruled in Ireland, and thus the relationship between police and public there had something in common with that in the rest of the United Kingdom. It is perhaps possible to perceive a United Kingdom approach to the problems of policing.

Policing Palestine 1920-36: Some Problems of Public Security under the Mandate

Tom Bowden

Policing Palestine 1920–36

> *Just Palestine Policemen a' doin' of their job,*
> *We come from every walk of life there be,*
> *We're pretty slick an' slippy, an' we 'aven't got a bob*
> *But we're known from Tel Aviv to Galilee.*
>
> *There's Christian, Jew and Arab in this ruddy 'oly land,*
> *As matey as a bunch of rattle snakes*
> *But if you'd give us coppers just a day or two's free hand,*
> *We'd guarantee we'd give the lot the shakes.*
>
> *Now there's Hussein El Mohammed and Moses Moshevix*
> *Plus Parliamentary members safe in Tooting,*
> *What's mucking up the country with their rotten politics*
> *And leaving British coppers to the shooting.*
>
> *We don't do no complainin' and believes a lot in Fate*
> *And verily we trust we're sons of Mars;*
> *But we're sent in open pick-ups in the manner of live bait*
> *While the Army tours the hills in armoured cars . . .*
> *Our brothers in the Army, they know the game as well*
> *And don't do all their fighting by the book*
> *So it's 'Use your boots and butts boys, go down and give 'em* [hell
> *They've knifed a British copper in the souk'.*
>
> *So Palestine Policemen they gets it in the back*
> *And at the Golden Gate they stand and stare*
> *And gaze upon St. Peter as he pops up from his shack*
> *With 'Well me boys, what 'ave you to declare?'*

We're only common coppers, sir, we never 'ad a bob,
We 'ave a few kind deeds, sir, and some vice,
But in the so-called 'Oly Land we always done our job
So now we'd like a bit of Paradise.

Epilogue—Roger Courtenay
Palestine Policeman (Herbert Jenkins, London, 1939)

The structure of the public security apparatus in Palestine
It is extremely difficult to compile an acceptable picture of the overall structure, content and distribution of the police forces in Palestine prior to the Arab Rebellion of 1936–39 primarily because the police organization itself was unstable. It seldom continued the same for more than three years at one time. Almost continual crisis conditions, rapidly changing administrative personnel on short tours of duty, chief administrators holding radically differing notions as to the precise role which the police should play, and, major reform attempts in 1921, 1922, 1925, 1926 and 1929, followed by minor ones in 1931 and 1935, all effected changes in the shape, condition and complement of the Palestine Police Force. Reforms during the period of the Arab Rebellion 1936–39 altered police structure even more.

It is important to note at the outset that the Palestine Police Force which came into being in 1925–26 as a result of Lord Plumer's reorganization,[1] was composed of the disparate police units which had policed Palestine from 1920–21 onwards—that is, the separately recruited British and Palestine Gendarmeries, the ghaffir forces and the almost purely Arab force guarding Trans-Jordan. Throughout both the early and later period, the British force was the élite unit.

Each constable recruited into the Palestine Police Force was to serve five years after an initial six months training at the police school. A salary of six pounds per month, (clothing and equipment free)[2] did not attract high quality recruits. The Force H.Q., located in Jerusalem, was divided into two segments. First, the Administrative Department which concerned itself with general police matters and the prison service. Second, as a separate unit, the Criminal Investigation Department. Throughout the period under discussion the force was distributed into the following seven districts:

[1] Lord Plumer was the High Commissioner of Palestine.
[2] *Palestine Police Manual* (State Archive, Prime Minister's Office, Jerusalem), 2.

District	Divisions
Jerusalem District	Urban, rural, Hebron
Southern (Jaffa) District	Jaffa, Ramat Gan, Tel Aviv, Ramle
Gaza District	Gaza, Beersheba
Northern (Haifa) District	Urban, rural
Nazareth District	Nazareth, Tiberias
Nablus District	Nablus, Tulkarm, Jenin
Frontier District	Northern Frontier, Safad, Acre[3]

Each of the Divisions was divided into areas controlled from stations and posts. A Superintendent and Deputy Superintendent were in charge of each district and a Deputy Superintendent and Assistant Superintendent in charge of each division which took its divisional name from that of the headquarters town, with, of course, the exception of the Frontier.

The British section of the police was composed of a curiously mixed personnel. An officer who served in the force wrote:

> Between us we represented every conceivable situation of life in the British Isles, from the heir of an impoverished earl, products of exclusive public schools, and graduates of famous universities to professional bruisers, coal miners, regular soldiers and really tough Tyneside Geordies who played a better game of football in their bare feet than they did with boots on.[4]

The British section could perhaps best be caricatured as an agglomerate of adventurers, escapers and marginal men with a salting of professional colonial service policemen from Ireland, India, Ceylon and elsewhere. The native Palestinian element of Jews and Arabs were drawn, in the main, from the uneducated, poorer sections of the community. The two sections of the force were kept apart, almost segregated. In the early period of the Mandate the British police were discouraged from learning either Arabic or Hebrew. As one serving British police officer noted 'Obviously we were at that time intended to be used not as real policemen but as tough shock troops'.[5]

Intelligence

For the containment of subversion, in the short-term at least,

[3] Ibid., 16.
[4] Lionel Morton, *Just the Job: Some Experiences of a Colonial Policeman* (London 1957), 19.
[5] Ibid., 20.

an efficient intelligence structure is an essential prerequisite. In Palestine the collection of political intelligence in particular was completely inadequate from 1920 to 1938—that is until the restructuring of security during the counter-insurgency campaign of 1938. In detailing the whole intelligence staff working for the Mandate Government, it is as well to remember that it seldom, if ever, functioned as a cohesive unit. A picture emerges in Palestine of mutually exclusive and warring intelligence departments.

The CID of the Palestine Police was the largest operational intelligence section covering the whole of Palestine. In addition, the intelligence section of the Trans-Jordan Frontier force operated in Trans-Jordan whilst a third intelligence agency, that of the Army Defence Headquarters Staff, operated in both Palestine and Trans-Jordan. There was thus much duplication of surveillance. However, the bulk of the 'hard' intelligence as opposed to hearsay, manufactured tales and rumour, came from Special Service Officers.[6] During the period 1920–36, a mere four Special Servicemen covered Palestine.[7] Prior to the 1936–39 rebellion they were stationed in Jerusalem, Haifa and at Amman and Ma'an in Trans-Jordan. As the rebellion escalated other Special Service officers were appointed to Jaffa and Nablus, key centres of Arab discontent, as well as to Nazareth and the Jordan Valley. Their duties were 'to procure information of a military, political and topographical nature and to keep in touch with feeling in the country by touring their districts'.[8]

Yet, despite the impressive array of information gathering units, the quantity and quality of information received were both extremely poor. Sir Herbert Dowbiggin reporting on the Palestine Police in 1930 designated the CID as 'the weakest spot in the force'.[9] Similarly, the Committee of Imperial Defence had noted in 1929, with reference to police intelligence,

> . . . we are informed that little information is forthcoming from it. For example, in 27 days out of 33 days during September and October (of 1929—immediately after the August riots in Jerusalem and elsewhere) the police had no information to publish in their daily situation reports . . . Not only must the police, owing to the nature of their present organization, rely largely on rumour for their information, but it has been reported that since the August outbreak the Pales-

[6] See Air 5/1244 PRO, London, for details.
[7] Ibid.
[8] Ibid.
[9] Cd. 5479 Peel Commission (1937), 191.

tinian personnel of the junior ranks of the police have shown a tendency to withhold information regarding events in their districts from their senior officers.[10]

Dowbiggin's recommendations for a new CID were not acted upon until two years later. In 1932 the CID was both thoroughly reorganized and strengthened.[11] The staff was further increased in 1934 to cope with the growing problem of illegal Jewish immigration. By 1935 there were some 51 CID officers operating within the Palestine Police alone. However, the reforms appear to have had little appreciable effect upon the collection and collation of hard political intelligence. Police intelligence remained inadequate until 1936 and almost completely dried up thereafter in the face of Arab terror and boycott. Selective assassination of Arab CID officers, usually the zealots, effectively neutralized the Arab CID as a reliable source of information. The Arab CID indeed became politically unreliable. If they did not actually transmit sensitive information to the Arab rebels they often sat upon information until it was of little use to the security forces. One incident, one of many documented, is worth detailing. Joshua Gordon of the Jewish Agency, reporting a meeting with Rice, Deputy Inspector General of police in 1936, observed that,

> I inquired whether he (Rice) was directly informed of the information which was being given to the British Crime Investigator Corporal Fisher by an Arab fellah woman with whom we (the Jewish Agency) had placed the police in contact. I understand that she had been giving valuable information about the movement and actions of a certain gang and I said that if Corporal Fisher was merely passing this information on to Abdin Bey, his superior officer, the British might spare themselves the trouble of obtaining this information . . . he (Rice) had not been getting the information at all and as we had not heard any results, it would appear that the information was merely buried by Abdin Bey.[12]

It was an incident which typified a general pattern of action throughout the Arab section of the Palestine police.

The Auxiliary Police

Auxiliary police units were established in Palestine to bolster the existing public security apparatus in times of crisis. Similarly, they

---

[10] CAB 24/209 Committee of Imperial Defence, 20 December 1929. (PRO).
[11] Cd. 5479 op. cit., 194–95.
[12] Central Zionist Archive (CZA) S.25/183—Miscellaneous documents on security 1933–1939. 1 July 1936 (Central Zionist Archive, Jerusalem).

enabled the release of trained policemen from passive routine to the more offensive, anti-terrorist actions becoming daily more necessary after the serious riots of 1929. There were, however, vital differences in the composition of these auxiliary units from the force proper. They were composed predominantly of Jewish personnel. It was because of this fact that both the civil and military command kept a very tight hold on the activities of the Auxiliaries. Both feared partisan policing, but above all offensive action, by a Jewish force operating under the imprimatur of the Mandate. The overall attitude of the Mandate Administration to the question of auxiliary policing by the Jews is effectively summarized in the following statements emanating initially from the High Commissioner's Office. A War Office document reported that,

> there was general agreement with the High Commissioner's opinion that Jews should be employed for defensive purposes only and only in areas mainly Jewish.[13]

The document also revealed the fear of offensive action by Jewish police units, many of whose men were simultaneously members of the illegal Haganah underground army. 'Arrangements might well be made', the document noted,

> for their training now in limited numbers with a view to using their services for protective work . . . if the need arises. Any such training should be carried out with the utmost discretion in order to avoid giving the impression in Palestine or outside Palestine, that HMG already foresee that after the publication of their decisions upon the Report of the Royal Commission (Peel Commission) a state of affairs will inevitably prevail in which the forces of authority will be ranged against the Arab population. As regards the employment of Jews even for defensive purposes in predominantly Moslem areas, it was agreed that this would be politically most undesirable . . . It was further agreed that in view of the possibility serious relations which might thereby be provoked in neighbouring Arab countries, the GOC should not, in any circumstances, decide to use Jews for offensive purposes without prior approval of HMG.[14]

Though it was eventually realized that there was a distinct need to utilize Jewish forces to preserve the Mandatory regime, the most rigid controls were always imposed upon their actions. It was only later, at the height of the Arab Rebellion, that Jewish Auxiliary units were granted more freedom of action.[15] At first, they were

[13] WO.32/4178 Respective functions of High Commissioner and GOC (PRO).
[14] Ibid.
[15] CZA S25/46 Keren Hayesod document 'Security in Palestine and Defence of the Yishuv' (Jerusalem, 25 July 1938).

specifically restricted to guarding fields, villages and their own settlements. Later they were allowed to accompany Jewish workers wherever they were required and ultimately became mobile units policing whole districts. From 1938 onwards, they became an important component part of the public security structure. Yet how were they composed? What was their complement and distribution? The few who have written about the Auxiliary Police have loosely referred to 'ghaffirs', 'settlement police', 'Supernumaries' as if they were one cohesive unit. By 1938 there were in fact five distinct classes of Auxiliary Police in Palestine. They are detailed below:

The Temporary Additional Police. This was a body of men enlisted for six months and having the same rates of pay and serving under the same regulations as the police proper. Most of the men were employed on general protection duties.

The Railway Protection Police. A self-explanatory unit who guarded and patrolled stations, block-houses and vulnerable and important bridges on the main railway line from Haifa to Lydda. The force was administered by an élite of British officers but was otherwise composed entirely of Jewish personnel.

Jewish Settlement Police. This unit was composed of Temporary Additional Police as well as volunteer, unpaid, special police enlisted after the onset of the Arab Rebellion in 1936. Its complement was something of a barometer of crisis since it rose and fell according to the level of internal disturbance. In effect it was the core of the Auxiliary Police units. Reorganized in 1938 they became a much more flexible, articulated unit with unified administration and command. Similarly, they were organized into 10 companies each commanded by a British police inspector seconded from the regular police. They were thus a mobile reserve as well as guardians of the Jewish settlements.

Supernumary Police. They were private police officers paid for by individual firms such as the Palestine Electricity Corporation, to guard private industrial property.

Ghaffirs. The ghaffirs were those auxiliaries, often from the Jewish settlement police who were exclusively employed as nightwatchmen.[16]

[16] CO. 814/13 Annual Report of the Mandate Administration (PRO).

Some problems of policing. Stress in the public security apparatus 1920–36

The police apparatus in Palestine reflected in miniature the complex problems which the Mandate Government faced. It was a creature of crisis, lacked legitimacy and internal cohesion and was without a definite notion of what its precise role was to be. From their inception the Palestine police were conceived of as a somewhat inadequate second best to the military apparatus. The major advantage of a quasi-military police force under civilian control was, for the Colonial Office, that it was cheap. Both HMG and the Colonial Office had stressed in 1920[17] that at £500 per man per annum the Military, operating as an internal security force, was too expensive. Civil policing in Palestine was thus instituted as an economic expedient and suffered under the continued application of economies down to 1929. Similarly, hastily recruited, organized and centralized under the British Military Government in July 1919[18] the police had, from their inception, little status and authority among either Jew, Arab or indeed, British communities. Their stature was hardly increased under the Military Government since they were not even allowed to investigate cases thoroughly—this was regarded as the preserve of the Courts and the Public Prosecutor. The police in fact operated as little more than drilled, uniformed, native errand boys for the military. Organized into district units they were also, from the outset, highly susceptible to local racial and religious influence. It was the British component, many of them ex-Royal Irish Constabulary men or Black and Tans, who gave the force its backbone. By contrast the native force possessed little unity of organization, systematic training, had not effected any significant formalized co-ordination between districts, and possessed no reserve upon which it could call in times of stress. Conditions in the force were at first so poor and the job held in such low esteem that in 1921, 60 per cent of the force resigned on the grounds of being badly housed and underpaid. This crisis and the inadequate manner in which disturbances in Haifa and Jaffa were combated forced both an inquiry and the first in a long line of piecemeal reforms[19]—none of which alleviated the major flaws in the police apparatus.

The force was improved organizationally in 1921 by the establishment of an HQ staff in Jerusalem. The security situation was also

[17] Cd. 5479 op. cit., 185.
[18] CZA S25/6167 Arms to Jewish Colonies.
[19] Sir Charles Jeffries, *The Colonial Police* (London 1952), 155.

somewhat eased by the institution of a mobile strike force, the Palestine Gendarmerie. A similar unit, to be known as the Arab Legion was created for Trans-Jordan. In 1922 these reforms were extended with the creation of a British Gendarmerie of 35 officers and 724 men, mostly transferred from the still disturbed, but now independent Ireland. The Palestine Gendarmerie, officered in the main by British policemen, but composed of Jews and Arabs, was financed from Mandatory funds whilst the British Gendarmerie was maintained directly from the United Kingdom. As an exercise in financial pruning, the substitution of these forces for the Military Garrison was clearly a success. The cost of the garrison as a whole, standing at £3 million in 1921–22 had by 1923–24 been reduced to £1½ million. It was thus merely an extension of the prevailing policy when in 1925 the mounted squadron of police and one company of the recently established British Gendarmerie were disbanded. The apparent calm in Palestine during 1924, 1925, and 1926 made it appear good policy to reduce the defences. Sir Herbert Samuel, the High Commissioner, was over-optimistic when he saw the country as pacified in 1925. He wrote that year:

> The spirit of lawlessness has ceased; the atmosphere is no longer electric; there have been no more raids from Trans-Jordan; all the brigands have been hunted down and either shot, executed or imprisoned . . . For some time past Palestine has been the most peaceful country of any in the Middle East.[20]

His report neglected the continuing brigandage in the hills and the disturbances in Jaffa, Nablus, and Tulkarm as well as the two small-scale revolts and incursions from the desert in 1922 and 1924 when both the Wahabis and Druzes from the Nejd had raided Mandatory outposts. There was a consistent undercurrent of antipathy, which was sure to revive when Jewish immigration escalated. The quiet was misleading.

However, in April 1925, the Security Conference held in Jerusalem[21] continued the policy of economies. Both Samuel, the High Commissioner and the Secretary of State for the Colonies felt that the British Gendarmerie should be reduced by some 200 men and its mounted cavalry unit disbanded altogether. Since Samuel was retiring it was decided not to apply the reforms but leave Lord Plumer, his successor, to assess them. Plumer, not only

---

[20] Cd. 5479 op. cit., 187.
[21] Cmd. 3530, 14.

reviewed Samuel's proposals but suggested sweeping reforms of his own which weakened the security apparatus still further. That reforms of such scale should follow those of 1920, 1921, 1922 and 1925, added to the aura of uncertainty in public security work, itself part of a wider feeling of impermanence. In his diary, Colonel Kisch of the Jewish Agency had written:

> MacNeill (Brigadier General A. J. MacNeill) who commands the British Gendarmerie is very sore with the Authorities who cannot come to any decision as to the future of his force. As a result over 200 of his best men have announced their intentions of resigning on completion of one year's service.[22]

Plumer had in fact recommended that both the Palestine and British Gendarmeries and the Arab Legion be abolished. This represented a radical change in the style of policing; it ended the aggressive, paramilitary stance of mobile gendarmeries and substituted for them an essentially static and defensive single unit, the Palestine Police. The bulk of the personnel of the Palestine Gendarmerie were to be absorbed into the Palestine Police. The remnant, organized into three new detachments, went to make up a Camel Corps, later known as the Trans-Jordan Frontier Force (TJFF). Those British Gendarmerie officers who remained being absorbed into the Palestine Police Force. In practice, the reforms merely compounded the operational weakness of police units not only because of the implicit force reductions but also because of the disarray the recommendations created. Plumers' recommendations remained in force from April 1926 to August 1929, when the riots of that month demonstrated just how inadequate internal public security forces had become. Kisch again wrote in his diary:

> On the subject of public security I unfortunately found myself in serious disagreement with Lord Plumer in respect of the measures he was introducing into the reorganization of the gendarmerie and the police . . . It was doubly difficult to make criticism effective, partly because of Lord Plumer's great authority as a Field Marshal, in matters of security, and partly because during his tenure of office Palestine in fact remained absolutely quiet. However, I was convinced that the security arrangements were dangerously inadequate and even if they might seem satisfactory in Lord Plumer's time, they could not be relied upon to keep the peace in Palestine, unaided by his great personal prestige as head of government.[23]

[22] F. H. Kisch, *Palestine Diary*, 14 February 1923 (London 1938), 31.
[23] Ibid., 235.

Thus 1926 was a major turning point on the public security front in Palestine. It was a year which also saw the Arab component of the force becoming increasingly predominant—despite their reluctance to prosecute rebellious fellow Arabs. The rearrangements of 1926 exaggerated the existing ethnic imbalance of the force. The Zionists were vociferous in their complaints. Kisch again stressed that,

> the new scheme does not take sufficiently into consideration the situation which would develop in Palestine in the event of any wave of Islamic fanaticism . . . Arab police cannot be relied upon for the protection of Jewish life and property . . . the Government is taking an unjustifiable risk in regard to the Jewish lives for which it is responsible.[24]

Chaim Weizmann also wrote at the time about his anxiety

> as to the possible effects of the far-reaching changes now in progress in the arrangements for defence and security of Palestine.[25]

Assessment of the data on the rearrangements makes this concern understandable. For instance, the disbanded Palestine Gendarmerie had been 50 per cent British, 15 per cent Jewish with a larger contingent of Jews in the officer corps. It was replaced by the TJFF, a predominantly Arab force. By the end of 1926 the TJFF consisted of 31 British officers, 35 Jews in technical work and 700 Arab officers and men. Similarly, the Palestine Police made up of 1,752 officers and men had a Jewish contingent of only 212 officers and men—1,300 being Arabs. The Jerusalem police force, focus of so much rioting and political violence, was particularly affected. In a city where Jews made up 60 per cent of the total population, out of 300 serving officers and men in the police, only 41 were Jews and of these 25 were employed in the police band.[26]

Yet the imbalance of the force ethnically or religiously was not solely a product or reflection of prevailing government policy moving, as it seemed at the time, increasingly towards Arab self-government.[27] It was also part product of self-exclusion from the

[24] CZA Jewish Agency Memorandum, 2 March 1936, 3. Kisch to the Chief Secretary of the Mandate Administration on behalf of the Zionist Executive.

[25] Ibid. Weizmann's letter to the Annual Meeting of the Permanent Mandates Commission, 1 May 1926.

[26] Ibid., 4.

[27] The Mandate Government had also begun to withdraw the sealed armouries in 1926 from the Jewish Colonies in which, for protective purposes, they had been established. The withdrawal was almost completed by 1929.

force by so many members of the Jewish Community. A member
of the Jewish Agency reported that,

> as regards the enlistment of Jews in the police, the actual situation is:
> Jews will not go into the police force for the sake of the job. In times
> of distress, unemployment, some may go, and they will leave again at
> the first opportunity. Only those will remain who have no prospects
> for other employment or who have no greater ambition than £7 a
> month for them and family for their lifetime. It will be agreed that
> those with such mentality are not the elements to build up the back-
> bone of the Jewish section of the Palestine Police. Already now there
> are loud complaints of the Jewish population about the 'element' of
> the Jewish policemen . . . A better element we will be able to get
> into the police only if we will be able to reach that part of the Jewish
> youth who will go into the police not for the job's sake, but for the
> sacrifice.[28]

The Jewish Community in Palestine thus perceived their policemen
as unskilled workers, poorly paid, intellectually inadequate and
marginally criminal. European Jewry in Palestine also expressed a
marked reluctance to serve in the exposed, dull and dangerous
rural areas. Tel Aviv and Jerusalem had more to offer.

The religious and ethnic imbalance in the force had serious
effects upon policing. Successful civil policing is dependent upon
the establishment of a mutual if somewhat distant respect between
police and public. With so few Jews in the local forces Jewish
citizens were most reluctant to go to Arab Officers with whom, very
often, they could not even communicate. Many complaints in the
available police records evidence this state of affairs. One such
complaint from a local council to the Jewish Agency emphasized
that,

> the number of policemen and officials in the Nazareth District is
> decreasing to a very noticeable degree . . . Previous to the disturb-
> ances (of 1929) two Jewish officials were employed in the District
> Administration and these either resigned or were discharged, so that
> today there is no Jewish official. The situation is such that a person
> not knowing English or Arabic cannot negotiate with the govern-
> ment. In the Nazareth police station there were four or six Jewish
> policemen and one Jewish officer up to the time of the disturbances
> . . . At present there is no Jewish policeman in Nazareth.[29]

---

[28] CZA S25/6170 Joshua Gordon to Kisch 17 July 1931. Jewish Numbers in
the police force, 1927–33.

[29] CZA S25/4374 Local Committee of Afuleh Bloc to Kisch 8 December 1929.

Thus both the position of Jews within the police force and the attitude of the Jewish community towards it was unsatisfactory. Of 439 Jewish constables enlisting during the years 1932–36, 255 were discharged or resigned.[30] Even those Jews and Arabs who remained in the force, working together reasonably well in quiet times, revealed their underlying mutual suspicion and distrust in times of crisis. Thus the police force, supposedly one of the supportive structures of the Mandate Government, was itself infected with the same fundamental cleavage that ran, like some massive geological fissure through the social, economic and political life of Palestine.

During the period 1920–36 the Arab section of the police became increasingly and dangerously unreliable in times of crisis. There were, of course, glorious exceptions. Yet in the main, there was, nor could be, little empathy with, nor lasting allegiance to the British Administration, when men of their own religion, blood, tribe and class were in direct opposition to that administration. A history of the Arab section of the Palestine Police is one of episodic collapse in the face of politico-religious tests and targetted terrorism.

One of the contributory factors in the total collapse of the Arab section of the police in 1938—they were eventually disarmed—was their inadequate training under stress. The riots of 1929, 1936 and the rebellion from 1936–39 all clearly demonstrated this failing. Again, Kisch, probably the most prolific and insightful writer of the period, wrote in the aftermath of the 1929 rioting that,

> During the recent disturbances it has become apparent that when faced by an actual Arab rising against Jews, the Arab police cannot be relied upon for offensive action. In some cases there is evidence of actual collusion on the part of the police . . . The rising in its earlier stages having been almost exclusively Moslem, the Christian Arab police were less affected than the Moslem Arabs . . . None of the police, however, . . . appear to have been equipped as regards training and discipline for effective action under fire. Both during the period of active rioting and during the subsequent period of tension, it became abundantly clear that the British police are effective out of all proportion to their number in dealing with such a situation.[31]

In Palestine the native Moslem policeman was in the unenviable position of being something of a 'Levantine man'—a man of the

---

[30] Cd. 5479 op. cit., 197.
[31] CZA S25/6167 Police Reorganisation, Dowbiggin Plan, 1929–30.

East serving the sophisticated, alien litigious codes of a modern industrial state. Is it not then valid to suggest that it was

> too much of a detached idealism to reckon with the hope that a native police officer who has hardly seen any Western government, who hardly conceives the Western maxims of objectivity and impartiality, even when he hears about them, will suddenly rise to the lofty heights of an umpire when it goes against his own flesh and blood, friend and benefactor . . . cease to be what he is only because he wears a uniform . . . it has to be realized that the ordinary policeman is drawn from the poorer classes of the population and possesses a very scanty education. He can read and write even in his own tongue with not too much ease. He does not know any foreign language at all. The subject of civics is something unknown to him. Soon after entering the police force he is bound, owing to the conditions offered to him, to continue in his free hours, the mode of life he has led before. He associates with the same people, reads or hears the same papers, and holds the same opinions . . . Under such circumstances there is not much probability of abandoning his Eastern conceptions of life and relations in favour of a people strange to him and suddenly, together with his uniform, acquire a Western sense of duty or *esprit de corps*.[32]

Many of the Arab police thus held an alternative allegiance to the feeble one they felt for the Mandate. By 1936 the Arab police had become so deficient in allegiance to the Mandate that they were much more of a threat to, than a guarantor of public security.

It is strange that as early as 1929, though the police force was seen to be deep in crisis after the riots in Jerusalem, the reform proposals failed to touch the heart of the problem—the question of allegiance. Had the native Palestine force been placed in barracks as were the Royal Irish Constabulary in Ireland it would perhaps have insulated them from some of the pressures they faced from extreme nationalists working in their communities. Dowbiggin's police reorganization plan of 1929–30 was to be the last systematic civilian attempt to rescue the security situation prior to the belated but eventually successful military reform undertaken during the counter-insurgency campaign of 1938.

Dowbiggin, described as 'the star police turn of the British Empire'[33] had been provided with his brief by a Government Imperial Defence Committee paper of 20 December 1929. Com-

---

[32] Ibid., Joshua Gordon of the Jewish Agency.
[33] The description it seems, is W. G. A. Ormsby-Gore's, Colonial Secretary. It was related to Kisch by Namier. See CZA S25/6167.

piled by the formidable triumvirate, Trenchard, Madden and Milne, it emphasized that,

> we are convinced that no additions to the military forces in Palestine would have the same preventive effect as a well organized and efficient police backed by an adequate intelligence department . . . we venture to express our strong conviction that reorganization required must amount to considerably more than merely an increase in the British section of the police force, which is now under consideration. We feel most strongly that the whole police force requires reorganization and that in particular, arrangements should be made to instil British influence, mentality and methods into the native force. We venture to recommend that an experienced and independent police official, such as an officer of high standing in the Indian police, should be invited to proceed to Palestine and report on the police reorganization.[34]

Once in Palestine, Dowbiggin quickly confirmed his reputation. His report, had it been speedily and efficiently implemented, may well have revitalized the security apparatus. He made a set of seminally important suggestions. Primarily, he stressed that there should be not only a clear conception and precise statement of the role of the police, but also, that in terms of the Administration itself there should be precise delineation of the respective powers of civil and military authorities. These problems were never satisfactorily resolved until the near collapse of the Mandate in 1938 concentrated the minds of those involved. The problem of allocating civil-military responsibilities, particularly with respect to the rebellion, led to a most bitter intra-administrative wrangle during the period 1936–38.[35] Dowbiggin also recognized the lack of an *esprit de force* as a major weakness. He indeed suggested that housing the police in barracks would be partially remedial, alleviating the boycott and ostracism of Arab officers. Barracks, on a national scale, were not constructed until 1939, by which time the rebellion had already been broken. Dowbiggin also advocated an increase in the British section of the police to 650 men, recognizing it as the vertebrae of the force; the reconstitution of a mobile strike force of 100 men which Plumer had destroyed; the need for a permanent Special Constabulary Reserve and, again in contradistinction to Plumer, he recommended an

[34] CAB. 24/209 PRO.
[35] See my 'The Politics of an Arab Rebellion' Parts I and II in *British Army Review*, No. 44, August 1973, and No. 45, December 1973, for a detailed account of the Rebellion.

increase in the number of sealed armouries for Jewish colonies. Above all, he identified the greatest weakness of the force as its CID and Intelligence section. Little was done to effectively re-mould this apparatus other than increase its personnel.[36]

Thus, Dowbiggin's was the final, failed reform of the public security apparatus prior to the rebellion of 1936–39. It has been pointed out elsewhere that,

> the maintenance of public order everywhere requires the constant intervention of law enforcement agencies their absence or neutralisation even in the well ordered society is conducive to violence and mob action.[37]

Palestine was not a well ordered society. The experience on the public security front 1920–36 confirms the contention made above that a policing vacuum induces disorder. In Palestine the police apparatus was seriously flawed prior to the onset of the Arab Rebellion 1936–39. Indeed, the flaws, particularly in the intelligence sphere led to a failure to monitor or check subversion, growing brigandage, and the organization by the Arab guerrillas of alternative authority structures. By 1929, the police were incapable of dealing adequately with a rash of spontaneous, disorganized, essentially urban riots. By 1936, little had been accomplished to make the force either detect, prevent or withstand the Arab Rebellion with its vigorous campaign of guerrilla warfare in the hills, assassins in the cities and nationalistic extreme political cells in most villages. The result was the almost complete collapse of the Mandate Government in 1938. It is perhaps worth recalling, in conclusion, Popper's dictum that 'institutions are like fortresses—they must be well designed and properly manned'.[38]

[36] Cd. 5479 op. cit., 'Public Security'.
[37] C. Leiden and K. Schmidt, *Politics of Violence and Revolution in the Modern World* (New York 1968), 20.
[38] Karl Popper, *The Poverty of Historicism* (New York 1964), 6.

The Crisis in the Prussian Schutzpolizei 1930-32

Eric D. Kohler

In the ever-expanding historiography of the Weimar Republic, comparatively little attention has been given to the Prussian Schutzpolizei, or Schupo. This organization of 85,000 men not only enforced the law but, owing to the regular Army's limited size and reliability, was also charged with defending German democracy against its myriad domestic enemies.[1] Although this force has usually been described as reliable and apolitical, it will be contended here that this was not the case, particularly in its officer corps after 1930.[2] Always top heavy with former military men, who chafed at labouring under civilian control while their Army comrades enjoyed virtual autonomy, the Schupo's officer ranks seethed with discontent throughout the Republic's fourteen-year history. Indeed, some new evidence indicates that this group not only welcomed Chancellor Franz von Papen's illegal dismissal of Prussia's republican government on 20 July 1932, but may well have been consulted in advance by the plotters, in order to secure its neutrality.

That former soldiers of dubious republican sympathies should have dominated the Schupo officer corps was no accident; both Wolfgang Heine, Prussia's Interior Minister after the November 1918 Revolution, and his successor after 1920 and fellow Social Democrat, Carl Severing, thought about their constabulary in paramilitary terms. Warned by the leaders of the Reichswehr that, because of Western demands for a rapid and radical reduction in the Army's size they would no longer be able to dispatch troops

---

[1] Brief treatments of the police appear in Carl Severing, *Mein Lebensweg* (2 vols. Cologne 1950); Albert Grzesinski, *Inside Germany* (Eng. trans.) (New York 1939); and Ferdinand Friedensburg, *Die Weimarer Republik* (Hannover 1957). A far more up-to-date but geographically limited treatment may be found in Hsi-huey Liang, *The Berlin Police in the Weimar Republic* (Berkeley 1970), and, by the same author, 'The Berlin Police and the Weimar Republic', *Journal of Contemporary History*, October 1969.

[2] Bernhard Weiss, *Polizei und Politik* (Berlin 1928), 11. Severing, op. cit., *passim*; Friedensburg, op. cit., 173.

to quell the unrest which frequently flared up in Germany's cities during the Republic's first two tumultuous years, both men strove to build a constabulary capable of replacing the military during such upheavals; both made special efforts to staff their force with demobilized soldiers, 'especially former [commissioned] and non-commissioned Army and Free Corps officers'.[3]

The result was a police officer corps consisting of 2,350 men, of whom, as late as 1931, more than half were former commissioned or noncommissioned Army officers; in the Republic's fourteen-year-history only 300 men, or 12 per cent of the Schupo officer corps, ever achieved their positions through promotion from the ranks.[4] Hostile towards both the state and their civilian chiefs, many of these men yearned to return to the military; it was not surprising that they missed no opportunity to subordinate themselves and their policemen to the Army command.

These tendencies were aggravated by two reforms inaugurated by Interior Minister Severing in 1922. In February he set up a series of police review boards, composed equally of officers and men, to adjudicate differences between them. Simultaneously he granted his Schupomen the right to organize and bargain collectively with his ministry (but not the right to strike). Irritated by the first of these measures, which they were convinced would harm discipline, the police officers were infuriated by the second, which encouraged the growth of a policemen's union, the *Allgemeiner Preussischer Polizeibeamten Verband* (or *Schrader Verband*, as it was frequently called, after its founder Ernst Schrader). When this union, which claimed to represent seventy per cent of the Schupo rank and file, demanded that anti-republican elements be purged from the police corps (and received some satisfaction in this respect after the assassination of Foreign Minister Walther Rathenau in June 1922), officer reaction against this group was rapidly transformed into paranoia. Thus, when in November 1923 President Ebert invoked the power to rule by

[3] Major Erich von Gilsa to Prussian State Ministry, 18 July 1919. *Akten des Preussischen Justiz-Ministeriums* (hereafter *APJM*), Geheimes Staatsarchiv, Berlin–Dahlem. Rep. 84a, vol. 3730; Severing to all Prussian Ministers, 11 June 1920, ibid., vol. 3731; Heine to former Prussian Interior Minister Bill Drews, 23 March 1921. Bill Drews Nachlass, Geheimes Staatsarchiv, Berlin–Dahlem. Item 10.

[4] *Protokoll der Preussentag der SPD 1928* (Berlin 1928), 17; Ludwig Dierske, 'War eine Abwehr des "Preussenschlags" von 20 Juli 1932 möglich?' *Zeitschrift für Politik*, 1970, 232.

decree granted under Article 48 of the Weimar Constitution, and control over the Prussian police temporarily passed into the Army's hands, several high-ranking Schupo officers petitioned the Reichswehr Command to make this subordination a permanent state of affiairs.[5] One such officer, Major von Buch, even proposed dissolving the Schupo, which in his words had become 'a private Social Democratic army', and replacing it with a new police force in which unions such as the *Schrader Verband* would have no place.[6]

The Army showed no interest in this last proposal. Fearing that any attempt to subordinate the Schupo to the Reichswehr permanently would damage the Army's political independence, its commander, General von Seeckt, refused to have anything to do with such plans. The disenchanted Schupo officers, abandoned by the military and left to fend for themselves, proceeded to form their own union, the *Verein der Polizeibeamten Preussens,* a group which eventually claimed the allegiance of ninety per cent of the Schupo officer corps, and which, almost immediately after its creation, began demanding supervisory rights over the Schrader Verband's activities.[7]

Paradoxically, this new union's militancy, which was aimed at crippling the *Schrader Verband,* stabilized the police situation over the next several years. The reason was the interest which the Officers Association's activities aroused among the Socialist and Democratic members of the Prussian Diet, a body in which these two parties, in coalition with the Catholic Centre, held a majority. Highly suspicious of the Association's aims and methods, these legislators forced it onto the path of moderation with continual threats of punitive action in the one area where the Schupo officers were extremely vulnerable: their security of tenure as civil servants bestowed upon them under the terms of a hastily-passed 1922 Police Law, which had granted them immunity to the summary dismissal and forced retirement which often characterized the careers of Prussia's higher civilian administrative

[5] Unsigned letter to General Arnold Ritter von Mohl, 3 December 1923. Kurt von Schleicher Nachlass, Bundesarchiv/Militärarchiv, Freiburg, No. N42/19.

[6] Von Buch to Schleicher, 16 December 1923. Schleicher Nachlass, No. N42/19.

[7] Hans Meier-Welcker, *Seeckt* (Frankfurt a/M. 1967), 338; Liang, *Berlin Police*, 70; *Stenographische Berichte des Preussischen Landtags* (hereafter *SB*), 8 October 1924, col. 24337 ff.

appointees. By common agreement the 1922 law was a temporary measure, slated for replacement as soon as the Inter-Allied Military Control Commission, which had been established by the victors of 1918 to supervise German disarmament—including the strength of the police—left German soil. The threat of a new police law, under whose terms the status of Schupo officers might be changed to that of political appointees, thus remained a very real one until the IMCC was withdrawn from the country in 1927.[8]

Strangely, when the time to rewrite the police law arrived, the legislature's republicans failed to make good their threats to 'take the sensible Bismarckian step' of transforming the Schupo's officers into political appointees.[9] Several factors account for this oversight. First, much of the Diet's time was consumed debating how to improve the lot of the rank and file. Second, threats of legislative reprisals against troublesome Schupo officers had brought about a détente between them and the *Schrader Verband*, thus lulling the Diet into believing that anti-republicanism within the officer corps had abated. Third, the Interior Ministry convinced the legislature that to change the officers' status would saddle it with an administrative nightmare. Finally, there existed a strong belief among Prussia's republicans that as long as the Schupo administration, particularly its twenty-two Police Presidencies, remained in the hands of reliable appointees, all would be well with the force. Unfortunately this was simply not the case: few republican appointees ever succeeded as municipal Police Presidents.[10]

Within eighteen months of the new police law's passage, the troubles which had characterized the relations between the Schupo officer corps and its civilian chiefs before 1924 flared anew. In June 1928, Police Col. Otto Dillenburger had to be removed from his East Berlin command after one of his men attacked the capital's Deputy Police President. Shortly thereafter, the Colonel resigned from the force to assume the presidency of the Associa-

[8] Wolfgang Runge, *Politik und Beamtentum im Parteienstaat* (Stuttgart 1965), 21; *SB*, 29 March 1927, col. 18617; 8 October 1924, col. 24338.

[9] Speech of the Democratic deputy Bartheld. *Preussischer Landtag Hauptausschuss*, 13 June 1927. Carl Severing Nachlass, Archiv der Friedrich Ebert Stiftung, Bad Godesberg, Folder 87/6 & 7.

[10] 'Der Polizeibeamte—ein Stiefkind des Staates', *Preussische Polizeibeamtenzeitung*, 20 February 1927; Severing Nachlass, Folder 87/6 & 7; Liang, 'Berlin Police and the Weimar Republic', 167; Speech of the People's Party deputy Mezenthin, *SB*, 27 February 1930, col. 11627.

tion of Prussian Police Officers, in order to carry on a cold war against both the Prussian Interior Ministry and the Berlin Police Presidium.[11] The following May an outbreak of communist violence in Berlin marked the opening of what became a three year guerrilla war between the Reds, the Nazis, and the Schupo for control of the capital's streets. Shortly thereafter, in late 1929, the huge police budget became the object of incessant political brawling in the Diet, when the diminution of Reich subsidies to the Prussian government forced the latter to cut expenditure on the constabulary.[12]

Although police salaries, like those of the Reichswehr, remained unaffected during the depression years, the cumulative pressure of incessant street fighting with Nazis and Communists, as well as continuing attacks on police expenditure in the Diet, began to depress the constabulary's morale, a decline which began to manifest itself during Autumn 1930. When the newly-elected Reichstag opened on 14 October, Nazi stormtroopers, celebrating their party's victory at the polls the month before, rioted in the area of the Potsdamer Platz and the Leipziger Strasse, the capital's shopping centre, while the Schupo stood by as idle spectators.[13]

It was this last event which finally moved Prussian Minister-President Otto Braun to take action. At the end of October he reappointed Severing, who had resigned from the Interior Ministry in 1926, to his old post. More importantly, he named Albert Grzesinski, an aggressive republicanizer of the Prussian bureaucracy, who had served as Severing's successor between 1926 and February 1930 (when his marital problems had forced his resignation from the cabinet), to the Berlin Police Presidency, a post which he had held in 1925–26.[14]

GRZESINSKI'S RETURN TO A POSITION of authority over the Schupo on 1 November 1930 marked the opening of the last, most bitter phase of that organization's relationship to its employer.

[11] Liang, *Berlin Police*, 64, 89.
[12] Ministerialdirigent Franz Tejessy to all Prussian Ministers, January 1930. Otto Braun Nachlass, International Institute for Social Research, Amsterdam, Folder 445/1.
[13] *SB*, 26 February 1930, col. 11566 ff., 27 February 1930, col. 11580 ff. Liang, *Berlin Police*, 110.
[14] On Grzesinski as Interior Minister, see Runge, op. cit., 146–48. On his marital difficulties, see E. D. Kohler, 'Otto Braun, Prussia and Democracy, 1872–1955', (Dissertation, Stanford University 1971), 367–70.

Where his predecessors had tolerated, ignored, or lightly reprimanded anti-republicanism within the force, the new Police President began demanding overt loyalty from every Schupo member, regardless of rank. Whether this programme was a workable one remains debatable. Probably it was a case of too little too late, an effort which, lacking Severing's wholehearted backing, was not only doomed to fail, but also produce the opposite effect to the one desired: instead of republicanizing the police, it succeeded only in widening the gulf between the force and its civilian superiors. Much of the blame for this can be laid at the feet of Severing, a small man who had a knack for compromising away far more than necessary. A good example of this was the Hellriegel case. Police Col. Fritz Hellriegel was one of the force's most ardent Republicans, and Grzesinski's candidate to replace the capital's Schupo Commander, Col. Magnus Heimannsberg, a man whom the new Police President believed had displayed excessive leniency towards unreliable subordinates. When in late October 1930 Grzesinski attempted to make this change, Severing not only stopped him, but also had Hellriegel transferred to Magdeburg. His reasons for this action were simple: not only was Heimannsberg (who had risen to his position from the ranks) enormously popular with the men on the force; more important, he was affiliated with the Catholic Centre Party, one of the government's coalition allies in the Diet. To this party, the Berlin Schupo Commander was an invaluable tool in its self-appointed role as arbiter of the capital's morals: without him, it might have encountered difficulties in carrying on its fight to keep contraceptive vending machines out of Berlin's men's rooms, to prevent the sale of pornography in the city's kiosks, and 'to keep tons of naked female flesh off theatre and cabaret stages'.[15]

Despite Severing's refusal to remove Heimannsberg from the Berlin Schupo Command, Grzesinski's efforts to exact republican loyalty from his police continued. This was demonstrated during the second half of 1931, in the aftermath of an abortive plebiscite to dissolve the Prussian Diet and elect a new one a full year before this became constitutionally necessary. This

---

[15] 'Der Kampf in Preussen geht los', *Hamburger Nachrichten*, 31 October 1930; 'Otto Braun der ungekrönte König von Preussen', typewritten interview manuscript for *L'étoile Belge*, 25 March 1932. Braun Nachlass, folder 600. Cf. speeches of the Centre Party deputy Stieler, *SB*, 17 October 1925, col. 4610 ff. and 27 February 1930, col. 11592.

referendum, which was sponsored by the militantly right-wing veterans organization, the Stahlhelm, the Nazis, and subsequently the Communists, was not the first such affair Germany had witnessed.[16] In 1926 there had occurred an ill-fated plebiscite, sponsored jointly by the communists and socialists, to expropriate the property of the country's former princes. Similarly, during Autumn 1929 there had taken place an election on a proposition which, if passed, would have rejected the Young Reparations Plan, signed that summer, and brought the statesmen who had accepted it on Germany's behalf to trial for treason. Under Article 73 of the Constitution this sort of legislation by popular vote was possible if those backing the proposed law could obtain the signatures of ten per cent of the electorate on petitions for a referendum. In practical terms this meant that non-signing voters, or voters who stayed away from the polls on election day if the plebiscite's backers obtained enough signatures to hold a vote, could ensure the proposition's defeat. For this reason the Prussian regime, during the 1929 plebiscite, exerted considerable pressure on its civil servants to avoid signing initiative petitions, and to stay away from the polls once those favouring the anti-Young Plan legislation obtained sufficient signatures to hold a special election. State employees who failed to heed the government's wishes were threatened with unfavourable fitness reports, negative promotion recommendations, or in the case of political appointees, dismissal from their posts.[17] By contrast, no such pressure was brought against the police. Two years later, during the parliamentary dissolution plebiscite, this policy was altered drastically—thanks to Grzesinski. On 8 August, the day of the referendum, the polling stations were placed under careful surveillance in order to ascertain which, if any, Schupo men or officers were voting for the proposed dissolution. Of the 47 Schupo officers who went to the polls, 33 were eligible for promotion to the rank of Police Major; all were subsequently passed over on the semi-annual police promotion list.[18]

[16] Initially the Communists opposed the plebiscite, but when in 1931 Severing prohibited them from holding a sports festival in the capital, they responded by endorsing the referendum. Severing, *Lebensweg*, II, 191.

[17] Hildegarde Pleyer, 'Politische Werbung in der Weimarer Republik' (Inaugural Dissertation, Münster 1959), 30.

[18] 'Volksentscheid Offiziere'. Typed list, Grzesinski Nachlass, International Institute for Social Research, Amsterdam, folder 1936.

Coming in Autumn 1931, just as the Reichswehr and Reich Interior Ministries were being combined under General Groener, the Berlin Police President's tough stand against the 'plebiscite officers', as these men came to be known, was politically unpropitious. Almost immediately after Grzesinski acted, the head of the Association of Prussian Police Officers, retired Police Col. Dillenburger, moved to exploit the situation by attempting to obtain the Army's intercession. On 7 November he asked Groener for a meeting, ostensibly for the purpose of getting acquainted. Possibly he was hoping to revive the scenario of 1923, when several high-ranking Schupo officers had pleaded with the Army Command to assume control over the Prussian police. Whether any meeting was held is unknown. In any case, word of what he was attempting reached Grzesinski, who warned Minister-President Braun that the 'gentlemen of the Reichswehr are learning . . . how to use the union between the Army and the Reich Interior Ministry to their advantage . . . in order to place the Army in control of the police and police practices'.[19]

At the same time as Dillenburger was trying to improve his relations with the military, he was busily pressing Severing to override Grzesinski's decision concerning the plebiscite officers. On 20 November he succeeded in persuading the Prussian Interior Minister to reinstate the men involved on the promotion list. Severing's motives for this decision were straightforward: looking ahead to the coming six months he anticipated that the impending Presidential and Prussian parliamentary elections, scheduled for Spring 1932, would bring on a 'crisis of the gravest magnitude', and he felt that a display of generosity towards the plebiscite officers would help to secure the Schupo's loyalty during this trouble-laden period and beyond.[20]

Grzesinski reacted strongly:

> I urge you . . . not to promote these officers. In my opinion .. . . their advancement will only alienate those officers who are loyal to the Republic, and will thereby damage the interests of the state . . . In my long experience, the absolute reliability of the police in case of serious internal difficulties is decisively influenced by their leaders' conduct. Officers who permit serious doubt to arise about their . . . loyalty by participating in plebiscites designed to undermine the

[19] Dillenburger to Groener, 7 November 1931. Schleicher Nachlass, no. N42/41; Grzesinski to Braun, 9 December 1931, Braun Nachlass, folder 400/2.
[20] Letter from Dillenburger to all Association of Prussian Police Officer

Republic do not deserve promotion . . . These officers can be promoted only to the disadvantage of other [more] loyal and efficient
men . . . This could produce most serious repercussions [among the
rank and file] in the case of disturbances . . . It appears to me that
a clear stand by you and your ministry on this question is absolutely
vital. No doubt should be permitted to arise as to whether or not
participation in the referendum was sanctioned by your office. The
ultimate consequences of a reversal could be fateful.[21]

If Severing was hoping that moderation would restore good relations between the Schupo officer corps and his ministry, he was
sadly mistaken. Indeed, the police officers interpreted his generosity
as a sign of weakness, and by the end of 1931 they were deliberately
staging incidents designed to embarrass their civilian chiefs. Thus
on the night of 24 November, after a republican youth rally, held
in the old Prussian Herrenhaus and addressed by Severing himself,
broke up, a police riot brigade attacked those leaving the building
for violating an open-air demonstration ban which had been
promulgated for certain districts in the aftermath of the May
1929 riots. When Grzesinski learned of this event the following
morning, he dispatched an angry rebuke to Heimannsberg, sar-
castically informing him that 'mass exits from unforbidden assem-
blies, held in closed halls, are not matters for police intervention',
and ordering him to remind his subordinates on the force of
that fact.[22]

Although Heimannsberg obeyed this last command, his efforts
had little effect. On the night of 2 December the republican
defence league, the *Reichsbanner Schwarz-Rot-Gold,* held a rally
at the Berlin Sportpalast. When the meeting ended and those
in attendance surged onto the streets around the Potsdamer Platz,
cheers went up for Braun and Severing. Thereupon Police Major
Andreas Levit, the officer in command of the area, ordered his
troops to charge the crowd. In the ensuing scuffle several dozen
persons were arrested for violating the open-air demonstration ban.
In a closely related incident, a brawl broke out between several
dozen rally participants and some Nazis when the former, shout-
ing republican slogans, marched past a tavern frequented by the
latter. In this instance, Levit had the marchers arrested for
disturbing the peace; only four of the Nazi brawlers were simi-

branches, 11 December 1931. Grzesinski Nachlass, folder 1954.
  [21] Grzesinski to Severing, 4 December 1931. Braun Nachlass, folder 300/3.
  [22] Grzesinski to Heimannsberg, 25 November 1931. Ibid., folder 300/7.

larly treated. These actions provoked an outcry from enraged republicans, and there followed an angry interpellation in the Diet.[23]

The Prussian government's response to this outrage was both feeble and inept. That Levit, a man with a five-year record of anti-republican activity (including the endorsement of both the Young Plan and Prussian Diet dissolution plebiscites), had been kept on the force was itself testimony to the Interior Ministry's lax and excessively tolerant personnel policies.[24] Given the Major's political attitude, he should have been dismissed from the Schupo immediately after the Reichsbanner incident, or at least suspended from duty until such time as disciplinary action, aimed at removing him from the force, could be brought to a successful conclusion. Instead of taking so decisive a step, the Prussian authorities hesitated, and in so doing brought down upon themselves a police crisis that ended only with the Braun-Severing government's removal from office on 20 July 1932.

On 4 December, two days after the Reichsbanner incident, Grzesinski informed Severing that he was having Levit's actions investigated and that he was convinced that

> a man like Levit can no longer remain a police officer, because he is temperamentally unsuited for such a post. Until now he has proven himself a brilliant Schupo officer, and has even been recommended for accelerated promotion, the justification for this being his outwardly correct behaviour, his keen . . . abilities, and his generally distinguished service. He knew how to conceal his true colours from his superiors. Perhaps this past year's . . . developments have confused him. Unfortunately, there is no way we can dismiss him from the force, since he already has more than ten years of service behind him . . . Only a disciplinary hearing aimed at his removal . . . remains. Should the investigation I have ordered . . . justify such a course, I should like to request that your decision on the matter should not be postponed.[25]

Given Levit's record, Grzesinski's praise of his 'outwardly correct' behaviour was grotesque. Certainly this equivocation on the part of the generally decisive Police President helps to explain Severing's hesitation in handling the case: instead of suspending Levit

[23] Severing, *Lebensweg*, II, 249 ff. Grzesinski to Severing, 11 December 1931. Grzesinski Nachlass, folder 1936; Liang, *Berlin Police*, 89.
[24] 'Volksentscheid Offiziere', Grzesinski Nachlass, folder 1936; Severing, *Lebensweg*, II, 294.
[25] Grzesinski to Severing, 4 December 1931. Braun Nachlass, folder 300.

pending a disciplinary hearing, he transferred him to a less sensitive post in Upper Silesia. Shortly thereafter the case was dropped, when Grzesinski concluded that the evidence warranting the Police Major's dismissal was insufficient; he had, after all, been enforcing the law during the Reichsbanner incident.[26]

As in the affair of the plebiscite officers, hesitation in the Levit case presented the enemies of the Braun-Severing cabinet with further proof of that regime's weakness. When Heimannsberg attempted to justify the Major's transfer by stating that he had demonstrated bad judgment in ordering the attack on the Reichsbanner, the Association of Prussian Police Officers and its rightwing friends in the Diet replied with a countercharge that Levit was being punished for enforcing the demonstration ban evenhandedly; the People's Party even went so far as to assert that the proceedings against the Major had been unconstitutional from the start.[27]

The Levit affair provided a catalyst for all the grievances that the Association had been accumulating against the Prussian Interior Ministry and the Berlin Police Presidium since Grzesinski's return to office in October 1930. On 8 December Dillenburger informed Severing that 'the actions taken against Levit were unjustified . . . the trust which we had in the Interior Minister was shattered by his conduct in the plebiscite officers case and there now exists a danger that we shall lose it completely'.[28]

This provoked an immediate reaction from the *Schrader Verband*, largest of the Prussian Police unions. On 12 December it issued a manifesto reminding the Officers' Association that they represented only a small minority within the Schupo, and that it 'disassociated itself from the goals of the Association of Prussian Police Officers. As before, it stands behind the Prussian government, especially Minister Severing'.[29] Backed with this declaration, Severing replied to Dillenburger that, as Interior Minister, he did not need the Association's confidence in order to continue in office, and that votes of confidence and no-confidence were prerogatives reserved to the Diet, not the police unions. There followed a conference between the two principals in the dispute and, in a

[26] Grzesinski to Severing, 14 December 1931. Grzesinski Nachlass, folder 1953.
[27] 'Verfassungswidrige Handlung', *Berliner Börsen-Zeitung*, 8 December 1931.
[28] 'Die Polizei-Offiziere gegen Severing', ibid., 9 December 1931.
[29] 'Polizeibeamtenschaft gegen Offizierevereinigung', *Vossische Zeitung*, 13 December 1931.

public letter to Severing dated 5 January 1932, Dillenburger backed down and apologized for the 'unintentional publication of the Association's feelings in the Levit case'. He promised that in future all differences between his union and the Interior Ministry would be settled in private conferences between the two parties.[30]

The termination of this conflict solved nothing: ill feeling between the Schupo officers and the Interior Ministry continued unabated. A review of the Levit case published in the Dillenburger organization's newspaper, *Der Polizei-Offizier*, on 1 February 1932, reiterated that the Major's only offence had been the impartial enforcement of the demonstration ban, and that he was being punished without benefit of due process. From this, the paper concluded that a

> grave danger has arisen . . . that the police are no longer the servants of the general public, the law and the Constitution . . . Rather, they have become the lackeys of the groups supporting the present regime . . . From now on they must divide the populace into two groups: those who support the government and those who do not . . . Stahl-helm demonstrations are to be handled differently from those of the Reichsbanner. This . . . is unconstitutional.[30a]

The continuation of this feud came at the worst possible time for the Braun-Severing government. With both President Hindenburg's term and the Prussian Diet's mandate slated to expire that spring, it faced two bitter and violent electoral contests within the space of a few weeks—three, if Hindenburg were forced into a runoff. Under such circumstances the Schupo's resources would be strained to the hilt. Moreover, given the spectacular gains the Nazis had been scoring at the polls during the past two years, there was little likelihood that the three coalition partners, the Democrats, Catholic Centrists, and Social Democrats, who had dominated the Diet since 1919, would retain their majority after the state elections. This in turn posed serious problems for the maintenance of order in Germany's largest state; under the Prussian Constitution, the Minister-President, who appointed the rest of the state cabinet, was elected by a simple legislative plurality. Should the elections give the Nazis many more seats in the Prussian Diet, and every sign indicated they would, the chance of the new legislature electing a National Socialist to the Minister-

[30] Severing, *Lebensweg*, II, 295; 'Der Polizeikonflikt beigelegt', *Vossische Zeitung*, 6 January 1932.

[30a] 'Betrachtungen zum Fall Levit', *Der Polizei-Offizier*, 1 February 1932.

Presidency and the latter appointing one of his party comrades to the all-important Interior Ministry—thereby giving the Nazis control over the Schupo—was real and frightening.[31] Hoping to circumvent this, the outgoing leaders contemplated altering the plurality rule governing the Minister-President's election. On 25 March, during its last session, the legislature (much against Minister-President Braun's wishes) changed the regulations governing the selection of his successor. Under the new procedure, a victorious candidate for the Minister-Presidency required not a plurality but an absolute majority of the legislature's votes: until such an individual emerged, the existing cabinet would continue in office as a caretaker government. Since it was believed that the Nazis would neither win a majority in the Prussian state elections nor be able to form a government commanding a legislative majority afterwards, the net effect of the new regulations was to guarantee the Braun-Severing regime's continuation in office after April 1932. This was by no means novel; by early 1932 the states of Bavaria, Saxony, Württemberg and Hesse were all being ruled by caretaker regimes.[32]

This scheme for prolonging the Prussian government's existence was unwelcome to the Reichswehr. Tired of the 'governing next to and against each other' which had characterized Reich-Prussian relations for more than a decade, the Army wanted the Braun-Severing cabinet out of office after the April elections. In its place, it intended to substitute a cabinet in which the Nazis would participate, but under no circumstances control the vital Interior Ministry. This arrangement, the generals hoped, would in turn win National Socialist toleration for the authoritarian non-parliamentary national government which they were planning to bring to power after the Presidential elections.[33] Until the end of March 1932 (i.e. as long as the possibility of removing the Prussian government by constitutional means remained open) the Army did nothing to interfere with the impending state elections. Nevertheless, the Reichswehr leaders, particularly General Freiherr von Hammerstein-Equord, began preparing for the possibility of the Braun-Severing regime's continuance in office after April. His

---

[31] *Vossische Zeitung*, 26 March 1932.
[32] *Vossische Zeitung*, 26 March 1932. On Braun's attitude, see Erwin Widder, 'Reich und Preussen vom Regierungsantritt Brünings bis zum Reichsstatthaltergesetz Hitlers' (Inaugural Dissertation, Frankfurt a/M. 1959), 98.
[33] F. L. Carsten, *The Reichswehr and Politics* (Oxford 1966), 330.

plan for meeting this contingency was simple: if the Prussian cabinet could not be removed from office by legal means, it would have to be removed by a coup.[34]

To a considerable extent the success of any such operation depended upon the Schupo's attitude. Although by no means as well armed as the Reichswehr, the police had the advantage of concentration: in the capital alone there were 16,000 Schupomen, half of whom were assigned to barracked riot squads which would be ready for instant action. Moreover, in the increasingly tense political atmosphere of the late twenties the Berlin Schupo Command had taken the precaution of drafting plans for the capital's defence against a rightist coup. In essence, these called for the isolation of the insurgents in the city's central government district and their subsequent expulsion from the metropolis with all the weaponry at the Schupo's disposal.[35] With slight modification this scheme could undoubtedly have been employed against any group, including the Reichswehr, bent on illegally removing the Prussian government from office. Alternatively, since any Army-sponsored action against the Braun-Severing regime would necessarily have to be a broad operation involving a substantial number of persons, and would therefore be difficult to conceal, the police might have been ordered out to guard Prussian government buildings at the first rumour of an Army/Reich-sponsored coup. Certainly the Prussian regime behaved throughout the spring of 1932 as if it wanted its enemies to believe that it and the Schupo were prepared for every eventuality. On 12 February Dr. Wilhelm Abegg, the State Secretary in the Interior Ministry and one of the Schupo's founders, told the Diet that 'the Schupo supports . . . the Constitution, is unquestionably united, stands behind the government, and is ready to perform all duties assigned to it for the Republic's defence'.[36]

Abegg's confidence was considerably less than justified. The Army, determined to prevent the Braun-Severing government from continuing in office beyond the spring elections, was now busily exploiting the serious differences which had arisen between the

[34] 'Freiherr von Hammerstein-Equord auf der Besprechung der Gruppen und Wehrkreisbefehlshaber im Reichswehr-Ministerium am 27 February 1932', *Vierteljahreshefte für Zeitgeschichte*, 1954, 442.

[35] 'Lehrgang für Polizeihauptleute', 10 November 1929. Braun Nachlass, folder 444.

[36] Dierske, 'Abwehr', op. cit., *SB*, 12 February 1932, col. 24068.

Schupo officers and their civilian chiefs. On 26 February the 'Economic-Political Information Service', a Nazi-oriented news bulletin which was sent to about thirty of Germany's principal commercial and financial leaders, and edited by Walther Funk, later the head of the Reichsbank, reported:

> According to several well-informed confidential sources, secret agreements have been concluded between the Reichswehr and most of the Prussian Schutzpolizei's senior officers. In essence, these concern the Schupo's subordination to the Army Command in case the Braun-Severing regime refuses to resign after the Prussian elections; e.g., remains in office as a caretaker government. The Left still expects that the Prussian state elections will not produce . . . a rightist majority, and that it will be impossible to build a rightist coalition government because of opposition from the Catholic Centre. It has repeatedly been stated that the Reich Interior and Reichswehr Ministries are planning to intervene in such a case by naming a Reich Commissar [for Prussia] . . . According to our informants . . . the Army anticipates resistance from the Prussian government, and especially the Socialists, to such a move. Consequently, the military has contacted the Schupo's commanders behind Severing's back. According to our sources, the Reichswehr has put the recent conflict between the Interior Minister and the Association of Prussian Police Officers to good use, and succeeded in obtaining . . . a pledge from the majority of Prussian police commanders that they will subordinate their forces to the Army in case of severe internal unrest. Our sources believe that both Braun and Severing have gotten wind of this affair. Having made the painful discovery that the majority of their police commanders have entered into an understanding with the Reichswehr Ministry, they have . . . accepted it. . . . Messrs Braun and Severing have discovered that their most powerful instrument is no longer in their hands . . . The Prussian government has supposedly given up all hopes of retaining power after the April elections, a fact which is underscored by news that the Prussian Social Democrats are planning to go into parliamentary opposition for a long time to come.[37]

Grzesinski, the first Prussian official to see this report, denied the 'likelihood' of its allegations on the ground that 'they proceed from false assumptions and fail to take into account the mentality of either the Schupo or Reichswehr officers'.[38] Coming from this perceptive man, the analysis was unusually complacent; once before, in 1923, a significant number of highly-placed Prussian police officers had attempted to have the Reichswehr assume control

---

[37] 'Die Preussische Schupo angeblich nicht mehr in der Hand von Severing?' Severing Nachlass, Binder A/16 1932 I.
[38] Grzesinski to Severing, 9 March 1932. Grzesinski Nachlass, folder 2021.

over their force—and failed only because of General von Seeckt's lack of interest in the arrangement. Since that time, thanks to the Prussian government's unwillingness to inaugurate it, little change had taken place in either the Schupo officer corps personnel or its members' political attitudes. Given the hostility between the Association of Prussian Police Officers and the State Interior Ministry over both the plebiscite officers and the Levit cases, there was little reason for the Schupo commanders and senior officers to reject an Army offer to remove from office the civilian chiefs with whom they had been quarrelling, with varying degrees of intensity, for the past thirty months. Moreover, the Berlin Police President should have been aware that if the Reich chose to dismiss the Prussian government under the emergency powers granted to the President under Article 48 of the Constitution, the Schupo would automatically come under Reichswehr control. Possibly he felt confident because the Army chiefs were not completely united over the wisdom of directly intervening in Prussian affairs: General Groener, the Reichswehr and Reich Interior Minister, was a reliable republican who could be trusted to oppose such tampering, while General von Schleicher, Chief of the Militäramt (the office in charge of relations between the Army and the country's various governments), had never looked favourably upon direct military intervention in police affairs.[39] Moreover, Grzesinski may have felt that the condescension which the military had long felt for the police and their work would prevent the two sides from ever cooperating.

These factors notwithstanding, the attitude of some other Reichswehr leaders, particularly General von Hammerstein, should have given the Prussian government cause for concern. In a report sent to the Foreign Office on 1 March 1932, Sir John Simon, the British Ambassador to Germany, noted that he had recently had dinner with Hammerstein, who had informed him that 'he had the Army well in hand'; his only regret was that the Reich government did not 'in the present circumstances control the Police in the different Federal states'. Nevertheless, Hammerstein continued, the national government would be able to obtain such control 'if the regime found it necessary to rule in virtue of the emergency paragraph in the Constitution'.[40]

[39] Thilo Vogelsang, *Kurt von Schleicher* (Göttingen 1965), 79.
[40] *Documents on British Foreign Policy*, II, 3, 101–02; Thomas Trumpp, 'Franz von Papen, der preussische-deutsche Dualismus und die NSDAP in Preussen' (Inaugural Dissertation, Tübingen 1964), 39.

If both the report of 26 February and Hammerstein's conversation with Simon a few days later lacked credibility in the eyes of Prussia's senior officials, a memo sent to Severing by Dr Rudolf Breitscheid, one of the Social Democratic leaders in the Reichstag, should have ended the regime's complacency. Writing on 6 May, he warned the Interior Minister that, according to an 'unimpeachable source', the topic of conversation at a recent meeting between some Reichswehr officers and the military attaché to the French League of Nations delegation in Geneva had been how the French government would react 'if the Prussian Schutzpolizei were placed under the Reichswehr's command'.[41]

With the appointment of von Papen to the Chancellorship on 1 June, rumours spread of an impending Reich takeover of what was by then a caretaker Prussian regime (the republican coalition having lost its legislative majority in the April elections). At this point Severing should have called out Schupo detachments to guard the Prussian Ministries in the capital, and in this way made it clear to the new Chancellor that the government of Germany's largest state was not prepared to make a quiet exit from the political stage. But, forewarned that the reliability of his Schupo officers was doubtful in case of trouble with the national government, he chose to do no more than deny the rumours concerning the impending appointment of a Reich Commissioner for Prussia. On 26 June Berlin's Social Democratic daily, *Vorwärts,* denied accounts in the Nazi press that Severing had requested a Reich takeover of the Schupo at a recent meeting with Freiherr von Gayl, his counterpart in the Papen government,[42] adding that the police forces were still firmly in the hand of the responsible Prussian Ministers, and that 'discipline has not been impaired in the slightest, despite several attempts to undermine the force's confidence in its superiors'.

In the case of the Schupo officer corps, this last assessment was overly optimistic. Caught between civilian superiors whom they had come to dislike and who were now obviously afraid to act, and the threat of an eventual Nazi takeover of the Interior Ministry

[41] Breitscheid to Severing, 6 May 1932. Severing Nachlass, Binder Tr. 4.1, item 6.

[42] In point of fact, Severing told Gayl that if the Reichstag elections scheduled for 31 July produced a legislature as 'unruly' as the Diet created by the Prussian elections of 24 April, he would 'understand' any Reich move to assume control over the Schupo. Severing, *Lebensweg,* II, 341.

(at that moment the National Socialists and the Catholic Centre party were discussing the formation of a coalition regime for Prussia), for which they had no desire either, the Schupo officers seem to have concluded that the appointment of a Reich Commissioner for Prussia and the subordination of the force to the Army Command constituted the ideal solution to their dilemma. During June and July 1932 their attitude was one of watchful waiting, reflected in considerable police tolerance towards Nazi outrages. In early June, when the ban on the wearing of the Nazi uniform in public promulgated on 14 April was still in effect (it was lifted on 14 June), Dr Goebbels, the capital's Gauleiter, was able to assemble fifty Stormtroopers, dress them in their uniforms, and parade them through downtown Berlin while the police stood by and did nothing to stop them.[43]

That Papen's illegal removal of the Prussian government on the morning of 20 July came as a relief to the Schupo officers is borne out by several pieces of evidence. That day no Schupo officer anywhere in Prussia lifted a finger to assist the Braun-Severing regime except Berlin Schupo Commander Heimannsberg and he, who wanted to call out his men in order to isolate the capital until such time as someone, preferably Minister-President Braun, Hindenburg's occasional hunting companion, could see the President and persuade him to revoke the decree, was refused permission to act by Severing himself, because the Minister was convinced that no one 'had the right to be brave with policemen's lives'.[44] Moreover, during and after the coup, several leading Schupo officers did everything in their power to assist in its smooth execution, thereby making the operation look like little more than a minor reshuffling of personnel, a peaceful, orderly, and legitimate transfer of power which no one opposed. These men included Police Col. Poten, Commandant of the Schupo Academy at Eiche-bei-Potsdam, who assumed Grzesinski's post, and Police Cols. Liebe, Giebel, and Niehoff of the Berlin police, all of whom subsequently swore falsely that Grzesinski's actions in the Levit case had been designed to transform the Schutzpolizei into a private

---

[43] Konrad Heiden, *Der Fuehrer* (Eng. trans.), (Boston 1944), 466.

[44] 'Bericht des ehemaligen Berliner Polizeikommandeurs, Magnus Heimannsberg', reprinted in Bracher, *Auflösung*, 735 ff.; Jakob Diel, 'Das Ermächtigungsgesetz', *Die Freiheit*, 1 October 1946, 26–29. On Severing's attitude, see *Lebensweg*, II, 347.

Social Democratic army.[45]   In addition, the success of the July coup enabled the officers to realize their ambition, dormant since 1923, to escape the control of their democratically-minded civilian superiors in matters pertaining to discipline. As one newspaper reported at the end of 1932:

> Whoever was familiar with the old Prussian constabulary will notice some definite changes in the Schupo . . . The comradeliness between officers and men which characterized the Republican police, has been replaced by the old tone of command. The police committees of officers and men, which were responsible, in the former's eyes, 'for the breakdown of discipline', have been disbanded . . . in the academies more stress is being placed upon military drill . . . and the monocles, which were strictly forbidden under Severing and Grzesinski, have made a remarkable comeback.
>
> The police is returning to its prewar image of spiked-helmeted (Pikelhaube) authoritarians, the bogeymen mothers used to conjure up whenever they wished to frighten misbehaving children.[46]

Additional evidence that the removal of the Braun-Severing regime enjoyed the support of the Schupo officers may be found in the fact that, in the wholesale housecleaning of the Prussian bureaucracy which followed the coup, only one professional police officer, the ever-loyal Heimannsberg, was removed from office, while another three were transferred to less significant posts.[47] Only after the Nazi takeover in 1933 was the Schupo purged of its 'unreliable' elements, and even then the casualty figures were comparatively light: of Prussia's 2,400 police officers, 294, or six fewer than the number who had risen to their positions through the ranks—a mere 12.8 per cent of the total of the force—were dismissed; of the state's 50,000 patrolmen, 1,370 (2.7 per cent) suffered the same fate.[48]

Seven months before the July coup, Grzesinski wrote to Severing that the 'reliability of the police . . . is determined by the reliability of its officers'.[49]   The evidence presented here indicates that the Schupo officers were never very reliable defenders of the

[45] 'Auszug aus einer Erklärung des Staatsminister a.D. und Polizeipräsident Grzesinski'. Konrad Adenauer Nachlass, Historisches Archiv der Stadt Köln, no. 902/11/1.

[46] 'Zurück zur Pickelhaube', *Der Montag Morgen*, 5 December 1932.

[47] Braun to Papen, 7 November 1932. *Akten der Reichskanzlei*, Bundesarchiv, Koblenz, R431/2281.

[48] Dierske, 'Abwehr', op. cit., 233.

[49] Grzesinski to Severing, 4 December 1931. Braun Nachlass, Folder 300.

Republic, and that the knowledge of this fact certainly influenced Severing's decision to acquiesce passively in Papen's coup.[50] For its failure to republicanize its police officers the Prussian government paid a bitter price. Given the ease with which this force was transformed into a reliable instrument of the totalitarian state after 1933, especially after Hitler subordinated it to the Army High Command, one may even legitimately question whether it was ever a dependable servant of Weimar democracy at all.

[50] Severing, *Lebensweg*, II, 247; E. Matthias, 'Die Sozialdemokratische Partei Deutschlands', in E. Matthias and E. Morsey (eds.), *Das Ende der Parteien 1933* (Düsseldorf 1960), 142.

Hitler's Personal Security*

Peter Hoffmann

From the early 1920s, Hitler enjoyed the attentions of a bodyguard, and precautions taken to protect his life against assassins became more and more elaborate after 1933. In 1934 Daimler-Benz Corporation began developing bullet-proof windshields and windows for his automobiles, and armoured cars were available for his use by 1938.[1] During the war especially, Hitler was increasingly surrounded by security guards, fences, perimeters, bunkers, and by elaborate precautions on his occasional public appearances. But in the autumn of 1939, Georg Elser, a cabinet-maker, was able to spend thirty to thirty-five nights, undetected by any security agents, in the Munich beer cellar, in preparation for his assassination attempt of 8 November 1939[2]; and Count Stauffenberg, a colonel and Chief of Staff of the Home Army, managed to bring into Hitler's immediate presence on three separate occasions in July 1944 four pounds of plastic explosive with chemical delay fuses, without ever arousing suspicion before the explosion of his bomb on 20 July 1944[3].

Elser's bomb, installed in a pillar in front of which Hitler used to give his annual address commemorating the 1923 putsch, killed eight people. Elser defeated whatever security precautions had

---

* Documents for which a repository is not given are in the possession of the author. All 'statements' and 'letters' were addressed to the author unless noted otherwise.

[1] Walter Hofer, 'Die Diktatur Hitlers bis zum Beginn des Zweiten Welt-krieges', *Handbuch der Deutschen Geschichte*, ed. Leo Just, IV, part 2 (Constance 1965), 29, 34; Friedrich Schmidt (formerly with RSD), letters, 8 February, 6 October 1966, 4 October 1967; Schmidt, letter to chairman of de-Nazification court in Camp Hammelburg, 27 April 1947; Gregor Karl (formerly with RSD), letters, 18 May 1966, 17 February 1968; Daimler-Benz Corporation Archive, Stuttgart-Untertürkheim.

[2] Johann Georg Elser, *Autobiographie eines Attentäters*, ed. Lothar Gruchmann (Stuttgart 1970); Anton Hoch, 'Das Attentat auf Hitler im Münchner Bürgerbräukeller 1939', *Vierteljahrshefte für Zeitgeschichte*, 1969, 383–413.

[3] Peter Hoffmann, *Widerstand, Staatsstreich, Attentat: Der Kampf der Opposition gegen Hitler* (Munich 1970), 451–73.

been taken. The provincial NSDAP (Nazi party) organization of Bavaria, rather than regular security officers, had been made responsible for Hitler's safety inside the beer cellar[4], and its measures were clearly inadequate. Hitler was saved only by a slight change of schedule that could not have been foreseen by the outsider Elser, nor was it planned as a security measure.[5]

Similarly, Stauffenberg's attempt—his third in nine days— failed through chance.[6] He was interrupted in his preparations and could use only one of the two packages of explosives he had brought with him, that is, half the amount considered necessary.[7] The force of the explosion was not sufficient to kill all those present at the conference. Hitler was again saved by luck, but the security breakdown that allowed Stauffenberg to come so close to success was quite different from that in Elser's case. Unlike Elser, Stauffenberg had a perfect disguise in the form of official duty that allowed him to enter Hitler's presence without arousing suspicion.

These security breakdowns raise the question whether or not all feasible steps were taken to ensure Hitler's personal safety. An examination of some typical security precautions designed to prevent attacks on Hitler's life (leaving aside ordinary accident prevention) might well give the superficial impression of thoroughness and impregnability.

Whether Hitler was travelling or staying in one of his headquarters, in the Berlin Chancellery, at the Berghof near Berchtesgaden, or in his apartment in Munich, he was always accompanied

[4] Order by Rudolf Hess, 9 March 1936, Bundesarchiv Koblenz (BA), EAP 173-e-10-12/90a.

[5] *Bericht Nr. 28* (by Alfred Rosenberg's liaison man in Hitler's Headquarters, reporting a table talk of Hitler's on 6 September 1941), typescript, dated *Führerhauptquartier* 7 September 1941, BA, R 6 o. Nr. This has not been published either in Henry Picker, *Hitlers Tischgespräche im Führerhauptquartier 1941-1942*, (Stuttgart 1965), or in Adolf Hitler, *Table Talk 1941-1944* (London 1953).

[6] Statements by Werner Vogel, 3 June, 1 July 1971; cf. Hoffmann, 'Opposition Annihilated: Punishing the 1944 Plot against Hitler', *The North American Review*, 1970, 3, 13; Hoffmann, *Widerstand*, 911-12.

[7] *Spiegelbild einer Verschwörung . . . Geheime Dokumente aus dem ehemaligen Reichssicherheitshauptamt* (Stuttgart 1961), 84; statements by Erich Kretz, the Headquarters chauffeur who drove Stauffenberg, 29 August 1965, 31 August 1966. Cf. Albert Widmann (a member of the investigating commission) in Bernd Wehner (also a member of the commission), 'Das Spiel ist aus', *Der Spiegel*, 23 March 1950; Hans Langemann, *Das Attentat: Eine kriminal-wissenschaftliche Studie zum politischen Kapitalverbrechen* (Hamburg 1956), 349, n. 57; Widmann, statement, 30 July 1968.

by his *Führer-Begleitkommando* (special detachment accompanying the Führer) composed of members of the SS bodyguard (*SS-Begleitkommando*), and of officers of the Secret Service (*Reichssicherheitsdienst* (RSD)).[8]

The function of the RSD in the early 1930s was to protect the head of government, members of the government, and to some extent their families; until 1934 it was known as the *Kriminalpolizeikommando z.b.V.* (criminal police squad for special duty). Then it was made a separate Reich authority by the Minister of Internal Affairs, Dr Frick.[9] In administrative matters, it was subordinated to the Secretary of State (after 1937 Reich Minister) and Chief of the Reich Chancellery, Dr Lammers, not, as one might expect, to Reichssicherheitshauptamt (RSHA), Reich Head Office for Security, under Himmler's authority.[10]

AT THE BEGINNING OF THE WAR, the status of the RSD detachment responsible for Hitler's security was changed slightly. Its members were now declared Wehrmacht officials for the duration of the war, administratively and militarily subordinated to the Chief of Army High Command (OKW), and possessing the rights and privileges of the Secret Military Police in the execution of their duties. Their uniform after November 1939 was the field-grey SS uniform.[11] This enabled them to move freely in areas dominated by Wehrmacht officers, and in turn mollified the Wehrmacht, which would have been offended by a display of many SS uniforms.

For its practical tasks in day-to-day operations around the person of Hitler, the RSD was under orders from Hitler himself or from his deputy, Rudolf Hess, and later from his secretary, Martin Bormann.[12] Only in theory, as a matter of hierarchical formality, was it subordinated to the supreme command of

[8] BA, R 43 II/1105.
[9] Schmidt, letters, 8 February 1966, 4 October 1967; Karl, letter, 18 May 1966; BA, R 43 II/1103–04. The RSD is not to be confused with the *Sicherheitsdienst (SD) des Reichsführers SS*, established by the Minister of Justice on 11 November 1938 'as an intelligence service for Party and State, particularly for the support of the Security Police'. All communication between SD and the Ministry was to be carried on exclusively through the Chief of the RSHA. BA, R 43 II/1104.
[10] Schmidt; BA, R 43 II/1105.
[11] Order by Keitel, 31 August 1939, BA, R 2/12160.
[12] *Befehlsverhältnisse, Allgemeine Aufgaben, Dienstsitz* of Kommondo z. b. V., 13 February 1935, BA, R 2/12159.

Reichsführer SS Himmler, who was also Chief of Police from 1936, and to his deputy Heydrich.[13] In reality, the immediate commanders of the RSD were the SS Lt. Gen. Hans Rattenhuber and his deputies, Peter Högl, Detective Inspector, Criminal Police, and Paul Kiesel, Police Inspector, and they all took orders directly from Hitler, Hess, or Bormann. Hitler also explicitly retained the right to appoint all members of the RSD personally.[14]

The bodyguards belonging to the RSD were, of course, chosen on the basis of their ability to do their job well. But political orthodoxy and loyalty were also strongly emphasized in their selection and appointment. There were in 1935 forty-five permanent members of the RSD of whom no more than twenty were detailed for Hitler's personal security; the rest were administrative personnel or guarded other members of the government. All were given security checks, and their financial situation and political reliability were looked into.[15]

Former members of the RSD are inclined to say that such matters as party membership and SS ranks (corresponding to civil-service ranks) entered into consideration only on grounds of formal efficiency. For instance, they assert that RSD officers were given SS ranks merely to enable them to perform their duties (observation, investigation of environment, surveillance of persons, etc.) without interference from Begleitkommando men who (before the war) wore the black SS uniform and regarded themselves as a special elite even among national-socialists. Actually, membership in the NSDAP and SS was important at all times, and at an earlier stage than some former RSD officers claim.

A law of 1936 provided that 'proven National Socialist candidates for higher government service who also meet the qualifications' for the positions for which they were candidates could be

[13] Hans Buchheim, *SS und Polizei im NS-Staat* (Duisdorf bei Bonn 1964), 47–51; Himmler's formal authority over the Führerschutzkommando was not definitively established until 22 October 1935; Lammers to Himmler, 22 October 1935, BA, R 43 II/1103.

[14] *Befehlsverhältnisse*, BA, R 2/12159; Högl to Brückner, 20 November 1939, BA, NS 10/136, 10/55, 10/124; Schmidt.

[15] BA, R 43 II/1103; order by Rattenhuber, 19 December 1939, BA, NS 10/136; Berlin Document Centre (BDC), NSDAP files; RSD files in National Archives, Washington D.C. (NA), T–175 roll 241, T–354 roll 193.

promoted at shorter intervals than the rest.[16] The preference shown to NSDAP and SS members for government service was general, and it applied to the RSD. Persons not eligible for SS and NSDAP membership were considered not eligible for RSD service. In May 1934 Göring, as Prussian Minister-President, and still Chief of the Secret State Police (Gestapo), stated that for the protection of Hitler only those could be considered suitable who were 'tried and trusted National-Socialists, and furthermore excellent criminal-police officers of unconditional reliability, utmost conscientiousness in fulfilment of duties, of good manners and sound physical health'. A search of the personnel files covering the years 1934–44 has turned up only one RSD officer who was a member of the SS but not also of the NSDAP. All others were members of both.[17]

Rattenhuber and Högl joined the NSDAP in 1934 and 1933, respectively; Kiesel became a member in 1937. Hans Baur, Hitler's pilot who also belonged to the RSD, was an NSDAP member from 1926.[18] The same general rule applied to the Begleit-kommando.

Personal loyalty was further ensured by elaborate swearing-in ceremonies. All regular military men and government officials had to take an oath, from 1934 in these words: 'I swear: I shall be faithful and obedient to the Führer of the German Reich and People, Adolf Hitler; I shall observe the laws and fulfil my official duties conscientiously, so help me God.'[19] Although RSD officers were first required to take the special oath for RSD men, an administration official insisted they must take the oath for all government officials as well, otherwise they could not have the status of government officials and the rights and privileges attaching thereto.[20] The additional oath required of RSD officers was even stronger: 'I swear to you, Adolf Hitler, as Führer and Chancellor of the German Reich, loyalty and courage. I vow to you and to my superiors designated by you obedience to the

---

[16] *Reichsgrundsätze über Einstellung, Anstellung und Beförderung der Reich- und Landesbeamten*, 1 October 1936, *Reichsgesetzblatt, Teil I, 1936* (Berlin 1936), 893.
[17] BA, R 43 II/1103-04; Göring to Lammers, 31 May 1934, BA, R 43 II/1103; *Ernennungsvorschläge*, BA, R 43 II/1103-04; BDC, NSDAP files.
[18] BDC files of Rattenhuber, Högl, Kiesel, and Bauer; BA, R 43 II/1103.
[19] Law of 20 August 1934, *Reichsgesetzblatt, Teil I, 1934* (Berlin 1934), 785.
[20] Hitler to Lammers, 17 January 1936, Lammers to Rattenhuber, 17 January 1936, BA, R 43 II/1103.

death. So help me God.' Moreover, Hitler always swore in RSD officers personally and insisted on retaining this privilege; swearing-in ceremonies were always held in front of the Munich Feldherrnhalle where sixteen supporters of Hitler had been killed by police on 9 November 1923; and the date of the ceremony was always 9 November.[21] While the regular oath retained loyalty to laws, the circumstances and the form of the special oath make clear that this one, using the familiar form of the second person singular, was the more binding. Personal loyalty was put above adherence to the law.

The SS-Begleitkommando was drawn from the SS-Leib-standarte Adolf Hitler (Hitler's personal SS guard), commanded by SS General Josef (Sepp) Dietrich. In 1939 about thirty members of the Leibstandarte were detailed for the protection of Hitler. Most were members of the NSDAP and had entered the party *en bloc*: a list of 1,400 of their names shows membership numbers from 5,506,805 to 5,508,254. The detachment for Hitler's protection was under the command, ultimately, of Hitler himself. For day-to-day operations it was commanded by Hitler's chief adjutant Wilhelm Brückner, SS Major Bruno Gesche (*Kommando I*), SS Major Peter Högl (*Kommando II*), SS Major Franz Schädle (*Kommando III*), and by Gesche's deputy, Adolf Dirr.[22] Gesche was transferred to a basic-training camp and then to the Russian front in April 1942, after over-indulgence in alcohol. In December 1942, Hitler ordered one of his personal SS adjutants, Richard Schulze, to take over the disciplinary and administrative powers of the Begleitkommando, including authority to issue guidelines for training and deployment, and to appoint and dismiss its members (though ultimately not without the approval of Hitler). He was not, however, put in immediate operational command.[23] Gesche was back in command by January 1943, but was finally removed, once again for over-drinking, on

[21] Lammers to Himmler, 22 October 1935, Rattenhuber to Lammers, 14 November 1935, BA, R 43 II/1103; Lammers, *Vermerk*, 3 January 1942, BA, R 43 II/1104.

[22] BDC, SS-Leibstandarte files; *Statistisches Jahrbuch der Schutzstaffel der NSDAP*, 1937, 1938. Schmidt; Karl; BA, NS 10/137, R 43 II/1105; Rattenhuber to Brückner, 18 November 1939, Högl to Brückner, 20 November 1939, BA, NS 10/136. Otto Günsche (Hitler's last SS adjutant), statement, 6 November 1972.

[23] Hitler order, 22 December 1942, NA, T-175 roll 43. See also Helmut Heiber, ed., *Hitlers Lagebesprechungen . . . 1942–45* (Stuttgart 1962), 36.

24 December 1944. Schädle was appointed provisional commanding officer.[24]

SECURITY REGULATIONS AT THE Chancellery were coordinated in March and April 1936 by Dr Lammers; there were honour guards of the SS and Wehrmacht in front. At Hitler's private residences there were only SS honour guards, but on special occasions such as Army Day they were replaced by Wehrmacht soldiers.[25] Regular police sentries from the 16th Police Precinct of Berlin had to watch for untrustworthy characters at the entrance and notify the doorman of their arrival if any appeared. The particular duties of the police sentries, the SS sentries, members of the Begleitkommando and of the RSD were clearly demarcated here. Among other things, the principal duty of the RSD was to watch every move of visitors who did not normally work in the Chancellery. Strange persons without proper identification were to be taken to the doorman, and, if no satisfactory identification could be made there, were to be arrested and taken to Police Precinct headquarters. All guards, porters, and doormen were strictly forbidden to divulge any information on Hitler's absence or presence. They were specifically told to answer questions from visitors or passersby in vague terms, certainly not by 'yes' or 'no'. On the other hand, a regulation issued a few days after the new Chancellery had been finished, said that the official standard was not to be flown when Hitler was not in the Chancellery, but that it was to be raised at the moment he drove through the main entrance into the inner court;[26] some forty privileged guests—Gauleiter, some government officials, the architect Speer and some others—could come to Hitler's lunch table whenever they wished, and could walk around in the Chancellery freely and unaccompanied.[27]

[24] SS-Hauptsturmführer Pfeiffer to Himmler, 17 July 1942, BDC, Himmler file; Bormann to Schädle, 17 December 1944, BDC, Bormann file. Günsche (statement 6 November 1972) says the order which also appointed him Schädle's superior never went into effect.

[25] BA, R43 II/1105. Colonel Schmundt (successor to Friedrich Hossbach as one of Hitler's Wehrmacht adjutants, and from October 1942 also Chief of the Army Personnel Office); Wolf Keilig, *Das deutsche Heer 1939–1945* (Bad Neuheim 1956) to OKW 25 March 1939, BA, NS 10/126.

[26] *Dienstanordnung*; Lammers to State Secretary Meissner, to SA Chief of Staff Lutze, to Dietrich, to the head of the 16th Police Precinct, and to others, 28 March 1936, BA, R 43 II/1105; Wünsche to SS-Leibstandarte Adolf Hitler, 18 January 1939, BA, NS 10/83.

[27] Albert Speer, *Erinnerungen* (Frankfurt/M. 1969), 131. This was true

A few days after Elser's near-successful assassination attempt, some changes were made in guard positions and guard-duty regulations. Several sentries and guards at the Chancellery who had been detailed by the Police Precinct for the periods of Hitler's absence were now replaced permanently by Begleitkommando officers whether Hitler was there or not. Other guard positions were manned twenty-four hours a day instead of merely during day-time. Patrolled areas were extended to provide a more continuous ring of guards around the Chancellery. In the weeks following, security was further intensified with specific reference to Elser's assassination attempt, and with the stated intention 'to avoid the recurrence of such acts of sabotage as that of 8 November 1939'. A special group of forty-one security guards was charged with observing all works, repairs, and maintenance activities performed in the Chancellery, and to increase surveillance of persons in the building.[28] Meanwhile, a general overhaul of security precautions was being prepared.

Under the date 9 March 1940, Heydrich sent to all high-level SS and Police commands a sixty-page instruction on 'security measures for the protection of leading persons of State and Party'. A special protection service section headed by SS Major Franz Schulz was created in the RSHA. It did not help Heydrich to gain much more control over security, although he declared the new section 'the central office for all security police measures and for all assassination reports'. Hitler's direct control through Bormann, Rattenhuber, and his personal adjutants was *expressis verbis* unaffected by the new arrangements, nor was Lammers' control reduced.[29]

Some discrepancies and division of delegated authority were present throughout the structure, in part intentionally, in part as a

---

throughout the war. Prominent and well known regular visitors were practically always unaccompanied. After 20 July 1944, they only had to have their brief-cases checked; Speer, letter, 11 May 1972.

[28] *Dienstanweisung*, 16 November 1939, BA, R 43 II/1101b; Wünsche to commanding officer of Leibstandarte, reserve battalion, 18 November 1939, BA, NS 10/83; Rattenhuber to RSD, 28 February 1940, BA, R 43 II/1104.

[29] *Richtlinien für die Handhabung des Sicherungsdienstes*, RSHA Amt IV, Berlin, February 1940, with Heydrich's covering letter containing general directives, 9 March 1940, NA, T–175 roll 383. This is the *Erlass* that Hoch had been unable to find; Hoch, 409–10 and n. 106. Hoch erroneously concluded from other information that Heydrich had managed to 'bring into his exclusive competence all security measures'.

result of indecision. But it was also desirable for practical reasons to allow the immediate leadership of the bodyguard enough latitude in making their own decisions as to what was necessary for security. At any rate, Heydrich's authority was very limited here, and he revealed the extent of the limitation in his own order of 9 March 1940 when he stated: 'The RSD (SS-Col. Rattenhuber, Chief) is the proper authority and responsible for the immediate and personal protection of the Führer and of those persons who are given a bodyguard. This authority is the same on *all* drives, trips, mass rallies, etc. Furthermore, the RSD is the proper authority and responsible for security measures in the Chancellery, in the private residence of the Führer and on the Obersalzberg. For all other security measures in the wider environs of these persons including routes of approach and departure, the Secret State Police is the proper authority and responsible. The wishes of the RSD in actual cases are to be accommodated . . . The Chief of the RSD has the right to give directions for carrying out security measures in the immediate environs of the Führer.'

Heydrich did manage to improve and intensify the long-range security precautions that were not under the control of Rattenhuber and his men, at least not during the months and years up to the last few days before an occasion requiring special security precautions. Areas of competence could also be defined more clearly, or even redrawn in some cases.

At places of regularly recurring gatherings with Hitler—Berlin, Munich, Nürnberg, Weimar, Hamburg, Hannover—the sites were in future to be kept under surveillance *at all times*.[30] The local Gestapo chiefs were made responsible for organizing, coordinating, and putting into effect all security measures in their districts. For all events in which Hitler, Göring, or Hess participated the regional Chief SS and Police officers were charged with the overall organization of precautions, but the local Gestapo remained responsible for carrying them out. Heydrich reserved for himself the authority to direct long-range security measures personally if a major event was planned for Berlin, or if one was planned at which he himself intended to be present. All this certainly took control over security out of the hands of party

---

[30] This is emphasized in both the *Richtlinien* and Heydrich's covering letter. Such places as the beer cellar were to be under constant surveillance, not only half a year in advance, as Hoch suggests.

functionaries, particularly with regard to the annual beer cellar gathering—obviously the most drastic and the most needed change wrought by Heydrich's new directive.

Most of the specific instructions in the new directive were a restatement and re-emphasis of long-standing principles and practices. All precautions were to be under constant review, to prevent them from becoming unthinking routine. The security intelligence services were to be specially active at home and abroad when the dates of recurring events were drawing near, and all reports of assassination plans were to be immediately and thoroughly followed up. Files were to be kept up to date on 'enemies of the State' living near sites to be protected, and also on the mentally ill who were at large, on professional criminals, on 'a-social elements', and on foreigners. Surveillance of foreigners, border points, roads, railroads, ports, airports, hotels, had to begin as soon as there was public knowledge of a forthcoming event, and in cases of regularly recurring events three months in advance. Even 'suspicious newspaper advertisements' were to be checked, and files kept on all persons living or working within a radius of 500 meters around the site of a recurring event. All persons were to be given security checks concerning their political and moral character, which had to be renewed, and not merely reviewed, at least once a year. Every change of address or employment within the security radius had to be recorded in the file at once. 'Unreliable' persons were to be 'removed' from the security radius where this was feasible.

In addition to constant observation of buildings, bridges, sewers, construction sites, attics, dubious hotels, etc., specialists such as watchmakers, electricians, and interior decorators were to be engaged to search for hidden explosives; they were to use the most up-to-date listening devices to detect any ticking noises—an obvious outcome of the Elser attempt. Security forces were also told to put together a collection of keys to all buildings, attics, basements and garages within the security radius around sites of regularly recurring events. Once a month at least, the site itself had to be investigated by specialists. Weapons shops, thefts of weapons and explosives were to be given special attention. In short: 'Nothing must be allowed to occur within the security radius that will not at the same time, at the latest, become known to the respective security office.' Special checks of the most thorough kind were to be made in the time between four weeks and one week before an event, and these had to include 'floors, walls, pillars, ceilings, furniture and decorations, podia and the like, cables, transformer stations, underpasses, overpasses, lamp-posts, monuments, advertisement pillars, sandboxes, garages, telephone booths, mailboxes, scaffolding, electric power lines, grandstands, pylons, flagpoles, etc. etc. and in this all applicable achievements of science and technology are to be employed such as listening, sensing, and screening devices, spotlights, etc. Furthermore, explosives experts must be called in to indicate on the basis of their experience the spots especially suited for assassination attempts with explosives.' Needless to say, even closer surveillance was to be maintained during the last days and hours before the event. If any preparatory work was still necessary, such as setting up stands, this was subject to the closest supervision. 'In particular, hollow spaces that will be closed in the course of such work must be very thoroughly examined before they are closed, and must be constantly observed afterwards.'[31] Even after the event, security was not to be relaxed, especially in places of regularly recurring events, because experience showed, said the directive, that assassins were capable of taking all circumstances into account, and that those proceeding systematically were likely to reconnoitre the site of an attempt in the confusion at the end of a mass meeting when a relaxation of precautions might be expected.

All this, however, was not enough, as some incidents showed. In the summer of 1940, Gestapo Chief Heinrich Müller of the RHSA was alarmed by the realization that it would be possible for an assassin or foreign agent who donned a uniform and carried a camera to gain admission to Hitler's immediate presence on such an occasion as his birthday reception. In the next year, Hitler's birthday reception was held at his military headquarters, probably as a result of Müller's alarm. But incidents of freak security breakdowns occurred as late as 1942, and those engaged in providing security had to be reminded as late as 1944 that

---

[31] This, incidentally, foiled Gersdorff's attempt to place a bomb on the speaker's rostrum to kill Hitler at the Memorial Day observances in Berlin on 21 March 1943; Hoffmann, 'The Attempt to Assassinate Hitler on 21 March, 1943', *Canadian Journal of History*, 1967, 77–78.

persons not employed in the Chancellery must never be allowed to move in it unaccompanied.[32]

PRECISELY DEFINED PROCEDURES were in effect for Hitler's public or announced trips and appearances, even before Heydrich's new directive.[33] A minute-by-minute programme of the event was arranged by a special department in the Propaganda Ministry and approved by Hitler personally. Before Elser's attempt on-the-spot preparations and arrangements were also under the immediate control of the Propaganda Ministry or of the regional Gauleiter. Security arrangements in the streets, at hotel entrances, assembly-hall entrances, etc. were the responsibility of the regional SS leader, to whom for such occasions all regional police were subordinated, 'and who was by order of the Reichsführer SS in most cases the senior police commander in his area'. Gauleiter and regional SS leaders were required to cooperate closely, but government representatives were excluded from participation in arrangements and the events themselves unless they got a special invitation from Hitler's adjutants.

When Hitler gave a speech in the Berlin Sports Palace on 30 May 1942 before 10,000 officer candidates, instructors, and invited guests, Heydrich's 1940 directives for such occasions were used with only minor modifications,[34] although an attempt on Heydrich's life had been made in Prague only three days before the event (Heydrich died later of his wounds).

This was merely referred to in the security orders for the Sports Palace in order to stress the need for tight security, which was as tight as it could be. The event itself was not made public and the audience were informed of the name of the speaker only when they arrived.

When Hitler rode in his car from the Chancellery to the Sports Palace, some 450 officers of the Gestapo, the Kriminalpolizei, and

[32] Müller to Rattenhuber, 3 June 1940, BA, R 43 II/1104; *Kriegstagebuch Nr. 5: Führer-Hauptquartier,* 1 January–30 April 1941, NA, T–78 roll 351; Rattenhuber to Hitler's adjutant's office, 17 March 1942, Lammers' *Dienstanweisung,* 30 September 1944, BA, R 43 II/1104.

[33] *Anordnung Nr. 34/36* by Rudolf Hess, 9 March 1936, BA, RG 1010/3183; Rattenhuber to Brückner, 29 May 1939, BA, NS 10/136.

[34] Security plans, BA, RG 1010/714; *Kriegstagebücher* nos. 1–6 of Hitler's headquarters, August 1939–July 1942, no. 6, NA, T–78 roll 351; there is a phonograph record of the speech in BA; the printed version of the speech in Picker, 493–504 is based on Picker's notes.

the RHSA were on hand. Since 26 May, there had always been sixteen officers in the Sports Palace to keep it under continuous surveillance, and uniformed policemen with police dogs constantly patrolled the grounds outside. While preparations were under way and scaffolding was being set up, an officer constantly patrolled the basement, another the attic, and still another was always stationed on the roof. The rest of the crew of sixteen had to watch the workmen and check all materials brought into the building. On 30 May, before the speech, eighty officers again thoroughly checked the entire building and occupied what were termed 'danger points', i.e. vantage points for would-be assassins. To ensure security and secrecy, the telephone booths in the building were occupied for the duration of the event by special army guards, and the use of the telephones was prohibited. No one was allowed to leave the building before Hitler had left it.

Entrance checks were made by army men reinforced by two police officers at each gate. On the day of the speech, fifteen police officers guarded the attic, the roof, and the roofs of all nearby buildings. One police officer was posted at the central light switches of the building. Throughout the building, police and SD officers were posted with specific instructions for watching the crowds, balconies, stairways, particularly those leading to the rostrum and the balconies. The basement doors and all windows and exit doors were locked and guarded by police officers. Buildings adjoining the Sports Palace, and buildings from which the main entrance and the approach area could be seen, were occupied by Gestapo officers, who were instructed to prevent anyone from going near a balcony or window in any of these buildings. Their roofs were also guarded. The occupants of these houses were registered by the police, and were told not to allow anyone who did not live there into their apartments during the speech.

Along the route, Gestapo officers were stationed on the second floor of all corner buildings, hotels and restaurants. The restaurants themselves were put under inconspicuous surveillance. Building sites, empty houses and lots, street sandboxes, piles of construction materials and scaffolding, railroad and subway entrances, bridges, public toilets, sewer shafts, were all checked and occupied by officers, and kept under close surveillance until after the event. Parks, gardens, gateways, airshafts and other hollow spaces,

163

balconies, mailboxes, hydrants, fire-extinguishers along the route and in the Sports Palace building were not forgotten. It was strictly forbidden to toss any flowers, letters, 'or other objects'; no one was allowed to climb a tree, fence, sign post, or vehicle of any kind. All policemen were required to watch out for suitcases, and especially for harmless-looking baskets and packages being deposited or otherwise appearing while Hitler's cars were passing. Parked cars had to be inspected, and 'Jews and other elements open to suspicion' had to be kept out of the security zone altogether. Police, Gestapo, and SD officers were stationed along the entire route, to keep the public on the sidewalks under observation, as well as the windows and balconies of the houses across the street.

Unless an insider was in the audience or happened to live along the route Hitler travelled on this occasion, there was little chance of any successful attempt on his life. Barring such an unlikely coincidence, and given secrecy, security precautions for the event must be considered complete and effective. There remained the outside chance of someone escaping the vigilance of the 450 security men; but even if all houses and sidewalks had been cleared altogether, there was always a residue of uncertainty, and to have taken more exhaustive measures would only have attracted the kind of attention that the authorities were trying to avoid.

On Hitler's unofficial journeys, when there was no need or no desire to inform the public about a trip, such as his private visits to his Munich apartment and his architect's atelier, one routine precaution was not to inform police or other authorities.[35] Hitler believed and repeatedly said that there was only the choice between security precautions as complete and elaborate as possible, such as those put on for occasions such as May Day, 30 January, or 8/9 November, or total secrecy and unpredictability of his movements.[36] If even a railroad official or some local policeman got wind of Hitler's approach, or if someone recognized him and telephoned ahead, there would be gendarmes all over the place standing guard so clumsily and conspicuously that everyone could only conclude that a great spectacle was about to occur. Naturally, crowds would gather, and then the well-intentioned security

[35] Rattenhuber to Brückner, 29 May 1939, BA, NS 10/136; cf. Speer, 52–62.
[36] Picker, 244, 306–07, 386–87; Rattenhuber to Brückner, 29 May 1939, BA, NS 10/136.

measures initiated by those eager and anxious policemen would be totally inadequate.

Yet, however small Hitler's entourage was on such occasions, it was difficult to conceal. A typical Führer-Begleitkommando for trips consisted of about eleven RSD officers, each with two loaded pistols and fifty extra rounds of ammunition, and stored in their automobiles six additional pistols with ninety-six rounds, six submachine-guns with 380 rounds, and one machine-gun with 4,500 rounds. There were also ten Begleitkommando men and at least one of Hitler's valets (who also had SS rank), and usually some adjutant such as Brückner, the driver Erich Kempka, the photographer Heinrich Hoffmann, the Press Chief Dietrich, the architect Speer. To increase security, Hitler insisted it was useful to lead an irregular daily life, to have habits that made his movements unpredictable, and to change plans frequently, at will, and on short notice.[37]

It has been mentioned that Hitler used armoured automobiles. Similar precautions were taken with other modes of travel. His special train, code-named 'Amerika' until November 1941, and afterwards known as 'Brandenburg', always carried guards and soldiers, and was regularly accompanied by heavy anti-aircraft guns. The planes he used during the war were armed with machine guns and had a parachute in every seat. Hitler could pull a red lever which would automatically parachute him down through a trap door under his seat.[38]

HITLER'S HEADQUARTERS AT Wolfschanze, about five miles east of Rastenburg (now Ketrzyn) in East Prussia, became in the course of the war the most heavily protected of all his residences. In the first few weeks Rommel was in charge of the headquarters installation and of security as provided by the army detachments. He was succeeded by Lt. Col. Gustav Streve, who had a reputation as a tough security man.[39]

[37] Merkblatt, 3 September 1939, BA, NS 10/126; order by Rattenhuber 19 December 1939, BA, NS 10/136; Merkblatt, June 1940, BA, Sammlung Schumacher 1492; Speer, 52–59; Picker, 306; statement by Erich Kempka, 19 August 1965.

[38] Kriegstagebücher, nos. 1–6; papers of Major (ret.) Josef Wolf (formerly commanding officer of Wolfschanze signals detachment); Bauer, 193, 260–61; Fabian von Schlabrendorff, Offiziere gegen Hitler (Frankfurt/M. 1959), 97.

[39] Kriegstagebücher, nos. 1–6; BDC, Rattenhuber file; statement by Helmuth Spaeter (formerly an officer with Führer-Begleit-Bataillon), 3 July 1965.

The general area was patrolled constantly; numerous military installations were located in the vicinity and integrated into security systems by the beginning of 1944. Access roads were under close surveillance, and a railroad running through the headquarters area was closed to the public, while all other railroads were patrolled by regular police, military police, and Gestapo and SD agents, as had become customary throughout Germany and German-occupied lands.[40]

An outer security fence surrounded two inner compounds, and was reinforced with heavy-machine-gun emplacements, anti-tank guns, anti-aircraft guns, and a mine belt. Each compound in turn had fences and security systems, with guards, checkpoints, foot patrols along the fences and within the entire compound areas, and ring-telephones for emergency alerts. Compound II contained the offices of the armed forces operational staff, headquarters commandant and his staff, mess halls, supply and utility plants, and a communications centre in a vast bunker. Compound I contained the bunkers of Hitler, Bormann, and later one for Göring; part of Keitel's offices and the barracks of the Army Personnel Office were constructed as air-raid-proof bunkers. There were also offices of the personal adjutants, of physicians, of the RSD and the Begleitkommando, and another large communications centre in a bunker.

Security precautions in Compound I were elaborate and comprehensive. As everywhere else, RSD and SS men were assigned to guard Hitler's person within his headquarters. If he walked from one bunker to another, he was followed by one or two security men. When he held his situation conference about midday, an RSD officer stood guard in front of the building, and another constantly patrolled the grounds around it. When Hitler walked his dog Blondi, bodyguards were around.

In 1943, a fenced-off area *within* Compound I was established as *Security Zone A*. It included Hitler's bunker and a few other buildings, such as Bormann's bunker and three mess halls. Special permits were required to enter, and there were RSD guards at the gates. Elaborate rules were set up for obtaining passes. All this was designed to 'maintain the secrecy of events, intentions, conferences, etc.' in Hitler's immediate environment;

---

[40] Cf. order by Rattenhuber, 19 December 1939, BA, NS 10/136.

and, 'besides secrecy, the reason for creating security zone A is the safety of the person of the Führer'.[41]

Security became so tight that an orderly of Keitel's whose office was within security zone A could not risk being found without a specific order if he walked the few yards from his own office to Hitler's bunker.[42] But during the periods of construction at Wolfschanze, and it was almost always under construction, the installation was swarming with some two or three hundred labourers, and it was very difficult to keep track of them at all times.[43] In fact, it was next to impossible, and security was partially defeated by the very efforts to increase it.

When Hitler finally moved back from Berghof to Wolfschanze on 14 July 1944, he was forced to stay in a building known as the guest bunker. His own bunker was under reconstruction to make it invulnerable to the heaviest aerial bombs then in use.[44] He held his daily midday situation conferences nearby in a hut with thin brick walls and a concrete roof. The two buildings, guest bunker and hut, were now enclosed by another special fence with a gate, and the new little compound was called the Führer's security zone. Again, RSD guards were posted at the gate, and special passes were required to enter, although such well known headquarters figures as Keitel or Jodl ordinarily did not have to show theirs, and they could also bring in other accredited officers on occasion.

External security arrangements were no less complete. All of Hitler's headquarters were surrounded by a network of military installations. There was a special battalion, drawn from the regular Army, for ground defence; a detachment for anti-aircraft defence and early warning against possible air raids; and a superbly equipped information section with a vast communications network

[41] Albert Bormann und [Rudolf] Schmundt, *Rundschreiben*, 20 September 1943; [Gustav] Streve, *Merkblatt über das Verhalten bei Alarm für die Belegschaft der Sperrkreise und Sonderzüge*, 14 October 1943, 5 May 1944; Schmundt, *Befehl zur Verteidigung des Führerhauptquartiers Wolfschanze*, 18 July 1944; Streve, *Zusatz zum Alarmbefehl für FHQu.* 23 July 1944, BA, EAP 105/33; *Kriegstagebücher*, no. 1; statement by General Herbert Büchs, 1 July 1964; *Grundlagen für die Befehlserteilung bei der Abwehr von Fallschirmjägern*, 1943/44, Wolf papers; [Heinz] Pieper (commanding officer in Führer-Begleit-Bataillon), *Erziehungs- und Ausbildungs-Richtlinien für das Führer-Grenadier-Bataillon*, 10 July 1944, Wolf papers; statement by Pieper, 24 July 1965.

[42] Vogel, 1 July 1971.

[43] Speer, 391.

[44] Karl Jesko von Puttkamer (formerly Hitler's naval adjutant), statement, 5 March 1964; Günsche.

within and outside Wolfschanze; and parachute units standing by to be dropped into Wolfschanze in case of an airborne attempt at a *coup de main*.[45] Such an attempt was highly unlikely in this land of forests, lakes and swamps around Wolfschanze, nor was it likely to occur in the mountainous Berghof district. But those responsible for Hitler's safety meant to be prepared for any eventuality. The orders given referred expressly not only to possible bombings and gas attacks, but also to possible attacks by parachute troops: 'In case of a parachute drop into the centre of the installation, defensive weapons will be aimed inward as well as outward . . . Wolfschanze will be defended to the last man.'[46]

Internal security seemed superfluous in the face of such complete external controls and protection. But bizarre instances of security breakdowns nevertheless occurred. In 1942, an intruder managed to climb over an outer fence. He was shot and killed by a guard; he was then discovered to have been a Polish labourer who had left his place of work and had apparently wanted to take a short cut on his way home. He carried only a small knapsack with some bread and meat, and a jack-knife.[47] In 1943, a colonel got off a courier train at Wolfschanze by mistake, thinking he was in Mauerwald. He wandered into Compound I, found an officers' mess, and was having breakfast when he was discovered by one of Hitler's personal adjutants. He refused to believe he was in Wolfschanze, until Hitler was pointed out to him where he was exercising his dog.[48]

THERE EMERGE FROM WHAT has been said three major contradictions: elaborate precautions and their dangerous, not infrequent breakdown; ineffectiveness of the various security measurers against insiders; and finally, Hitler's own contribution to the defeat of security when he took unneccessary risks.[49]

---

[45] Büchs.
[46] Streve, *Merkblatt*, 5 May 1944.
[47] *Kriegstagebücher*, Nr. 6.
[48] Puttkamer.
[49] During the campaign in Poland, he exposed himself to gunfire and bombing; *Kriegstagebücher*, no. 1. In February 1943 he visited a front headquarters that was already threatened by Russian tanks, and barely escaped being trapped there; [Martin Bormann], *Daten aus alten Notizbüchern 1934–1943*, Hoover Institution, Stanford, California, *NSDAP Hauptarchiv*, reel 1 folder 16; Baur, 231; *Kriegstagebuch des Oberkommandos der Wehrmacht* (*Wermachtführungsstab*) *1940–45*, III (Frankfurt/M. 1963), 136–37.

There was, of course, no defence against a disguise as complete as Stauffenberg's. Hitler's legendary instinct failed him completely in this case. He was equally unprotected against other would-be assassins if they belonged to the officials and officers with whom he had personal contact for governmental and military purposes. Dr Erich Kordt, who hoped to kill Hitler in November 1939 and found himself thwarted by circumstances arising from the aftermath of Elser's attempt, was high up in Ribbentrop's Ministry and a familiar figure in the Chancellery. Eberhard von Breitenbuch accompanied Field Marshal Busch as *aide-de-camp* on visits to Hitler in the spring of 1944 on several occasions, and he too planned an assassination attempt. Colonel von Tresckow, his *aide-de-camp* Fabian von Schlabrendorff, and Colonel Freiherr von Gersdorff, who made assassination attempts, all had contact with Hitler through official business.[50] These are only a few examples. Access to Hitler was not a serious problem for several of the conspirators, although it was usually difficult to find individuals who had the opportunity and were also willing and able to make use of it. Several conspirators who did have access to Hitler, and who eventually gave their lives in the fight against him, confessed that they were simply not able to kill the man although they had excellent opportunities.[51]

The idea of using explosives rather than pistols or knives in assassination attempts was in part a response to such inhibitions; moreover, some very effective security precautions around Hitler's person could be evaded only by using explosives: all his visitors were virtually always under close surveillance by RSD officers and SS adjutants, so that it appeared quite impossible to draw a pistol in Hitler's presence, let alone to shoot accurately. Hitler himself said that an attempt with a bomb had a far better chance of success than shooting.[52]

[50] Hoffmann, *Widerstand*, 302–04, 309–55, 389–92; Consul Susanne Simonis (in 1939 in close contact with Kordt), letter, 8 March 1971.

[51] Statement by Axel Freiherr von dem Bussche, 8 July 1971.

[52] There were regulations forbidding persons in Hitler's presence to put their hands into their pockets. Count Strachwitz, a highly decorated tank commander, once reached into his pocket for a handkerchief in Hitler's presence when he was about to receive one of his many medals for bravery, but before he could withdraw his hand it was gripped by an SS adjutant; Count Strachwitz von Grosse-Zauche und Caminetz, letter, 20 January 1966; cf. Heiber, 439; statement by Heinz Sasse (formerly a Porpaganda Ministry cameraman), 1 July 1971; Picker, 387.

Screening and surveillance methods that still applied to high-ranking lieutenants and advisers were much less effective among Hitler's constant immediate entourage. The number of those allowed to eat at his table, for instance, was reduced drastically after September 1942, mainly as a result of an angry exchange of words between Hitler and General Jodl on 7 September, and not primarily as a security measure; but there were still thirty-eight persons on the list of Dining Room 1 that was used by Hitler in Wolfschanze.[53] Those who were allowed to take meals with him, some of whom sat at tea with him every night, were his most loyal henchmen, including Keitel, Bormann, Dietrich, Hewel, Jodl, Schmundt, adjutants, physicians, Rattenhuber, the pilot Baur and the driver Kempka, the film reporter Walter Frentz whom Hitler liked, the photographer Heinrich Hoffmann, and others. Servants, typists, and secretaries, forty-three persons in all, were assigned to Dining Room 2. Any of these could have come to the conclusion that Hitler must be removed to save Germany from ruin. They could easily have used explosives.

Hitler's valets were loyal and trusted members of the Begleit-kommando. The female secretaries were his admirers, and some were married to Begleitkommando men.[54] In this intimate sphere, there was still an inevitable residue of uncertainty; elaborate precautions on the one hand, and, on the other, personal trust to the point of negligence, and unnecessary risk-taking. Hitler did not require his cook to taste his food in front of him before he ate. He simply trusted his cooks. He was not physically a coward, but he was frequently preoccupied with his personal security, and he claimed great expertise in the business of protecting his life against assassins. He acknowledged that an 'idealist' prepared to risk his life could murder him with relative ease, but he himself

---

[53] Walter Warlimont, *Im Hauptquartier der deutschen Wehrmacht 1939–1945* (Frankfurt/M. 1962), 267–69; [Franz] Halder, *Kriegstagebuch*, III (Stuttgart 1963), 518–19; Bormann und Schmundt, *Rundschreiben*, 20 September 1943. On Hitler's alleged fear of being poisoned see Heinrich Hoffmann, *Hitler was my Friend* (London 1955), 201–02.

[54] BDC files on Hans Junge and Heinz Linge. Cf. H. R. Trevor-Roper, *The Last Days of Hitler, passim*.

contributed to making this possible. He would explain in great detail how attacks on his automobile could be foiled; but he often defeated elaborate precautions by taking unnecessary risks.[55] In his own judgment, he owed his narrow escapes in 1938 (Maurice Bavaud's attempt), in 1939 (Elser), and in 1944 to 'accidental lucky circumstances', to 'marked accidents', and to 'Providence'.[56] Security was defeated by laxity on occasions, by freak incidents on others, and frequently by insiders, and by Hitler himself. There were increased security precautions, but there is no evidence of a massive and comprehensive clamp-down after any of the attempts on Hitler's life.

The question why the many attempts and plans failed is not the primary topic of this study. Its purpose was to discover, by investigating selected aspects of security precautions, whether adequate security was provided for Hitler so far as it was possible under the circumstances. What emerges is that gaps and contradictions as well as great thoroughness characterized the security system, and that only some of the gaps could have been closed. There were definite limits to the feasible security precautions, even if Hitler had accepted (as he did not) the role of a mysterious rarely-seen man-behind-the-scenes. The fact that he was not assassinated does not in itself indicate full effectiveness of security measures; at least four or five attempts came within a hair's breadth of success, and Hitler escaped *after* and *although* security had been defeated. Until 1940, even 'ordinary' assassins, the type by whom every head of government is threatened, and whom Hitler called 'idealists', were not effectively foiled by security, as Elser's case shows. As Hitler's ability to rule and to lead declined with his failing health, and with the failures of the war, the dangers to his life increased as fewer and fewer considered his person sacrosanct. No increase of security could prevent insiders from acting.

[55]*Trial of the Major War Criminals before the International Military Tribunal: Nuremberg 14 November 1945–1 October 1946*, XXV (Nuremberg 1947), 330; Picker, 307–08; *Kriegstagebücher*, nos. 1–6; *Kriegstagebuch des Oberkommandos der Wehrmacht*, 136–37; Baur, 231.
[56]*Bericht Nr.28*; Picker, 306; Heiber, 620. The details Hitler mentioned from memory are not all accurate; e.g. he dated Bavaud's attempt a year back to 1937.

Maurice Bavaud's Attempt to Assassinate Hitler in 1938

Peter Hoffmann

Political assassination was rife in the early years of Weimar Germany, and Hitler, in common with many other political figures, attracted this kind of political violence. Even before the real beginning of his political career, in March or April 1919, he appears to have been in some danger of becoming a victim of political execution at the hands of the Soviet government that was then in power in Bavaria.[1] In 1933, when he became the Reich's Chancellor, and in 1934 when he became the President, he also attracted those attempts that were normally directed at persons in such positions.

On 3 March 1933, a ship's carpenter named Kurt Lutter was arrested in Königsberg and accused of having led a group of communists who were plotting to assassinate Hitler with explosives at a *Reichstag* election rally in Königsberg on 4 March.[2] Rumours and threats against Hitler's life came to the attention of the Gestapo throughout the twelve years of National Socialist rule.[3] In November 1935 the adjutant to the Führer and Reich's Chancellor, Captain Wiedemann, who had served in World War I as personnel officer in the regiment where Hitler had served as corporal, received information from the *Reichssicherungsdienst-Kommando* of the Prussian Secret State Police (*Preussische Geheime Staatspolizei*), that a vast conspiracy had formed in Paris and Prague with the aim of killing Hitler and some of his close associates.[4] Nothing happened, but more rumours, reports and attempts followed in 1936 and 1937.[5] In December 1936, a

[1] Werner Maser, *Adolf Hitler: Legende, Mythos, Wirklichkeit* (München 1971), 159–60.

[2] *Oberreichsanwalt* to *Reichsminister der Justiz* 1 June 1933, *Bundesarchiv* (henceforth: BA) R 43 II/1519.

[3] BA RG 1010/3183; R 43 II/991; NS 29/vorl. 435.

[4] BA R 43 II/991; Fritz Wiedemann, *Der Mann der Feldherr werden wollte: Erlebnisse und Erfahrungen des Vorgesetzten Hitlers im l. Weltkrieg und seines späteren Persönlichen Adjutanten* (Velbert 1964), 23.

[5] BA R 43 II/991.

student named Helmut Hirsch, who was connected with Otto Strasser and the *Schwarze Front* in Prague, came to Germany in order to blow up a party building in Nürnberg and to murder Julius Streicher or possibly Hitler himself; he was arrested, tried, and sentenced to death in 1937.[6] After 1937, the number of threats against the life of the Führer and Reich's Chancellor increased.[7] A group of German émigrés, Jews and *Schwarze Front* sympathizers plotted in Czechoslovakia to kill Hitler in 1937 and 1938. Also in 1938 new sources of plots opened up in Switzerland and Great Britain, while the opposition inside Germany was getting ready to launch its own attempts to overthrow and assassinate Hitler.[8]

Of course it did not become public knowledge until 1969 that the military attaché of the British Embassy in Berlin, then Colonel Mason-MacFarlane, in the summer of 1938 proposed to do away with Hitler personally through the use of a high-powered rifle,[9] and was told by his government that such a procedure would be unsportsmanlike.[10] But it was brought to the attention of the German authorities that there was a great deal of talk about assassination attempts against Hitler in Switzerland and in Czechoslovakia,[11] and some incidents became known publicly. In 1936, a Jewish student of medicine in Bern, Switzerland, who had hoped to assassinate Hitler, murdered instead his deputy-leader in Switzerland, Wilhelm Gustloff.[12] There were in Switzerland several anti-Hitler groups at work with various objectives, some of them plotting assassination, and their activities were not entirely secret.[13] They were particularly active in 1938, and an 'Anti-Hitler-Organization' was formed with the purpose of finding and fitting out a group of assassins against Hitler and his closest associates.[14]

[6] Peter Hoffmann, *Widerstand, Staatsstreich, Attentat: Der Kampf der Opposition gegen Hitler* (München 1970), 297–98.

[7] BA RG 1010/3183; R 43 II/1101b; *Auswärtiges Amt/Politisches Archiv* (henceforth: AA/PA) 83–69 A.g.

[8] Hoffmann, op. cit., 298–302; AA/PA 83–69g; BA NS 29/vorl. 435.

[9] Ewen Butler, 'I talked of plan to kill Hitler', *The Times*, 6 August 1969, 1.

[10] *Der Spiegel* Nr. 32, 4 August 1969, 18.

[11] AA/PA 83–69g 28.1.; BA NS 29/vorl. 435.

[12] *The Times*, 5 February 1936, 12; 6 February 1936, 14; 7 February 1936, 13; 13 February 1936, 12; 10 December 1936, 13; 15 December 1936, 15; David Frankfurter, 'I kill a Nazi Gauleiter: Memoir of a Jewish Assassin', *Commentary* 9 (1950), 133–41; cf. Walter Wolf, *Faschismus in der Schweiz: Die Geschichte der Frontenbewegungen in der deutschen Schweiz, 1930–1945* (Zürich 1969), 271–73.

[13] Hoffmann, op. cit., 299; cf. note 46.

[14] Ibid.

In April 1938, the Gestapo communicated to the *Auswärtiges Amt* detailed information on assassination plans originating in Italy and with connections in Switzerland and Great Britain.[15] It was also in 1938 that Alexander Foote, an Englishman working as a Soviet spy, made discreet inquiries into the question of how Hitler might best be assassinated.[16] By September 1938, the nucleus of the German conspiracy against Hitler which, in the course of the next six years, prepared a dozen or so attempts against the dictator's life, had formed, and an attempt to murder Hitler was to be made if war or a diplomatic defeat for Hitler resulted from the Sudeten Crisis in 1938.[17] In November 1938, Georg Elser reconnoitred the terrain for his 8 November 1939 bombing of the annual gathering in Munich's *Bürgerbräukeller* commemorating the *putsch* of 1923 that had failed.[18] After his arrest, Elser gave among his motives the fact that in the autumn of 1938 there was general talk of war among labourers, that he himself was convinced that war was imminent because Hitler wanted to annex more territories besides the Sudetenland, and that he believed the way to prevent war was to remove Hitler.[19] This was indeed a widespread opinion, and, together with the prevailing international situation in 1938, it formed the context in which Maurice Bavaud came to his own decision to murder Adolf Hitler.

IN MAURICE BAVAUD'S PERSONALITY one finds a dynamic drive to action combined with a taste for adventure. Since he was in search of a great and worthy task, Bavaud was easily 'influenced' by certain kinds of unusual reading matter and personal advice.

Bavaud's father was a postal official in Neuchâtel, Switzerland. His mother ran a small vegetable business. They were not poor, but neither were they wealthy, considering that they had three sons (Maurice was the eldest) and three daughters. One son and one daughter worked in the mother's shop, and a younger son and

[15] AA/PA 83–69g 21.4. (111g).
[16] Alexander Foote, *Handbook for Spies* (London 1953), 30–33.
[17] Hoffmann, op. cit., 301–2.
[18] Johann Georg Elser, *Autobiographie eines Attentäters: Aussage zum Sprengstoffanschlag im Bürgerbräukeller, München am 8. November 1939*, Lothar Gruchmann (ed.) (Stuttgart 1970), 85–89.
[19] Elser, op. cit., 81–84.

a younger daughter were still at school.[20]   The family lived in a
peculiar environment: they were very orthodox and strict Catholics
who spoke only French, in a Protestant town where most people
understood both French and German.[21]

Maurice Bavaud was born in Neuchâtel on 15 January 1916.
He attended primary school there, and secondary school until
he was sixteen.[22] Early in 1932 he became an apprentice in technical draughtsmanship with Favag in Neuchâtel, a firm that produced electrical apparatus. After the conclusion of his apprenticeship in 1935, he worked in the firm for two months.[23]

During his apprenticeship when he was between sixteen and
nineteen years old, Maurice Bavaud joined two organizations.
One was the Catholic St Joseph's Association for young people
which was led by a vicar.[24] Its activities included religious

[20] *Der Oberreichsanwalt beim Volksgerichtshof, Anklageschrift 20 Nov. 1939*
indicting Maurice Bavaud for attempting to assassinate Hitler, 2–3, *Politisches
Archiv des Auswärtigen Amts* (AA/PA) R 2318g; Dossier Maurice Bavaud,
Eidgenössisches Politisches Departement. Bavaud's attempt on Hitler's life is
virtually unknown. Aside from short and vague reports in Swiss newspapers after
the war, and aside from distorted and cryptic, almost unrecognizable references
in Hitler's *Table Talk* (Henry Picker, *Hitlers Tischgespräche im Führerhauptquartier 1941–42* [Stuttgart 1965], 306, 387; *Hitler's Secret Conversations 1941–
1944* [New York 1961], 426–27), nothing was published on the attempt until 1969.
Only a brief mention is made of it in this author's *Widerstand*, 299. Since then, and
after some frustrated efforts, he has gained access to the documents relating to
Bavaud's trial and execution which are kept in the *Politisches Archiv* in the *Auswärtiges Amt* of the Federal Republic of Germany, and to the dossier in the
Eidgenössisches Politisches Departement (henceforth: EPD) in Bern, Switzerland;
he has also interviewed Maurice Bavaud's parents. The files of the *Volksgerichtshof*, the special court for political offences in which Maurice Bavaud was tried,
were destroyed in large part in the last months of the war. On 3 February 1945,
the *Volksgerichtshof* building received a direct hit in an air raid and burst into
flames (Fabian von Schlabrendorff, *The Secret War against Hitler* [Toronto,
London 1965], 325–26). During the collapse of the Third Reich many documents
were burned, others were destroyed during the shelling of Berlin by the Red
Army. Several railway-carloads of documents were strewn along the tracks near
Berlin and partly salvaged by Allied authorities (Allen Welsh Dulles, *Verschwörung in Deutschland* [Kassel 1949], 185, 189). A large body of the surviving
documents are at present in the custody of the Berlin Document Centre (they
contain nothing on the cases of Bavaud or Gerbohay). The *Deutsches Zentral-
archiv* in Merseburg also has considerable holdings of *Volksgerichtshof* files which
include some material on the two cases; what exactly is there beyond the indictments and the sentence against Bavaud (which are also in the *Auswärtiges Amt/
Politisches Archiv*) has not yet been revealed to me by the authorities of the *DDR*.
[21] Interview with Alfred and Hélène Bavaud, 9 July 1971; EPD Dossier Bavaud.
[22] *Anklageschrift* Bavaud, 3.
[23] Ibid.
[24] Ibid.

exercises, sports and games. The other organization which Bavaud joined only in the winter of 1934/35 was the *Nationale Front*, the most important of a number of Swiss Fascist political parties.[25] The *Nationale Front* propagated essentially the ideology of German National Socialism, even to the point of abandoning the independent existence of Switzerland. They were anti-semitic, anti-democratic, anti-liberal, anti-marxist, anti-communist, anti-parliamentary, and they subscribed to racist *völkisch* and pan-German ideas and goals.[26] They were not content with unrestrained, vulgar and violently aggressive propaganda. Bombs exploded in the offices of rival political parties in August 1933 and in January 1934; in June 1935 explosives were set off in the Zürich *Schauspielhaus* during the staging of Brecht's *Dreigroschenoper*.[27] Terror squads beat up opponents and harmless citizens, they defaced synagogues and abused Jews, and they broke up meetings of rival groups. Some of them fought back, there were battles also with the police and street-fighting and rioting were not uncommon.[28] The *Nationale Front* adopted the Hitler salute, many of its members donned uniforms and organized troopers similar to the SA.[29] Hitler's policies in Germany were supported wholeheartedly by them, their newspaper hailed the murders of SA leaders in Germany in June and July 1934 (*Röhm-Putsch*) as swift justice —although the leader of the *Nationale Front*, Dr Rolf Henne, subsequently condemned the *methods*—and Hitler's aggressive and unscrupulous foreign policy including the rape of Czechoslovakia found the enthusiastic approval of the *Nationale Front*.[30]

Bavaud was dissatisfied with the local leadership of the *Nationale Front* in Neuchâtel.[31] At any rate, the movement failed to gain much support in the French-speaking part of Switzerland—not surprisingly for a pan-German movement.[32] Bavaud left the group,

[25] *Anklageschrift* Bavaud, 3; sentence of *Volksgerichtshof*, 2. *Senat*, of 18 December 1939 (copy, for *Auswärtiges Amt*), 2, AA/PA R 2597/g; Wolf, op. cit., 12, 18, 113–398.

[26] Ibid., 113–15.

[27] Ibid., 215–27.

[28] Ibid.

[29] Ibid., 249–50.

[30] Ibid., 255–64.

[31] *Anklageschrift* Bavaud, 3. How much of the ideas of the *Nationale Front* he adopted is unclear; during pre-trial interrogations in the spring of 1939, he steadfastly maintained that he was an anti-Semite (*Anklageschrift* Bavaud, 37), but he had also claimed to be an ardent admirer of National Socialism just in order to get close to Hitler.

[32] Wolf, op. cit., 125–26.

probably not least because of its pan-German tenets,[33] but he had demonstrated a keen interest in political affairs, and he had become familiar with the large, disturbing, violent, fascinating phenomenon of Fascism and of National-Socialist Germany, and with the most controversial political events and ideas of the day.

Shortly before Bavaud gave up his membership in the *Nationale Front*, he decided to become a priest and a missionary.[34] Apparently he had read a book describing the life of a missionary in the Congo basin, and he contacted the *Congrégation du Saint-Ésprit*. A Church office for missions in Fribourg arranged for him to enter a seminary, the Ecole-Saint-Ilan-Langueux near Saint-Brieuc in the Bretagne.[35] In October 1935, Bavaud entered the seminary, together with five other Swiss students, and began preparatory training that was to last four years. He spent vacation periods with his parents in Neuchâtel, but from a vacation begun in July 1938 he did not return to Saint-Ilan.[36] He refused to continue his theological studies.[37] During his trial, he said that he had then already made his decision to travel to Germany to assassinate Hitler.[38] What had prompted him to make it?

At Saint-Ilan, Maurice Bavaud had been under the influence of a friend and co-student, Marcel Gerbohay.[39] This was revealed by Bavaud after he had received his death sentence, in letters to his parents,[40] and it was confirmed by Marcel Gerbohay himself

[33] Sentence, 2–3.

[34] *Anklageschrift* Bavaud, 3; sentence, 3.

[35] *Anklageschrift* Bavaud, 4; sentence, 3; letters from École Saint-Ilan, 15 February 1972, and from a former fellow-student, Père Charles Rappo, 20 June 1972.

[36] *Anklageschrift* Bavaud, 4–5; sentence, 3.

[37] Alfred Bavaud to EPD 16 January 1939, EPD Dossier Bavaud.

[38] Sentence, 3.

[39] M. Gerbohay was born on 3 May 1917; *Der Oberreichsanwalt beim Volksgerichtshof, Anklageschrift* against Gerbohay 5 November 1942, 1, AA/PA R 7273.

[40] EPD Dossier Bavaud. The connection before and the continued communication after Bavaud's departure for Germany between himself and Gerbohay was a matter of record long before Bavaud's trial. *Anklageschrift* Bavaud, 10–12. Bavaud had written to Gerbohay from Baden-Baden, and a letter from Gerbohay arrived there after Bavaud had left for Berlin. Bavaud could not deny in pre-trial interrogations his connection with Gerbohay. Nevertheless, he tried his best to protect his friend by offering the story of highly-placed German instigators. Bavaud also did not mention the *Compagnie du Mystère* when he told his interrogators about his relations with Gerbohay (*Anklageschrift* Gerbohay, 3–11).

who was arrested by the German authorities in France on 1 January 1942.[41] A fellow student describes Bavaud as 'sentimental, calm, slow', and as 'of average intellect, and agreeable conversation', while Gerbohay, in the words of the same classmate, was 'ultra-sensitive, nervous' and 'very intelligent'.[42] Gerbohay, who had apparently had contact with Russian émigrés in Paris, had entered the seminary a year before Bavaud, but he fell ill, and from October 1937 to July 1938 he was in the same class with Bavaud. He had strange dreams and talked in his sleep in what appeared to be a Slavic language. Bavaud asked Gerbohay about some of the strange things he said while dreaming (they slept in a large dormitory hall with the rest of the students). Gerbohay then told Bavaud that he was really the son of a Russian grand-duke and a member of the Romanov family, whose aim it was to destroy communism and Jewry in Russia, and to resume power.[43]

After his death sentence, Bavaud made these statements, and Gerbohay confirmed them after he was arrested in 1942.[44] During pre-trial interrogations, Bavaud had claimed to be acting at the inducement of a highly-placed German protector who had convinced him that Hitler must be killed because he was too peace-loving and therefore not likely to use the very strong *Wehrmacht* for pan-German territorial goals; therefore, Hitler was an obstacle to the protectors' own political aspirations.[45] Bavaud steadfastly refused to reveal the name of the protector until some time after he had been sentenced to death.[46]

[41] *Anklageschrift* Gerbohay, 2–11.
[42] Rappo.
[43] Ibid. The Gestapo later tried to find out from Bavaud's and Gerbohay's classmates if it was true that Gerbohay was a member of the Romanov family (letter from Père Emile Jacquot 8 September 1972).
[44] *Anklageschrift* Gerbohay, 3–11; *Führerinformation* by Justice Ministry 7 September 1942, BA R 22/4089.
[45] *Anklageschrift* Gerbohay, 6–8; *Anklageschrift* Bavaud, 13; sentence, 15–16.
[46] Ibid.; EPD Dossier Bavaud; Dr Roland Freisler (then *Staatssekretär* in the Justice Ministry) to *Auswärtiges Amt* 12 February 1941, AA/PA R 5239g. There are references to alleged contacts of M. Bavaud with an anti-Hitler organization in a letter of M. Gerbohay to Alexander Desilvestri, one of the members of the *Compagnie du Mystère*. In this letter, written after Bavaud's arrest had become known to Gerbohay, the latter denied that he instigated Bavaud's attempt. The letter is reproduced in German translation in *Anklageschrift* Gerbohay, 16–18; it was apparently turned up by the investigations of the Gestapo in Switzerland (EPD Dossier Bavaud). Another reference to connections of Bavaud with anti-Hitler groups is equally untrustworthy though somewhat less obviously motivated. It mentions an *Anti-Hitler-Organisation (AHO)*

During the trial, Bavaud gave up the protector story which was considered a mystification by the court.[47] He claimed he acted entirely on his own, and that on the basis of what he had read in the Swiss press, and of what he had been told by Catholic émigrés from Germany, he had considered Hitler a danger for mankind.[48] Foremost among his motives, Bavaud said, were religious and ecclesiastical ones: he hoped to help the suppressed Catholic Church in Germany, and to serve mankind and Christendom. This, he said had been in part an outgrowth of his conviction that he had an inner calling for missionary activity.[49] It was true, he said, that he had exaggerated his own role; but he insisted that he was not mad, and that he had acted for serious reasons.[50] The experts consulted by the court and the court itself accepted this and judged Maurice Bavaud sane.[51] His defence counsel pleaded for leniency on grounds that his client had merely made preparations to assassinate Hitler, but had not acted; but the lawyer made no attempt to plead insanity of his client.[52] Nor were the attempts of the Swiss Government to save the life of the condemned man based on any plea of insanity.[53]

[47] Sentence, 16.
[48] Ibid., 16–17.
[49] Ibid.
[50] *Anklageschrift* Bavaud, 37, 41; sentence, 21.
[51] Sentence, 21.
[52] Sentence, 21; *Der Stellvertretende Präsident des Volksgerichtshofes* to *NS-Rechtswahrerbund* 5 January 1940, EPD Dossier Bavaud.
[53] Correspondence on the case in *Akten betreffend Strafverfolgung von Ausländern wegen in Deutschland begangenen Hoch- und Landesverrats: Strafrecht—Strafverfolgung Geheim*, 1939–42, AA/PA; EPD Dossier Bavaud.

operating in Switzerland; allegedly, Bavaud made contact with this group before going to Germany. However, none of the sources pointing in this direction can be demonstrated to have been produced before or even during the war, all appear to have been produced after the war (Alhard Gelpke, *Exposé Nr. 2: Über einige Comités, die während der Hitlerzeit im Dienste des Abendlandes wirkten*, typescript, n.p., May 1956, Hoover Institution Library Ts Germany G 321; Dr Alhard Gelpke, letter dated 25 January 1972; [Alhard] Gelpke, *Exposé bf. den gemeinsamen privaten deutsch/schweiz. Geheimdienst der Jahre 1930/45*, carbon copy of typescript, n.p. n.d.; [Dr Wilhelm Abegg], *Archiv-Notiz bf. Attentatsplan eines schweiz. Theologie-Studenten*, carbon copy of typescript, dated Zürich 1937 but written after the war according to its *post scriptum*: 'Bis Hitlers Tod nur in Steno u. zwar in G. zu archivieren'. The Steno, according to Dr Gelpke, has been destroyed; at any rate, the date is not confirmed in the results of the investigation of Bavaud's activities before October 1938. Cf. also Alardus [= Dr Alhard Gelpke], *Krieg in Sicht*? [Privately publ. by Dr Alhard Gelpke, Zürich ca. 1959] 64).

The historian cannot find any cause to dispute these opinions. Despite similarly bizarre circumstances in other cases of lone assassins trying to do away with Hitler, few people would seriously suggest that Elser, Kordt, Tresckow, Schlabrendorff, Gersdorff, Bussche, Breitenbuch or Stauffenberg—all of whom tried it—were insane.[54]

The mixture of fact and fiction became more intelligible after Bavaud's further revelations, and after their confirmation by Gerbohay. Religious fervour was certainly among Bavaud's motivating forces;[55] anti-communism was taught at Saint-Ilan;[56] Hitler's anti-clericalism was seen by Bavaud and his friends as an indirect pro-communism;[57] anti-semitism (which Bavaud claimed to embrace but which seems unlikely to have been part of his motivation) was likely and not at all far-fetched;[58] the mysterious protector actually existed in the person of Marcel Gerbohay; and the pan-German goals turned out to be part of Gerbohay's plan to gain his 'rightful' Romanov throne.[59]

[54] Cf. Hoffmann, op. cit., passim.
[55] EPD Dossier Bavaud, passim; Bavaud to his family 5 April 1940, EPD Dossier Bavaud; *Anklageschrift* Bavaud, 3, 41; sentence, 16–17; interview with Alfred and Hélène Bavaud.
[56] *Anklageschrift* Bavaud, 4; *Anklageschrift* Gerbohay, 5–6.
[57] *Anklageschrift* Gerbohay, 5–6.
[58] Bavaud insisted in pre-trial interrogations that he was an anti-Semite; *Anklageschrift* Bavaud, 37.
[59] *Anklageschrift* Gerbohay, 4–9. Gerbohay claimed in his own pre-trial interrogations that he never consciously declared himself the true heir to the Romanov throne, but that he allowed his friends to believe he was when they interpreted what he said in his dreams in this way (*Anklageschrift* Gerbohay, 5). Gerbohay was considered something of a confidence man by many of his fellow students at Saint-Ilan (*Geheime Staatspolizei* Berlin to *Oberreichsanwalt beim Volksgerichtshof* 21 January 1941, AA/PA R 5239g/41); he did admit that he let his friends believe he was a Romanov because this gave him greater influence over them (*Anklageschrift* Gerbohay, 5). There exists the possibility that Gerbohay dreamed and dream-talked not entirely involuntarily. Gerbohay's motives and his apparent pathological egomania and lying were not explored in the formal indictment against him (*Anklageschrift* Gerbohay, 20–21). The Reich's prosecutor was content to emphasize Gerbohay's belief that Hitler was an enemy of France and of Catholicism; that Gerbohay *therefore* hated Hitler; and to allow the possibility that Gerbohay also hoped to accelerate the process leading to a collision between Germany and the Soviet Union, and thus to the destruction of communism and to the weakening of Germany.

Which motivating force was strongest in Maurice Bavaud cannot be determined on the basis of the limited evidence available. However, everything that is revealed about the relationship between Maurice Bavaud and Marcel Gerbohay indicates a friendship so close, a loyalty so great—at least on the part of Maurice Bavaud—that 'love' seems a more appropriate term.[60] What Bavaud wrote to his parents between 19 December 1939 and 8 February 1940 points in this direction;[61] two references in his letter to his parents of 5 April 1940 must be interpreted in this way: 'Ah! si j'étais resté à Saint Ilan, au service de Dieu, si je n'avais pas quitté le créateur pour la créature, ce qui est éternal pour ce qui est périssible, la lumière pour les ténèbres, je ne serais pas ici'.[62] And: 'Enfin, comme ma faute consistait en faiblesse et en passion et non pas en une orgueilleuse mauvaise volonté, j'ai fini par remporter la victoire car Dieu est avant tout la bonté et la miséricorde même. Mais il n'est pas moins vrai qu'il est très dur de mourir pour des motifs plus que terre à terre alors qu'avant j'avais orienté ma vie dans la voie de Jésus Christ'.[63] 'Creature', 'weakness', and 'passion' can only be understood as references to Marcel Gerbohay.[64]

[60] *Anklageschrift* Bavaud, 7, 36, 37; *Anklageschrift* Gerbohay, 3, 5. The sentence against Bavaud does not mention Gerbohay: the court did not suspect the importance of this friend, nor was the court struck by the interchangeability of the descriptions used by Bavaud variously in reference to the protector and to Gerbohay.

[61] *Reichsminister der Justiz* to *Auswärtiges Amt*, 8 February 1940 and 12 February 1940, AA/PA R 278g/40 and R 5239g/41; *Geheime Staatspolizei* Berlin to *Oberreichsanwalt beim Volksgerichtshof* 21 January 1941, AA/PA R 5239g/41.

[62] EPD Dossier Bavaud.

[63] Ibid.

[64] In an interview with an official of the *Eidgenössisches Politisches Departement* on 11 June 1941, Maurice Bavaud's parents showed the official the last letter of their son in which, according to the official's report, he had written that 'a forty-year old, ambitious man, to whom he was deeply devoted, had induced him to the deed he had attempted;' EPD Dossier Bavaud. The letter itself has not been available for corroboration so that the possibility of an error in the figure forty cannot be excluded. Gerbohay, born in 1917, was twenty-four at the time of the interview. There are no other references in the entire available material that would indicate the existence of an instigator besides Gerbohay. Other references from other letters of Maurice Bavaud cited by the official all point to Gerbohay: Bavaud wrote that the German authorities seemed to have extended their investigations of the case to the Collège de Saint-Ilan; that the spiritual author of his assassination attempt appears to have cowardly denied his co-responsibility; that he was deeply depressed and disillusioned by the behaviour of his supposed intimate friend (EPD Dossier Bavaud).

In other letters to his family, Maurice Bavaud referred even more openly to his infatuation with Gerbohay, and Gerbohay's exploitation of it. When he was arrested, Bavaud had with him a photograph of Gerbohay and he also carried a note in Gerbohay's hand that said: 'Cet homme est sous ma protection immédiate et n'a rien fait qui ne soit selon mes ordres'.[65]

But it was not Marcel Gerbohay alone who led the would-be assassin to action. If the motivating forces mentioned earlier had prepared Bavaud for his role, a group of friends that formed around Marcel Gerbohay made it socially acceptable and indeed compulsory to act. The group formed during the academic year 1937–38, under the leadership of Marcel Gerbohay. They frequently discussed politics, particularly in connection with Adolf Hitler and his position vis-à-vis the Catholic Church and communism.[66] They concluded that Hitler, who was trying to preserve peace, must be a friend of communism and an enemy of Catholicism and of France, and in general a destroyer of mankind—in short, an incarnation of Satan.[67] Founded on their common hatred of Hitler and communism, the group constituted itself as the *Compagnie du Mystère*.[68] Their goal: to move against Hitler with any means

[65] *Anklageschrift* Bavaud, 13–14, 30, 33–5, 44–5; sentence, 14; *Anklageschrift* Gerbohay, 8–9, 15–16. The signature 'ARH' was written to look like a secret symbol, with lines drawn through the letters; the investigating authorities misread and misinterpreted the letters to mean that *A*dolf *H*itler was to be killed by *B*avaud. Bavaud denied that this was the correct interpretation and insisted the letters represented the initials of his German protector. He also denied the correctness of the graphological expertise according to which he himself had written the note and the inscription on Gerbohay's photograph (*Anklageschrift* Bavaud, 35, 38). In 1942, after Bavaud's execution, Gerbohay admitted that he had written the note, and so the graphological expertise must also have been wrong concerning the inscription, although the indictment against Gerbohay continued to name Bavaud as the writer of the inscription (*Anklageschrift* Gerbohay, 8–9, 15–16). Gerbohay said the meaning of the letters A, R and H was *Amour envers la patrie, Renoncement à soi-même, Honneur* (*Anklageschrift* Gerbohay, 9).

[66] *Anklageschrift* Gerbohay, 5–8.

[67] Ibid.

[68] *Anklageschrift* Gerbohay, 6–8. Bavaud does not seem to have mentioned the *Compagnie du Mystère* while in German custody; the term does not appear in documents produced before the arrest of Gerbohay (*Führerinformation* of *Reichsminister der Justiz* 7 September 1942, BA R 22/4089). The Gestapo came up with the names of those who allegedly belonged to the group; the Roumanian Mathias Tomansky, the Alsatian Raymond Bleny, Fernand de Cools from Martinique, Emile Jacquot from Paris, the Swiss Alexander Desilvestri, the Frenchman Emile Arribard; some others are said to have belonged as well, but they are not named.

available if he in any way cooperated with communism. A plan was hatched to send Maurice Bavaud to Germany, since he had relatives there. Bavaud was to try to be received by Hitler, and to persuade him to make war on Soviet Russia.[69] The group as a whole does not seem to have been involved in the assassination plot, which, judging by the available records, was devised by Maurice Bavaud and Marcel Gerbohay alone.[70]

If the complex motivations of the *Compagnie du Mystère* were contradictory, it may be hindsight that makes them seem so. The uncanny affinities between National Socialism and Soviet Communism were observed by many in the 1930s; the occasional cooperation of the NSDAP and the KPD in the turbulent months before Hitler became Chancellor, the terror methods employed by the extreme Left and the extreme Right—these were obvious superficial manifestations of the totalitarianism common to both.[71] In 1939, when Hitler and Stalin made their pact and divided Poland and the Baltic countries between them a few days before Hitler's attack on Poland,[72] and when Stalin, so far from aiding the Poles against the fascists, took over his share, and then carried the war into Finland—then, not everyone had the prophetic gift to predict that Hitler would attack the Soviet Union in 1941. The motivations of the *Compagnie du Mystère* may seem irrational, they may seem bizarre; the actions of Maurice Bavaud were not.

In July 1938, Maurice Bavaud and Marcel Gerbohay left Saint-Ilan at the beginning of the summer vacation. As far as Rennes, they took the same train.[73] Then Gerbohay took a train to his home town, Pacé, and Bavaud took one to Neuchâtel. On the train to Rennes, Gerbohay confessed to his friend that he was not really a descendant of the Romanovs.[74] But this did not change Bavaud's determination to act. Apparently, Gerbohay later wrote to Bavaud that he was after all the exalted personality he had allowed Bavaud to believe him to be in Saint-Ilan.[75]

[69] *Anklageschrift* Gerbohay, 6.

[70] *Anklageschrift* Gerbohay, 5–9; Jacquot; Rappo.

[71] Karl Dietrich Bracher, Wolfgang Sauer, Gerhard Schulz, *Die national-sozialistische Machtergreifung: Studien zur Errichtung des totalitären Herrschafts systems in Deutschland* (Köln, Opladen 1962), passim; Bruno Gebhardt, *Handbuch der deutschen Geschichte*, Vol. 4 (Stuttgart 1959), 173–79; Alan Bullock, *Hitler: A Study in Tyranny* (New York 1964), 229–30.

[72] *Akten zur deutschen auswärtigen Politik*, Series D, vol. VII, documento.229.

[73] *Anklageschrift* Gerbohay, 6–7.

[74] *Anklageschrift* Gerbohay, 7. Gerbohay and Bavaud confirmed this independently during interrogations.

[75] Bavaud's statements after his condemnation are cited in *Anklageschrift* Gerbohay, 7.

Bavaud insisted that he believed this new assertion on the part of Gerbohay, who then expressed in letters sent to Bavaud at his Neuchâtel address the expectation that Bavaud, out of his passionate devotion to his friend, would remove Hitler, the obstacle to Gerbohay's ambitions.[76]

Gerbohay denied only the motivation, not the fact that he had urged Bavaud to assassinate the Führer.[77] Gerbohay claimed that his motivation was not his 'right' to the Romanov throne, but his belief that communism must be destroyed by Germany, and that if Hitler refused to do it, he had to be removed. Therefore, he said, he had instructed Maurice Bavaud to kill the Führer if he did not succeed in persuading him to declare war on the Soviet Union.[78]

WHEN MAURICE BAVAUD CAME HOME to Neuchâtel for the summer vacation of 1938, he decided before the end of July not to return to Saint-Ilan, and he wrote this to the director of the seminary.[79] Then he tried in vain to find a job as a draughtsman, and, in the meantime, he worked in his mother's vegetable business.[80] During this time, he began learning German and Russian.[81] He also tried to become familiar with Hitler's ideas by reading the French edition of *Mein Kampf*, and a collection of speeches by Hitler entitled *Ma Doctrine*.[82] He believed it would be easier for him to gain access to Hitler's presence if he passed himself off as an ardent adherent of National Socialism.[83] He also took out a subscription to the German National Socialist magazine *Weltdienst*

[76] *Anklageschrift* Gerbohay, 7.

[77] Ibid.

[78] *Anklageschrift* Gerbohay, 7–8; Bavaud's letter to his parents, written between 19 December 1939 and 8 February 1940, in which he confirms the inducement by Gerbohay is referred to in *Reichsminister der Justiz* to *Auswärtiges Amt* 8 February 1940 and 12 February 1941, AA/PA R 278g/40 and R 5239g/41; and, in the report of the official who visited the Bavaud family on 11 June 1941, EPD Dossier Bavaud. In his pretrial and trial statements, Bavaud had attributed these same ideas to a mysterious prominent German with whom he claimed to have been in contact in Neuchâtel, Baden-Baden, Berlin and Munich (*Anklageschrift* Bavaud, 6–7, 12–13, 33, 36–37; sentence, 15).

[79] *Anklageschrift* Bavaud, 4–5; sentence, 3–4.

[80] Ibid.

[81] Ibid.

[82] *Anklageschrift* Bavaud, 6; sentence, 4; Adolf Hitler, *Ma Doctrine* (Paris 1938).

[83] Sentence, 4.

in the first days of October 1938.[84] Then he prepared for his trip to Germany by having his passport renewed for four weeks on 4 October, and by taking 600 Swiss Francs from the safe in his mother's vegetable business on 8 October.[85] On Sunday, 9 October, he left for Baden-Baden early in the morning, and arrived there at 2 p.m. in the afternoon.[86]

Bavaud went straight to the home of his great-aunt, Frau Karoline Gutterer, and declared that he had come to find employment as a draughtsman.[87] He always pretended that he was an enthusiastic admirer of National Socialism and of Hitler. Although Bavaud received active assistance from his relatives, he was unable to find a job.[88] While he was in Baden-Baden with his relatives, there was nothing to do but to take walks with the six-year-old grandson of his great-aunt, whose father was *Ministerialdirektor* Leopold Gutterer, a fairly high-ranking official in Dr Joseph Goebbels' *Ministerium für Volksaufklärung und Propaganda*.[89] He also wrote some postcards to his friend Marcel Gerbohay in which he expressed his admiration for Germany.[90] Gerbohay answered with a short letter exhorting Bavaud not to be taken in by Germany's present greatness, and 'to obey God's commandments'.[91] But Bavaud never received this letter, it arrived at his relatives' address after he had left them.[92]

---

[84] *Anklageschrift* Bavaud, 7–8; sentence, 4.

[85] *Anklageschrift* Bavaud, 8; sentence, 4–5.

[86] Ibid.; *Anklageschrift* Gerbohay, 10.

[87] *Anklageschrift* Bavaud, 9, 43; sentence, 5. Frau Gutterer née Nofaier was a sister of one of Bavaud's grandmothers.

[88] *Anklageschrift* Bavaud, 9–10; sentence, 5.

[89] *Anklageschrift* Bavaud, 10–11; sentence, 5. Gutterer wanted nothing to do with his relative; he informed the Gestapo of Bavaud's arrival in Baden-Baden, he warned his parents to be careful and not to allow Bavaud to use his, Gutterer's, name in looking for work. He told the author on 31 July 1972 that he did not know Bavaud.

[90] *Anklageschrift* Gerbohay, 10–11; *Anklageschrift* Bavaud, 11–13.

[91] *Anklageschrift* Bavaud, 11–12; as has been noted above, in Bavaud's trial the court concentrated on convicting the accused and did not make a serious effort to clear up the background of the assassination attempt; they disregarded the many links with Gerbohay, and the striking affinity between Gerbohay and the mysterious protector as described by Bavaud. Thus the sentence attaches no importance to the short letter from Gerbohay. In the trial of Gerbohay, the court did recognize this letter as one of his efforts to spur Bavaud into action (*Anklageschrift* Gerbohay, 10–11).

[92] Ibid. Bavaud's great-aunt and great-uncle, warned by their son, turned over the letter to the Gestapo where it was opened, translated, and then sent on to Maurice Bavaud's parents in Neuchâtel.

On 20 October, after his most promising prospect for a job had failed to materialize on 19 October, Bavaud told his relatives he was going to Mannheim to try and find a job there; in fact he booked his luggage through to Berlin at the railroad station, and before going there himself, took a train to Basel.[93] There he bought a 6.35 mm. calibre Schmeisser pistol with ten rounds of ammunition, and then he took a train to Berlin where he arrived on 21 October.[94] Here he hoped to come close enough to Hitler for an attempt on his life. The first night be stayed in a hotel, the Alexandra, and on 22 October he rented a furnished room, and bought twenty-five more rounds of ammunition for his pistol.[95] But then he read in a French newspaper, the Parisian *Le Jour*, that Hitler was at his house near Berchtesgaden at the time.[96]

So on 24 October, Bavaud took a train to Berchtesgaden, leaving behind in his furnished room the French edition of *Mein Kampf*, and the collection entitled *Ma Doctrine*, besides some other personal effects.[97] He arrived on 25 October and took a room in the Hotel Stiftskeller. While in Berchtesgaden, he took prolonged walks in the environs, and he practised target-shooting, taking shots at trees from about 7 to 8 meters.[98] He used up about twenty-five rounds of ammunition. Once he tried to find out from a policeman how one might get close to Hitler's Berghof, but he was told that no one could get through the fences and gates.[99]

In reality, it would have been possible. On occasions, large throngs of visitors were allowed to stand waiting for the Führer to pass on the Obersalzberg,[100] and security was somewhat lax generally. Some forty SS men patrolled the grounds around the Berghof,[101] but the area was large and partly wooded, and construction was going on constantly.[102] It was difficult to control the labourers who worked on the site regularly, and at times there were large security gaps, not all of which were closed before November

[93] *Anklageschrift* Bavaud, 14; sentence, 6; *Anklageschrift* Gerbohay, 11.
[94] Ibid.
[95] *Anklageschrift* Bavaud, 15–16; sentence, 6–7; *Anklageschrift* Gerbohay, 11.
[96] Ibid. On Hitler's itinerary, see below, 15.
[97] *Anklageschrift* Bavaud, 17–18; sentence, 7–8.
[98] Ibid.
[99] Ibid.
[100] Wiedemann, op. cit., 79–80.
[101] *Chef des Reichssicherheitsdienstes* Rattenhuber to Personal Adjutant Brückner 15 November 1937, BA NS 10/55.
[102] [Martin Bormann,] *Daten aus alten Notizbüchern 1934–1943*. Hoover Institution, Stanford, California, *NSDAP Hauptarchiv* reel 1 folder 16, passim; Albert Speer, *Erinnerungen* (Berlin 1969), 98–100.

1938, nor even before the beginning of the war.[103]   In November and December 1937, a dangerous situation had been pointed out to Martin Bormann and to Hitler's Personal Adjutant Brückner. The Chief of the Secret Service (*Reichssicherheitsdienst*) *SS-Standartenführer* Rattenhuber, stated urgently that under prevailing conditions anyone could *drive* onto the Obersalzberg because the guard post at the *Schiessstättbrücke* had been removed.[104]

Bavaud did not find a suitable gap in the security system, but he struck up an acquaintance with some Berchtesgaden schoolteachers, two gentlemen named Ehrenspeck and Reuther, with whom he spent a number of afternoons in Berchtesgaden inns and cafés.   He told them he was an admirer of National-Socialist Germany and of the Führer, and eventually he asked them how he might go about seeing the Führer.[105]   They told him that it was probably impossible in Berchtesgaden.   Bavaud, Ehrenspeck and Reuther sat talking about this one day in a café when a Major Deckert who sat at a table nearby contributed to the conversation. Major of Police Karl Deckert, then a captain, had been specially charged in 1936 with the creation and supervision of an internal security service in the *Reichskanzlei,* under the authority of *Staatssekretär* Dr Lammers and as his adjutant; he at the time worked in the Berchtesgaden branch of the *Reichskanzlei.*[106]   Deckert said that a personal interview with Hitler was indeed out of the question because the Führer was currently so busy that he had not even seen Foreign Minister Ribbentrop and the Chief of the Chancellery Dr Lammers who had been waiting for interviews.[107]

Hitler was away from the Berghof from 25 October until 27 October.[108]   He was on a trip visiting Pressburg, Vienna, the Sudetenland and Nikolsburg, from which he returned to the Obersalzberg on 28 October.[109]   On 1 November, Hitler left the

[103] Rattenhuber to Brückner 15 November 1937 and Rattenhuber to Bormann 13 December 1937, BA NS 10/55.

[104] Ibid.

[105] *Anklageschrift* Bavaud, 18–19; sentence, 8; *Anklageschrift* Gerbohay, 12.

[106] *Anklageschrift* Bavaud, 19–20; sentence, 8; *Anklageschrift* Gerbohay, 12. Deckert, *Anordnung für den Sicherheitsdienst der Reichskanzlei* 25 April 1936, BA R 43 II/1105; letter from *Bundesarchiv* 7 June 1972.

[107] *Anklageschrift* Bavaud, 19.

[108] [Martin Bormann, *Tagebuch* 16 June–24 November 1938], BA NS 10/125; [Bormann], *Daten aus alten Notizbüchern*; Max Domarus, *Hitler: Reden und Proklamationen 1932–1945*, vol. 1 (München 1965), 961.

[109] Ibid.

Berghof for Munich.[110] On 2 November, he took the brand-new *Autobahn* from Munich to Nürnberg (it was opened to the public on 5 November) to inspect construction work on the party rally area; on 5 and 6 November he was in Weimar to give a speech, and by 8 November he was back in Munich.[111]

Major Deckert suggested, however, that the memorial festivities in Munich on 8 and 9 November at which Hitler was to be present might offer a good opportunity to see him, at least from a distance.[112] Besides other useful hints, Ehrenspeck translated for Bavaud Deckert's suggestion that an interview with Hitler might be obtained with the help of an introductory letter from some influential person, or by talking with Dr Lammers first.[113] Now Maurice Bavaud had a plan.

The march of 9 November was established in 1935 as the official *Nationalsozialistische Prozession*, as the Munich *Gauleitung* put it in organizational directives in 1936.[114] This first commemorative procession carried the sarcophagi of the sixteen who were shot near *Feldherrnhalle* on 9 November 1923 to the *Feldherrnhalle* for a commemorative observance, and thence on to the *Ehrentempel* at Königsplatz which were made their mausoleums. Marches were held again in 1936 and 1937,[115] but the 1938 march was the last one.[116] It is not clear whether or not the 1939 march was cancelled because of Bavaud's attempt. Elser's attempt was not the reason; Hitler did not receive any news about it until his special train had reached Nürnberg, late on the night of 8–9 November 1939.[117] Although there are strong reasons that can serve as rationalizations for Hitler's unusually early departure from the *Bürgerbräukeller* on the evening of 8 November 1939, just thirteen

[110] [Bormann], *Daten aus alten Notizbüchern.*
[111] *Völkischer Beobachter* 4 November 1938, 1; 6 November 1938, 1; 10 November 1938, 1–5.
[112] *Anklageschrift* Bavaud, 19–20; sentence, 8; *Anklageschrift* Gerbohay, 12.
[113] Ibid.
[114] *Bemerkungen zum Programm 8./9. November 1936*, BA NS 10/124; *Völkischer Beobachter* 9–12 November 1935.
[115] *Völkischer Beobachter* 10 November 1936, 1; 10 November 1937, 1.
[116] Max Domarus, *Hitler: Reden und Proklamationen 1932–1945*, Vol. II (Neustadt a.d.Aisch 1963), 1414, 1603; *Regie-Programm für den 8./9. November 1939 in München, Gesamtleitung: Gaupropagandaleiter Pg. Karl Wenzel*, BA NS 10/126.
[117] Anton Hoch, 'Das Attentat auf Hitler im Münchner Bürgerbräukeller 1939', *Vierteljahrshefte für Zeitgeschichte* 17 (1969), 411; Domarus, op. cit., 1414–15.

minutes before the explosion of Georg Elser's bomb that killed eight where Hitler had been standing, there persists an uncertainty.[118] On 7 September 1941, Hitler still pondered the question whether or not to abolish the march in future, because it combined the entire leadership of the Reich in a very small place where they were highly endangered.[119]

On 31 October Maurice Bavaud obliged the two teachers by participating in their French classes and by serving as a demonstration subject, being a native speaker. Then he took a train to Munich, and on his arrival he obtained a room in the Hotel Stadt Wien.[120] Next he went about securing a seat on one of the grandstands for the march of 9 November. He went from one place to another, to City Hall, to the Foreign Press Office, to the guard at *Feldherrnhalle,* and everywhere he was told that there were no more admission cards. Finally, at the Office for the Ninth of November, by passing himself off as representing newspapers in Western Switzerland, he managed to obtain a complimentary ticket for the grandstand opposite *Heiliggeist-Kirche.* He was the only foreigner, as it turned out, who got a complimentary ticket.[121] He was never asked for identification.[122]

The *Heiliggeist-Kirche* grandstand was as good a spot as Bavaud could have hoped for. It was situated at the west end of a street named Tal through which the marchers were going to come, from the *Bürgerbräukeller,* across the *Ludwigsbrücke* and through the *Isartor,* marching westward. Only a few yards from the *Heiliggeist-Kirche* grandstand, they would turn north into Dienerstrasse which led into Residenzstrasse and to the *Feldherrnhalle* on Odeonsplatz.

During the following days, Bavaud bought some more ammunition, went to the Ammersee near Herrsching, rented a boat,

---

[118] Hoch, op. cit., 410–11; Hoffmann, op. cit., 303–6. Hitler himself said in September 1941 that he owed his life to the fact that because of bad weather he had taken the overnight train back to Berlin instead of the plane next morning; *Bericht Nr. 28.* In May 1942 he explained that he had to be in Berlin the next day because of an urgent conference. (Picker, op. cit., 306. Cf. Hoch, op. cit., 410–11; Hoffmann, op. cit., 303–6 and 755, n. 33).

[119] *Bericht Nr. 28.*

[120] *Anklageschrift* Bavaud, 20; sentence, 9.

[121] *Anklageschrift* Bavaud, 20–22; sentence, 9; *Anklageschrift* Gerbohay, 13. All circumstances related above are confirmed by *Stabsleiter* Emil Senftinger, then *Geschäftsführer* of the *Amt für den 9. November,* in a letter to the author dated 15 May 1972.

[122] Ibid.

and continued his exercises in marksmanship by taking shots at small paper vessels he put into the water from his boat. One day he used printed targets that he put on trees in the forests near Pasing.[123]

Back in Munich, he bought a copy of the programme for the festivities of 8 and 9 November; they were being sold in the streets.[124] He used it to draw into a city map of Munich the exact route of the march, and then he walked the entire route to determine which would be the best spot for shooting Hitler.[125] His conclusion was that, as Deckert, Ehrenspeck and Reuther had already suggested to him, the Café City provided the best opportunity: one could sit at a table inside, and step out directly into the street a moment or two before the marchers arrived. The street was so narrow there that one could not fail to have point-blank range.[126] Bavaud also considered standing on a table or chair inside and shooting through the window. But finally he gave up the café idea in favour of the grandstand.[127]

On the morning of 9 November, Maurice Bavaud went to take his seat on the grandstand so early that he managed to get one in the very first row. The pistol was loaded, in his overcoat pocket.[128] From here he hoped to shoot Hitler, provided the distance proved to be short enough. If it did not—he could not calculate exactly how far Hitler would be from his position—he wanted to leave his place, run up to the marchers, and take his shots from closer up.[129]

As the marchers approached, Bavaud realized that Hitler was at too great a distance from his place, on the far side of the street, almost twice as far away as the targets he had practised with, too far for even a remote chance of an accurate shot, and the Führer was flanked on both sides by people like Göring and Himmler.[130] Bavaud found it impossible to carry out his alternative plan, because a dense cordon of uniformed SA troopers two men deep

---

[123] *Anklageschrift* Bavaud, 23; sentence, 9–10; *Anklageschrift* Gerbohay, 13.
[124] Ibid.; it had also been announced in the *Völkischer Beobachter* of 8 November 1938, 8, that the march was to follow once again the route of 1923.
[125] Ibid.
[126] *Anklageschrift* Bavaud, 23–24; sentence, 10; *Anklageschrift* Gerbohay, 13.
[127] Ibid.
[128] Ibid.
[129] Ibid.
[130] *Anklageschrift* Bavaud, 24; sentence, 10, 18; *Anklageschrift* Gerbohay, 14.

made it impossible either to get a clear shot, or to approach the marchers.[131]

Back in his hotel room, Bavaud began hatching his next plan. He now decided to try using a forged letter for introduction that would look as if it had been written by the former French Minister President Flandin, hoping for an interview with Hitler during which he might shoot him.[132] In 'Flandin's letter', Hitler was asked to see Bavaud who had another, private letter for the Führer. Just in case the ruse might work, Bavaud also prepared an envelope addressed to Hitler containing a blank sheet which presumably was to be the private letter.[133]

With his letters and his pistol, Bavaud took a train to Berchtesgaden on 10 November. He arrived between 5 and 6 p.m., hired a taxi, and told the driver to take him to the Obersalzberg.[134] Bavaud was stopped by the gendarmes at the *Schiessstättbrücke,* he declared he came directly from Paris to hand a letter to the Führer; the gendarmes telephoned, but finally they told him that Hitler was not on the Obersalzberg.[135] Bavaud went straight back to the railroad station and took a train back to Munich.[136]

Now he hoped to see Hitler in Munich. But he developed doubts about the appearance of his 'letter of introduction': the hand-written note might look suspicious, it would be better to use a type-written letter.[137] He rented a typewriter and wrote a new letter and new envelopes, but he used the name of the National-

[131] *Anklageschrift* Bavaud, 24; sentence, 10–11; *Anklageschrift* Gerbohay, 14. As Hitler told it in his *Table Talk* of 7 September 1941 *(Bericht Nr. 28)*, it was impossible for Bavaud to take his shots because of the forest of arms raised for the Hitler salute in front of him. Other details were inaccurate in Hitler's reminiscences: he said the attempt was made in 1937, and he called Bavaud a Swiss headwaiter. In Picker, op. cit., 306 and 387 where *Table Talks* of 3 May and 4 June 1942 are recorded, Hitler referred to a Swiss assassin who had stalked him on the Berghof for three months; he did not mention a year; other details are somewhat more accurate. Hitler was informed repeatedly about this attempt and the development of the prosecution; one report from the Ministry of Justice is dated 7 September 1942, another 14 October 1942; BA R 22/3090 and R 22/4089.

[132] *Anklageschrift* Bavaud, 24–25; sentence, 11; *Anklageschrift* Gerbohay, 14; Picker, op. cit., 306, 387, with some factual errors.

[133] *Anklageschrift* Bavaud, 25; sentence, 11; *Anklageschrift* Gerbohay, 14.

[134] Ibid.

[135] Ibid.; this was true: Hitler gave a speech to representatives of the press in Munich on this day.

[136] *Anklageschrift* Bavaud, 25; sentence, 11; *Anklageschrift* Gerbohay, 14.

[137] *Anklageschrift* Bavaud, 25–26; sentence, 11–12; *Anklageschrift* Gerbohay, 14.

Radical Member of the Chamber of Deputies Pierre Taittinger instead of Flandin's. He feared that Hitler's advisers might be familiar with Flandin's signature, and that the forgery might be discovered before he had a chance for his attempt on the Führer's life.[138]

On 12 November Bavaud went to the *Braunes Haus* on Königsplatz with his letters and the loaded pistol, hoping to find Hitler there.[139] After the language barrier had been overcome with the assistance of an office worker who knew French, and who translated between Bavaud and an SS-*Hauptsturmführer* who was the guard on duty, and after a telephone call by the guard, Bavaud was led across Briennerstrasse to the *Haus des Führers*. Here he was received by *Landgerichtsdirektor* Dr Kurt Hanssen who was *Reichsleiter* Bormann's assistant for such matters.[140] Once again, Maurice Bavaud was told that he could not see Hitler. Dr Hanssen suggested that he send the letter through the mail, or hand it to him and he would see that Hitler got it. When Bavaud insisted that he must see Hitler personally, Dr Hanssen told him that he might get in touch with the *Reichskanzlei*.[141]

In view of the events of these few days, Dr Hanssen's suggestion illustrates some of the weaknesses of security surrounding the person of Hitler. Although on occasions when Hitler made public appearances there were usually enough bodyguards around to watch the crowds,[142] and although it was not likely at any time that Maurice Bavaud would have been allowed to see Hitler alone, he could have got close enough to make the situation dangerous. In the opinion of the People's Court, Bavaud had in fact represented an acute danger for the Führer's life on two separate occasions (9 and 12 November).[143] This was certainly a time to exercise the greatest possible caution, from the point of view of Hitler's security, and it is surprising that the security network was not any

---

[138] *Anklageschrift* Bavaud, 26–27; sentence, 12–13; *Anklageschrift* Gerbohay, 14.

[139] *Anklageschrift* Bavaud, 28; sentence, 13; *Anklageschrift* Gerbohay, 15.

[140] *Anklageschrift* Bavaud, 28–29; sentence, 13; *Anklageschrift* Gerbohay, 15, For the topography of *Königsplatz* and nearby streets see Karl Fiehler (ed.). *München baut auf* (München n.d.), 69–71.

[141] *Anklageschrift* Bavaud, 29; sentence, 13; *Anklageschrift* Gerbohay, 15.

[142] Cf. Jochen von Lang (ed.), *Adolf Hitler: Gesichter eines Diktators* (Hamburg 1968), passim; Heinrich Hoffmann Collection, National Archives, Washington, D.C.; Hoffmann, op. cit., 639–69.

[143] Sentence. 17–21.

tighter. On 7 November 1938, the Legation Councillor Ernst vom Rath in the German Embassy in Paris was shot by Herschel Grynszpan.[144] Two days later, in its 9 November edition, the official NSDAP newspaper *Völkischer Beobachter* devoted two full pages to the assassination; one article was headed '*Ein neuer Fall Gustloff: Der jüdische Mordanschlag in Paris*'. Dr Goebbels in his lead article of 12 November also drew the parallel between the two cases.[145] But he had given the signal for the most horrible pogrom in Germany since the 1880s on 9 November, and on 10 November Jewish stores, homes, synagogues were vandalized, broken into, robbed and burned, and countless Jews were beaten and killed by SA thugs. The events of the day became notorious as the *Reichskristallnacht*.[146]

Hitler was still in Munich on 10 November; he gave a secret speech to representatives of the press and told them to get it into their heads that they must prepare the German people for war and drive out all that rotten pacifism.[147] The speech was given in the *Haus des Führers*. But on 11 November, Hitler left for Berchtesgaden.[148] He was back in Munich on 14 November.

Maurice Bavaud had reached the end of the line, but not because of security precautions on the part of those responsible for Hitler's safety: he had no more money to wait for a suitable opportunity.[149] Not yet ready to admit failure, he made a last frantic effort. He took the train to Bischofswiesen on 12 November, hoping to get an interview with Hitler through the *Reichskanzlei* offices there, near the Berghof.[150] His financial resources had dwindled to five

[144] On the circumstances of and surrounding the assassination of Ernst vom Rath, and on the connection of it with the attempts of the German and Polish governments to get rid of several tens of thousands of Jews, see Helmut Heiber, 'Der Fall Grünspan', *Vierteljahrshefte für Zeitgeschichte* 5 (1957), 134–72; *Völkischer Beobachter* 8 and 9 November 1938, 2–3. On the prosecution and survival of Grynszpan see also Raul Hilberg, *The Destruction of the European Jews* (Chicago 1961), 655; on 23, Hilberg incorrectly gives 9 November as the date of the assassination.

[145] *Völkischer Beobachter* 12 November 1938, 1. On the Gustloff case, cf. note 12, above.

[146] Helmut Krausnick, 'Judenverfolgung', in Hans Buchheim, Martin Broszat, Hans-Adolf Jacobsen, Helmut Krausnick, *Anatomie des SS-Staates*, vol. II (München 1967), 275–79; cf. Speer, op. cit., 125–27.

[147] Wilhelm Treue (ed.), 'Rede Hitlers vor der deutschen Presse (10 November 1938)', *Vierteljahrshefte für Zeitgeschichte* 6 (1958), 175–91; cf. Domarus, op. cit., vol. I, 973–77.

[148] [Bormann,] *Daten aus alten Notizbüchern*.

[149] *Anklageschrift* Bavaud, 29; sentence, 13–14.

[150] *Anklageschrift* Bavaud, 29; sentence, 13–14; *Anklageschrift* Gerbohay, 15.

marks, and he decided to reach the *Reichskanzlei* offices on foot. But then darkness fell, and it occurred to Bavaud that at this hour, and on a Saturday to boot, he was not likely to find anyone in the *Reichskanzlei* offices who could be of any help to him.[151] At this point, he gave up his efforts to kill Hitler.

MAURICE BAVAUD WENT BACK to the Bischofswiesen railway station and bought a ticket to Freilassing. Apparently, he planned to cross the border into France, but he did not have enough money to buy a ticket that would take him far enough. After he had paid for the ticket to Freilassing, and for some food, he only had one mark and fifty-two pfennigs left.[152] In Freilassing, the cars of Bavaud's train were added to the fast Vienna-Paris train, and in Munich Bavaud went over into one of the cars going to Paris. He had little hope of getting into France, but he was specially anxious to avoid arrest in Munich where his efforts to approach Hitler might be discovered quickly.[153] The next stop was Augsburg, but soon after the train had left Munich, a conductor caught Bavaud without a valid ticket and unable to buy one. He was ordered off the train in Augsburg and handed over to the railway police who turned him over to the *Geheime Staatspolizei* because he was a foreigner.[154]

After his arrest by the Gestapo, all the incriminating items were found on Bavaud's person: the RM 1.52; the 'letter of introduction from Pierre Taittinger'; the envelope addressed to Hitler with the blank sheet in it; the photograph of Marcel Gerbohay; the loaded pistol, and of course the railway ticket from Bischofswiesen to Freilassing.[155] Gerbohay's picture bore his dedication 'Credo in stellam tuam. Sumus unum corpus unum cor una anima ubicumque et semper'.[156] But Bavaud had overestimated the ingenuity of the Gestapo. Although the pistol in his possession duly aroused the suspicion of his interrogators, he was not accused of any attempt on Hitler's life until weeks later. He said it was only a hobby for him to have a pistol, that he was an enthusiastic admirer of the National-Socialist movement and of the great accomplishments of

[151] Ibid.
[152] Ibid.
[153] *Anklageschrift* Bavaud, 29–30; sentence, 14; *Anklageschrift* Gerbohay, 15.
[154] Ibid.
[155] *Anklageschrift* Bavaud, 30–31; sentence, 14; *Anklageschrift* Gerbohay, 15.
[156] *Anklageschrift* Bavaud, 30; *Anklageschrift* Gerbohay, 15–16.

the Führer, and that he had wanted to see him to ask him about his position vis-à-vis Swiss neutrality.[157] That the Gestapo were not particularly suspicious is indicated by the fact that the first interrogation was not conducted until Monday, 14 November, although Bavaud was arrested on the preceding Saturday.[158]

At first Bavaud stubbornly stuck to his basic story when he was intensively interrogated by the Gestapo from 24 to 31 January 1939.[159] He changed it gradually, largely under the impact of the results of Gestapo investigations. They proved to him that he had not, as he had claimed, bought the pistol in Neuchâtel in August 1938, but that he had made a trip to Basel for it on 20 October; thereupon Bavaud said he had despaired of finding a job and had thought of suicide. When it was pointed out to him that he had by no means attempted to commit suicide, but instead had travelled straight to Berlin and then to Berchtesgarden, Munich and Bischofswiesen, all the while making every effort to see the Führer, Bavaud broke down and said, 'Le soupçon qu'on a contre moi est une réalité'.[160] Now he admitted his attempts to assassinate Hitler and described the full details of his efforts, but he still kept to himself most of the background and motivation, especially the role of his friend Marcel Gerbohay, and he never mentioned the *Compagnie du Mystère*.[161]

Having been held by the Gestapo without warrant, and when the Gestapo had obviously found Bavaud relatively harmless, he was turned over to the District Court of Augsburg on 24 November.[162] The court issued an official arrest warrant, and on 6 December Bavaud was sentenced to two months and one week in jail for ticket fraud and illegal possession of a weapon. The court could not give him any credit for his time in the Gestapo jail, but they remitted one week of the total term for the two weeks he was held before sentencing. He served his term in Augsburg jail from 14 December 1938 to 14 February 1939.

After this, Bavaud was transferred to Berlin into the custody of the People's Court. He was now charged with having attempted to

[157] *Anklageschrift* Bavaud, 31.
[158] Ibid.
[159] *Anklageschrift* Bavaud, 31–4.
[160] *Anklageschrift* Bavaud, 34.
[161] *Anklageschrift* Bavaud, 34 and passim; sentence, 15 and passim; *Anklageschrift* Gerbohay, 6.
[162] *Anklageschrift* Bavaud, 31; sentence, 15; Swiss Consulate in Munich to EPD 1 April 1939, EPD Dossier Bavaud.

assassinate Hitler.[163] He was held pending trial *(Untersuchungshaft)* in Moabit Prison from 1 March to 19 December 1939, and, pending execution, in Plötzensee Prison from 19 December 1939 to 14 May 1941.[164] During this time, Bavaud was interrogated on several occasions, specifically by a judge from 25 February to 1 March and on 27 and 28 March, 1939; by police on 14 and 15 February 1940; and again by a judge on 9 May 1941.[165]

Since his confession to the Gestapo in January 1939, Bavaud never withdrew his admission of guilt, but he protected his friend Gerbohay until after his conviction, according to his own later explanation, in the hope of being regarded as eccentric, and also hoping to draw a lighter sentence by avoiding any charges of conspiracy.[166] These explanations, however, probably do not reflect Bavaud's primary concern at the time. Even in the proceedings early in 1939, he admitted that he was aware that attempts on the Führer's life carried the death penalty; that in point of fact he had reconciled himself to any penalty he might receive; and that he had expected to be set upon and killed by the other parade-watchers on 9 November had he been able to take his shots at the Führer from the grandstand.[167] However, he stated his belief that the powerful person who had sent him would also be able to protect him against punishment.[168]

The trial was held on 18 December 1939 before the 2nd *Senat* of the People's Court. The court was convinced that Maurice Bavaud had in fact committed the crimes of which he was accused —two fully developed attempts on Hitler's life, on 9 and 12 November 1938 in Munich; that this had been proven by the accused's full confession as well as by the investigation and evidence; and, that, far from having been or being either temporarily or permanently insane, a possibility which both medical experts and Bavaud himself rejected, Bavaud had gone about carrying out his plan with exemplary circumspection, shrewdness, intelligence and skill.[169] Because of the seriousness of the offence,

---

[163] *Anklageschrift* Bavaud, passim.
[164] *Anklageschrift* Bavaud, 1; file card of Plötzensee Prison, photocopy, EPD Dossier Bavaud.
[165] *Anklageschrift* Bavaud, 35, 37; *Anklageschrift* Gerbohay, 19–21.
[166] Sentence, 16; *Anklageschrift* Gerbohay, 20. The second alleged reason given by Bavaud is contradicted by his allegation of influential Germans who had put him up to his attempts, but he apparently hoped that these claims would also fall into the court's category of eccentricity, and in any case he dropped this allegation in his trial.
[167] *Anklageschrift* Bavaud, 35.
[168] Ibid.
[169] Sentence, 17–21.

197

the acute danger to Hitler's life, and the complete lack of extenuating circumstances, Maurice Bavaud was sentenced to death on the basis of § 5, No. 1 of the Reich President's Decree for the Protection of People and State of 28 February 1933.[170] Since this decree was specifically directed against communist acts of violence, it really was not applicable to Bavaud's case. Nevertheless, it was used before 1939 in the repression of the Churches, and it was used subsequently against other *Staatsfeinde* including the conspirators of 20 July 1944.[171]

If the proceedings were a sad comment on the state of the German legal system, this was compounded by the subsequent treatment of the lawyer who had defended Maurice Bavaud, Dr Franz Wallau.[172] Wallau had asked for acquittal on grounds that only preparatory actions had been proven. This was certainly a debatable point, and in the light of all the evidence most people who were involved, including Hitler, the court, and Bavaud himself were adamant that only accidental circumstances had prevented the Führer's assassination.[173] Wallau merely did his best for his client, as he should have, but the People's Court held that defence counsel had grossly misconceived his duties, and that he ought to be expelled from the *NS-Rechtswahrerbund*, the official party- and government-controlled professional organization. The *Anwaltskammer*, the old pre-

[170] Ibid.; *Reichsgesetzblatt Teil I 1933* (Berlin 1933), 83. Bracher argues persuasively that the *Verordnung des Reichspräsidenten zum Schutz von Volk und Staat* of 28 February 1933 actually lacked legal validity since the motivation it claimed, 'zur Abwehr kommunistischer staatsgefährdender Gewaltakte', had no correspondence in fact: not before the *Reichsgericht* had dealt with the *Reichstag* fire, because there was no proof of it being a communist act of violence; and not after the trial of the arsonist because no conspiracy had been established (Bracher, op. cit., 84–87). The decree was legally untenable in general because it imposed the death penalty for mere attempts which were not punishable by death under regular criminal law: 'Das versuchte Verbrechen oder Vergehen ist milder zu bestrafen als das vollendete. Ist das vollendete Verbrechen mit dem Tode oder mit lebenslänglichem Zuchthaus bedroht, so tritt Zuchthausstrafe nicht unter drei Jahren ein, neben welcher auf Zulässigkeit von Polizeiaufsicht erkannt werden kann'. (*Strafgesetzbuch für das Deutsche Reich mit Nebengesetzen*, neunundzwanzigste Auflage bearbeitet von Dr Eduard Kohlrausch [Berlin, Leipzig 1930], 5, § 44).
[171] Bracher, op. cit., 85.
[172] *Der Stellvertretende Präsident des Volksgerichtshofes* to *NS-Rechtswahrerbund* 5 January 1940, EPD Dossier Bavaud.
[173] *Anklageschrift* Bavaud, 1–2, 34, 37, 41; sentence, passim; *Anklageschrift* Gerbohay, passim; *Bericht Nr. 28*; Picker, op. cit., 306, 387; *Stellv. Präsident des Volksgerichtshofes*.

Nazi Bar Association, refused to begin proceedings against Wallau, was then forced to hold them after all, and found no fault with Dr Wallau. But the *NS-Rechtswahrerbund* expelled him anyway.[174]

M. ALFRED BAVAUD HAD BEGUN formal inquiries after the fate of his eldest son on 16 January 1939 when he wrote to the *Eidgenössisches Politisches Departement* requesting that they obtain for him some information. He had learned from the Gutterers in Baden-Baden that his son had given Mannheim as his next stop in his quest for a job.[175] But the Gutterers had checked with the Swiss Consulate in Mannheim, and nothing was known there about Maurice Bavaud.[176] Inquiries were made, and it did not take very long for the Swiss Consulate in Mannheim to receive information from the Gestapo office in Karlsruhe, as by now a full-scale investigation was under way, after Maurice Bavaud's confession in January. But the reply dated 22 February 1939 that the Consulate received and which it passed on to the *Eidgenössisches Politisches Departement* said that Bavaud was serving a jail term of several month's length in Augsburg, for fraud, although this had ended on 14 February.[177] M. Alfred Bavaud was given this information by the *Eidgenössisches Politisches Departement* under the date of 2 March 1939. Upon his immediate request for details, he received word at the beginning of April that Maurice Bavaud had served two months and a week in Augsburg jail for railway-ticket fraud, and that he was now detained in Berlin-Moabit jail under suspicion of having committed a political crime, pending prosecution.[178]

Now the Swiss Legation in Berlin was deputed by the *Eidgenössisches Politisches Departement* to look into the matter to see what could be done for Maurice Bavaud, to find out what the charges were, and to provide counsel for him. All inquiries had to be made through the *Auswärtiges Amt*, a time-consuming process. By the end of May 1939, all that had been learned was that the charges would remain secret until the Reich's prosecutor had handed up the formal accusation, and that no lawyer could be appointed for Maurice Bavaud until then.[179] However, some short

---

[174] Affidavit by *Justizrat* Dr Viereck 12 November 1945, EPD Dossier Bavaud.
[175] Alfred Bavaud to EPD 16 January 1939, EPD Dossier Bavaud.
[176] Ibid.
[177] Ibid.; *Anklageschrift* Bavaud, 31; sentence, 15.
[178] Gestapo Karlsruhe to Swiss Consulate in Mannheim 22 February 1939, Swiss Consulate in Munich to EPD 1 April 1939, EPD Dossier Bavaud.
[179] EPD Dossier Bavaud.

letters were transmitted between Maurice Bavaud and his father.[180]

Only on 22 November 1939 was the Swiss Legation in Berlin able to inform Bern that Maurice Bavaud had been formally charged with 'activity against the State' on 21 October 1939.[181] On the same day, the Legation asked the *Auswärtiges Amt* for more details. The Ministry of Justice authorized the *Auswärtiges Amt* on 6 December 1939 to inform the Legation confidentially of the charge: attempt to murder a member of the government.[182] But the Legation was not informed of the formal indictment until 20 December, two days after Maurice Bavaud had already been sentenced to death.[183] It was learned, however, that Bavaud had been given a lawyer who spoke French as well as German. Even on 21 December, the Swiss Legation was inquiring at the Foreign Office what date had been set for the trial.[184] Only on 3 January 1940 did the Legation receive word that Bavaud had already been sentenced to death, still without specific information about the crimes of which he had been convicted, and they were also left in the dark as to whether the death sentence had been carried out or not.[185] But an official of the Legation was told in the *Auswärtiges Amt* on 3 January, in strict confidence, that Maurice Bavaud had come to Germany to assassinate Hitler, how he went about it, and that apparently the death sentence had not been carried out as yet.[186]

Obviously, the matter was a sensitive one. The Swiss Government and its Legation considered the possibility that Bavaud was insane, but there seemed to be no hint of this in the evidence, and the court appeared not to have found any. There appeared to be no legal grounds for a request that the laws of a foreign country be set aside in a case clearly falling under the foreign government's jurisdiction.[187] It might have put the Swiss Government in a very ambiguous position if the Legation had asked for clemency; they

[180] Ibid.
[181] EPD Dossier Bavaud; the formal indictment is dated 20 November 1939; AA/PA Strafsachen Ref. III Bd. 1 Forts. Band 2; the Swiss Minister in Berlin Frölicher to *Auswärtiges Amt* 22 November 1939, AA/PA R 2284g.
[182] Dr Roland Freisler to *Hofrat* Schimpke 6 December 1939, AA/PA R 2425g.
[183] Draft verbal note of *Auswärtiges Amt* to Swiss Legation 20 December 1939, AA/PA R 2538g/R 2557g/39; Frölicher to Minister Feldscher (Chief of *Abteilung für Auswärtiges* in EPD) 21 December 1939, EPD Dossier Bavaud.
[184] AA/PA R 2557g.
[185] Frölicher to Feldscher 4 January 1940, EPD Dossier Bavaud; draft verbal note of *Auswärtiges Amt* to Swiss Legation 31 December 1939, AA/PA R 2557g.
[186] Frölicher to Feldscher 4 January 1940, EPD Dossier Bavaud.
[187] EPD to Swiss Legation in Berlin 14 February 1941, EPD Dossier Bavaud.

were already embarrassed by the attempt of a Swiss citizen to assassinate Hitler. On the other hand, an execution would raise many questions in Switzerland, and it would then be difficult to maintain the secrecy that the German Government had requested in order to prevent other potential assassins from developing similar plans. The murder of Gustoff had not been forgotten, nor that of Rath.[188] The Swiss Legation also had to consider, besides the fate of a human being, the potential dangers that any vigorous efforts to have him spared or freed might have upon the military and international position of Switzerland. The war had begun in September 1939, and there was talk of an impending German invasion of Switzerland. This apparent danger was compounded a few months later by the defeat of France. Energetic efforts to save the life of Maurice Bavaud, who actually insisted that he had tried to assassinate Hitler, could not seem in the circumstances to be in the best interests of Switzerland.

Further efforts were made, and the Swiss authorities and Maurice Bavaud's parents learned more about the crime of which he had been convicted. More letters passed back and forth between the condemned man and his parents.[189] But Maurice Bavaud remained alive for more than a year and a half after his conviction neither because of his parents' efforts to win clemency for him, nor because of any efforts on the part of the Swiss authorities.

The parents spared no efforts. Alfred Bavaud, Maurice's father, submitted several petitions for clemency in 1940, one addressed directly to the Führer in December 1940.[190] It had not been until 10 June 1940 that Alfred Bavaud had learned that his son had been condemned to death, and he learned it only from his son's seventh post-trial letter, the one from Plötzensee Prison dated 5 April 1940; the other six had not been passed on.[191] Alfred Bavaud asked the *Eidgenössisches Politisches Departement* to intervene without delay,

---

[188] See above, 2, 19; cf. the accusations levelled against Switzerland after the murder of Gustloff cited by Wolf, op. cit., 271; see also Edgar Bonjour, *Histoire de la Neutralité Suisse*, 6 vols. (Neuchâtel 1971).

[189] AA/PA 83–69g, R 5530g/40, R5404g/40, R 5653g/40, R 6189g/40, R 6533g/40, R 6012g/40; EPD Dossier Bavaud.

[190] German Consulate in Lausanne to German Legation in Bern 2 January 1941, German Legation in Berne to Foreign Office 22 January 1941, AA/PA R 5225g/41, R 5237g/41.

[191] Alfred Bavaud to EPD 10 June 1940, EPD Dossier Bavaud; the Swiss Government had been requested by the German Foreign Office to keep the affair secret, even from the parents.

and to use all its influence to obtain a milder sentence.[192] One of Maurice's brothers, a *sergeant* in the Swiss Army, also petitioned the Swiss Government to intervene on Maurice's behalf.[193]. On 27 May 1941, Alfred Bavaud again asked his government to intervene with the German authorities to obtain clemency for his son.[194] He asked repeatedly if an exchange could be arranged.

The Swiss Government was not in a position, as has been seen, to make forceful representations on behalf of Maurice Bavaud, and they saw no basis for requesting an exchange.[195] Immediately after the Swiss Government had learned that Maurice Bavaud had been sentenced to death for his attempts to assassinate Hitler, the Swiss Legation in Berlin declared orally to an official of the German Foreign Office that they would refrain from any formal request for clemency, although the Swiss Government would prefer that the death sentence was not carried out.[196] The Swiss Government, however, did go further in its efforts in the days immediately following. The chief of the *Division des Affaires Etrangères*, Minister Feldscher, asked the German Legation in Bern on 16 January 1940, in the name of the *Bundesrat*, to pass on to the German authorities a request that the death sentence be commuted.[197] As late as June 1941, the *Eidgenössisches Politisches Departement* continued its efforts to save the life of Maurice Bavaud, after he had been executed: the Swiss Government had not been informed of the impending execution.[198] They first learned about it through Maurice Bavaud's last letter to his parents, dated 12 May 1941 and received in the first days of June. Only then, upon a telegraphed request from the *Eidgenössisches Politisches Departement*, was the Swiss Legation in Berlin able to report that the death penalty had already been carried out.[199] The German Legation in

[192] Ibid.

[193] EPD Dossier Bavaud.

[194] Ibid.

[195] *Eidgenössisches Politisches Departement* to Swiss Legation in Berlin 14 February 1941, EPD Dossier Bavaud.

[196] *Auswärtiges Amt* to *Reichsminister der Justiz* 11 January 1940, AA/PA R 63g.

[197] Telegram of German Legation in Bern to *Auswärtiges Amt* 16 January 1940, AA/PA R 125g; German Legation in Bern to *Auswärtiges Amt* 22 January 1941, AA/PA R 5237g/41.

[198] *Eidgenössisches Politisches Departement* to Swiss Legation in Berlin 5 June 1941 and 7 June 1941, EPD Dossier Bavaud.

[199] *Eidgenössisches Politisches Departement* to Swiss Legation in Berlin (telegram) 7 June 1941 and telegraphed reply of the same day, EPD Dossier Bavaud.

Bern and the German Consulate in Lausanne had been informed of this, but they had apparently informed neither the parents nor the Swiss Government.[200]

The German Government had never been inclined towards extending clemency. The *Auswärtiges Amt* wrote to the Minister of Justice on 11 January 1940 that it had no objections against carrying out the execution of Maurice Bavaud.[201] The Ministry of Justice informed the Foreign Office on 26 January 1940 that clemency would not be considered and that the death sentence would be carried out.[202] This position was reiterated after the father's petition of December 1940,[203] and again a few days before the execution.[204]

What kept Maurice Bavaud alive for a year and a half after his condemnation was the newly awakened interest of the Gestapo in clearing up the mysterious ramifications of his assassination attempts. In a letter to his parents, the condemned man had revealed more about the connection of his attempts with Marcel Gerbohay and the *Compagnie du Mystère*. The letter was, of course, read by the police, the execution had been delayed, and the investigation was resumed by the Gestapo.[205] The Gestapo interrogated Maurice Bavaud on 14 and 15 February 1940, and on 9 May 1941 he was interrogated by an official of the judiciary administration.[206] In the meantime, inquiries had been made to determine the complicity of Maurice Gerbohay and of other co-students of Maurice Bavaud in Switzerland and in France. Maurice's father learned that such inquiries were made in Neuchâtel in 1940,[207] and students and professors of the Collège de Saint-Ilan

[200] *Auswärtiges Amt* to German Legation in Bern and German Consulate in Lausanne 24 May 1941 (draft), AA/PA R 5695g/41.

[201] *Auswärtiges Amt* to *Reichsminister der Justiz* 2 and 11 January 1940 (drafts), AA/PA R 2557g/40 and R 63g/40.

[202] *Reichsminister der Justiz* to *Auswärtiges Amt* 26 January 1940, AA/PA R 169g.

[203] *Auswärtiges Amt* to *Reichsminister der Justiz* 8 March 1941 (draft), AA/PA R 5237g/41.

[204] *Reichsminister der Justiz* to *Auswärtiges Amt* 7 May 1941, AA/PA R 5695g/41.

[205] *Reichsminister der Justiz* to *Auswärtiges Amt* 8 February 1940 and 12 February 1941, AA/PA R 278g/40 and R 5239g/41; *Geheime Staatspolizei* Berlin to *Oberreichsanwalt beim Volksgerichtshof* 21 January 1941 (copy), AA/PA R 5239g/41.

[206] *Anklageschrift* Gerbohay, 19–21.

[207] Alfred Bavaud to *Eidgenössisches Politisches Departement* 15 September 1940, EPD Dossier Bavaud: '. . . il y a eu au mois de mai et juin une nouvelle enquête conduite par la police fédérale, les condisciples de mon fils ont été interrogés . . .'

were interrogated intensively by the Gestapo in 1941.[208] On 6 May 1941, it was decided to have Maurice Bavaud executed, and to suspend the prosecution of the alleged instigator for the time being.[209] It was later resumed with the result that Gerbohay was arrested on 1 January 1942.[210]

On 12 May 1941, Maurice Bavaud wrote to his parents that he expected to be executed the next day.[211] Five days after his last interrogation, Maurice Bavaud was executed at 6 a.m. on 14 May 1941 in Plötzensee Prison.[212]

[208] Abbé Lucien Rozo (since September 1939 Supérieur of the Seminary of Saint-Ilan) letter dated 2 May 1972; the predecessors of Abbé Rozo are all deceased.

[209] *Reichsminister der Justiz* to *Auswärtiges Amt* 7 May 1941, AA/PA R 5695g.

[210] *Anklageschrift* Gerbohay, 1. Gerbohay was sentenced to death by the People's Court on 1 February 1943 and executed in Plötzensee on 9 April 1943; *Mordregister*, BA EC 941 N.

[211] *Eidgenössisches Politisches Departement* to Swiss Legation in Berlin 7 June 1941, EPD Dossier Bavaud.

[212] *Reichsminister der Justiz* to *Austwärtiges Amt* 15 May 1941, AA/PA R 5727g: file card of Plötzensee Prison (photocopy), EPD Dossier Bavaud.

The SD:
The Significance of
Organization and Image

George C. Browder

The Nazi police state was built on a fusion of Heinrich Himmler's
SS with the police forces of Germany. The heart of the SS and
Police system was Sipo *(Sicherheitspolizei)* and the Security Service
of the SS *(Sicherheitsdienst des Reichsführers SS)*. The exact relationship between the SD and Sipo and the real nature and role of
the SD have been points of controversy because of inconsistencies in
definitions and descriptions of 'the SD'. This problem may have
arisen spontaneously, but was later intentionally exaggerated.

As we shall see, the men of the SD, the Gestapo, the Reich
Criminal Police (major branches of Sipo) and other related organizations could not agree on their roles, their relationships or on the
areas of their jurisdiction. They were divided into rival factions,
each with a different view of itself and different views of the other.
When survivors of these organizations testified at Nuremberg, they
insisted on the separateness of each police organization, the SD, and
the *Einsatzgruppen* (the mass murder squads of the Eastern front).

* This article is an elaboration of some ideas originally presented in a paper
at the meeting of the American Historical Association, Washington, DC, 30
December 1969. The final form has benefited greatly from the criticisms of
Roger Daniels, Robert Koehl, Robert Wolfe and several others. The author
would also like to express his thanks for the support given by the National
Endowment for the Humanities and the State University of New York Research
Foundation, and the generous assistance of the staffs of the US Document Center,
Berlin, and the National Archives, Washington, DC. Although material from the
Bundesarchiv, Koblenz, and other German archives was not needed to support
this article, the help of their staffs has also been invaluable.

Their positions were based on an intentional obfuscation of the nature of 'the SD'.[1]

Of what importance is this historical and scholarly inability to settle on a precise definition of 'the SD' or its relation to Sipo? A clear picture of the elastic, *plural* character of organizations like the SD is essential to an understanding of the 'successes' of the Third Reich. Perhaps more importantly, an exploration of the 'multiple definitions' of the SD will increase our understanding of how ill-defined functions, confusing organizational structures and unrealistic self-images helped lead so many otherwise respectable and talented men to play their roles in the machinery of police terror and genocide.

The origin of the problem lies in the history of the SD. It began in 1931 as a special intelligence staff office of the SS *(Schutzstaffel)*, which was then only a small élite security and police force of the National Socialist Movement. Since it grew out of the SS, which had been, in turn, a component of the Storm Troopers (the *Sturmabteilung* or SA), the SD naturally developed a self-image as an élite within élites.[2] However, neither the nature of its éliteness nor its mission was ever clearly defined.

The nascent SD drew its first mission from its parent organization, the SS. As bodyguard for Party leaders and speakers, the early SS acquired some intelligence functions, including watching the Party for spies and undesirables and reporting on any improprieties in the SA, the rather uncontrollable strong-arm squads. In 1931, Heinrich Himmler (Reichsführer of the SS since 1929) decided to create a special intelligence agency. By the fall of 1932, after some evolution, the *Sicherheitsdienst des Reichsführers* SS, the SD, emerged as an autonomous branch of the SS under the command of Reinhard Heydrich.[3] In addition to spying on enemies, the SD

---

[1] For the full text of the trial, International Military Tribunal, *Trial of the Major War Criminals before the International Military Tribunal*, 42 vols. (Nuremberg 1947–49), henceforth referred to as *IMT*. The Gestapo and SD were charged as criminal organizations, *IMT*, 1:262–68. The defence picture of the SD emerged from such testimonies and affidavits as Werner Best, *IMT*, 20:123–55; Rolf Heinz Hoeppner, 20:185–236; Wilhelm Höttl, 9:228–31, 256–60; Otto Ohlendorf, 4:311–54; and Hans Rössner, 20:236–62. (Most of the more thorough pretrial interrogations are part of record group 238, National Archives, Washington, DC, henceforth cited as NA/RG 238.) The defence summarized its documents and affidavits in 21:319–30.

[2] The most recent and complete history of the SS, including Sipo and SD, is Heinz Höhne, *Der Orden unter dem Totenkopf, Die Geschichte der SS* (Gütersloh 1967).

[3] Shlomo Aronson, *Reinhard Heydrich und die Frühgeschichte von Gestapo und SD* (Stuttgart 1971), 55–65 covers the birth of the SD.

became a watchdog of the Movement: a guardian of morals and ideology whose job it was to pry into the Party and its organizations, including the SA and the SS, and to ferret out infiltrators and deviationists.

Actually, the mission soon went beyond spying. Heydrich strove to develop his SD into the sole intelligence agency of the Movement, with the mission of keeping the Nazi leadership fully informed on everything it needed to know to lead the nation. Heydrich's model for the SD was a national intelligence service, based not on police spies and informers, but on every citizen who would feel a patriotic duty to give information.

Meanwhile, the prospect of seizing power emphasized the necessity of insuring the internal security of the future Reich. Between 1932 and 1935, Himmler and Heydrich developed an added role for the SD as the core of a future political police force which would in turn be the centre of an SS-controlled Reich police force guaranteeing internal security. The police civil servants had to be welded into a hard core, blindly obedient to the orders of the Nazi leadership. Through ideological indoctrination, the police had to be freed from the divisive and restrictive theories of the liberal, constitutional state so they could be imbued with the spirit of the Movement and the *Volk*. In short, a revolution of attitude was needed, and Himmler and Heydrich meant to use the SS and SD as the vehicles of that revolution.[4] The resulting political police shaped by the SD would be the watchdog of the Nazi state, of its administrative machinery (including the more ordinary police forces) and of that pillar of the German state, the Army. As with the SD relation to the Movement, here was a concept of éliteness vis-à-vis the organs of the state.

By 1935, the SD's ill-defined functions and ambiguous self-image was rife with potential contradictions. On the one hand, it was the

---

[4] For an after-the-fact boast about their long-range designs on the police, Heydrich's introduction to *Organisation und Meldedienst der Reichskriminalpolizei* (Berlin 1939), US National Archives Microfilm Publications, Microcopy T-175, *Records of the Reichsführer SS and Chief of the German Police*, Roll 451, Frame 2967012 (hereafter T-175/451/Frame or folder number). Other than oral tradition, there are no pre-1935 sources to prove that this was a plan of action predating 1933; among other places, the oral tradition has found print in Wilhelm Höttl, *The Secret Front: The Story of Nazi Political Espionage* (New York 1954), 21, 45; Aronson quotes oral sources, Heydrich's wife, Freiher v. Eberstein and Werner Best, to trace the idea back as far as 1932–33 (*Heydrich*, 107, 134, 169).

internal watchdog of the nation and the Movement with its spies and informers whom people might fear and distrust. Yet at the same time, it sought to be an information service to keep the leadership in tune with the true mood of the people. As such, it would rely on all public-spirited citizens as agents. In this capacity, its image would have to rise above that of either Party informers or secret police spies. From yet another perspective, the SD was to absorb and revolutionize all suitable members of the political police and other state agencies essential to the internal security of the new Reich. To improve conformity and insure security, this police force had to terrorize by its image of cold, brutal efficiency. Obviously, such vaguely-conceived functions were not easily compatible. Even so, the contradictions were not acute, because the 'mission' of 'the SD' was not yet clearly defined.

Not only do these ambivalent beginnings help explain the confusingly complex character of the later SD, but they also made it possible for this organization to attract the several different and incompatible types who would perpetuate and elaborate the internal contradictions. The early membership of the SD provides us with further insight into both the reality of the élitist self-image and the confusing development of the organization.

Most efforts to characterize Sipo and SD membership have relied on descriptions left by former members, opponents and victims, and are consequently distorted. The best impressions are those which can be drawn from Shlomo Aronson's and Alwin Ramme's books, mainly describing men who achieved middle and high-ranking positions. A quantitative study drawn from every rank and branch of Sipo and SD is badly needed to expand on this impression of the leadership. The author has undertaken such a project with only limited success in developing a random sample of SD membership. Although it is premature to present results, a few safe generalizations can be made. They and the impressions derived from this reasearch provide the basis for the descriptions in this article. Unfortunately, because of a lack of rosters for all ranks, this sample is limited to SD men who eventually became officers, and therefore still have a relatively élite bias.[5]

[5] Aronson, *Heydrich*; and Alwin Ramme, *Der Sicherheitsdienst der SS: Zu seiner Funktion im faschistischen Machtapparat und im Besetzungsregime des sogenannten Generalgouvernements Polen* (Berlin 1970). The sample was drawn from men identified as SD officers in the annual *Dienstaltersliste der Schutzstaffel der NSDAP*, 1934–38, T-175/204 and 205 (henceforth DAL). It consists

The SD began as a very small hand-picked group, and did not begin to grow significantly until the latter part of 1933. By the autumn of that year, its total membership was probably around two to three hundred. It may have reached one thousand toward the end of 1935 and tripled in size the following year. It had definitely exceeded three thousand by January 1937.[6]

The only safe generalization about SD membership is that they were a mixed bag, including all types who were drawn into the Nazi Movement. Approximately one-quarter of the membership had shared the trench and *Freikorps* experiences which generated the anti-communist activism and aggressive xenophobic nationalism described in Robert Waite's study of the Free Corps. Most of the remainder belonged to the younger generation analyzed so insightfully in Peter Loewenberg's article on the 'Nazi Youth Cohort'. Their characters had been moulded amid the deprivations and emotions of wartime and the humiliating peace which followed. Then the jolt of the depression released their pent up tensions in revolutionary activism. Many of the autobiographical summaries written by SD men read like passages from one of these works.[7]

As part of their élitist self-image, former SD men have asserted that few of their number were originally in the SS. They liked to see themselves as providing a superior element. They also insisted that few were really imbued with the Nazi or SS ideology. Subse-

[6] Höhne, *Der Orden*, 195, gives a two-hundred-man estimate for autumn 1933; and Ramme, *Der Sicherheitsdienst*, 35, estimates close to three hundred for the end of 1932. Although both figures are significantly higher than Nuremberg testimonies, they provide a range more consistent with all known information. The growth pattern from 1934 through 1936 is based on the growth of the officer corps listed in the DAL. The figures for 1937 and 1938 (*Statistisches Jahrbuch der Schutzstaffel der NSDAP*, 1937, T-175/204/4042259, 1938, Ibid., 4042315) represent the *total SD* (all '*hauptamtlich, ehrenamtlich und zugeteilte*' SS members) but probably no 'clandestine members' (see n. 44).

[7] Robert G. L. Waite, *Vanguard of Nazism* (Cambridge 1952): and Peter Loewenberg, 'The Psychological Origins of the Nazi Youth Cohort', *The American Historical Review*, 76 (December 1971): 1457–1502. Most BDC/SSO and RuSHA files contain one or more handwritten *Lebensläufe*.

of all officers in the 1934 DAL, and one out of every twenty-five new SD officers for each subsequent year. This produced sixty-four officers and men as of 1933 (probably twenty to twenty-five per cent of the total), sixty-eight officers and men who joined from 1934 through June 1936, and fifty-six who joined subsequently. The biographical data was derived from the SS personnel files (SS Officers' and Race and Settlement Main Office files) at the US Document Center, Berlin (hereafter BDC/SSO and RuSHA).

quently, many writers interpreted this to mean that they joined and served for either self-seeking or 'more idealistic' reasons.[8] However, of the 188 men in our SD sample, 115 came into the SD from the SS and 161 were previously members of the NSDAP. Of the latter, no breakdown of 1933 band-wagon jumpers vs. earlier members and 'Old Fighters' is yet available, but the balance is not in favour of latecomers. Even most of the latecomers and non-Party members seem to have been fellow travellers during the Weimar years.

The lives of many of these men had been disrupted by the hard times and the social malaise of Germany in the twenties and thirties. A large number had their professional or educational careers interrupted or terminated before entering the SD, and many had suffered from long periods of unemployment or had moved about from job to job. Unable to cope with their problems, they liked to complain that their hardships resulted from their political dedication or from Jewish-directed harassment — they saw their fate as inseparable from the persecution and degradation of Germany. For them, the SS and SD were a solution to all these problems.

There is an apparent correlation between those who suffered significant economic and social dislocation before entering the SD and those who got into trouble while in the SD. Several were the subjects of strong disciplinary action, a number resigned or were expelled from the SD, and many were denied promotions. Some were lost souls who could adjust to neither the Nazi revolution nor the society they were helping to destroy. Some were simply amoral adventurers and misfits. After 1934, the freebooters and misfits continued to trickle in, but their types became unwelcome as the SD sought respectability.

Among the early membership, this social rootlessness made some of them ready tools for whatever action their leaders considered necessary, and they often performed the illegal 'dirty work': blackmail, kidnapping and executions. For many, the first major task of this sort was probably the Röhm purge in 1934,[9] and the last was the final solution of the Jewish problem. Adolf Eichmann can be

[8] Hoeppner's testimony, *IMT*, 20:194 has been quoted for the estimate that only ten per cent of the SD came from the SS; and Höttl, *Secret Front*, 22 was usually cited to the effect that there was little identity between the SD and men imbued with the Nazi ideology.

[9] Orb, *Nationalsozialismus*, provides us with what were apparently inside stories about which SD men did the 'dirty work' in the purge and which men were shocked or incensed by it.

cited as an infamous example, but the lesser known Alfred Naujocks was more typical. He was involved in counterfeiting, kidnapping and assassination, and also conducted the phony border incidents preceding the invasion of Poland. Even Heydrich, who commanded the SD, was a man who could not fit into his first profession, the naval officers' corps. His biographer, Shlomo Aronson, has concluded that he became a loyal servant of the men and order which gave him a place of esteem.[10]

Such men could never have been happy in an ordinary job. They required an organization with special importance. They had to be involved in Germany's revolution; most of all, however, they had a strong personal need to be part of some sort of élite. They were probably attracted by the aura of a 'secret service'. Both the missions and the alleged éliteness of the SS and SD satisfied these needs on several counts.

Judging from its early membership, the SD hardly lived up to an élitist image. Throughout its history, members were drawn in for purely pragmatic reasons, often for the sole purpose of penetrating another branch of the Movement or a state office such as the police. Even the SS membership criteria for 'racial éliteness' were not applied strictly to SD personnel. The process of coordinating Sipo and SD with SS membership standards was not begun until June 1938, and even then an essential person could be included if he was considered racially a *'fast ausgeglichener Mischling'*.[11]

Nevertheless, the early membership did include the first of that

[10] Eichmann is well described in Hannah Arendt, *Eichmann in Jerusalem, A Report on the Banality of Evil* (New York 1964). The colourful career of Alfred Naujocks is revealed in his Nuremberg interrogations (NA/RG 238) and in the journalistic biography written with his cooperation by Günter Peis, *The Man Who Started the War*. Aronson, *Heydrich*, 25–38, 254.

[11] RdErl. d. RFSSuCdDP, *Aufnahme von Angehörigen der Sicherheitspolizei in den Schutzstaffeln der NSDAP*, 23 June 1938, Germany, *Ministerialblatt des Reichs-und Preußischen Ministeriums des Innern*, 1089–91, and subsequent decrees and memoranda can be found in US National Archives Microfilm Publications, Microcopy T-580, *Captured German Documents Microfilmed at the Berlin Document Centre*, Roll 93, Folder, 457 (hereafter T-580/93/457); and T-175/241/EAP 173-b-10-05/48. US National Archives Microfilm Publications, Microcopy T-354, *Miscellaneous SS Records: Einwandererzentralstelle, Waffen-SS und SS-Oberabschnitte*, Roll 453, Folder Fulda-Werra 118, and Roll 454, Folder Fulda-Werra 121 (hereafter T-354/453/Folder or frame number) contains communications and orders from the SS Race and Settlement Main Office from 1936 through 1939 dealing with the infusion of Gestapo and Kripo personnel into the SD and SD candidates into the SS—who could be accepted, who could not, and why.

group which has traditionally been called the 'intellectuals' or 'academicians'. The label 'intellectuals' was used as both a pejorative and laudatory reference to SD members by contemporaries, and it appears in many memoirs. Historians from Reitlinger to Höhne have employed it, including Aronson, who seems to prefer 'academicians'. Some of these men clearly fit Daniel Lerner's definition of intellectuals: 'those persons who are predisposed—through temperament, family, education, occupation, etc.—to manipulate the symbolic rather than the material environment'.[12]

It should be noted, however, that the term 'intellectuals' has been used too loosely. It is true that before 1933 at least twenty per cent of the SD officer corps had completed university studies, usually receiving a doctorate. Thereafter, academic degrees would be even more important to SD careers. However, the majority of the men who held advanced degrees would be more properly called professional men than intellectuals, for they were physicians, engineers, lawyers and civil servants of the higher ranks. Even so, they all seem to have been attracted by the aura of membership in an 'intellectual élite' which would provide the proper direction for the new Germany.[13] Therefore, since 'intellectual' was an important part of the SD image, especially for this type of man, the label remains appropriate for them.

Regardless of what we call them, these men were jurists, college professors, political scientists, economists and historians who desired to have an influence on their society commensurate with their education and talents. They were committed to Nazism as the only road to a better future for Germany, but each had his own view of what National Socialism should be, and each hoped to use his position in the SD to shape the Nazi *Weltanschauung* in his chosen direction. This category is always identified with Otto Ohlendorf, who later developed the more idealistic SD mission of providing objective situation reports to inform and direct the leadership. They hoped to steer the Movement along the 'proper' path and

[12] Daniel Lerner, 'The Nazi Elite', Harold D. Laswell and Daniel Lerner (eds.), *World Revolutionary Elites* (Cambridge, Mass. 1965), 203. See n. 13.

[13] Cf. Ramme, *Sicherheitsdienst*, 76 f. on educational backgrounds. Considering the full spectrum of SD men often identified as 'intellectuals', perhaps Robert Koehl's 'social engineers' would be a better term ('Toward an SS Typology: Social Engineers', *The American Journal of Economics and Sociology*, 18 [January 1959]: 113–26).

protect the leadership from the misguided advice, half-truths and lies of the sycophants and self-seekers surrounding Hitler.[14]

In their self-deluding role, most of these men were quite sincere and 'idealistic' in the sense that they were pursuing what they considered to be idealistic goals for the nation. They cannot be dismissed as cynical self-seekers. The recruitment appeal which they provided for many of Germany's other frustrated intellectuals helped the SD to realize its image of a patriotic intelligence service. Nevertheless, labels like 'intellectual' and 'idealist' should by no means be taken to mean that they were not racists. Some were blatantly so, others merely accepted part of the Nazi view. Many might have originally looked askance at more vulgar racist talk and considered themselves above the common sort who would resort to violence and inhuman acts. However, few made any serious effort to head off such action, and, when caught up in it, would soon justify it as necessary and even supervise genocide. Others would quietly drop out when they saw what was coming.[15]

From the above, one can see that despite its élitist self-image, before the Nazi seizure of power the SD was a less than significant organization of mixed quality. It included men who could serve as informers or conduct any other cloak and dagger function. There

---

[14] The character and 'idealism' of the 'intellectuals' is well revealed in the Nuremberg testimonies and interrogations of Otto Ohlendorf and others such as Rolf Heinz Hoeppner, (see n. 1); NA/RG 238/Interrogations of Dr Wilhelm Höttl, 2 October 1945, and 4 October 1945, 5f. An example of how Ohlendorf tried to shape Nazi policy can be found in NA/RB 238/Ohlendorf testimonies, 29 October 1945, 2–6, 3 December 1945, 19–21, and *Vernehmung des Zeugen Otto Ohlendorf am 23. Juni 1947*, 17. Kersten, *Memoirs*, 206–20, contains a revealing sketch of Ohlendorf, his plans, and his conflicts with Himmler and other Nazi leaders.

[15] In the fall of 1939, both Ohlendorf and Werner Best apparently had breaches with Himmler and Heydrich over the first genocide plans in Poland (NA/RG 238/Ohlendorf interrogation, 23 June 1947, 17, and Walter Schellenberg, *Memoiren* [Köln 1959], 71 n.) Ohlendorf claimed to have proposed minority regulations, apparently resembling extreme segregation, and to have been opposed by extremists on the racial question; nevertheless, when called to service in the *Einsatzgruppen* he did his duty (NA/RG 238/Ohlendorf interrogation, 3 December 1945, 19–21; and Ohlendorf testimony, *IMT*, 4:353f.). Franz Six, pioneer in SD ideological and racial research, thought the November Pogrom of 1938 a 'shame and a scandal' because it occurred without orders, but he accepted any Führer orders, since they came from the head of state. He considered the execution of women and children deplorable, but killing male Jews was proper because they were potential bearers of arms (Office of United States Counsel for Prosecution of Axis Criminality, *Trials of the War Criminals*, 15 vols. [Washington 1946–48], 4:523, hereafter *TWC*.)

were also those who could build a reliable information service for the leadership. However, when Hitler came to office in January 1933, the SD was hardly an élite force ready to seize power or to take over the reins of state through a powerful, centralized political police force. When that became part of the SD mission, the next major element of SD membership, the policemen, were added.

It took three to six years to weld together the basic structure of the SS and the police system. The process began during 1933 and 1934 when Himmler gradually acquired command of the political police forces of each of the separate states *(Länder)*, the final coup being the inclusion of the Prussian Gestapo in April 1934. The Gestapo, or *Geheime Staatspolizei* (Secret State Police), were the political police force of Prussia, formed in 1933-34 by Hermann Göring. Gestapo headquarters in Berlin became the central office for Himmler as Political Police Commander of each of the German states. Under the actual command of Heydrich, this collection of police offices was welded into a *de facto* unity which became official with the establishment of a Reich-wide Gestapo in the summer of 1936.[16]

Meanwhile, in June 1936, Himmler had officially become Chief of *all* police forces in Germany. Most important, he was given the double title of Reichsführer SS and Chief of the German Police, which implied that he was simultaneously a leader in the Movement and an officer of the state. The significance of this dual position lay in the fact that those of his subordinates who were both SS members and policemen could receive orders from him in either capacity, legal police orders or Führer orders, and no one could distinguish between the two. For himself, Himmler could choose between those orders he received either through civil administrative or Party channels, or he could short circuit the whole system by appealing directly to Hitler. As a result, it became veritably impossible for either Party or state to control him or his agencies.[17]

No sooner was Himmler's position officially recognized than he assigned Heydrich a similar duel command, Chief of the Security Police (a state agency) and the SD (an SS and Party organization

---

[16] Aronson, *Heydrich*, Chapters 3-5, on the consolidation of the political police under Himmler and Heydrich.

[17] The full implications of Himmler's double title are best explained in Hans Buchheim, 'Die SS – Das Herrschaftsinstrument', in *Anatomie des SS-Staates*, vol. 1 (Olten 1965), 59-67.

financed through the Party and not part of the civil administration). The Security Police (Sipo) were a fusion of the new Reich-wide Gestapo and the Reich Criminal Police, united under Heydrich's command.[18]

Although Himmler and Heydrich commanded these police forces, there was no other official connection between the SS or SD and the police. The police were state agencies; the SS and SD were only organizations of the Nazi Movement. Consequently, Himmler and Heydrich deliberately encouraged an overlapping of personnel. Before the power seizure, the SS and SD had managed to attract some professional policemen as members. In 1933 and 1934, Heydrich drew certain key officers from the political police of the *Länder* into the SD. After 1935, he began a concentrated effort to make all suitable political policemen members of the SD. After 1936, the criminal police were also included. Those among them who fitted his purpose rose rapidly, because their professional know-how was immediately important, even indispensable. The small amateur SD did not provide the necessary police instrument for winning the internal power struggle, and both Himmler and Heydrich needed the professionals.[19]

In the summer of 1935, a survey of Gestapo personnel was compiled; its results are worth citing here as an example of the early interrelations. By that time, almost thirty per cent of the 608 people in the Berlin Gestapo Office were already members of the SD; however, in the entire Prussian Gestapo of more than 2,500, the proportion of SD men was less than nine per cent. Even so, about twenty per cent of the total did belong to various branches of the SS, and they were soon to be incorporated *in toto* into the SD.[20]

Heydrich's major motive for drawing his policemen into the SD was probably to tighten control over them. As their superior in the police system, he could only require them to obey legal orders, but

[18] Order of the RFSSuCdDP, 26 June 1936, T-175/423/2951255; and Buchheim, 'Die SS,' 63-65.

[19] Heydrich's appreciation of trained police personnel is revealed in his introduction to *Organisation und Meldedienst der Reichskriminalpolizei*, T-175/451/2967012 f.

[20] *Namentliches Verzeichnis der bei der Preußischen Geheimen Staatspolizei, stellv. Chef und Inspekteur und bei dem Geheimen Staatspolizeiamt in Berlin, beschäftigen männlichen Personen nach dem Stande vom 25. Juni 1935*, and similar reports for most of the Prussian *Staatspolizeistelle*, BDC/Mappe Polizei.

as members of the SS under his command in the SD, they were sworn to obey absolutely any order from Himmler or himself as a Führer order.[21]

As members of the SD, professional policemen were usually considered distinct, because most of them joined after the seizure of power. Consequently, there were many doubts as to their ideological commitment and motivation. The SS and Police empire being built by Himmler based its primary appeal to these professionals on the promise of releasing them from the more confusing liberal constitutional limitations that supposedly 'handcuffed' the police. They would have a free hand to perform their mission, i.e., protecting society from its antisocial elements. When this appeal was fused with the élitist image of the SS, the combined effect must have been most seductive. As members in the élite corps, they would now have a moral obligation to impose order and authority on the nation. Here was a self-image which could smother the negative picture of the police as the oppressors of the people, and which would help the policeman cope with whatever conflicts might arise from his role as law enforcer. Such appeals, coupled with the desire to keep a secure job, were sufficient for the majority of the pre-Nazi police to continue under Nazi and SS command. It is only fair to say that most of these policemen apparently expected that proper professional procedures would guard against serious abuse, and many were disturbed by subsequent developments.

For overall direction and the execution of the more extreme actions, Himmler and Heydrich relied upon a type of policemen usually called 'Gestapoists', but perhaps better labelled 'radical enforcers'. Such policemen wanted a free hand to eliminate antisocial elements, which they were willing to define in the most abstract terms. They argued that such people should have no rights and deserved no consideration, and always sloughed over the problem of distinguishing antisocials from good citizens. Their willingness to take on the duties of judge, jury and sometimes executioner meant that they too became easily involved in illegal 'dirty work'. It is usually emphasized that before being drawn into the SD, most of them had no real commitment to Nazism, and their lack of standing in the Movement made them especially beholden to Heydrich, who safe-guarded their careers. Nevertheless, they were

---

[21] For an elaboration of the significance of the concept of *Führer Befehl*, see Buchheim, 'Befehl und Gehorsam', *Anatomie*, 1: especially, 314–80.

almost unanimously right-wing nationalists, strongly anti-communist and often anti-semitic. Their real commitment, however, was to the absolutely free execution of their mission, which became an end in itself, taking them to the sort of radical extremes which made them most suitable tools for the police state. They were, therefore, looked down upon by the rest of the SD and by many other Nazis as blind and dangerous functionaries.[22] They added further confusion and incompatibility to the SD membership.

The last Gestapo chief, Heinrich Müller. was typical of these radical enforcers. He embodied their more extreme attitudes, and was the object of much fear and disgust from the 'more responsible' SD men. Unfortunately, his more extreme attitudes were rarely committed to writing, and we rely most heavily on other people's— usually his enemies'—descriptions.[23] As a professional policeman during the Weimar period, he had already gone beyond accepted legal restraints in his work against Leftist movements,[24] and under the Nazis he found the freedom he craved. Aside from believing in strong-arm tactics, he favoured a very minimal statement of police powers — i.e., they must be free to do whatever is necessary to carry out their mission.[25]

However, the use of Müller or the 'radical enforcer' as an example of the Gestapoist image can be misleading, for the Gestapo was by no means a uniform corps. To begin with, most professional policemen did not possess this 'radical enforcer' mentality. Furthermore, the professional policemen of the Gestapo were also joined

[22] Most of the literature on open-ended power tor the police was written by Sipo and SD's major propagandist, Werner Best, who provided the arguments for the 'radical enforcers'. Most widely published was *Die Deutsche Polizei* (Darmstadt 1941). A very concise statement can be found in 'Neubegründung des Polizeirechts', *Jahrbuch der Akademie für deutsches Recht*, 1937, 132–38, US National Archives Microfilm Publications, Microcopy T-82, Records of Nazi Cultural and Research Institutions, Roll 25, Item ADR-26, File Number 5224/4/37 (hereafter T-82/25/ADR-26/5224/4/37). After helping to establish extraordinary police power, Best broke with Heydrich partly over the extremes to which things were moving (see n. 15). On SD contempt for Gestapoists, Schellenberg, *The Schellenberg Memoirs* (London 1956), 177 f.; and for Party attitudes, letters of *Gauamtsleiter* and *Gauleiter* for Upper Bavaria to Deputy Führer, NSDAP, 12 December 1936, BDC/Party Correspondence File/Heinrich Müller.

[23] Schellenberg, *Memoirs*, 91.

[24] Letters of *Gauleitung Upper Bavaria to Deputy Führer*, NSDAP, 12 December 1936, BDC/Party Correspondence File/Müller.

[25] Müller to Best, *Ausserung zu der vorläufigen Formulierung des Polizei-Begriffes*, 5 May 1937, T-82/25/ADR-26/5224/4/37.

by a diverse group of former civilians. Between 1933 and 1936, untold hundreds of men entered the Gestapo from the SS and SD, giving its police professionalism a transfusion of the 'lay' revolutionary spirit. Many came over with proper civil service status from other offices of the state; a few were assigned to special positions directly; and many others rose through the ranks beginning as employees—even chauffeurs. After 1936, and especially after 1938, all new Security Police recruits had to meet SS standards and were recruited and indoctrinated simultaneously by the SD and their police office. By September 1939, the process of mutual penetration produced at least three thousand SD members in a Security Police of approximately twenty thousand, with the majority of these SD men in the Gestapo.[26] Still later, as manpower requirements rose, the ranks of the Gestapo were swollen by a wide variety of temporary personnel. Although it would come under the command of Heinrich Müller, a 'radical enforcer' of professional police origin, the Gestapo was never a monolithic body epitomized in one man.

As for the personnel of the Reich Criminal Police, they also had a distinct self-image and character which added further diversity to Sipo and SD. The German criminal police had traditionally stood aloof from and often disdained the political police because of their involvement in political work. To further complicate matters, the Reich Criminal Police had been fused into a centralized force in part as a counter to the Gestapo and the SD in the struggle for police power in the Third Reich. They were co-ordinated with Sipo and SD when Himmler won that struggle. The more technical nature of detective work impeded Nazi penetration and made the pre-Nazi, trained professionals indispensable; however, the criminal police had their share of 'radical enforcers', and their organization was by no means immune to the effects of growth and SD pentration.[27]

Meanwhile, by 1936, with the inclusion of growing numbers of

[26] T-175/239/EAP 173-b-05/2J contains material on the final requirements for careers in Sipo and SD, and some interesting exchanges between Best and Schellenberg over the relative time to be devoted to more traditional police and legal training vs. SD indoctrination. The three-thousand-man figure for 1939 is based on Merkel's defence summation, *IMT*, 21:506, and is probably an underestimate.

[27] On disdain for political police work, Hsi-Huey Liang, *The Berlin Police Force in the Weimar Republic* (Berkeley 1970), 122–24. The RuSHA files cited in n. 11 also deal with the inclusion of Kripo personnel into the SD.

professional policemen, the character of the SD was becoming even more diverse than that of the Sipo. Himmler's acquisition of police power complicated its already mixed mission and self-image. Riding on the coat-tails of the evolving Gestapo, the SD in 1934 had been recognized by the Party as its only official organ for internal intelligence; it then attained recognition and official co-operation from the military and from a succession of state administrative offices and the Foreign Ministry. Paradoxically, the very process of official recognition destroyed the SD's *raison d'être*. Every acknowledgment contained a limitation of the SD's field of action. The SD changed from a freewheeling cloak and dagger squad into a semi-official agency hedged in by bureaucratic struggles for competence. The legitimate position of the Gestapo especially undermined the SD's function. As the enemies of the Movement became outlawed as enemies of the state, the police could handle their prosecution and the SD was reduced to an auxiliary; it was officially denied any role in executive actions.[28]

As the SD found itself being edged out, its members grew increasingly insecure about their future. The result was greater competition, friction and hostility with the Gestapo, whom they considered their intellectual and ideological inferiors.[29]

As a result, the SD began to search for more distinct missions and a more secure reason for its existence. The search led in three directions. The first was very much in line with Himmlerian ideology — what he referred to as the 'ideological intelligence' role of the SD. The emphasis was to be on the investigation of the more

[28] Hess, *Anordnung*, 9 June 1934, Heydrich, *Befehl*, 8 December 1935, and Hess *Rundschreiben*, 14 February 1936, T-580/93/457; the first agreement with the military was *Vereinbarung betr. Aufgabentrennung auf dem Gebiete der Abwehr zwischen Wehrmacht einerseits und der Gestapo und SDdRFSS andererseits*, 17 January 1935, T-175/402/2926114 f.; *Zusammenarbeit der Behörden der allgemeinen und inneren Verwaltung mit dem Sicherheitsdienst des Reichsführers = SS (SD)*, 11 November 1938, and an elaboration of this order, 22 November 1938, T-175/414/2939671–73. Unofficial SD *Auswärtiges Amt* cooperation can be traced back to at least November 1938, when Ribbentrop approved payment to the SD for clandestine operations in Czechoslovakia (*Auswärtiges Amt* memo, 29 November 1938, NA/RG 238(NG-3325). An official recognition of RSHA foreign intelligence came on 26 October 1939, which, although it has not been found, is discussed in *Auswärtiges Amt, Aufzeichnung über den Einsatz des SD im Ausland*, 9 August 1940, NA/RG 238/NG-2316. Hoeppner testimony, *IMT*, 20:190 f.; and Ohlendorf testimony, 4:352 f.

[29] Aronson, *Heydrich*, Chapter 6, provides the best treatment of the early competition and its long-range effects.

abstract enemies of the *Volk* — the Jews, for instance, and the connections between 'international Jewry' and the more precisely defined enemies of the state under police jurisdiction. Instead of investigating the activities of Communist cells, ideological intelligence was concerned with studying the long-range objectives of international Communism.[30] Unfortunately, these investigations were not clearly distinct from Gestapo work, and ultimately led to more conflict and competition.

The second direction would develop the SD into a foreign intelligence agency. The SD had dabbled in intelligence and fifth column activities in foreign countries since at least 1933. This role involved more conflict and competition with state offices, especially with the *Abwehr* (miliary intelligence) and the Foreign Ministry, and a number of Party offices. The SD was slow in establishing a real foothold in the realm of foreign intelligence, and its activities did not really become significant until the war years. From then on, it fought a slow, but winning battle for a monopoly of foreign intelligence activities.[31]

The third direction in the search for a distinct mission eventually proved to be the answer for the more 'idealistic intellectuals'. The SD was to gather information to produce 'situation reports' to guide and enlighten Nazi leadership. The SD was not to be a spy network, but a reporting system on every sphere of German life and all developments of importance in business, the economy, arts and letters, the state administration and every other institution of German life. Moods and opinions from the highest to the lowest levels were to be presented 'objectively'. The SD man was not to ferret out troublemakers, but to keep the leadership in touch with the realities of German life.[32] In this way, the official mission of the SD would be that of a most comprehensive secret Gallup Poll rather than a police force or spy network.

[30] Himmler, 'Wesen und Aufgabe der SS und der Polizei', *IMT*, 29:223 f.; Arendt, *Eichmann*, 37, 40 f.; and statement of Dieter Wisliceny, Bratislawa, 18 November 1946, in Leon Poliakov and Josef Wulf, *Das Dritte Reich und die Juden* (Berlin 1955), 87 f.

[31] The agreements with the military and Foreign Ministry (n. 28) pertain to early SD foreign intelligence activities. The subsequent struggle for monopoly is described in Schellenberg, *Memoiren*.

[32] NA/RG 238/Ohlendorf testimony, 26 November 1945 (1500–1715), 2; and *Vernehmung des Zeugen Otto Ohlendorf am 23. Juni 1947 vom 10.30–12.00*, 14–16. The history of the development of the situation reports is summarized in Boberach, *Meldungen aus dem Reich*, 7–17; and Arthur L. Smith, 'Life in Wartime Germany: Colonel Ohlendorf's Opinion Service', *Public Opinion Quarterly* (Spring 1972), 1–7.

This turmoil over a mission for the SD helped to further cloud the reality of what 'the SD' had become. By the late 1930s, the increasingly varied membership and a number of not necessarily compatible missions were producing a severe case of 'multiple schizophrenia' from which the SD self-image never recovered. From the broadest point of view, 'the SD' had become two distinct things: the *functioning SD*, consisting of the SD members in SD offices responsible for a wide variety of intelligence duties; and the *total SD*, a manpower pool, which included many policemen as members of the SS through the SD. The *total SD* was to be an élite above Party and state whose mission it was to convert the Sipo and the *functioning SD* into the future internal security force of the Reich. To belong to the *functioning SD* was to belong automatically to the *total SD*.

SD membership had become so complex, its different images so incompatible that one might say it had become schizophrenic. Within the *total SD*, it was impossible to reconcile the terroristic police work and illegal 'dirty work' with the image of the *functioning SD* as the 'idealistic intellectuals' wanted to see it.

During 1938 and 1939, while Himmler and Heydrich developed plans for solving some of their more pragmatic problems, they inadvertently inflamed this SD crisis of identity. Organizationally, the product of these plans was the fusion of the Sipo and SD into a more unified command under a semiofficial state office, the Reich Security Main Office (RSHA). After more than a year of organizational development, the RSHA acquired a seven-office structure: (I) Personnel (Sipo and SD); (II) Organization, Administration and Law (Sipo and SD); (III) SD Internal Intelligence; (IV) Gestapo (Sipo); (V) Criminal Police (Sipo); (VI) SD Foreign Intelligence; (VII) Ideological Investigation (SD). The RSHA was the *de facto* central headquarters for the entire structure of Sipo and SD.[33]

As part of Heydrich's effort to keep the organization from being controlled by his professional policemen, he intended the administrative and personnel offices (I and II) of the new RSHA to be run by the 'proper sort' of personnel from the *total SD*, and in reality

[33] The 1938–39 staff studies for the reorganization of Sipo and SD can be found in T-175/239/EAP 173-b-05/1A, -05/2B, -05/2J, -05/2K, -05/2L, -05/2M, -10-16/2, and T-175/432/EAP 173-b-05/2F. The final seven-office structure found expression in the *Geschäftsverteilungsplan der RSHA*, 1 March 1941, T-175/232/2721071–150.

to be administrative offices of the *total SD* rather than mere state offices which also administered the *functioning SD*. Legalistic, technical and real power problems prevented him from creating a *de jure* RSHA of the sort he planned;[34] however, given time and a peacetime rate of growth, Heydrich's *de facto* organization and its recruitment and training programme might well have succeeded in creating the Sipo and SD he desired.

It is precisely this sort of web of legalistic and conceptual distinctions which lies at the heart of the shifting sands of image and reality which helped to suck men into the extremes of Sipo and SD work. The distinction between RSHA offices as state offices or as offices of the *total SD* standing above state and law is a case in point. For instance, Hans Buchheim's analysis of the RSHA offices was excellent as far as it went. He was clear about the mixture of the formerly separate Sipo and SD offices in Office I; however, he did not discuss the role of the *total SD* in this conjunction, although he treated it thoroughly elsewhere. Instead, he emphasized legal organizational problems in discussing Office I. Perhaps that is what induced Heinz Höhne to emphasize that Office I was an office of the *state*, thereby obscuring its significance.[35] If this confuses scholars today, one can be sure such subtle distinctions clouded the minds of the men who lived with them. They made the crisis less pressing for the SD man who had to weigh 'legal' orders and assignments against his moral conscience, already weakened by racist doctrines.

To make matters worse, when the RSHA was formed, the other part of the SD's schizophrenic self-image, the older *functioning SD*, was broken down into three separate missions represented by the offices finally numbered II, VI and VII. Office III was SD Internal Intelligence, Otto Ohlendorf's idealistic and intellectual information service, which was to give proper guidance to National Socialism. As part of the process of maintaining its self-image, this SD office was relieved of all distasteful responsibilities for the prosecution of

[34] Heydrich's plans for *Ämter* I and II evolved in Schellenberg's memoranda, 4 and 25 April, 1939, T-175/239/2728107 f., 2728633, 2728639–42. On the hindering of these plans, Schellenberg, *Memoiren*, 34; and Ohlendorf testimony, *IMT*, 4: 326-28. The difference between the plans and Himmler's order establishing the RSHA are obvious, *Die Zussammenfassung der Zentralen Ämter der Sicherheitspolizei und des SD*, 27 September 1939, 361-L, *IMT*, 38:102–4.
[35] Buchheim, 'Die SS', 76 f.; and Höhne, *Der Orden*, 237.

or direct spying on the enemies of the Reich.[36]

Office VII, Ideological Investigation, fitted the SD intellectual mould as the archival service for all branches of Sipo and SD, and as the agency for the more ideologically oriented racial investigations.[37] Here the SD intellectuals gathered the 'scientific' knowledge to convince themselves of the necessity for 'unpleasant' racial programmes.

Office VI was SD Foreign Intelligence, where 'the SD' image had a different twist. Under the leadership of Walter Schellenberg, there was an aspiration to become the sole foreign intelligence agency of the Third Reich. They strove for an image of the professional intelligence service, autonomous, independent of the unsavoury element of Sipo and SD (especially the Gestapo), and free from partisan interests. They sought to advise the leadership in foreign affairs. Of course, these men could not limit their image to an academic and scientific respectability like that sought by the rest of the functioning SD. By its very nature, secret service work in foreign countries implies an extra-legal and amoral derring-do which they had no desire to deny. It was part of their carefully cultivated image — the only image that former SD men bragged about in their memoirs. Even the less sensational Schellenberg had lapses which revealed his romantic inclinations; for instance, his descriptions of his office with secret microphones, electronic gadgets and hidden machine guns could have come straight out of James Bond. The romantic secret service agent with a licence to kill was part of their identity, but it too was an élitist concept. The rootless dirty-work

[36] Ohlendorf testimony, *IMT*, 4:328. For the transfer of SD offices related to executive actions, RSHA, *Überleitung des Arbeitsgebietes III 2 des Sicherheitsdienstes RFSS auf die Geheime Staatspolizei*, 13 October 1939, T-175/239/2728778–81; Schellenberg memorandum, 24 February 1939, T-175/239/278177–80, expresses the intent to limit the SD mission to pure intelligence; and CdSuSD, *Geschäftsverteilungsplan des Reichssicherheitshauptamtes*, 1 February 1940, T-175/232/2720809–14. For examples of the SD's idealistic self-image and the concept of the role of its reports, SD instructions, *Lageberichterstattung auf dem Gebiet: Allgemeine Propaganda, Presse, Schrifttum, Rundfunk*, 12 September 1940, *Zur Einfügung in die Arbeitsanweisung III A Rechtsordnung und Reichsaufbau*, 10 November 1941, and *Arbeitsanweisung für die Referate III A 4III C*, 1 August 1941, T-175/225/2763720–23, 54–57, 84–87.

[37] In the first organization of the RSHA, it was numbered *Amt* II; its final position was set by CdSuSD, *Geschäftsverteilungsplan*, 1 March 1941, T-175/232/2721142–49. For an example of the *Amt* VII archival work, *Tätigkeitsbericht des Amtes VII für den Monat September 1942*, T-175/466/2986785–95.

man was a blot on the desired image of the sophisticated, suave professional.[38]

At about the same time as the creation of the RSHA, another problem arose to further complicate the SD image. It was the Special Action Groups, the *Einsatzgruppen* of the Sipo and SD. These were police teams which had followed the Army into Austria, Czechoslovakia and then Poland. Their role in the Polish invasion presaged their mission as mass murder squads on the Russian front. These *Einsatzgruppen* were commanded by officers of the *total SD,* but their ranks were filled with men often drawn from outside Sipo and SD. Nevertheless, all of these men wore SD insignia and were paid and administered through the Sipo and SD system.[39]

At this point, the rather confused development of 'the SD' needs to be summarized. After the official fusion of 1936, Sipo and SD became nominally united under Heydrich's command. By the autumn of 1939, when their organizational relations were further tightened and the intermixture of their personnel was increasing rapidly, Sipo and SD really became a single body transcending both Party and state structures. Consisting of the Security Police (the Gestapo and the Criminal Police) and the SD, this organ was centrally commanded by Heydrich through the Reich Security Main Office. It must be considered a single unit, Sipo-and-SD, the Security Force of the Third Reich, which included the *Einsatzgruppen.* Sometimes this conglomerate was erroneously called 'the SD'.[40] By the end of the war, Sipo and SD probably included over fifty thousand personnel, plus twenty-one thousand attached personnel, including *Einsatzgruppen.*[41]

[38] CdSuSD, *Geschäftsverteilungsplan,* 1 February 1940, T-175/232/2720821–24, The development of Schellenberg's desire to free *Amt* VI of the stigma of association with other elements of the SS, Sipo and SD can be traced in the latter part of his *Memoirs* (also see n. 48); for his romantic lapses, 241 f.

[39] At Nuremberg, Ohlendorf frankly revealed the administrative and personnel relationship between RSHA, Sipo and SD, and the *Einstatzgruppen, IMT,* 4: 313–25, 354.

[40] Ohlendorf testimony, *IMT,* 4: 328.

[41] The estimates of the final size of Sipo vary widely, but the most accurate seems to be 32,000 to 35,000 for the Gestapo (allowing for growth after the end-of-1944 estimate in Gestapo Affidavit 31, *IMT,* 21: 295. This is consistent with an RSHA report containing *Iststärkenachweisung der Sicherheitspolizei . . . und des SD, Stand 1.1.1944,* T-175/240/2730236, which gives 31,374 as a total), and 15,000 to 20,000 for the Kripo (Schellenberg's estimate, *IMT,* 4: 380). The estimate for attached personnel is in Affidavit 31; however, an undetermined percentage of the attached personnel worked under SD offices and *Amt Mil.,* a late addition to RSHA.

Within the personnel of this mixture of organizations was an élite core, the bulk of the leadership and all new recruits, who were members of the SS through the SD. This smaller body of men constituted the *total SD,* the élite corps which was supposed to imbue the future Security Force of the Third Reich with the proper spirit. At the beginning of the war, at least fifteen per cent of Sipo personnel were members of this *total SD;* there are no reliable estimates for what happened thereafter.[42]

More than one third of the offices in the organizational structure of Sipo and SD were also 'the SD' — that is, those branches under the RSHA responsible for executing SD intelligence missions. These offices and their personnel, only part of the *total SD,* were the *functioning SD.* Since this functioning SD now fell under three separate offices, it had ceased to be a single organization.[43] Members of each branch frequently tended to refer to their group as 'the SD'. The full-fledged members of this *functioning SD* undoubtedly exceeded seven thousand by the end of the war.[44]

This was the confusion which was brought to trial at Nuremberg when 'the SD' was charged as a criminal organization. Properly speaking, the SD was at least two things: the *total SD* and the *functioning SD.* However, if one ever wishes to understand the

[42] The estimate given by the Gestapo defence for September 1939 (see n. 26) was fifteen per cent. Given the problems inherent in defining SD membership (see n. 44), it is presently impossible to arrive at reasonably reliable figures for the *total SD* or the *functioning SD,* as a basis for testing this estimate.

[43] Hoeppner testimony, *IMT,* 20:187.

[44] The *Iststärkenachweisung* for Sipo and SD, 1 January 1944, T-175/240/2730236, listed the *SD des RFSS* at 6,482. Considering the size of the *total SD* at the end of 1938 (n. 6), this must represent the *functioning SD.* Schellenberg (*IMT,* 4:380) estimated the final size of his *Amt* VI at four hundred, and Ohlendorf (*IMT,* 4:329, 351) estimated all 'employees' of his *Amt* III at three thousand. *Amt* VII may have resembled *Amt* VI in size. The difference between these Nuremberg estimates and the over seven-thousand estimate of this paper lies in the problem of defining 'SD membership'. This problem makes it extremely difficult to give any reliable estimates of the size of the SD. As in the SS, proper SD membership consisted of two categories: official, salaried *(hauptamtlich)* members, and part-time, unsalaried *(ehrenamtlich)* members (the more common English translation of *ehrenamtlich* as 'honorary' does not fit this particular usage). Both types manned the offices of the SD, but statistics in some cases may only list the 'salaried employees'. The problem is made greater by the existence of several types of clandestine membership or affiliation with the SD which did not fall under either the *hauptamtlich* or *ehrenamtlich* category. Few of these clandestine types would appear in statistics, only some left records indicating membership, and the majority had only an affiliation rather than true membership (i.e., the trusted agents or V-men of *Amt* III whom Ohlendorf, nevertheless, referred to loosely as 'honorary members' [*IMT,* 4:329]).

225

complexity of the Nuremberg testimonies, documents of the Nazi period, or the statements of any surviving oral sources, he must realize that 'the SD' is a term the definition of which changes radically according to context. In common usage, 'the SD' could be all of Sipo and SD or the *Einsatzgruppen*. Used more accurately, 'the SD' was the *total SD* or the *functioning SD* or any one of its three component offices. 'The SD' was several different things to each individual who used the term and to each member of the *total SD*. This confusion not only provided an obscurantist defence at Nuremberg, but also a trap which many men built for themselves and others between 1933 and 1945.

The trap was the image of an élite organization so vaguely defined that it seemed to fulfil the needs of a wide variety of men. The *total SD* was supposed to be a highly selective inner élite which would be the Security Force of the Third Reich. Given time, Heydrich might have been able to build the sort of disciplined and devoted élite corps he and Himmler visualized. Unfortunately for his plans, the necessities of war and the unexpected inclusion of such vast territory so greatly overextended the Sipo and SD that Heydrich, his successor, Ernst Kaltenbrunner, and each of their agencies were constantly forced to modify and compromise their plans and ideals. Sipo and SD and its inner élite, the *total SD,* were flooded with the new personnel necessary for their ever-expanding functions. Many military personnel no longer suitable for active duty and old, often retired police bureaucrats filled the ranks of Sipo and SD.[45] The *total SD* could not possibly keep up with its mission.

This is not to say that 'the Sipo' absorbed 'the SD'. Both organizations were overwhelmed by the numbers needed for their expanded functions. Arguments about who absorbed whom become meaningless.

The upshot was that the *total SD* became a synthesis of ideological revolution, expediency and necessity — an overblown collection of romantic revolutionaries and bureaucrats, idealists

[45] On the extensive use of drafted personnel, RFSSuCdDP, *Pensionierte Kriminalbeamte im Verstärkten Polizeischutz*, 12 August 1938; and CdS, *Kennziffer z111c (Einstellung von Ersatzkräften)*, 20 September 1938, T-175/240/ 2729961, 2729969 f., which show this was a recognized necessity even before the war began; Bilfinger testimony, *IMT*, 12: 49 f.; and Schellenberg, *Memoirs*, 413. On efforts at caution in selecting older personnel, CdS order, *Einstellung von Berufssoldaten in den hauptamtlichen Dienst der Sipo u. SD*, August 1940, T-175/277/5488408–10.

and self-seekers, and adventurers and experts. Nevertheless although it may have failed in its 'revolutionary mission' in the face of wartime problems, it succeeded frighteningly well in holding together the mixed components of the machinery for police terror. It succeeded in tapping the services of thousands of men whose self-image remained that of the professional police — not part of 'the SD', not really drawn into the SS, not tainted by 'political' work. Regardless of the image of the branch to which he belonged, the professional detective could find himself doing Gestapo work, and any Sipo man could be involved in the execution of Nazi racial programmes. If he needed it, the organizational maze allowed him the myth that this work was not part of his professional service, merely extra unpleasant assignments.[46]

The *functioning SD* also failed to live up to its idealistic images. It is true that those SD offices under Eichmann which acquired the executive function of solving the Jewish problem were transferred to the Gestapo,[47] ridding the *functioning SD* of those *directly* involved in genocide. Even so, adventurers such as Alfred Naujocks remained in offices of the *functioning SD* as long as there were extralegal jobs to be done. In defence of their self-images, SD idealists tried to purge themselves of the likes of Naujocks. Schellenberg boasted of it in his memoirs, while Naujocks developed a well-earned persecution complex.[48]

Nevertheless, the SD 'intellectuals' strove in vain for respectability and service commensurate with their brand of idealism. They never controlled the decision-making process of the Third Reich. On the contrary, when SD reports made it increasingly obvious that the war and the Movement were lost, the barons of the Reich, like Bormann, Goebbels and Himmler, obstructed the circulation of SD reports and finally denied the SD access to official sources of information-gathering.[49] As for Schellenberg's Foreign Intelligence Office, its absorption of *Abwehr* (military intelligence) in the final months of the war was a victory in defeat. Even

[46] Merkel's defence summation, *IMT*, 21: 507 f., 512 f., 532.
[47] See n. 36 on the transfer of offices.
[48] On the 'persecution' of Naujocks, Peis, *The Man Who Started the War*, 167–69, 186. For Schellenberg's version of his general purge of *Amt* VI, *Memoirs*, 221 f., 233 f.
[49] Boberach, *Meldungen aus dem Reich*, 27–30. For Ohlendorf's version of his defeat, NA/RG 238/testimony, 29 October 1945, 2–4, 7 f.

if his office could have affected strategic and foreign policy decisions, it was too late. This other half of the SD self-image also met with failure.

From the above, it should be obvious that the picture of the SD as an idealistic intelligence service was not conjured up entirely for the defence at Nuremberg. The Otto Ohlendorfs and Walter Schellenbergs strove for it throughout the history of the Third Reich. They vainly sought to separate themselves from the unpleasant and distasteful activities of the Gestapo and from much of what the *total SD* implied.[50] Try as they might, however, they were members of this *total SD*. They could still be required to spy and inform, but worst of all, they might have to serve in the infamous *Einsatzgruppen*, where they were called upon to participate personally in mass murder.

SD defendants and witnesses at Nuremberg repeatedly confused the issue, referring sometimes to the *total SD*, sometimes to the *functioning SD*, and at other times to 'the SD' as if it were only one specific office. They sought to differentiate themselves from the Gestapo and other SD personnel involved in criminal acts. Like the police, they always refused to acknowledge any commitment to the *total SD*. In this way, they were also able to deny a direct relationship between *their* definition of the SD and the *Einsatzgruppen*, for instance. They argued that their service in the murder squads was the result of a draft which temporarily removed them from their SD offices.[51]

Such a wilful fragmentation of the various aspects of the SD was much more than a phony defence in a trial for their lives. There was much more at stake, as revealed by Ohlendorf's frank, sometimes almost penitent confession of his role as head of an *Einsatzgruppe* responsible for the murder of approximately ninety thousand Jews. Since he was unable to deny that role to himself or to anyone else, he tried to depict it as an unpleasant duty separate from his chosen mission. Such a man as Ohlendorf was not just pleading for his life, but for his self-image. He fell back on the argument that he had obligations to society and to

[50] For efforts to involve *Amt* III in police spying and Ohlendorf's resistance, NA/RG 238/testimony, 25 October 1945 (p.m.), 16; and for Schellenberg's disdain for and frustrated effort to avoid an executive assignment, *Memoirs*, 409–11.

[51] Ohlendorf testimony, *IMT*, 4:328; Hoeppner testimony, *IMT*, 20:198, 203–33; and Höttl testimony, *IMT*, 11:229, cf. 256.

law and order, and, therefore, had to submit to men and institutions too powerful for him to resist.

The frustrated intellectuals could not admit to themselves that the ideology which they sought to direct had captured them and carried them along to the inhumane and self-destructive conclusions which were inherent in the logic of their own racist world view. They could not admit that, like any other member of the *total SD*, they had been seduced by a shifting image of inner élitism and that they had prostituted themselves in vain. Instead, they clung stubbornly and blindly to their idealistic self-image. They tried to separate their roles in the SD and their definition of the SD from the totality of their involvement in and their indispensable contribution to the Third Reich.

Had Arthur Nebe, head of the Criminal Police, survived his involvement in the attempt to assassinate Hitler, his efforts to defend his role as an *Einsatzgruppen* leader would have been equally revealing. Undoubtedly, his justifications would have been similar to those of the intellectuals.

The members of the *total SD* had only two things in common: a basic attitude which could fit in with the flexible Nazi *Weltanschauung*, and a strong need to be a member of an élite. Their inability to agree on the details of the ideology or on what constituted their éliteness within Teutonic éliteness allowed many SD members to be self-righteously idealistic while serving in the efficient terror instrument of the Nazi police state. It enabled completely incompatible types to work together, while providing fulfilment only for the amoral opportunists and allowing only the most perverted 'radical enforcers' to come near consistently realizing their self-image.

Otto Ohlendorf, the Sicherheitsdienst and Public Opinion in Nazi Germany

Lawrence D. Stokes

The history of the *Sicherheitsdienst* (Security Service or SD) of the *Reichsführer* SS falls into three phases. The first preceded the Nazi 'assumption of power' on 30 January 1933 and was the beginning of the organization under Reinhard Heydrich. The second period, from 1933 to 1936, saw the SD's efforts to establish itself within the 'new order' alongside the other major Nazi police instrument, the Gestapo.[1] The last phase began when Otto Ohlendorf, later head of the Third Department (*Amt* III) of the wartime 'Main Office for National Security' (*Reichssicherheitshauptamt* or RSHA), joined the SD and ended with his arrest in 1945. From its founding until 1936 the SD primarily helped detect individuals and groups dangerous to Hitler's rule, including those within the Nazi party. After Ohlendorf entered it and especially following the outbreak of war, the SD also attempted to provide the Nazi leadership with a continuous and unbiased picture of German public opinion. It thereby became the most important and controversial office reporting on popular morale and attitudes towards the regime.[2] The difficulties it encountered

---

[1] The evolution of the SD up to 1936 and its complementary although often conflicting relations with the Gestapo are traced in Shlomo Aronson, *Reinhard Heydrich und die Frühgeschichte von Gestapo und SD* (Stuttgart 1971); see also L. D. Stokes, 'The *Sicherheitsdienst* (SD) of the *Reichsführer* SS and German Public Opinion, September 1939–June 1941', unpublished Ph.D. dissertation, Johns Hopkins University 1972, chs. 1 and 2.

[2] In addition to the SD and the Gestapo other offices included the regional heads of governmental administration (the *Regierungspräsidenten*); the 'Information Office' of the Labour Front; the local offices of Joseph Goebbels' Ministry of Propaganda; the party 'indoctrination officers' (*Schulungsleiter*) under Alfred Rosenberg; local, county and provincial Nazi leaders (*Ortsgruppen-, Kreis-* and *Gauleiter*); and, during the closing months of the war, the Propaganda Department of the *Wehrmacht* High Command. See Stokes, op. cit., 12 ff. and the literature cited there: also Franz Dröge, *Der zerredete Widerstand. Zur Soziologie und Publizistik des Gerüchts im 2. Weltkrieg* (Düsseldorf 1970), ch. 2.

largely resulted from the essential dichotomy in the SD's status: it was both a police agency supplying members to execute Nazism's criminal acts[3] and simultaneously sought to be an impartial monitor of popular opinion, even claiming to be a substitute 'loyal opposition'. Its schizophrenic nature condemned the SD to ineffectualness within the Nazi system, whose leaders wanted to know public opinion but not follow its dictates if these threatened their retention of power. Force, not consent, was the basis of Hitler's rule.

OTTO OHLENDORF, more than either Heydrich or Heinrich Himmler, was identified with the SD during its final phase. His command of a mobile killing squad (*Einsatzgruppe* D) of the 'Security Police and the SD' in Russia between June 1941 and June 1942, which killed some 90,000 men, women and children, has left Ohlendorf with the reputation of an 'intellectual thug', an 'academic gangster', and a cold-blooded mass murderer. The death sentence an American military court imposed on him was carried out in Landsberg prison on 8 June 1951.[4] The publication of some of

[3] Cf. Alwin Ramme, *Der Sicherheitsdienst der SS. Zu seiner Funktion im faschistischen Machtapparat und im Besatzungsregime des sogenannten Generalgouvernements Polen* (East Berlin 1970).

[4] Edward Crankshaw, *Gestapo: Instrument of Tyranny* (New York 1956), 100; Walter Laqueur, 'Rewriting History', *Commentary*, LV (March 1973), 55. The participation of SD members in the *Einsatzgruppen* is the best illustration of the organization's dual function; Ohlendorf's experiences are a case in point. He was sharply critical of the harsh treatment accorded the Polish and Ukrainian populations by such Nazis as *Reichskommissar* Erich Koch and advocated instead a rational *Ostpolitik* including support for the anti-Soviet army recruited among Russian prisoners-of-war led by General Andrei Vlasov. He also tried to evade service in the east and initially protested at Hitler's order to kill all Jews, communist functionaries, and gypsies in the rear of the German forces. The mental strain involved in shooting defenceless populations, he argued, made the task impossible. His concern for the psychological effects of such operations on those carrying them out was nevertheless outweighed by his conviction that, in Germany's life-and-death struggle against 'Bolshevism', even the most ruthless acts decreed by the Führer had to be performed. The executions, he maintained, not only sought to achieve security, 'but also permanent security because the Jewish [and gypsy] children would [otherwise] grow up and surely, being the children of parents who had been killed, they would constitute a danger no smaller than that of their parents'. Furthermore, Jews played so significant a part in the administration of the USSR and in the partisan movement that their execution *en masse* was necessary if Stalin's regime was to be destroyed. Mainly to ease the 'moral strain' on his men, Ohlendorf ordered that the shootings be conducted 'in the most humane and military manner possible'—with submachine guns and rifles while the naked victims stood in an anti-tank ditch. He insisted (wrongly) that it

the wartime public opinion reports produced by Ohlendorf's *Amt III*,[5] however, has lately directed attention to other activities of this 'Grand Inquisitor . . . with a pedantic mania for regarding everything as an object of scientific analysis', this 'paragon' and 'Saint-Juste germanique' who tirelessly pointed out to Nazi leaders the consequences of their policies.[6] Historians have thereby been encouraged also to re-examine National Socialism's impact upon Germany and the German people.[7]

Ohlendorf was born on 4 February 1907, the youngest child of a Protestant and national–liberal farmer in Hoheneggelsen, near Hildesheim.[8] This rural background helped form his ideal of an

[5] Heinz Boberach (ed.), *Meldungen aus dem Reich. Auswahl aus den geheimen Lageberichten des Sicherheitsdienstes der SS 1939–1944* (Berlin 1965). A comprehensive supplementary collection of Nazi police documents on church topics has also been edited by Boberach, *Berichte des SD und der Gestapo über Kirchen und Kirchenvolk in Deutschland 1934–1944* (Mainz 1971).

[6] Gerald Reitlinger, *The SS: Alibi of a Nation, 1922–1945* (London 1957; 2nd rev. ed.), 43; Heinz Höhne, *Der Orden unter dem Totenkopf. Die Geschichte der SS* (Gütersloh 1967), 218; François Bayle, *Psychologie et éthique du national-socialisme: Étude anthropologique des dirigeants SS* (Paris 1953), 36.

[7] Cf. Hartmut Jäckel, ' "Meldungen aus dem Reich". Die deutsche Heimatfront 1939–1945', *Der Monat*, no. 212, 1966, 48–57; Marlis G. Steinert, *Hitlers Krieg und die Deutschen. Stimmung und Haltung der deutschen Bevölkerung im Zweiten Weltkrieg* (Düsseldorf 1970), 588 ff.; Stokes, op. cit., especially 516–25 (conclusion).

[8] The details of his biography are found in *Trials of War Criminals before the Nuremberg Military Tribunals* (Washington 1949), IV, 223 ff., testimony of Otto Ohlendorf (Case no. 9, the 'Einsatzgruppen Case', hereafter *TWC*); unless otherwise indicated, all subsequent quotations from the published transcript of Ohlendorf's trial are his own testimony. See also Internationaler Militärgerichtshof Nürnberg (hereafter *IMG*), *Der Prozess gegen die Hauptkriegsverbrecher vor dem internationalen Militärgerichtshof Nürnberg 14. November 1945–1. Oktober 1946* (Nürnberg 1947 f.), IV, 344–45, testimony of Otto Ohlendorf; Aronson, op. cit., 210–14; Höhne, op. cit., 197–98, 217 ff.; Boberach (ed.), *Meldungen*, xiii ff.

was impossible to evade service in the *Einsatzgruppen*: the only alternatives were an SS court-martial followed by a 'gruesome' death sentence or a 'senseless martyrdom through suicide'. All he could do, Ohlendorf pleaded, was to save a few individual Jews from execution and try to win over the rest of the population for the occupier. Like other SD members, Ohlendorf was prepared to 'solve' any problem put to him by the Führer, who was alone responsible for Germany's fate. He applied the same scientific precision with which he had studied Nazism's enemies to destroying them. Ohlendorf thus seemed to personify 'Dr Jekyll and Mr Hyde': notwithstanding his self-confessed crimes, shocked spectators at his trial often felt sympathy for the 'upright-looking . . . straightforward, honest character' of the scholarly monitor of German public opinion. Even the Vice-Chancellor of the Federal Republic tried in vain to prevent his hanging as contrary to the provisions of the 'Basic Law' which abolished the death penalty. Cf. Stokes, op cit., 90–92, 152, 164 ff., 167–72; Sven Steenberg, *Vlasov* (New York 1970), especially 129–33; G. M. Gilbert, *Nuremberg Diary* (New York 1947), 101; Reinhard Henkys, *Die nationalsozialistischen Gewaltverbrechen. Geschichte und Gericht* (Stuttgart 1965; 2nd rev. ed.), 204.

harmonious social order resting upon small-scale entrepreneurs. He eventually studied law and economics at Leipzig and Göttingen, passing his bar examinations in July 1933. His ambition was to teach economics in a university.

Ohlendorf's Nazi career had begun in 1925, at eighteen years of age, when he joined the *Sturmabteilung Hitler* and soon afterwards the party. His motives combined attraction to the national, social and worker aspects of the movement (without the Marxism of the socialists) and rejection of the 'bourgeois class selfishness' of the German National People's Party. What developed into continual disagreement with his superiors began almost immediately: 'In 1926 there were the first differences between myself and my superiors in the party. I did not agree with . . . [their] personal and factual views. Therefore, from 1926 to 1933 I did not work within the official party'.

In October 1933, Ohlendorf became an assistant to Jens Peter Jessen, Professor of Economics at the *Institut für Weltwirtschaft*, Kiel University. He only held the post a few months. The two objected strenuously to so-called 'national Bolshevist' (meaning collectivist and state socialist) tendencies in the local party which, they claimed, were spreading to many government ministries. As a result, Ohlendorf was arrested at the party's behest in February 1934; Jessen barely escaped the same fate. The latter was forced, though, to leave Kiel; Ohlendorf was dismissed too 'because I was a factor of political unrest there'. After this experience he wrote to his wife: 'Something in me has been shaken. I don't any longer have the same carefree certainty with which I struggled for our [idea of] National Socialism'. Ohlendorf never overcame his disillusionment with the reality of National Socialism, although he kept trying to 'reform' Hitler's movement in a direction he could approve.

After the Kiel fiasco, Ohlendorf moved to Berlin where he and Jessen wanted to build an economics institute to oppose 'national Bolshevist' influences in the party with 'real representatives of National Socialism'. But these plans, too, were ruined after Alfred Rosenberg attacked Jessen in the *Völkischer Beobachter*. Another position was lost following party protests that Ohlendorf was too critical of Nazi agricultural policy. Finally he joined the party censorship commission.[9] In effect, the movement he wanted to serve had rejected him.

[9] *TWC*, IV, 226–27.

Ohlendorf's entrance into the SD, which seemed his last chance in the party, was arranged by Jessen who had been offered a post as specialist for economic questions in SD headquarters (*Hauptamt*) by the director of its Central Division II/2, Reinhard Höhn.[10] Jessen declined, and recommended Ohlendorf instead. Höhn was impressed with his 'very critical political opinions concerning practical National Socialism' which, he said, were 'just what the SD was looking for'. Höhn wanted to shift the emphasis of the SD's work from observing opponents of the regime (*Gegnerbeobachtung*), as it had hitherto chiefly done, to reporting on broad spheres of German life (*Lebensgebietsarbeit*). He described the SD to Ohlendorf as an organization which, 'since there was no more public criticism . . . would have as its mission to inform the leading organizations of the party and the state about National Socialist developments, and especially as regards wrong tendencies, abuses, etc.'. This conception of the SD was adopted by Ohlendorf and determined his work in it throughout the Third Reich.

Ohlendorf's first task was to set up his own section (*Hauptabteilung* II/23, 'the economy') which would direct an economic intelligence network to provide 'all the information in the field of economics which [it] was essential for National Socialist leaders to know concerning mistaken developments'. He found Höhn's Central Division, however, only in its initial stages, with some twenty members lacking secretarial, clerical and other assistance, and virtually no corresponding apparatus at the local level.[11] 'No one knew in detail what was wanted. Individual questions were taken up such as accidentally fell to an embryonic organization. The natural interests of its head [Höhn] constituted practically the entire content . . . . He was a political scientist and university professor, and therefore the first work of [Central

[10] For the biography of Höhn, a 'Nazi intellectual' whose career in the Third Reich resembled Ohlendorf's, see Aronson, op. cit., 212, 216, 305 n. 74; also Alfred Schweder, *Politische Polizei* (Berlin 1937), 152 f., 156 f., 189. For the structure of the SD when Ohlendorf joined it, see Stokes, op. cit., 74 ff.; Hans Buchheim, *Die SS—Das Herrschaftsinstrument. Befehl und Gehorsam* (Olten & Freiburg 1965), 240–41; Boberach (ed.), *Berichte*, xxxiv–xxxv.

[11] Höhn's Central Division was in its infancy, not the SD as a whole, as the literature on the organization usually implies; see, for example, Aronson, op. cit., 213. This error has led to a blurring of the SD's dual function: *Gegnerbeobachtung* and *-bekämpfung* continued to be carried on after Ohlendorf joined it, just as *Lebensgebietsarbeit* had also existed almost from its origins. Cf. Stokes, op. cit., 37, 77–80. His contribution was to continue Höhn's efforts to strengthen the one without abandoning the other.

Division II/2 of] the SD involved the universities and political science'. Notwithstanding these handicaps, Ohlendorf soon created an intelligence structure which gathered information about German economic life and employed specialists to analyse trends and evaluate their significance. Himmler was impressed with Ohlendorf's reports, although his first major investigation (of the German railway and communication network) was considered too controversial for publication and was locked away in Heydrich's safe.

Early in 1937, Höhn appointed Ohlendorf his deputy with special responsibility for applying his system of economic reporting to other *Lebensgebiete*. Heydrich's decree of 4 September 1937 defined the purpose of the work: 'The task of situation reporting (*Lageberichterstattung*) in the various areas of [German] life can only be one of revealing to what extent National Socialist ideology has asserted itself in each of these, and recording what resistance [it has encountered] and if so from whom; only from this point of view are reports about cultural or material questions or those affecting national life to be made'.[12] On a small scale, 'the basis for [a] comprehensive information service was worked out and organized' — the later *Amt* III of the RSHA. Central Division II/2 had three sections which together 'encompassed all the spheres of national life': (i) Culture, learning (*Wissenschaft*), education and 'folkdom' (*Volkstum*, that is ethnic, racial and minority questions); (ii) Administration and law, party and state, universities and student organizations; and (iii) The economy. These, in turn, were further subdivided: II/231, for example, handled agricultural and II/236 labour and social welfare questions. Beginning in January 1938 the Central Division received monthly reports from its regional offices based on the observations and analyses of SD officials, informants and volunteer 'specialists'. The format of the annual situation report (*Jahreslagebericht*) for 1938 was a graphic representation of the SD's two broad areas of work: whereas the opening part dealt with the various opponents of the regime, the remainder analysed the impact of developments during the preceding twelve months in the fields of law, administration, culture, learning, the economy and social policy.[13]

[12] Quoted in Boberach (ed.), *Meldungen*, xiv; see also Höhne, op. cit., 220.
[13] Friedrich Zipfel, *Kirchenkampf in Deutschland 1933–1945* (Berlin 1965), 458–85, document 53; *TWC*, IV, 228; Höhne, op. cit., 219; Dröge, op. cit., 230, n. 22; Aronson, op. cit., 213; Boberach (ed.), *Meldungen*, xiv–xv; Boberach (ed.), *Berichte*, 301–30, document 14.

Ohlendorf's initial period of activity in the SD was brief and indicative of some of the problems he subsequently faced as head of *Amt* III. His departure from the organization stemmed from differences with Himmler over two issues: one was the relationship between intelligence gathering and its evaluation, the other Ohlendorf's response to the course of Nazi economic policy. Central Division II/2 was not content merely to assemble information on the different *Lebensgebiete* in order to assess the extent of their Nazification, as Heydrich decreed. It also promoted alternative policies in certain areas when such seemed called for. One example was the SD's objection to efforts by various party organizations to dismiss non-Nazi university professors. According to Ohlendorf, '[we] pointed out that opportunist young careerists (*Kulturritter*) were certainly not suitable substitutes for the knowledge of the older teachers'. Another, which conjured up a more powerful array of opponents, involved SD resistance to the industrial undertakings of Göring's 'Four Year Plan' and the agricultural policies pursued by Walther Darré, head of the 'Reich Food Estate'. In an undated memorandum on 'The Economy in the National Socialist State', Ohlendorf attacked the *Reichsmarschall's* rearmament programme for producing 'unparalleled' economic tensions by 'strengthening large firms, weakening the others, eliminating private initiative in countless areas, instead promoting huge marketing and retailing organizations with all their disadvantages [and] interference in setting prices and wages'. In Ohlendorf's view, small and medium-sized independent businesses constituted 'the real social basis of the German economy'. But precisely these were endangered by Göring's 'national bolshevism' which used the plea of state necessity to take them over. As for Nazi agricultural policy, rigid governmental control of prices and land kept rural income down and prevented the sale of farms heavily burdened by debt. The methods the SD employed in these controversies were significant: 'We not only sought to record the actual [course of] these developments and to point out the catastrophic results of the closing of plants and of the structural changes, but also intervened in individual instances by personal conferences backed up with our intelligence material'.[14]

[14] *TWC*, IV, 228–29; Höhne, op. cit., 218–19; Felix Kersten, *Memoirs 1940–1945* (New York 1957), 207–8, entry for 29 August 1943. On Ohlendorf's opposition to the even more pronounced 'collectivistic and socialistic' features of the Nazi wartime economy, see Stokes, op. cit., 173–75.

Ohlendorf thus used the SD to gather information which he then utilized within the government in advocating his own economic and social policies.

As happened frequently after 1939, Himmler sided with Ohlendorf's opponents, particularly Darré, whose ideological support was essential to the *Reichsführer*'s racial mythology.[15] '[This was the beginning of] a perpetual struggle, of defeats, victories and still more defeats for the SD and myself'. Himmler was not interested in the economic questions at issue; instead, he objected to the SD's reporting because it was directed against Darré. Thereupon, Ohlendorf recalled, Himmler called him on the carpet for the first time and described him as a pessimist, an epithet which stuck for the remainder of the Third Reich. The *Reichsführer* denounced the SD for meddling in business, agricultural and university affairs which were the party's exclusive responsibility. It had only been intended as an intelligence service to combat the regime's enemies; anything else harmed the overall interests of the SS. Himmler thereby attempted to delimit the SD's *Lebensgebietsarbeit*. Moreover, in distinguishing between gathering information and advocating policies based on the data collected, he pointed to a basic conflict concerning the SD's functions which during the war again divided Ohlendorf and himself.

In the course of 1937, Reinhard Höhn was ousted from the SD.[16] This change in the leadership of Central Division II/2 was accompanied by alterations in the emphasis and method of its work. What Ohlendorf called the 'scientific' approach to reporting on *Lebensgebiete* was abandoned and its proponents 'put on the shelf'. Ohlendorf was confined once more to dealing with economic questions and wanted to quit the SD entirely. Heydrich at first refused but after lengthy negotiations agreed to permit him to give up full-time employment with the SD. In June 1938 he became business manager of the 900,000 member *Reichsgruppe Handel* (one of the seven broad divisions of the Nazi economy) in the Ministry of Economics, and the following November its managing director. From that vantage point he continued his fight against Nazism's 'economic collectivization'. This ended Otto Ohlendorf's first tour of duty with the SD.

[15] Cf. Josef Ackermann, *Heinrich Himmler als Ideologe* (Göttingen 1970), who calls Darré Himmler's 'intellectual mentor'.

[16] For the background to Höhn's removal, the discovery of sharp criticism of Hitler and the party in his pre-1933 writings, see Helmut Heiber, *Walter Frank und sein Reichsinstitut für Geschichte des neuen Deutschlands* (Stuttgart 1966), 880–937.

WHEN OHLENDORF RETURNED TO THE SD in the autumn of 1939 as part of his wartime service obligation, he sought to continue its work along the lines he and Höhn had pursued three years earlier. His ideal of a domestic intelligence agency,[17] formulated after the war, stemmed from his view that, whatever their political form and ideology, complex modern states characterized by an increasing fragmentation and specialization of their citizens' activities could only be led for the benefit of all through some measure of 'social engineering'.[18] Individualists acting autonomously could no longer ensure cultural and material progress; instead 'direction in the [different] areas of life and the shaping of classes' was needed. Particular interests should be controlled and guided by the state with its superior vision, commitment to the common good and ability to reconcile differences; otherwise, 'backward conditions, undesirable interruptions and errors' in social development would occur. 'In this regard, a comprehensive view of the diverse problems in individual areas [of national life] is of special importance, in order to perceive the common prerequisites for their orderly solution and to take into consideration the effects of government measures'. This required an intelligence service to supply factual information and simultaneously observe the course of developments. Such an agency must operate independent of the interests it reported on and of the fluctuating opinions of government and bureaucracy. It had to express its views without consideration of persons 'and without stubbornly adhering to [political] doctrines'. A technocratically impartial intelligence service was particularly needed in states organized on the 'Führer principle' without the correctives of a free press and parliament; yet every government should possess such an agency in order to make correct decisions based on sufficient and impartial information which a particularized civil service could not provide. Therefore an internal intelligence service had to be created entirely separate from existing administrative organs (although supplying them with needed information) and 'directly subordinate to the head of government'. Every effort had been made, Ohlendorf

---

[17] 'Der innenpolitische, lebensgebietsmässige Nachrichtendienst in Deutschland', memorandum composed in mid-May 1945 for Count Schwerin von Krosigk, chief minister in the 'Provisional Government' of Grand Admiral Karl Dönitz at Flensburg, quoted in Boberach (ed.), *Meldungen*, 533–39.

[18] Cf. Robert L. Koehl, 'Toward an SS Typology: Social Engineers', *American Journal of Economics and Sociology*, XVIII (1959), 113–26.

asserted, to prevent the SD's attachment to other institutions and agencies. But he conceded that his chief goal, to transform his organization into 'an instrument of the *highest* leadership of the state', had 'in no way' been realized. Immediate subordination to the supreme political authority, however, along with complete independence, could alone ensure objective intelligence reporting.

Ohlendorf's conception of the function of a domestic intelligence agency rested on his experience with the SD. Once in power, he said, the Nazi party needed to obtain a clear picture of Germany's multifarious cultural and social institutions, their needs and potential for suitably National Socialist development — an idealized description of the brutal procedure of *Gleichschaltung*. Some of the regime's policies had adverse effects, leading to developments 'in completely wrong directions' such as 'national bolshevism'. The resulting problems could be solved only if the Nazi leadership was made aware of the situation. 'I thus had the idea of creating an organ which, in the absence of public criticism, would nevertheless put the leadership of the state in a position to learn and take into account existing or emerging opinion among the people'. The SD had to 'point out when [party and government] measures aroused opposition' and so 'reveal the sort of things that come out in open discussion under a parliamentary regime'.[19] Furthermore, his organization furnished an 'outlet for unresolved tensions and an indicator of urgent needs felt by the people'.

According to Ohlendorf, his aim thus went far beyond the SD's initial concern with combatting Nazism's political and ideological enemies (which nevertheless remained an important part of its work). To understand the social reality behind opposition to the dictatorship, Ohlendorf 'developed a staff within the Security Service . . . which specialized in . . . factually-oriented problems'. Looking at political, economic, social, cultural, scientific and administrative developments from the public's viewpoint rather than in a doctrinaire Nazi fashion, he claimed, was unique in Hitler's Reich. Only thoroughly qualified, reputable persons with practical experience in the areas covered were employed to analyse the information, which was collected by local, mostly volunteer informants recruited 'without reference to party membership'. Final evaluation of the assembled data was done by a small group of

[19] Kersten, op. cit., 210–11, entry for 2 September 1943.

specialists, largely drawn from the government departments or outside organizations concerned, within *Amt* III. It sent regional SD offices detailed questionnaires which provided an overall view of each field and indicated problems requiring investigation. Information was then compiled by continual reporting of the 'opinions, worries and wishes' of those working in the different areas and of the general public.

The results of this 'polling' were communicated to the appropriate government departments, along with suggestions for action — a reflection again of a fundamental dilemma of the SD: how to separate the gathering of intelligence from the exploitation of it. 'The particular value of this centralized evaluation [of information] lay in the fact that all areas of observation were thereby seen in relation to one another. The result was that within [*Amt* III of] the RSHA, the division into departments and specialties was overcome by a unified view of the ongoing development of the entire community.' Some departments, Ohlendorf observed, took increasing advantage of the SD's work. More significantly,

> among experts and in wide circles of the population, *Amt* III was increasingly looked upon as a suitable forum to transmit legitimate misgivings and desires to the leadership of the state, to express criticism of policies, conditions and tendencies, and to point out more appropriate courses. Hence it followed that very soon the SD occupied a position vis-à-vis both government departments and especially a party leadership hardening into dogmatism as the impartial representative of a healthy public opinion of the real nature of the German people and their needs.

Countless ordinary citizens therefore volunteered information about the unsuitability and misconduct of office-holders, which was also forwarded to the agency involved. Afterwards, Ohlendorf emphatically denied the SD had wielded, or even desired, executive authority; on the contrary, 'it sought to clarify situations and exercise persuasion using facts, rather than intervene directly to shape events' which was the Gestapo's task — an abstention not true in every case.[20]

[20] In addition to Ohlendorf's post-war memorandum, see his testimony in *TWC*, IV, 268, and *IMG*, IV, 390–91; ibid., XX, 214, 262–63, testimony of Rolf Heinz Hoeppner and Hans Rössner; Kersten, op. cit., 211 f., 212–14, entries for 4 and 7 September 1943; Dröge, op. cit., 57–58; Helmut Heiber (ed.), *Reichsführer!* . . . *Briefe an und von Himmler* (Stuttgart 1968), 183, document 192.

Ohlendorf's account of the lofty objectives, impartial operations and positive results of the work of *Amt* III was intended, among other things, to distinguish the SD's activities from those of the Nazi party in general and the Gestapo in particular, with which it was linked in the RSHA, in the eyes of Germany's conquerors. He also tried to picture as harmless an organization Germans rightly feared. The SD's role in suppressing opposition to the regime at home and applying Nazi racial principles in the occupied territories made it more dangerous than the innocuous public-opinion-polling agency depicted at Nürnberg. Nevertheless, two of Ohlendorf's claims for the SD were partly justified: firstly it did enjoy a reputation as a vehicle by which 'loyal' criticism of measures and personalities could penetrate the top levels of the Nazi government.[21] In view of the insurmountable difficulties Ohlendorf himself encountered trying to shape policy on the basis of his intelligence information, however, it is doubtful whether expressions of popular 'opposition' which reached the leadership via the SD significantly influenced events. Secondly, the bi-weekly *Meldungen aus dem Reich* produced by *Amt* III, notwithstanding Ohlendorf's ambition to employ it to alter various government actions, is nonetheless the most unbiased, reliable and comprehensive compilation of German 'public opinion' produced by any Nazi agency during the war.[22] To this extent, the practice of the SD corresponded to Ohlendorf's ideal.

THE ORGANIZATION OF THE SD was patterned on Heydrich's vague conception (derived from reading adventure novels) of the English Secret Service. Whereas the French, following Fouché, employed police spies and paid agents for intelligence work, 'every decent Englishman is ready to aid the Secret Service, regarding it as his obvious duty, without requiring any special obligation'. British power, Heydrich believed, 'was really based on the Secret Service, for the best informed have a great advantage over others'; and in the English view, 'intelligence work [was] a matter for gentlemen . . . an honourable task'. Therefore, he told his subordinates

[21] *IMG*, IX, 86, testimony of Field Marshal Erhard Milch; ibid., XXI, 553–54, statement of Dr Merkel (defence lawyer for the Gestapo); ibid., XXI, 353–77, 690–706 and XXII, 9–57, final summation by Dr Gawlik (defence lawyer for the SD); ibid., XXII, 345, statement of French prosecutor M. Auguste Champetier de Ribes; ibid., XLII, document SD-65, sworn statement of Professor Gerhard Ritter; Zipfel, op. cit., 154.
[22] Cf. Stokes, op. cit., ch. 4; also Dröge, op. cit., 59–60.

in September 1932, the SD's network of informants (*Vertrauens-leute*, or V-*Leute*) who would comprise the bulk of the organiza-tion would not be hired spies but rather persons of irreproachable character, idealistic and unpaid, whose personal achievements, professional qualifications and objective, realistic judgement would command public respect.[23]

After 1935 the SD consisted of a headquarters in Berlin beneath which were ranged regional (*Oberabschnitt*), district (*Abschnitt*) and local (*Aussenstelle*) offices; informants made up the base of the pyramid. Each *Oberabschnitt*, staffed by full-time (*hauptamt-lich*) SD members, was sub-divided into two or three district offices. The several *Aussenstellen* belonging to each *Abschnitt* employed both full- and part-time (*ehrenamtlich*) personnel who sent their accumulated information to the responsible *Abschnitt*, which co-ordinated and then forwarded it to the next highest level. Headquarters itself comprised three divisions and Ohlendorf had first joined one of these.[24]

The SD leadership, recruited from among lawyers and academics, engineers, former soldiers and businessmen, was generally on a par with the highly qualified German civil service. This preference for university-trained leaders again reflected the influence of Heydrich's model, the British Secret Service. The lower levels of the organization were trained according to an established pattern. Candidates had first to pass through either a National Socialist Leadership School or SS-*Junkerschule* (cadet school). Courses were then conducted at the SD's own institution at Bernau, near Berlin; the initial programme, in January 1935, included lectures on Nazism's chief 'ideological opponents' (freemasonry, Judaism, Catholicism) as well as instruction in observing the press and the economy, especially for evidence of corruption. The headquarters divisions also had facilities to prepare recruits for SD careers.[25]

[23] Kersten, op. cit., 219–20, entry for 18 June 1944; Aronson, op. cit., 60–61. In his memorial address following Heydrich's assassination in June 1942, Himmler declared that the SD only employed persons who were 'personally decent, politically progressive and technically expert, loyal to the Führer and our people, [who were] on the whole free of selfish interests and for the most part ready to serve without any sort of financial reward or public recognition, solely for the sake of the cause'. Quoted in Aronson, op. cit., 140–41.

[24] Stokes, op. cit., 56–58, 74–77; Heinrich Orb, *Nationalsozialismus. 13 Jahre Machtrausch* (Olten 1945), 62 ff., 67 ff., 81 ff.; Boberach (ed.), *Berichte*, xxxvi.

[25] Stokes, op. cit., 81–84; Boberach (ed.), *Berichte*, 900–903, document 1; Dröge, op. cit., 58–59. For a perhaps typical example of an SD aspirant who passed through most of these stages, see the personal file of Marcel Zschunke in US National Archives, Washington, DC, Microfilm Publications, Records of the Reich Leader of the SS and Chief of the German Police, Microcopy T-175, Roll 240, Frames 2730019–2730221 (hereafter *RFSS* with the appropriate micro-copy, roll and frame numbers).

The SD's professional staff was supplemented by specialists attached to the subordinate offices who furnished regular reports on specific questions in their fields of competence. These experts included judges, leading bureaucrats, employers, factory managers, doctors, teachers from every type of school, artists and professors. SD 'study groups' (*Arbeitsgemeinschaften*) at several universities furnished advice on academic matters. In July 1939 the SD office in Koblenz, for example, was employing twenty-four specialists (including four professors) on a part-time basis, along with thirteen regular SD members and two secretaries. It had four *Aussenstellen* to which reported some forty informants in surrounding towns and villages, among whom were civil servants, local police officials, a veterinarian, a doctor and a teacher. Perhaps 10 per cent of the 30,000 SD informers belonged to the SS, rather more to the party; others were known opponents of the regime. Finally, secrecy was emphasized. An order of 22 June 1936 forbade the revelation of the names of SD members, V-*Leute* or other employees to any party or government office. 'The SD can only fulfil its onerous tasks as an intelligence organization in the service of the party, state and people if the network of associates is kept absolutely secret.' Moreover, 'in order to protect the reputations of all citizens, in case a deliberately false report is submitted, insofar as an SS member is involved, severe punishment will follow; in the case of V-*Leute*, criminal proceedings will be initiated against him by the state prosecutor'.[26] How rigorously this stipulation was enforced is impossible to say; the phenomenon of 'denunciation' was widespread in Nazi Germany and SD informants probably contributed to this in part.

The *modus operandi* of the *Vertrauensleute* can be glimpsed in their activities vis-à-vis the churches, a chief object of SD attention. A 1937 directive from SD-*Oberabschnitt Nordwest* (Hanover) pointed out that, because the Gestapo could not act against church-affiliated organizations without prior permission from the Ministry

[26] *IMG*, XX, 214, testimony of Rolf Heinz Hoeppner; ibid., XLII, 465–68, document SD-65, sworn statement of Professor Gerhard Ritter; *RFSS*, T-175, 240, 2730223/4, 'Befehl für den SD Nr. 25/36: Namensnennung von SD-Angehörigen'; Boberach (ed.), *Meldungen*, xiv–xv; Boberach (ed.), *Berichte*, xxxvii–xxxix; Höhne, op. cit., 201–2; Werner Best, *Die deutsche Polizei* (Darmstadt 1940), 91–92; Manfred Wolfson, 'Constraint and Choice in the SS Leadership', *Western Political Quarterly*, XVIII, 1965, 560–61; Steinert, op. cit., 44–45; Dröge, op. cit., 51–54, 230, n. 19.

of Church Affairs, even to secure their membership lists, the SD 'had . . . taken over the duty of making good this weakness from the point of view of intelligence gathering'. Each *Aussenstelle* should therefore place at least one informant in every village in its area. Since the V-*Leute* had to be generally knowledgeable and 'able to think logically and factually', teachers, local party, SA and SS leaders, farm officials (*Ortsbauernführer*), veterinarians and pensioned civil servants were most suitable. They were to blanket their communities with a network of helpers who were not to know they were working for the SD. The *Vertrauensleute* 'daily noted down in indelible pencil and telegram style . . . on message pads' each piece of information they received, such as 'Lutheran pastor Kirchhoff preached on Sunday, 4.2., in the church before 120 parishioners and said that the results of the school elections in the Saar had been falsified. — signed W'. Every *Aussenstelle* was to report fresh information immediately to its superior office. If these provisions were followed, the directive proudly concluded, the SD would be exactly informed 'about every action hostile to the state' and would be 'the world's best intelligence service'. Martin Bormann's ban in January 1939 on party members simultaneously holding minor church posts was therefore not entirely welcomed by the SD: 'This decree . . . has to some extent had an unfavourable effect from the intelligence point of view, since precisely organists and sacristans were often very valuable bearers of information'.[27] Whether the quality of the SD's informants corresponded to the claims of Heydrich and Ohlendorf, or rather (as the regime's opponents maintained) constituted the 'scum' of German society, recognizable by the 'fish-like' look in their eyes, under National Socialism they did not need to feel ashamed of their activity: Hitler himself began his political career as an informant for the Bavarian Ministry of War.[28]

Within the *Reichssicherheitshauptamt*, established on 1 October 1939, Ohlendorf's *Amt* III was variously designated SD-*Inland* (the domestic SD, to distinguish it from *Amt* VI, SD-*Ausland*, the organization's foreign intelligence service) and *Deutsche*

[27] Zipfel, op. cit., 106–7 and n. 141, 379–84, document 35; Höhne, op. cit., 200–201; Johann Neuhäusler, *Kreuz und Hakenkreuz. Der Kampf des National-sozialismus gegen die katholische Kirche und den kirchlichen Widerstand* (Munich 1946), I, 360–82; Boberach (ed.), *Berichte*, 902–5, document 2.

[28] Ernst Deuerlein, 'Hitlers Eintritt in die Politik und die Reichswehr', *Vierteljahrshefte für Zeitgeschichte*, VII (1959), 185, Höhne, op. cit., 10.

Lebensgebiete or 'German Areas of Life'.[29]   Its internal structure indicates the SD's wartime range of interests. Besides a business office to look after internal administration, *Amt* III had four main sections dealing with legal and constitutional questions, 'folkdom', culture and the economy. Section III/A had five desks, including ones for 'general questions of *Lebensgebietsarbeit'*, legal developments, constitutional and administrative law, and police law and jurisdiction. Under section III/B were desks for 'Volkstumsarbeit' (the affairs of ethnic-German groups within and outside the Reich's borders), minorities, 'racial and public health', nationality and naturalization, and the occupied territories. The cultural sphere of section III/C was divided among four desks: learning, education and religious life, 'popular culture' and art, and press, publications and radio. Finally III/D, the largest section, by 1943 had the following desks: the economic press and publications; the colonial economy; economic, trade and labour legislation; the occupied western territories; the occupied eastern territories; agriculture; commerce, communications and handicrafts; financial, currency, banking, stock market and insurance matters; industry and power; and labour and social questions.[30]   Under the RSHA, *Amt* III's regional offices were redesignated SD-*Leitabschnitte* and SD-*Abschnitte* of which there were some forty by April 1943 subdivided into one or more *Hauptaussenstellen* and directing around 500 individual *Aussenstellen*.[31]   Responsibilities were strictly centralized: each *Abschnitt* was allowed to handle only local matters; those of 'general and national importance' were referred to Berlin.

[29] *IMG*, IV, 361–64, testimony of Otto Ohlendorf; ibid., XXX, 253, document 2346-PS; ibid., XXXVIII, 102–4, document 361-L; Höhne, op. cit., 234 ff., 237–38; Buchheim, op. cit., 71–72, 76–77; Zipfel, op. cit., 149–50.
[30] *RFSS*, T-175, 232, 2720801–24, 'Geschäftsverteilungsplan des Reichssicherheitshauptamtes, Stand vom 1.2.1940'; *IMG*, XXXVIII, 1–24, document 185-L, 'Organisation und Geschäftsverteilungsplan des Reichssicherheitshauptamtes vom 1. März 1941'; ibid., XXXVIII, 60–85, document 219-L, 'Organisation und Geschäftsverteilungsplan des Reichssicherheitshauptamtes der SS nach dem Stand vom 1. Oktober 1943'. As originally set up, *Amt* III also included a desk dealing with 'National Socialism' which evidently disappeared early in 1940. Cf. *RFSS*, T-175, 232, 2720831 ff., undated organizational plan of the RSHA, probably from the period between 1 February and 21 March 1940; *TWC*, IV, 214–16, document No–4234, sworn statement of Werner Braune.
[31] *RFSS*, T-175, 232, 2720725–65, 'Dienststellenverzeichnis der Sicherheitspolizei und des SD', April 1943; ibid., 2721192–201, 'Änderung des Zuständigkeitsbereiches der Sicherheitspolizei und des SD', 1 June 1944; Boberach (ed.), *Berichte*, xxxvi–xxxvii.

Regular directives from headquarters assured uniform reporting. Most significantly, 'all conflicts or difficulties with government, party and *Wehrmacht* offices . . . whether settled locally or not' had to be reported to the RSHA.[32] On this issue Ohlendorf's conception of the SD eventually shattered.

THE FIRST *MELDUNGEN AUS DEM REICH* produced by *Amt* III appeared on 9 October 1939. The reports initially comprised five sections of varying length reflecting the organization of SD-*Inland:* 'general mood and situation', 'opponents' (discontinued in September 1940 by the Gestapo), 'cultural areas', 'law and administration' and 'the economy'. Another section, ' "folkdom" and public health', was added in April 1940. The section on popular morale and reactions to the war was supplemented after May 1940 by detailed analysis of public response to the propaganda media: the press, radio and films, especially newreels. That on the economy was very extensive, doubtless due to Ohlendorf's special interest in that field. Until mid-May 1940 the reports were compiled three times each week, afterwards twice weekly. Their size varied from twelve to over thirty double-spaced typed pages, averaging twenty; lengthy appendices on special topics were often included.[33]

The opening section analysed the opinions of the population on political, military and other events of the past few days. These included operations on the war fronts, speeches or announcements by Hitler and other Nazi leaders and, particularly during battle-field lulls, the impact of economic developments on morale. The reports thus constitute 'a continuous commentary on the history of the war' viewed from the home front.[34] Later especially, *Amt* III also tried to determine trends in German opinion; when such projections pointed to defeat, Ohlendorf was again branded a pessimist and the SD's reporting activities virtually terminated.

Goebbels' Ministry of Propaganda was obviously affected by

[32] *IMG*, XXXVIII, 105–110, document 316-L; Boberach (ed.), *Meldungen*, xv–xvi; Best, op. cit., 56.

[33] Boberach (ed.), *Meldungen*, xvi–xvii. For a summary of the contents of the different sections of the reports, see Stokes, op. cit., 193–210.

[34] Boberach (ed.), *Meldungen*, ix. In addition to the representative selection of the reports printed in *Meldungen*, see Stokes, op. cit., chs. 6 and 7, for an analysis of German opinion and morale during the first eighteen months of the war; also Steinert, op. cit., 91 ff.

reports from *Amt* III on popular morale, and examined them very carefully. In his conferences to decide the daily propaganda programme, Goebbels demanded that 'the situation and morale reports of the SD, the *Gau[leiter]*, etc., should always be corrected in cases in which superficial reporting or false information can be demonstrated in order to train [*sic*] these agencies to report factually'. But once satisfied of their accuracy, he regularly utilized them in shaping propaganda.[35] The historian of these meetings concludes that

> Goebbels' propaganda would never have been so effective if he had not learned in a relatively unvarnished form especially from the SD reports how the populace in the different parts of the Reich reacted to [it], to films and radio programmes, to press announcements and speeches, and where dissent, criticism and annoyance were produced. . . . Without [this] knowledge of the morale of the people he would never have been in a position to head off its possible decline by corresponding propaganda measures and reaffirm confidence in the leadership . . . . Thus on occasion the impression arises that the real Minister of Propaganda did not reside in the Prince Leopold Palace [Goebbels' Berlin headquarters], but rather at a desk in the Prinz-Albrecht-Strasse, in [*Amt* III of] the *Reichssicherheitshauptamt*. For Goebbels the SD reports soon became his most important reading.[36]

Goebbels' attitude changed drastically when the SD later began to report less favourably about his work. But at the outset, Goebbels was remarkably receptive to the SD's information. Victory made this easy; as defeat loomed up, however, he attacked Ohlendorf and *Amt* III as the bearers of unwelcome news. The narrow limits the Nazi dictatorship allowed even to 'loyal criticism' were soon reached.

To what extent other Nazi departments and leaders read and made use of the *Meldungen aus dem Reich* is uncertain. The reports were neither numbered nor bore distribution lists, so it is impossible to determine exactly who received them. *Amt* III's immediate superiors, Himmler and first Heydrich and later Ernst Kaltenbrunner, certainly did.[37] Hermann Göring approvingly dis-

---

[35] Willi A. Boelcke (ed.), *Kriegspropaganda 1939–1941. Geheime Ministerkonferenzen im Reichspropagandaministerium* (Stuttgart 1966), 211, 228, entries for 26 October and 20 November 1939. Numerous examples of the influence of the SD reports on propaganda policy are given in Stokes, op. cit., 212–16.

[36] Boelcke (ed.), op. cit., 45–46.

[37] Kersten, op. cit., 39, 300–1; *IMG*, IV, 371, testimony of Otto Ohlendorf; ibid., XI, 355, testimony of Ernst Kaltenbrunner; ibid., XXIX, 110 ff., document 1919-PS, speech of Himmler at Posen, October 1943; ibid., XXXI, 324–25, document 2939-PS, sworn statement of Walter Schellenberg; Heiber (ed.), *Reichsführer!*, 69, document 55.

cussed the first ones in meetings of the 'Ministerial Council for the Defence of the Reich'. According to Ohlendorf, Göring also defended the reports in 1940, 'when a number of *Gauleiter* objected strongly to [them]'. Despite some reservations, the Minister of Justice after 1942, Otto Thierack, considered them a 'valuable means of guiding the administration of justice'. The Ministry of Finance, Nazi party treasurer, the Interior Ministry and party ideologist Alfred Rosenberg were sent copies. Since the reports were stamped 'secret' and 'for the personal information of the recipient only', they could not be passed on; lesser officials, such as broadcaster Hans Fritzsche, only saw sections dealing with their own work. It therefore appears that, until Goebbels intervened early in 1943, all Nazi ministers and party *Reichsleiter* received the reports. After that date, 'subscribers' were reduced but included the Propaganda Minister, Göring, Bormann and Hans Lammers, chief of the Reich Chancellery.[38]

Nazi wartime policy was principally determined by Hitler. Himmler, however, adamantly refused to transmit the *Meldungen aus dem Reich* to him. Felix Kersten often 'found [Rudolf] Brandt [Himmlers' secretary] in despair because Himmler was filing away the SD's reports . . . instead of taking them with him to discuss with Hitler'. Only 'in the rarest cases, and even then with the greatest caution and reserve' did the *Reichsführer* inform Hitler of some of the consequences of his decisions. 'He never wanted to put himself in the position with Hitler where he would be making use of [the SD's] reports to criticize orders which emanated from the Führer.' Himmler complained Ohlendorf's 'pet idea' was that 'I should let the Führer see his reports. But they're usually so pessimistic that this is quite out of the question; they would only impair the Führer's capacity for action'. Whether accurate or not was beside the point. 'Details which are unhelpful must be kept from the Führer, however important they may appear', Himmler declared. 'His task is to lead us to victory; I must keep from him anything which might interfere with this

---

[38] Boberach (ed.), *Meldungen*, xvii–xviii, xxiv, xxvi; Boberach (ed.), *Berichte*, xxxiii; *IMG*, IV, 391, testimony of Otto Ohlendorf; *TWC*, IV, 269; Buchheim, op. cit., 68–69; Hans-Günther Seraphim (ed.), *Das politische Tagebuch Alfred Rosenbergs 1934/35 und 1939/40* (Göttingen 1956), 116, entry for 10 May 1940; Joseph Wulf, *Presse und Funk im Dritten Reich. Eine Dokumentation* (Gütersloh 1964), 366 ff.

task, even if Herr Ohlendorf does not share this view.'[39]

The head of *Amt* III poured out his frustration to Kersten.

> If only the leadership would make use of this intelligence system as a conscience to test all its enactments, I would regard my life's work in this field as accomplished. . . . The Higher Command [of the *Wehrmacht*] receives daily and hourly reports of the exact situation on all fronts and makes its dispositions accordingly. The same ought to apply to the home front. The Führer and high officials in the party and the government ought to know every measure's effect without regarding this as a personal attack on them. But apparently it's going to be another generation before we can get this idea accepted. It wouldn't be so bad in peacetime, but now we're engaged in a life-and-death struggle. . . . Bormann always keeps [my reports] from the Führer. This is absolutely fatal, since they deal with the home front, for which the party is responsible. . . . The *Reichsführer,* who as head of the intelligence service is the proper person to do so, doesn't dare lay my reports before the Führer, even when he believes they're true . . . . The *Reichsführer* considers that the Führer ought not to be troubled with matters which might interfere with his lofty conceptions and arouse his displeasure. You surely know how everybody close to the Führer is constantly striving to keep any unpleasant news from reaching him. The *Reichsführer* is no exception. . . . I'm convinced that if the true situation was revealed to the Führer, then measures would be taken. What wouldn't I give to be able to put before the Führer the overwhelming mass of material which we possess about the situation on the home front.

Instead, Ohlendorf never got to 'know Hitler personally nor did I ever have the possibility of submitting a report to him or even speaking to him'. What he considered 'the tragedy of the SD' was that only the last reports produced by *Amt* III in late 1944 and early 1945 reached the Führer. 'The true state of public opinion depicted by the SD'. Ohlendorf lamented, 'was not reflected in Nazi policy. This applied not only to individual departments and administrative officials, for whom the criticism voiced was often very disagreeable, but also unfortunately to the central leadership of the Reich and even the Führer who to an entirely inadequate extent took notice or was informed of the facts, thoughts and suggestions put forward [by the SD].'[40]

[39] Kersten, op. cit., 211–12,2 15–16, 300–1, entries for 4 and 18 September 1943. On Hitler's increasing unwillingness to listen to reports which contradicted his own impressions and his deep aversion to all forms of criticism, see Stokes, op. cit., 221–25.

[40] Kersten, op. cit., 212–14, entry for 7 September 1943; *TWC*, IV, 238; 'Der innenpolitische, lebensgebeitsmässige Nachrichtendienst in Deutschland', part iv, quoted in Boberach (ed.), *Meldungen*, 538.

There was a final irony in the relationship between *Amt* III and the Führer it sought to serve. Almost the only evidence that Hitler reached a decision based on information supplied by the SD is found in his *Table Talk*. On 22 March 1942, Bormann showed him a report from the SD that the following day every German Catholic priest would read from the pulpit a pastoral letter accusing the government of breaking the 1935 concordat on a wide range of subjects. Hitler was therefore able to issue advance instructions to the press 'not to engage in polemics' against the bishops, but rather to silence their protests by stressing the support Catholics fighting in the *Wehrmacht* were daily according the regime. Thus Hitler, like Himmler, found the SD's chief value in precisely the aspect of its activities Ohlendorf sought to de-emphasize: as an adjunct of the Gestapo combatting the regime's enemies. The point was underscored in the Führer's informal eulogy for Reinhard Heydrich. Aside from 65,000 'asocial' [*sic*!] Germans who fled the Reich after the 'assumption of power', Hitler said, this element had either been confined to concentration camps or else shot. In 'breaking such necks', Heydrich and his SD had performed 'a service which is all the more to be valued since the courts showed themselves incapable of rising to the task'.[41] This could serve as an epitaph for the SD.

THE HISTORY OF *AMT* III largely concerns Ohlendorf's efforts to realize his ambitions for the SD. These provoked even stronger opposition than before the war. Clashes with the Nazi party again touched off difficulties with Himmler which finally led to Ohlendorf's dismissal and ended the SD's domestic intelligence activities. The party resented an organization which prepared reports on all spheres of German life — including the reception of party measures by the populace. The SD ignored the party's sensitivity to such control; in December 1940, for example, regional SD officials were ordered to report anything the *Gauleiter* said concerning postwar economic planning.[42]

Party leaders responded sharply. *Gauleiter* Friedrich Florian

[41] Henry Picker (ed.), *Hitlers Tischgespräche im Führerhauptquartier 1941–1942* (Stuttgart 1965, 2nd rev. ed. by Percy Ernst Schramm *et al.*), 198–99, 392, entries for 22 March and 7 June 1942; see also Boberach (ed.), *Berichte*, xxxiii, 384–85 n. 5; Steinert, op. cit., 20–21.

[42] *TWC*, IV, 232–33; Boberach (ed.), *Meldungen*, xviii; also Stokes, op. cit., ch. 8.

angrily wrote to Martin Bormann on 30 November 1942, referring to questionnaires sent to *Vertrauensleute* in SD-*Leitabschnitt* Düsseldorf requesting information on party ceremonies (*Feiergestaltung*):

> My suspicion, hitherto unfortunately impossible to prove, that the SD is meddling in party matters, is unequivocally confirmed by this questionnaire. I am forced to resort to measures of self-defence and . . . will forbid every party official and employee to take on tasks on behalf of the SD or else make doing so dependent on the permission of the individual's local leader or myself.

Gauleiter Karl Weinrich of Hesse also complained in January 1943 that after watching with astonishment the behaviour of the SD and the Gestapo for years, the former seemed worse than the latter. Many SD agents, declared Weinrich, were 'odd fish' and moreover party novices, vintage 1940; if they continued reporting internal Nazi affairs, he would charge them with anti-party activity. 'I forbid once and for all this sort of snooping by the SD. We are not living in Russia that we have to be shadowed by the GPU.' Local leaders tried to remove informants from the party. 'Who of you is the so-called *Vertrauensmann* of the SD?' *Kreisleiter* Kampe of Danzig asked a meeting of his officials. When one indicated he was, Kampe berated him as an 'unpatriotic and spineless' undercover agent. The audience applauded with shouts of 'spy!' and 'Cheka methods!'. The informant was thereupon told to choose between the party and the SD — he could not simultaneously obey his *Gauleiter* and 'Herr Himmler'. The Labour Front and the SA, too, forbade co-operation with the SD. One SA leader, also an SD official, received this order in March 1943: 'According to the regulations of SA group Weichsel, no SA man can serve in the SD. Within eight days you must send a sworn, written declaration that you have quit the SD. If you do not, you must be dropped from the SA'. Some V-*Leute* were denounced as party enemies and summoned before party courts, others were boycotted by Nazi functionaries in their locality.[43]

Although its information on party matters was often valuable, Himmler was ready to heed complaints about the SD because of temperamental and political differences between himself and the head of *Amt* III. He considered Ohlendorf an 'unbearable,

[43] Höhne, op. cit., 16–17, 391–92; Buchheim, op. cit., 74; Boberach (ed.), *Meldungen*, xviii; Steinert, op. cit., 41.

humourless Prussian, an unsoldierly type, a defeatist and [a] damned intellectual'. Ohlendorf, in turn, constantly criticized the *Reichsführer*'s own policies and ambitions. This outspokenness contributed to a steady deterioration in relations beginning soon after Ohlendorf rejoined the SD. He told Felix Kersten:

> There are men [in Germany] . . . who would like to put the Führer . . . in the place of God. Then they would be able to issue the divine commands as representing the nation and satisfy their own desire for power without any trouble. They all talk of the totalitarian state, which is simply a new version of the old absolutist state—in which they would be absolute and irresponsible masters. . . . [Himmler] should be entirely opposed to the . . . conception of a totalitarian state, if only from his knowledge of the Germanic state and his respect for Germanic ideals. . . . Of course it's not easy to accept . . . when you've got power—and the police force—in the hollow of your hand; and it's even more difficult when that's going to bring you into conflict with men like Göring or [Robert] Ley.

Ohlendorf accused Himmler of imitating Hitler in fostering administrative anarchy by appointing several individuals to perform the same task. The *Reichsführer,* in his eyes, was the 'personification of dualism' and 'a parasite' on the German people, 'not so much because of what he did, but because of what he did not do'. Himmler's power was an 'empty shell' because he refused to use it 'to create orderly conditions' within the Reich.[44] Yet disorder was precisely the essence of Nazism. The SD owed its existence after 1933 to the perpetuation of the very dualism that Ohlendorf wanted to remove from the Nazi state.[45]

What finally brought about Ohlendorf's downfall were attacks on the SD by two powerful figures, Joseph Goebbels and Martin Bormann. Together they furnished Himmler with the means of removing Ohlendorf. All three charged that he and the SD's reports were excessively pessimistic. As Germany's situation deteriorated, Goebbels complained about the 'defeatism' in the reports. By this he largely meant the mounting public criticism of Nazi propaganda the SD registered. His dissatisfaction climaxed with its evaluation of reactions to his dramatic 'total war' speech

[44] *TWC*, IV, 233–35, 243, 283; Höhne, op. cit., 16, 220, 393–94; Kersten, op. cit., 207–10, 212–14, entries for 29 and 30 August and 7 September 1943; Heiber (ed.), *Reichsführer!,* 122–23, document 116.

[45] For a discussion of this important theme, see Stokes, op. cit., 68; Aronson, op. cit., 214–15; Ernst Fraenkel, *The Dual State: A Contribution to the Theory of Dictatorship* (New York 1941).

on 18 February 1943. Goebbels responded to the SD's critique on the effectiveness of his speech by banning its reports within his ministry because they 'tended to encourage defeatist impressions of popular morale and prospects in the war even among leading circles of the party and the state'. Furthermore, the reports informed government officials about party affairs which solely concerned the party chancellery (that is, Bormann). This two-pronged assault on the SD's allegedly 'negative' attitude towards the war and its meddling in party matters was intended to win allies against Ohlendorf. Goebbels wanted to 'change the nature' of the reports through closer 'collaboration' between himself and *Amt* III. 'If the SD material, which in itself is good, is sifted politically and brought into line with the political views of the *Gauleiter* and the Reich Propaganda Offices, it can develop into a good source of information.' But this would have destroyed the independence Ohlendorf demanded. Himmler, who sometimes tore up and returned reports to Ohlendorf on the same grounds that Goebbels objected to them, was reluctant to support his un-manageable subordinate. Goebbels noted on 12 May 1943: 'Himmler is now ready to have the SD reporting stopped, or at all events to stop supplying it to every sort of minister, as its effect is too defeatist. Himmler now wants to have a special report made up by the SD for me personally, containing everything which has hitherto been submitted to a larger circle'.[46]

Following Goebbels' intervention, in June 1943 the comprehensive *Meldungen aus dem Reich* was replaced by 'SD Reports on Domestic Questions' dealing with individual topics and available only to government departments and leading Nazis who needed to see them. Even this drastic curtailment did not satisfy *Amt* III's enemies, including many in the SS besides Himmler. *Waffen*-SS commanders, for example, resented SD reports of public criticism of the poor quality and training of officers, heavy casualties, unnecessary brutality and alleged police functions of

[46] See Boelcke (ed.), op. cit., 80; Steinert, op. cit., 43–44; Ernest K. Bramsted, *Goebbels and National Socialist Propaganda 1925–1945* (East Lansing 1965), 53 f., 256 ff., 264 ff., 271 ff.; Louis P. Lochner (ed.), *The Goebbels Diaries* (London 1948), 4–5, 101, 131, 142, 144 f., 158, 163 f., 179, 258–59, 293, entries for 22 January, 26 March, 23, 28 and 29 April, 13 and 18 May, 12 December 1942, 17 April 1943, and 12 May 1943; Günter Moltmann, 'Goebbels Rede zum totalen Krieg am 18. Februar 1943', *Vierteljahrshefte für Zeitgeschichte*, XII, 1964, 13–43; *RFSS*, T-175, 264, 2758775/6, 'Meldungen aus dem Reich', 22 February 1943, section 'Allgemeines'.

their formations.[47] The sharpest attack came from Gunter d'Alquen, editor of the SS newspaper *Das Schwarze Korps* and once Ohlendorf's ally. D'Alquen, like Ohlendorf, thought the regime required 'constructive opposition' to avoid 'hardening of the arteries', and wanted his newspaper to provide it. To publicize 'the attitudes, opinions and experiences of the people' regarding bureaucratic ineptitude and party corruption, he obtained information from SD files. For several years this was readily forthcoming. Co-operation ceased, however, when Ohlendorf complained *Das Schwarze Korps* was defaming entire professions, including lawyers — Ohlendorf's own and a favourite Nazi target. He also objected to the newspaper's call to check black-marketeering by closing corner shops and small businesses. Ohlendorf demanded d'Alquen consult the SD before raising issues, a censorship the editor refused. Ohlendorf's views, he replied, 'were out of line with the basic ideas of National Socialism and the special interests of the SS'. Although Ohlendorf cut the newspaper off from SD sources, Himmler refused his request to dismiss d'Alquen.[48] So another effective propagandist joined Ohlendorf's opponents.

Goebbels' efforts to turn the party leadership against the SD were successful. On 2 February 1943 Bormann wrote to Himmler: 'Not long ago I pointed out to you that various *Gauleiter* have the impression the SD sees its role as supervising party officials and the work of the party. It appears urgently necessary to me that you clear up these questions in a circular to the *Gauleiter* as soon as possible'. The *Reichsführer* reassured him that 'as before' the SD had 'strict orders not to concern itself with internal party affairs'. Ohlendorf's relations with Himmler continued to worsen; the latter told Kersten:

> To be quite frank . . . I don't care for the man. . . . He has no sense of humour, he's one of those unbearable people who always know better. Having his gold party-badge and being one of the first recruits to the SS, he regards himself as the Galahad [*Gralshüter*] of National Socialism and thinks that all is lost when things happen which conflict with his ideology. He's like a schoolmaster watching over me to see that I do things properly. Yet he hasn't the slightest idea of tactics. If I were to listen to him, I would have to take official action over every one of his reports and make bitter enemies on all sides.

[47] Boberach (ed.), *Meldungen*, xxvi; *IMG*, XLII, 318, sworn statement of Walter Huppenkothen; Höhne, op. cit., 18, 404, 444–45; Dröge, op. cit., 56.
[48] Aronson, op. cit., 139; Höhne, op. cit., 198, 204–9, 398; Helmut Heiber and Hildegard von Kotze (ed.), *Facsimile Querschnitt durch das Schwarze Korps* (Munich 1968), 8–20; Boberach (ed.), *Meldungen*, xxiv–xxv.

In mid-1943 Himmler acceded to demands that the SD abandon public-opinion reporting. '[It] was . . . now that the actual crisis of the SD started', Ohlendorf testified, 'because after Stalingrad conditions in Germany became more and more difficult. The more difficult . . . these became, the more critical . . . became the reports of the SD. And now Himmler was no longer prepared to cover this activity on the part of the SD, but on the contrary, he used the complaints of his colleagues . . . and pushed them on to the SD.'[49]

First Himmler assigned the SD 'more useful' tasks: in decrees of 7 and 24 September 1943, he transferred some responsibilities from his new Ministry of the Interior and the regular police (*Ordnungspolizei*) to *Amt* III. Kaltenbrunner, Heydrich's successor, who initially had thought of dismissing Ohlendorf but soon came to value his organization, urged him 'to stop the [*Meldungen aus dem Reich*], or at least to camouflage them as reports on opponents or sabotage'.[50] Bormann, however, pressed for the elimination of the SD whose V-*Leute* 'evidently only came from oppositional circles'; their reports were mouthpieces for defeatism. On 27 April 1944 he again complained to Himmler, this time about the SD's claim to assess the qualifications and political attitudes of civil servants before promotion. Although the SD had long influenced personnel decisions, Bormann now declared this solely the party's duty. After threatening 'to speak to the Führer' which would put the head of *Amt* III 'where he belonged' and assign his subordinates 'to more productive work', Bormann forbade party officials, organizations and employees 'down to the charwomen' to co-operate at all with the SD.

As Ohlendorf observed to Kersten on 13 June, his 'hands were now tied' in a manner which prevented him from accomplishing very much. The last of the 'SD Reports on Domestic Questions' appeared in July 1944. Ohlendorf conceded *Amt* III had sometimes judged events too severely and been prone to 'wag their fingers', giving the impression the SD was 'somehow negative or oppositional' and operating 'against the . . . party'.[51] But this

[49] Höhne, op. cit., 392–93; Kersten, op. cit., 215–16, entry for 18 September 1943; *TWC*, IV, 236–37; Boberach (ed.), *Meldungen*, xxvii.

[50] *IMG*, XI, 267 f., 355, testimony of Ernst Kaltenbrunner; ibid., XXXI, 324–25, document 2939-PS, sworn statement of Walter Schellenberg; Wilhelm Hoettl, *The Secret Front: The Story of Nazi Political Espionage* (New York 1954), 38–40.

[51] *TWC*, IV, 238; Boberach (ed.), *Meldungen*, xviii, xxvii–xxviii; Höhne, op. cit., 129, 394; *RFSS*, T-175, 267, 2762294–311, speech by Ohlendorf before *Amt* III and SD regional leaders, 31 October 1944.

'self-criticism' came too late. Until April 1945 only random reports on specific problems (such as civilian evacuation from fighting zones) emanated from Ohlendorf's office. Bormann attacked even these: 'anonymous persons who bear no responsibility whatsoever' were criticizing without consulting those who did, mostly party officials. Ironically, the regime during its final weeks had to create an *ad hoc* alternative to the SD: inexperienced and inadequately equipped soldiers kept the Nazi leadership informed of German morale while the populace awaited the disintegration of the Third Reich.[52]

ALTHOUGH CRITICAL OF ASPECTS of the Nazi dictatorship, Ohlendorf would not join the German Resistance to overthrow Hitler. He had no illusions about the war's probable outcome; when asked at Nürnberg whether he had 'anticipated the defeat of Germany', Ohlendorf replied: 'The SD in its reports pointed out the many difficulties which might make the success of the war questionable, that is why [Himmler] called me a defeatist'. Nevertheless he opposed altering the government by force. Postwar reforms, however, were possible and necessary.[53] Professor Jessen, who had allegedly steered Ohlendorf into the SD to control Nazism's worst sides, could not win him over to the Resistance. Thanks to the *Meldungen aus dem Reich* he enjoyed a reputation, according to Hans Fritzsche, as 'the mouthpiece of an opposition which otherwise could never have been expressed'. He also prepared plans for a future National Socialist state in which the party occupied merely an advisory position without political or administrative power. Nevertheless, to Ohlendorf those who actively contemplated a Germany without Hitler 'denied their past and surrounded their oath sworn to the Führer with a tissue of lies and treachery'. This hostility continued even after the war; thus Ohlendorf was cool to Albert Speer's plan to assassinate Hitler early in 1945 when he learned of it at Nürnberg.[54]

[52] Boberach (ed.), *Meldungen*, xxviii; Steinert, op. cit., 42; Dröge, op. cit., 56 f.; *TWC*, IV, 238, 269; Aryeh L. Unger, 'The Public Opinion Reports of the Nazi Party', *Public Opinion Quarterly*, XXIX, 1965–66, 580; Volker R. Berghahn, 'Meinungsforschung im "Dritten Reich": Die Mundpropaganda-Aktion der Wehrmacht im letzten Kriegshalbjahr', *Militärgeschichtliche Mitteilungen*, I, 1967, 83–119.
[53] *TWC*, IV, 234; Höhne, op. cit., 472–73.
[54] Eberhard Zeller, *Geist der Freiheit. Der 20. Juli* (Munich 1963, 4th rev. ed.), 88 f., 501 n. 32: Gerhard Ritter, *Carl Goerdeler und die deutsche Widerstandsbewegung* (Stuttgart 1956), 419–20; Höhne, op. cit., 475–77; *IMG*, IV, 380–81, testimony of Otto Ohlendorf; Albert Speer, *Erinnerungen* (Berlin 1969), 462.

But Ohlendorf did try to rescue the conspirators' ideas for his own projected postwar Germany. At his request, Carl Goerdeler and Johannes Popitz in their death cells prepared lengthy memoranda on the Reich's administrative and territorial reconstruction, the future division of power among national, state and communal governments, the transition to a peace-time economy, the rebuilding of German cities and industries, and questions of finance, law, labour procurement and social policy. At the end of 1944, meetings between *Amt* III and Interior Ministry representatives were held to discuss the memoranda. Ohlendorf wanted to preserve the tradition of impartial and expert administration that Goerdeler and Popitz represented.[55]

During the curious denouement to the Third Reich at Flensburg under Admiral Karl Dönitz, Ohlendorf's chief interest was 'to salvage what he considered useful parts of the SS apparatus — in particular . . . *Amt* III — and perhaps even improve on them in the absence of the Führer'. He transferred several SD members to Dönitz's headquarters where they continued collecting and analysing intelligence. Their 'Daily Report No. 1, regarding the Morale and Opinions of the Population' of 6 May was modelled on the *Meldungen aus dem Reich*. Like *Amt* III, the now re-designated 'News Office' aimed to report developments objectively; but it also provided a forum for those led by Ohlendorf unwilling entirely to abandon National Socialism.[56]

The Flensburg interlude seemed an opportunity finally to realize Ohlendorf's ideal for the SD. His solution for postwar Germany was a government 'conducted along National Socialist lines' with a reconstructed *Amt* III providing accurate intelligence to help it apprehend national needs. Ohlendorf impressed on Dönitz the need 'precisely at the present moment' for an intelligence service to furnish 'objective' information about 'the factual problems of the different *Lebensgebiete* and the impact of government measures' and so facilitate co-operation with the occupier.

[55] Ritter, op. cit., 417 ff., 448 ff., 546–47 n. 28–33; Werner Münchheimer, 'Die Verfassungs- und Verwaltungsreformpläne der deutschen Opposition gegen Hitler zum 20. Juli 1944', *Europa-Archiv*, V, 1950, 3187–95.

[56] James G. McDowell, 'The Captive Government: A Study of the Flensburg Enclave and the German Surrender in World War II, April–May 1945', unpublished Ph.D. dissertation, Johns Hopkins University, 1964, 226–27, 235–39, 442–50; Marlis G. Steinert, *Die 23 Tage der Regierung Dönitz* (Düsseldorf 1967), 146 ff., 311–12; *IMG*, XX, 261, testimony of Hans Rössner.

Unfortunately, 'pronouncements by the Allied military government as well as public discussion abroad and also in Germany have revealed that false impressions exist of the nature, tasks and real importance of the SD, at least insofar as my former office is concerned'. To combat these 'misunderstandings' which had led the Allies to dissolve the SD, to outline 'its possible role within the framework of the present Reich government', to rehabilitate himself and *Amt* III in Allied eyes and to prepare to participate 'in future [political] developments in the Reich and in the area of Europe', the SD's work had to be clarified. In time, Ohlendorf maintained, the SD had become distinct from its 'accidental' administrative connection with the police and the Nazi party, which continually tried to restrict its activities and subordinate it to their own, narrower interests. The uncomfortable criticism the SD levelled at party organizations and officials led *Amt* III to be maligned as a 'secret service'. But government policy was often not based on its recommendations; thus people overestimated the SD's influence. It was imperative, though, that the SD continue. Both the German people and the occupier could better overcome the onerous problems left after the war by utilizing the 'objective appraisal of conditions in the country' that Ohlendorf and his organization could provide.[57]

Dönitz decided it would be 'inopportune' to forward Ohlendorf's proposal to the Allies. Its future was settled when both were arrested on 23 May.[58] This ended the SD's history, except for its condemnation as a criminal organization before the International Military Tribunal.

HOW EFFECTIVE WAS OHLENDORF'S SD as a monitor of public opinion in Nazi Germany? There are limitations on the reliability of its reports, mainly arising from the SD's structure. It depended for intelligence primarily on a corps of volunteer informants, whose activity rested upon two potentially weak pillars: anonymity and chance. The secrecy surrounding *Amt* III removed effective checks on the correctness of the information gathered. The V-*Leute* reported conversations overheard or provoked at work, in

---

[57] 'Der innenpolitische, lebensgebietsmässige Nachrichtendienst in Deutschland', covering letter and parts iv and v, quoted in Boberach (ed.), *Meldungen*, 533 f., 538 f.; McDowell, op. cit., 557 f., 562, 609; Steinert, *Die 23 Tage*, 158–59; Kersten, op. cit., 211–12, entry for 4 September 1943.

[58] McDowell, op. cit., 442 ff., 600–1; Steinert, *Die 23 Tage*, 147 f., 376, n. 440; *TWC*, IV, 242.

pubs and restaurants, shops and offices, on trains and street-cars, and among relatives, friends and acquaintances. Each *Aussen-stelle* accumulated as much 'raw material' as possible from which, multiplied many times over, *Amt* III finally assessed German opinion. Ohlendorf tried to recruit the best quality informants; nevertheless, the anonymity of their reporting lessened the certitude of accuracy. Furthermore, if the *V-Leute* wanted to uncover the 'real' feelings of Germans on sensitive subjects, their questioning could not be overly conspicuous. They relied on accidental encounters for much information. Most were not specially trained for their work, as full-time SD members were.[59] The broad basis upon which the reliability of their reports ultimately depended was the SD's least 'professional' aspect.

Amt III aimed to produce a 'mosaic of impressions', 'typical examples' extracted from each area of national life, in order to build up a 'valid survey of the entire Reich'. Its informants were told to depict popular morale 'factually, clearly, reliably and responsibly, just as it is, not as it could or should be'. A directive of 2 August 1941 stipulated that they be recruited 'from the point of view . . . that the portion of the work in the area which they carry out shows all the features of the [entire] area, since every intelligence organization must evaluate the part as representative of the whole'.[60] Wolfgang Kraus and Gabriel Almond, among the first to examine the SD reports, emphasized that no quantitative techniques were employed by Ohlendorf's organization. While many SD members and informants thought themselves agents of a national 'Gallup poll', they were completely innocent of the sampling, interviewing and other procedures characteristic of contemporary opinion surveying. In any case, using such techniques was a practical impossibility in Nazi Germany. *Amt* III and the regional offices checked the data from the *Aussenstellen* by employing their own *V-Leute* to report on the same subjects in the same fashion; they also received letters sent by the public to the Propaganda Ministry as well as its regular reports. The best guarantee of accuracy, however, was the idealism motivating the

[59] *IMG*, XX, 214, 263, testimony of Rolf Heinz Hoeppner and Hans Rössner; Kersten, op. cit., 212–14, entry for 7 September 1943; Boberach (ed.), *Berichte*, xxxix–xl; Steinert, *Hitlers Krieg*, 44.

[60] *IMG*, IV, 390–91, testimony of Otto Ohlendorf; ibid., XX, 263, testimony of Hans Rössner; Kersten, op. cit., 212–14, entry for 7 September 1943; Boberach (ed.), *Meldungen*, xv; Steinert, *Hitlers Krieg*, 40.

great majority of informants working voluntarily and without salary because they were convinced such an agency was needed. Kraus and Almond concluded that 'this elaborate organization produced what unquestionably constituted both the most comprehensive and the most objective morale reports in Germany'. Compared with the SD, those prepared by the Nazi party appear superficial, implausible and 'rose coloured'. According to A. L. Unger,

> it is clear that in general the . . . [SD] had less motive for concealing the unpleasant truths about public opinion than had the local organizations of the party . . . The [SD] had no vested interest in concealing manifestations of popular discontent. *Menschenführung* ('leading the people') was not the responsibility of the SD. . . . The impression gained from reading the [SD] reports as a whole is that the SD allowed few inhibitions to stand in its way in presenting a picture of public opinion that was wholly unadorned and, for the Nazi leadership, often highly unflattering.[61]

Police reports are directly related to the events, personalities and institutions with which they deal. They can no more escape their environment than can the conscientiously impartial historian describing a period far removed from his own. No greater scepticism, though, need be afforded to the authenticity of what Ohlendorf and *Amt* III recorded in the 'internal newspaper' of the RSHA than to most other historical sources. This would needlessly deprive us of 'an indispensable source for the internal situation in Germany during the war' and what 'unless all evidence deceives [are] the most revealing . . . and certainly the most interesting . . . domestic political documents' to survive the Third Reich.[62]

[61] Wolfgang H. Kraus and Gabriel A. Almond, 'Resistance and Repression under the Nazis' in Almond (ed.), *The Struggle for Democracy in Germany* (Chapel Hill 1949), 37–40; Dröge, op. cit., 53; Unger, op. cit., 572, 578; also Berghahn, op. cit., 83; 'Der Sicherheitsdienst', *Der Spiegel*, 15 December 1965; Daniel Lerner, *SYKEWAR: Psychological Warfare against Germany, D-Day to VE-Day* (New York 1949), 294 ff.; Boberach (ed.), *Berichte*, xli.

[62] Walter Laqueur, 'Nazism and the Nazis', *Encounter*, XXII, (1964), 40; Jäckel, op. cit., 50–51.

The North-West Mounted Police and the Klondike Gold Rush

W. R. Morrison

The career of the North-West Mounted Police during the Klondike (or Yukon) gold rush of 1897—99 is one episode in the history of Canada with which foreigners are generally familiar. People who know little else of this country can remember pictures of dog-teams, northern lights, and 'mounties' who 'always get their man'. Thanks to a large amount of literature written about the period, not the least influential of which has been the poetry of Robert W. Service, this era in Canadian history has acquired an image which is more romantic than scholarly. Nonetheless there is more to the subject than simple melodrama. The gold rush provides an opportunity to study the methods of operation of the NWMP,[1] showing clearly some of the strengths and weaknesses of this remarkable force. It illustrates the Canadian system of coping with the challenge of a mining frontier, in striking contrast to the system used by the government of the United States. It also illustrates how flexible a body of police can be, given the proper stimulus.

The great discovery of gold was made in August 1896 on Bonanza Creek, a few miles from the present town of Dawson, which is located at the confluence of the Yukon and Klondike Rivers. Although this event precipitated the rush,[2]

---

[1] After 1904 the Royal Northwest Mounted Police; since 1920 the Royal Canadian Mounted Police.
[2] The best history of the period is Pierre Berton, *Klondike Fever* (New York 1958).

it was not the first occasion on which gold had been found in the area. Two or three hundred miners had been active along the Yukon River since 1886, and small discoveries of gold were regularly made. Most of the early miners in the Yukon were Americans, and since there were no officials of the Canadian government in the region at all before 1894, except for an occasional surveyor, the miners had set up a form of self-government suited to their own needs. This was based on the code of laws developed in the California gold fields, and its basic institution was the 'miners' meeting' — a sort of direct democracy, by which any miner with a grievance could call an assembly of his fellows, who would hear the case, discuss it, and give out a decision or sentence as required. Each locality in the Yukon, as in the neighbouring gold fields of Alaska, made its own by-laws and mining regulations; the usual penalty for infractions of these laws was expulsion from the community.

Thus, this remote part of the Dominion of Canada operated at that time under a system which, in the best tradition expounded by Frederick Jackson Turner, sprang directly from the American idea of the self-governing community, unhampered by external controls and conducting its affairs as it saw fit. This system was bound to come into conflict with that of the Canadian government, which saw its distant possessions not as crucibles of self-government, but as communities to be put under the benevolent but complete control of the central government.

Although the government at Ottawa viewed the situation in the Yukon with unease, it took no formal action until complaints began to trickle down from the north. These came from the traders and the missionaries — the two groups in Yukon society which stood to benefit most from government intervention. The traders, most of whom were also Americans, feared the threat to commerce posed by the possibility of a mining society in complete disorder. The missionaries, in particular the Anglican Bishop of Selkirk, William Carpenter Bompas, deplored the influence of the miners on the local Indians. As early as 1893, Bompas begged the government to regulate the flow of liquor in the Yukon, which, he said, was causing his charges to spend 'nights of debauch'[3] and was endangering relations between Indians and whites. The miners had taught the Indians the art of making a concoction called 'hoo-chin-oo' (from which 'hooch'), a mixture of molasses, sugar, and dried fruit, which made them violent and sometimes poisoned them.

So the frontier made its traditional appeal for law and order. The Dominion government of the day was not slow to react in this case, for the nineteenth century territorial quarrels between Canada and the United States, especially the Oregon crisis of 1846, stood as examples to apprehensive Canadians of the results of permitting Americans to occupy an area in dispute or under question. The example of California, and to a lesser extent British Columbia, showed what could happen if public order were neglected during a gold rush. The North-West Rebellion of 1885 had, perhaps, taught the government the dangers of procrastination.

And the tools for the task were at hand, for the government had in the NWMP a body of men the adaptability and flexibility of which had been proven for over twenty years in the development of the Canadian prairies. Those in command of the police welcomed the suggestion that their activities should be extended to the far north-west, particularly since it appeared that their initial mission — the pacification of the prairie Indians — was nearly complete.

Thus it was with considerable dispatch and enthusiasm that the commander of the police, Commissioner L. W. Herchmer, responded to a resolution of the Canadian Privy Council, approved by the Governor-General on 26 May 1894, to send a police officer into the Yukon:

> it is highly desirable that immediate provision be made for the regulation and control of the traffic in intoxicating liquor, for the administration of the lands containing the precious metals, for the collection of customs duties upon the extensive imports being made into that section of Canada from the United States . . . for the protection of the Indians and for the administration of justice generally.[4]

[3] Letters from Bompas to T. M. Daly, Superintendent General of Indian Affairs, Ottawa, May 1893 and 9 December 1893, Charles Constantine Papers, Public Archives of Canada, MG 30, E-2, v. 3.
[4] A copy is in *ibid*.

Two members of the NWMP were sent on a reconaissance mission to the Yukon in the summer of 1894, and in the next year a party of twenty, commanded by Inspector Charles Constantine, left Regina for the north, reaching the mining region at the end of July. The men built a police post, Fort Constantine, on the bank of the Yukon River about twenty miles from the Alaska boundary, and Constantine wrote proudly in January 1896 that he was making his annual report from 'the most northerly military or semi-military post in the British Empire'.[5]

HOW WERE THE POLICE RECEIVED by this heterogeneous group of men in the Yukon? Perhaps surprisingly, there was only one real challenge to their authority, and coming in the summer of 1896, it marked as nothing else could have done the passing of the old free way of life in the Yukon, and the replacement of the older system of justice by the new. The facts of the incident were as follows: two owners of a claim at Glacier Creek leased it to a third man, who defaulted on the payments to his labourers and left the country. A miners' meeting was called, and the men seized the claim in lieu of wages, then sold it to a fourth man. Thereupon the original owners appealed to the police for redress. When the new owner arrived at the police office, which was also the recording office, and was refused registration of his purchase, he left 'breathing defiance'. Constantine realized 'that this was the turning-point, and should I give them their way or recognize them in any manner, trouble would never cease'. He immediately sent an officer and ten men to the disputed claim with orders to act circumspectly but firmly, and sent a note to the miners' leaders warning them to desist. This they did; the claim was handed back to its original owners (the workers were never paid), and the only challenge to police authority in the Yukon ever presented by an organized group collapsed. The traditional system of justice obtained from the miners' meeting had given way to police law; the old order had passed in the

5 NWMP *Report* 1895 (Ottawa 1896), 7.

Yukon, and American-style frontier democracy had been replaced by British authoritarian paternalism.[6]

Thus when the great discovery of gold took place, the police were unchallenged in the Yukon. This was fortunate for Canada, for between 1897 and 1899 about thirty thousand people — again, largely Americans — descended on the Yukon, which was made a separate Territory in June 1898. Police reinforcements were rushed north, and by the end of November 1899 there were 254 police stationed in thirty-three posts in the Yukon and the adjacent parts of British Columbia.

When in the summer of 1897 the discovery became generally known in the south, all sorts of unlikely people chartered all manner of unlikely craft — for passage was at a premium — and hurried north. Little was actually known of the Yukon by the general public, especially in the United States, and the devices for finding gold which were fobbed off on credulous green-horns in Seattle and Victoria would have done credit to P. T. Barnum. Of course the flotsam of society went north as well, those whose trade it was to 'mine the miners' — the thieves, gamblers, murderers, and what one writer euphemistically called the 'ladies of ultimate accessibility'.[7] By the thousands they streamed over the trail of '98 — from Dyea and Skagway in Alaska over the Chilkoot and White Passes into northwestern British Columbia, to the headwaters of the Yukon River, then down the river to the new city of Dawson, which in 1898 became the largest city in Canada west of Winnipeg. These were to cause the police much work, as were those who became public charges through their own incompetence or bad luck.

ONCE THE MOUNTED POLICE arrived in force in the Yukon, they quickly made their presence felt in all aspects of the life of the community, legal or other. It was as if the police, under their new commander in the Yukon, Superintendent (later Major-General Sir) S. B. Steele, were determined to avoid the example of Skagway, which was generally

[6] RCMP Papers, PAC, RG 18, B-1, v. 123: See also M. H. E. Hayne, *Pioneers of the Klondyke* (London 1897), 124.
[7] M. Morgan, *One Man's Gold Rush* (Seattle 1967), 162.

cited as the horrible result of what was likely to happen in an unpoliced society. The police were fond of comparing the lawlessness of Skagway with the relative order of Dawson. According to Supt. Steele, for example, the tempo of lawlessness increased as one approached the Canadian border, and then it ceased:

> murder, robbery, and petty theft were of common occurrence, the 'shell game' could be seen at every turn of the trail, operations being pushed with the utmost vigour, so as not to lose the golden opportunity which they would not be able to find or take advantage of on the other side of the line in British territory.[8]

While providing a haven for crime-weary travellers and collecting substantial sums in customs duties for the Dominion government, the police were also busy laying the physical foundations of their authority in the Yukon. Detachments were quickly set up on the various gold-bearing creeks, down the length of the Yukon River, and at all points of entry into the Territory. In cooperation with the Commissioner of the Yukon, the civilian official appointed by Ottawa to govern the Territory, a flood of Territorial and police general orders was sent out, with the object of regularizing society as much as possible. The indefatigable Supt. Steele settled down to a routine which would have killed a lesser man; his description of his working day shows what was expected of an officer of the NWMP in the Yukon at that time:

> my working hours were at least nineteen. I retired to rest about 2 a.m. or later, rose at six, was out of doors at seven, walked five miles for exercise between that hour and eight, two and a half miles up the Klondyke on the ice and back over the mountain, visited every institution under me each day, sat on boards and committees until midnight, attended to the routine of the Yukon command without an adjutant, saw every prisoner daily, and was in the town station at midnight to see how things were going.[9]

At the detachments, which normally comprised two to four men, the police, although expected to show initiative, were by no means left to their own devices. Each detachment had

[8]S. B. Steele, *Forty Years in Canada* (Toronto 1918), 296.
[9]Ibid. 324.

a prescribed daily routine; the one for the post at Lake Bennett in October 1898 is typical:

Reveille	6:30 a.m.
Morning stables	7:00
Breakfast	7:30
Fatigue	8:30 or as may be required
Noon stables	11:30
Dinner	12:30 p.m.
Fatigue or exercise	2:30 or as may be necessary
Evening stables	4:30
Supper	5:30
Last post (roll call)	10:00
Lights out	10:15[10]

This rigorous schedule, which does not include the police duties which were a part of every day, such as customs and general criminal work, was of course modified depending on circumstances. Some of the detachments had no horses (that at Lake Bennett had only two), a fact which must have lightened the work considerably.

One of the most interesting features of police work in the Yukon was the pragmatic attitude adopted by the force towards the unusual problems posed by conditions there. In more than one instance the police, in the interests of common sense, acted quite outside the law. One example comes from the spring of 1898, when a motley collection of boats lay on the shores of Lakes Bennett and Lindeman, waiting for the break-up of ice to permit downstream passage to Dawson. Unfortunately for the Klondikers, two major sets of rapids lay in their path, at White Horse and at Miles Canyon. The inexperienced gold seekers attempted these dangerous rapids in their crazy boats, once the ice disappeared, without guides and without much common sense. Several men were drowned, whereupon Steele began a system of registration for the boats, and drew up rules for the passage of all craft through Miles Canyon. In this he acted quite arbitrarily, admitting, as he said, 'there are many of your countrymen who have said that the Mounted Police

[10] RCMP Papers, PAC, RG 18, D-2, v. 12.

make the laws as they go along, and I am going to do so now, for your own good'.[11]

In November of the same year the possibility arose in Dawson that the existing supplies of food might not be sufficient to carry the community through the winter. The police were especially apprehensive, for lack of food inevitably meant disorder, while the destitute, for lack of anywhere else to go, generally applied to the police for aid they could not always afford to give. It was also difficult to distinguish between real and counterfeit cases of need. Thus on 18 November 1898 Steele issued a proclamation stating that no one would be permitted to enter the Yukon without satisfying the police that he had with him two months' provisions and $500 in cash, or six months' provisions and $200 in cash. Notices to this effect were posted in Skagway and the main coastal cities of Canada and the United States. This ruling was quite illegal, as the Department of Justice informed the police the following July. Steele was told that his actions were illegal, but that this fact should not be made public until the emergency no longer existed.[12]

These two incidents raise an important question about the work of the police in the Yukon. They were not cases of flexible interpretation of the law; this is done by all police forces, and was to be expected in the Yukon. These were matters of actual invention of non-existent law to fit a certain situation. One might argue that extraordinary conditions require extraordinary measures; yet they still leave the historian with an uneasy feeling. Perhaps they may be explained most easily by saying that neither the police nor any other branch of officialdom at that time was as sensitive to the nuances of civil liberties as their counterparts are today, and the police must, in fairness, be judged by the political theories prevailing in Canada in 1900, which were more authoritarian than those of our own time. A great deal of police work in the Yukon consisted of exercising a more-or less benevolent control over the safety of others, men who were too foolish or too careless to look after themselves.

[11] Quoted in Berton, op cit. 281.
[12] RCMP Papers, PAC, RG 18, B-1, v. 159.

From this situation a feeling of paternalism was bound to develop.

In the summer of 1898, with the rush to the Yukon well under way, it seemed to the police as if a wave of crime had descended on them. The community spirit which had prevailed among the miners before the rush disappeared with the influx of those, honest or not, who were unaccustomed to the old code of ethics. Formerly, miners had been able to leave their supplies cached on the trails in perfect safety, but with the advent of the Klondikers, the police reported that 'a man has to sit on his cache with a shot-gun'.[13] At first petty criminals were summarily told to leave the country, since it was more convenient, though illegal, to throw them out than to feed them in jail. Many others were simply turned back at the border posts, at the discretion of the police there. After the new NWMP headquarters in Dawson were completed, the police applied corrective therapy to thieves in the form of ten hours' work per day on the enormous woodpile behind the barracks.

Although some crimes were committed on the creeks and the trails, most of them, except for smuggling and bootlegging, tended to take place in Dawson. The police in some respects took a pragmatic view of this crime, especially where moral standards were concerned. Given the social conditions of a mining town, it seemed to the police that the eradication of gambling and prostitution was patently impossible; indeed, perhaps it was even undesirable, despite the protestations of the local clergy to the contrary. If vice was too prevalent, too popular, and perhaps too essential to suppress, then it should at least be kept under control and practised honestly. To this end the prostitutes were herded into their own ghetto, much to the rage of the citizens who lived there already, and were later deported across the river to Klondike City, or 'Lousetown', as it was popularly called. They were also given regular medical examinations, until this practice was forbidden by Ottawa as giving too much sanction to their trade.[14] On the other hand, women were forbidden to drink in saloons, and no liquor was served in dance-halls. All

[13] NWMP *Report* 1897 (Ottawa 1898), 309.
[14] Department of the Interior, Northern Administration Branch Papers, PAC, RG 85, v. 658, f. 3418.

gambling was forbidden which involved the 'house' getting a percentage of the stake; institutionalized gambling was thus prevented. These measures gave the police a considerable degree of control over such nominally illegal operations, without making it necessary for them to be abolished altogether. Eventually, gambling was suppressed, and prostitution driven underground, but these developments, much desired by upright citizens, did not come about until after 1901, when the Yukon was fast declining in population and importance.

There was never much serious crime in the Yukon. There were a few murders, all of which were rapidly solved by the police. It was not a good country for murderers; as one observer put it, the police were 'rapid, simple, and severe in their methods'.[15] As was learned then and later, the north, though huge, is not a good place to hide. The few exits from the Yukon were closely and constantly guarded, and it was all but impossible to live off the land. The police kept careful track of the movements of suspicious characters, and frequently advised them to leave the country even when they were innocent of any proven crime. As a result the Yukon was, for a mining community, amazingly quiet. The comparison which the police delighted in making between the sink of iniquity at Skagway and the model of good order at Dawson spoke volumes for 'what a motley throng can achieve under British institutions'.[16]

The other side of police work in the Yukon lay in the numerous civil duties they performed. Since these duties, as opposed to the strictly regulatory, were possibly the most durable of their contributions, it is a pity that this was the work the police liked the least. Most members of the NWMP had come to the Yukon expecting to expand their energies in catching criminals, but much of their work consisted of more prosaic tasks. The list is impressive: they kept the penitentiary prisoners and the lunatics (in adjacent cells), and acted as magistrates and justices of the peace. They looked after the welfare of the Indians and ran the Yukon postal service.

[15] A. N. C. Treadgold, *Report on the Gold Fields of the Klondike* (London 1899), 69.
[16] Ibid. 70.

They acted as land agents, mining recorders, coroners, and returning officers at elections. They served writs and notices for all levels of government, accompanied the tax collector on his rounds, or collected taxes themselves. They acted as escorts for visiting dignitaries and orderlies for the courts. They assigned two men every night to guard the Dawson banks. They enforced the customs and the gold-smuggling laws.

Not all these duties were performed gladly; in fact the complaints from the police were vehement and continuous, their burden being that it was unfair to expect the police to prevent crime and to be versatile civil servants at the same time, especially since they were generally not paid for these extra duties. As one officer put it, the police were 'at the disposal of any department which wants to save expenses by calling upon the police to do work which properly belongs to its employees'.[17] The jobs which involved some element of adventure, such as carrying the winter mail, were reasonably popular, for they afforded the police an opportunity to show their mettle. A mail patrol in the winter of 1898—99 provided this example:

> delayed between Bennett and Caribou owing to drifting ice and heavy wind. One dog died on route . . . Mail delayed one day at Thirty Mile owing to horses being unable to go further. Between Five Fingers and Hootchikoo one sleigh with five bags of mail . . . went through the ice. Constable Davis and Special Constable Garson got into the river up to the waist to get the sleigh out . . . delayed one day . . . drying mail.[18]

The duty which the police disliked most was that connected with the customs service; much of this involved clerical routine, a task for which they were neither suited nor trained. It also caused unpleasant clashes with the public. All people entering the Yukon were physically searched for liquor and for goods on which duty had not been paid; those leaving the country were searched for gold. There were complaints that the police were extortionists, when they were in fact charging only the prescribed rate. The police were highly sensitive to attacks on their public image, especially since

---

[17] NWMP *Report* 1902 (Ottawa 1903), III, 5.
[18] RCMP Papers, PAC, RG 18, B-1, v. 147.

their authority rested to a considerable extent on their reputation. They therefore chafed at duties which cast them in the role of rapacious tax-gatherers. Nor were they pleased by civil servants who came north expecting police to act as their batmen. They were not unwilling to work, but they wished their special status to be recognized. And in fact their reputation was high among their contemporaries in the Yukon. The three daily newspapers published in Dawson during the gold rush, two of which were strongly critical of the government, had nothing but praise for the police. The *Klondike Nugget* (30 August 1898) stated that 'The only good thing that can be said of the government of the Yukon District is that we have an excellent police and court . . . The debit side covers several pages.'

Examined as individuals the police naturally show a wide variation in competence, enthusiasm, and character, and it should come as no surprise that there were frequent lapses from the strict path of duty. Many traps existed to snare the susceptible. The police were exceedingly ill-paid; during the Klondike period the basic rate of pay for a constable was fifty cents a day, and after three years service, seventy-five cents. In addition, men on Yukon service were given fifty cents a day hardship allowance. In contrast, common labourers in Dawson could make between five and ten dollars a day in wages, though the fact that room and board was provided for the police reduces this contrast somewhat. But a basic fact of police service was that no one entered it for profit; most of the recruits were out for adventure. Even this was not sufficient to fill the ranks with Canadians; the force had to advertise for recruits in Britain, where young men were unaware of or indifferent to the purchasing power of a dollar in the Yukon. At the same time, some men volunteered for Yukon service for a free ride north, hoping to purchase a discharge and stake a claim — a practice which the authorities discouraged. With a fair number of idealists and opportunists in the force, it was inevitable that disenchantment would set in for many, and the police reports every year noted that it was almost impossible to get men to re-enlist in the Yukon.

With this in mind, it may be surprising to discover that

instances of serious crime among the police were quite rare. There were a few cases of theft; one constable guarding the Bank of British North America stole a small sum from the manager's desk, while another stole $2,300 from the Board of License Commissioners.[19] A special constable embezzled $1,100 from the Dawson dog pound.[20] But there was not much of this sort of thing; most of the reductions in rank, fines, and dismissals handed out to the police were for service offences, of which there were a great many. The records of the Dawson detachment are full of accounts of police who were punished for visiting brothels, being drunk in dance-halls, and the like. 'Breaking barracks' was a daily occurrence. Most of their sins were sins of the flesh, and as such were perhaps more easily excused by the Klondikers than crimes of violence or dishonesty.

Under the conditions the police had to endure, and with their miserable pay, it speaks well for the fibre of the force that serious derelictions of duty were so few, and that the challenges of the Yukon were met as well as they were. For every record of a sergeant reduced to the ranks for drunkenness, or an officer in disgrace, there are many accounts of the sort of heroism which so caught the attention of the public and the writers of popular fiction. If the police were not perfect, they were undoubtedly closer to perfection than was the average Klondiker, and that is all, perhaps, that can reasonably be expected of the character of a police force.

The Yukon rush was not long-lived; it was virtually over by the end of 1899, when new discoveries in Alaska drew off much of the population. Gold continued to be extracted from the Yukon creek-beds, but by giant dredges rather than by hand. The passing of the boom was a blessing to the police in one way, insofar as most of the criminals left the Territory along with its prosperity. The number of police in the Yukon was reduced from a high of three hundred to about forty by the beginning of the first world war, and the men remaining settled into a less spectacular routine of police duty which has persisted to the present day.

[19]General Yukon Order 2048, 30 May 1903, and Yukon Order 225, 22 April 1899. Copies kindly furnished by S. W. Horrall, RCMP Headquarters, Ottawa.
[20]RCMP Papers, PAC, RG 18, D-1, v. 7.

The Mayor and the Police— The Political Role of the Police in Society

Cyril D. Robinson

This article will examine the relationship between the mayor and the police in the big American city. More specifically, it will discuss the use of the police to shield the mayor from responsibility for problems arising out of long-time neglect of city problems, especially those found in ghetto communities.

The reference to the 'mayor's responsibility' is not to be taken literally. His relationship to other city authorities, to state and federal government, to semi-governmental bodies and to private interests, is complex. 'Mayor' is used as the central figure in a vortex of forces — one who is visible, somewhat in the same way in which the police will be described as being central and visible. Today's problems did not arise under the administration of any one mayor, nor is it clear that, even if he did all that he could, these problems could be substantially reduced through the means within his control. Nevertheless, to the extent that they become politically visible, he must deal with them. 'Mayor' or 'police' therefore, should be seen as the description of two teams, subject to periodic substitutions, playing a (usually) friendly game of catch, the ball being responsibility for tackling the city's problems.

WHEN AMERICAN OFFICIALS discuss the 'crime problem' today, they are talking about areas in the big central city with large concentrations of low-income blacks living in ghetto conditions.

Chicago is one of these cities. It is in certain ways unique, particularly in its unity of governmental and political structure. Nevertheless, the interaction of the police department with other parts of the government is sufficiently typical of large northern cities to make comparisons possible.

Like many of America's huge cities, Chicago's growth has been rapid and undisciplined. From 200 inhabitants in 1883, the year

277

of its incorporation, it grew to 3,620,962 in 1950. In 1910, 2 per cent of the city population was black; in the 1970 census they accounted for 32.7 per cent, but the city's total population, like that of most large northern American cities, had declined as many of the middle-class whites moved to the suburbs.

More than 85 per cent of the black population of Chicago live in communities in which at least 85 per cent of the population is black. Chicago is now more segregated than it was a generation ago. It is these ghetto areas that police are asked to control. Police are held in such low esteem by some ghetto residents that riots have been touched off by a minor police contact with black citizens.

The purpose of this paper is not, however, to discuss the causes of riots, or poor police-community relations as such. Nevertheless, the reaction between the police and alienated groups does help to make explicit the role of the police in a way that their day-to-day activities may not.

Simply stated, the political role of the police is to accept the punishment that might otherwise be received by their employers. The police serve as the convenient scapegoat for a variety of error, ineptitude, malfeasance, misfeasance and nonfeasance, committed or permitted by other institutions. In recent years, police have been shot, stoned, beaten and insulted from the left, while being honoured, supported and pampered from the right. The same government that created or allowed to be created the conditions that led to ghetto riots places the police in a position to accept, as representatives of the State, the abuse of the abused. For their performance, the State, in turn, lavishes praise upon them.

What explains their acceptance of public punishment for the sins of others, and in doing so, what services, if any, do they render to other institutions in society, and what services do they receive in return? One explanation for the maltreatment of the police by the political left is their contention that the police represent the power of the State by which the governing class maintains its dominance. This view has been accepted by Marxist and non-Marxist criminologists alike. Joseph D. Lohman, a criminologist, a former Cook County, Illinois, sheriff and state treasurer, described the police function as supporting and enforcing 'the dominant political, social, and economic interests of the town, and only incidentally to enforce the law'.[1] Hence, from the viewpoint of the under-privileged or the under-represented, they are fair game. While such a view may be politically attractive to some, it does not explain why the police, who are largely drawn from the working class, allow themselves to be so used. Even less does it explain why, to the extent that the police are recognized as representatives of others, the anger of the aggrieved should be directed at them rather than their principals.

This confusion of where the 'real target' lies seems to arise from such factors as the increasing remoteness and diffusion of the governing class, as well as changes in the composition of the police. A contributing factor, though perhaps in the long run a less fundamental one, is the decentralization of the American law enforcement system.

IN BIG CITIES, THE USUAL form of government is an elected mayor and city council. A municipal code or city charter sets forth the powers of the mayor and his relationship to the police

---

[1] A. Niederhoffer, *Behind the Shield* (New York 1967), 12. The conventional view of police function is that expressed in a 1970 survey of the Chicago police department by the International Association of Chiefs of Police.

The police shall:
1. Protect and preserve life and property.
2. Prevent and suppress crime.
3. Enforce statutes and ordinances.
4. Investigate crimes for the purpose of identifying offenders and establishing a case suitable for presentation in court.
5. Apprehend offenders either at the time they commit offences or after warrants of arrest for them have been issued.
6. Preserve the public peace and tranquility.
7. Provide a wide variety of public services which at a given time are unavailable elsewhere.

Modern writers about the police scene . . . tend to define the police role into two or three basic terms. These include 'order maintenance', 'law enforcement', and 'service functions'. In this perspective, the police have three responsibilities. The first is to discourage, prevent or otherwise cope with many types of disorderly conduct. The second responsibility is somewhat more precise although not completely so; it suggests that the police take official action when there is a reasonable unanimity of opinion that a clear-cut breach of the law has occurred. The third responsibility is that the police will provide certain services to individual citizens—services which tend to increase their comfort and well-being.
(*A Survey of the Police Department*, Chicago, Illinois, vol. II, Operational Services 542 [International Association of Chiefs of Police June 1970]).

and other departments. In Chicago, the mayor is the 'chief executive officer'. The municipal code (there is no city charter) establishes 'an executive department of the municipal government of the city which shall be known as the department of police'. With the exception of the superintendent of police, the mayor appoints all department heads with the advice and consent of the city council. The police superintendent is appointed by the mayor from the three persons suggested by a police board, the members of which are appointed by the mayor by and with the consent of the city council. Thereafter, the superintendent is to serve 'at the pleasure of the mayor'. The Superintendent 'shall be the executive officer of the police department' and he alone 'shall be responsible for the general management and control of the police department and shall have full and complete authority to administer the department in a manner consistent with the ordinances of the city, the laws of the State, and the rules and regulations of the police board'.

The police board is to 'adopt rules and regulations for the governance of the police department' but 'the board's power' to adopt such rules and regulations 'does not include authority to administer or direct the operations of the police department, or the superintendent of police'. This statutory monstrosity might be expected to lead to jurisdictional squabbles if either the superintendent or the board were to seek more power. In practice, neither does because the mayor controls both.

How this formal system works depends to a large extent on the mayor. A strong mayor ordinarily means that the executive departments are led with a firm hand. Even though the system is based on the principles of separation of powers and checks and balances, the removal power of the mayor and his designation as chief executive officer should be enough to ensure his command of the police department. Several decentralizing aspects, however, substantially weaken his control. Laws governing the appointment of the police chief, the civil service and the police boards, as well as the laws to be enforced by the police, are products of the state legislature. Ordinances promulgated by the city council must be in accord with these laws. It is the Civil Service Board that controls hiring and promotion through the rank of captain and it is the city council that prescribes the duties of the police and determines their salaries and departmental budgets. Police procedures are determined in part by the state legislature, in part by the state courts, and to a considerable degree by the United States Supreme Court. The correctional system is essentially state run.

While the exceptions of violations of city ordinances and federal law, the state's attorney, an elected county official responsible to that governmental unit, will prosecute persons arrested by the city police. On the periphery are the sheriff and coroner, elected county officers who have uncertain and shadowy roles in city law enforcement. Each elective office encourages personal advancement, best achieved by an appearance of individual activity rather than of co-operative effort. Further complicating the task is the recent entry of the federal government into local law enforcement through the Omnibus Crime Control and Safe Streets Act of 1968. This act sifts federal money through a series of state, regional and local commissions. Grants normally are applied for and granted to police departments rather than to cities.

In addition, as both a unifying and decentralizing factor, is the political party, an ubiquitous and all-powerful force in Chicago. One significant result of all this is that city government does not and in the nature of things perhaps cannot agree on common goals and on a common programme for city law enforcement. Far from having commonly agreed goals, the various units are often antagonistic to each other.

NOTHING, HOWEVER, IS MORE important in the relationship between the mayor and the police than the question of political interference from the mayor's office. Calls for police departments to be free of political control or interference have been frequent throughout police history, appear to be nationwide, and part of a larger movement to take the city government 'out of politics' through the employment of city managers and the like. 'Political control' has usually meant that police chiefs would rise and fall with the fortunes of the mayor;[2] that the department would be used to further the mayor's career by campaigning for the mayor's

[2] The chief evil . . . lies in the insecure, short term of service of the chief or executive head of the police force and in his being subject while in office to the control by politicians in the discharge of his duties . . . The average term of service . . . is considerably under five years . . . in 10 cities having a population of 500,000 and over the average service of the chief is a mere 2·41 years. In one of our great cities, Chicago, there were 14 chiefs of police in 30 years.
(The Citizen's Police Committee, *Chicago Police Problems* [1931 reissue 1969; hereafter cited as *Chicago Police Problems*], 3).

candidates, to favour the mayor's friends, to arrest and harass his enemies, and to enforce laws on a politically selective basis. From the early 1900s until the mid-1930s grand juries, vice commissions, citizen committees, evangelists, suffragettes, anti-vice crusaders, and finally a string of governmental commissions tried to purge the evil.

Chicago came to be a symbol of official corruption; 'In 1928 a special grand jury declared the Chicago Police Department to be "rotten to the core . . ."' Although other parts of the criminal justice system were likewise condemned, the major push for reform was reserved for the police. Aside from suggested internal organizational reforms, the one consistent call was against 'political interference' in police affairs. The Wickersham Commission called for the removal of 'the corrupting influence of politics . . . from the police organization',[3] and the Citizen's Police Committee of Chicago warned that it would be impossible to achieve improvement in the department 'while the commissioner is compelled to dispense political favours in their several forms'.[4] These two similar sounding statements mask profound differences of approach to the responsibility of the mayor for police behaviour.

The Wickersham Commission argued from the well-known fact of the time:

> The chief is usually appointed by the mayor . . . such appointment is, however, never a guaranty of competency for the place of the person appointed, but is simply an assurance that he is the personal appointee of the mayor and subject to his arbitary control, or, more likely, that he is satisfactory to the party politicians whom the mayor felt obliged to consult before he dared risk confirmation of his nominee.[5]

'The chief evil', it was thus argued, 'lies in the insecure, short term of service of the chief . . . of police and in his being subject while in office to the control by politicians in the discharge of his duties.'[6] It was this 'lack of independence' that must be countered.[7] The mayor was given this control over the tenure

---

[3] *National Commission on Law Observance and Enforcement*: No. 14, *Report on Police* (US Government Printing Office 1931; hereafter referred to as the *Wickersham Report*), 140, 1–3.

[4] *Chicago Police Problems*, 44.

[5] *Wickersham Report*, 2. The commission points to one horrendous example where the mayor 'appointed his tailor as chief of police because he had been his tailor for 20 years and he knew he was a good tailor and so necessarily would make a good chief of police'. (Ibid., 3).

[6] Ibid., 1.

[7] Ibid., 3.

of the chief because the American people,

> jealous of their liberties . . . have hesitated to place too much power
> in the hands of the police. Accordingly, every known political device
> has been experimented with in order to fix responsibility for police
> service without placing the head of the department and the members
> thereof beyond the pale of the people . . . Limiting the powers of the
> police executive by placing absolute control of police under the
> mayor, commissioners, or city manager has opened the door for every
> conceivable type of incompetency, political corruption, and organi-
> zation demoralization. The theory that the mayor, representing the
> people, will exercise wisdom in conducting the business of the city
> and, being directly responsible to the electors, will do his utmost to
> protect lives and property of inhabitants and preserve the peace, has
> been badly shattered, judged by the calibre of police service which is
> to be found in the majority of the communities in this country.[8]

The commission also disputed another argument for mayoral
control, that mayors:

> put into operation progressive policies and at the same time keep the
> police in harmony with modern trends . . . There is a preponderant
> amount of evidence that mayors . . . have more often than not pre-
> vented the adoption of progressive methods and have seriously im-
> paired the efficiency of active police organizations.[9]

To the commission, the answer appeared obvious:

> The head of the department should be selected at large for compe-
> tence, a leader, preferably a man of considerable police experience,
> and removable from office only after preferment of charges and a
> public hearing.[10]

The Citizens Police Committee came to an opposite conclusion.[11]

> The whole police problem has reached a point where no police adminis-
> trator, regardless of his competence, can hope to solve it alone and
> unaided.

[8] Ibid., 49.
[9] Ibid., 50.
[10] Ibid., 140. By 'at large' the commission meant outside the department.
[11] The reasons for this divergence may be as follows: *Wickersham* was an
exposé of conditions of the entire criminal justice system; it was dealing with the
national problem and solutions had to be broadly applicable. *Chicago Police
Problems* was initiated at the request of the then commissioner of police. The
committee 'confined its attention to the administrative functioning of the Police
Department. Questions of police corruption have been excluded'. The study was
'conducted largely from the police viewpoint and therefore will commend itself
to many police officers'. *Chicago Police Problems*, xi–xii, n. 3, 9, 17, 29–30,
44–45, 271–73.

The mayor of Chicago, and he alone, can dictate the kind and quality of police administration which the city shall receive.[12] . . . The control and direction of the police force in a complex urban community like Chicago is and ought to remain in the mayor's hands. This does not mean that the mayor should be police commissioner, or that he should directly concern himself with the details of police administration. It does mean, however, that the policies of the Police Department must be in general harmony with the views of the social groups which the mayor represents . . . It is vain to expect either good police work or reasonable continuity of police leadership until the voters of Chicago are able to elect consecutively a series of mayors who possess the courage and foresight to see the police problem within its feasible limitations, but who will also insist that the police force exists for the protection of persons and property rather than for other extraneous and at times extra-legal purposes . . . the voters of the city are confronted not with a police problem alone, but with the even larger problem of civic control.[13]

The two reports agreed that political interference, that is, the use of the police force for the partisan interests of the city administration, debased the department; they agreed that it was important to have a competent police chief who had public support. Apparently, it would be the mayor in each case who would make the selection. To the Wickersham Commission it was an administrative problem. They would create a police chief secure in tenure and hence a department 'independent' of the mayor, and thus of partisan interests. To the Citizen's Committee the problem was political. They would rely on the chief executive of the city not only to appoint a competent chief but to control and to direct the overall policies of the department. The mayor, in turn, would have to be controlled by 'a compelling public opinion'.

The Wickersham view, then, was that the department should be free of 'political interference' in order to attain 'independence' from the mayor, and the view of the Citizen's Committee was that the mayor should have the double responsibility of formulating a law enforcement policy for 'a complex urban community', and of ensuring that the department conform its actions to that policy.

While this larger problem of civic control has been ignored, the call for freedom from political interference has found a use never intended by these commissions — as a means of avoiding respon-

[12] *Chicago Police Problems*, xi, n. 3.
[13] *Chicago Police Problems*, 45, n. 3.

sibility for police action that might prove embarrassing to the mayors' administration. It has meant that the police department determines, or at least has the visible authority to determine, what is law enforcement and what is not, what the goals of law enforcement should be, what laws should be enforced and to what degree.

This tendency is encouraged by legislatures which on the one hand set few if any standards or limitations on police pursuit of law breakers, but on the other hand pass laws against gambling, drug use and like offences that invite the police to commit illegal acts of enforcement. All these factors combine to give to the police the attributes of an independent governmental unit; the department has been allowed to pursue its own goals even where these have been inconsistent with the aims of another part of the system.[14]

'Independence' of the police must offer certain advantages to other parts of the governmental structure. Otherwise, it would not persist. This independence depends, in the last analysis, on its acknowledgement by other institutions, particularly the office of the mayor. But, as we shall see, the mayor receives considerable benefit from his apparent ceding of power.

If there are problems in the city that reach a point of violence, they are not created by the police. In so far as blame can be assigned, it rests on those who make or influence policy, the legislature, the mayor, the prosecutor, or even the 'governing class'. But it is the police who must go into these 'crime' areas in an attempt to keep them from boiling over, and friction naturally develops between them and the population being policed. When they are attacked for their 'brutality' they are defended by the mayor, but he cannot intervene because that would be political interference. It follows that neither the mayor nor other senior officials are responsible for police actions.

This is a mask that may be slipped on and off as needed. Where the department has behaved well, the mayor is still in a position to take the credit. What are the gains to the police department and what are the gains to the mayor through the use of such a strategy? The police department, of course, has control over its

[14] An excellent elaboration of such a system of accommodations may be found in W. S. Sayre and H. Kaufman, *Governing New York City* (New York 1960), 290–91; see also 412, 428–31.

policies, goals and personnel; it becomes almost immune to criticism from other parts of the city administration; its solidarity is reinforced; the security and tenure of the higher-ups are strengthened and prolonged, and attacks bring it support from the administration and from groups which support the administration's policies.

The mayor gains because, when the police department commits serious errors of judgment, he can avoid criticism of both himself and the police by speaking of the important principle of freedom from political interference rather than about the particular incident. This does not prevent him from defending the police nor the police from thanking the mayor for his support.

Such interplay may be illustrated by a series of colloquies arising out of the disturbances attending the 1968 Democratic convention in Chicago. On 3 December 1968, just after the publication of the Walker Report criticizing the Chicago police for their actions,[15] Chicago's mayor Richard J. Daley, was asked during a news conference if he would handle the convention 'disorders differently today'. He answered:

> Who handled it? What do you mean? Do you have me out there responsible for an individual policeman? . . . out there directing them as to what to do? If you ask me if I support the Chicago Police Department and the National Guard in their actions, the answer would be an unequivocal yes.[16]

Similar comments followed in March 1969, when former Vice-President Hubert Humphrey, commenting on his electoral defeat, called the mayor's handling of the protestors during the convention a 'tragedy'.[17] The mayor responded:

> I had nothing to do with setting up the Convention or running the police department . . . Daley gave no orders to the police department. I defy you or anyone else to show that I did. No one runs the police department but Supt. (James B.) Conlisk.[18]

Further evidence will be cited to support the assertion that the part played by the police in society is that of buffer between the governing group and the more agitated groups of the governed. By 'governing group', is not meant a so-called 'power élite', lurk-

[15] D. Walker, *Rights in Conflict* (New York 1968).
[16] *The New York Times*, 4 December 1968, 29, col. 1.
[17] *Chicago Tribune*, 6 March 1969, 2, col. 6.
[18] *Chicago Daily News*, 6 March 1969, 8, col. 6.

ing somewhere in the background, but rather the group that visibly does the governing, a managing class, who may or may not, represent such an élite. But, regardless of whom this governing group represents, the police, as well as other governmental units mentioned (the legislature, the prosecutor), play this game on their own behalf, in order to protect their respective interests and territories.

Looked at in this fashion frictions between blacks and police, between students and police, between anti-war demonstrators and police, are not simply the result of poor co-ordination, the refusal to hire minority policemen, inadequate pay, hiring policies, or training in community relations, or any of the many other factors frequently assigned as causes of police-community frictions. Such conflict must be seen as one of the *benefits* the city administration receives from the police — a group on which neglected minorities may expend their energies.

In fact, programmes of police reform propose the police to the community as both a cause of and solution to community problems. Problems of housing, discrimination, bad schools, and lack of employment are turned back on the police. What might otherwise appear as the failure of the city administration to preserve the elements of a livable society becomes first a citizen and then a police failure to maintain order. All groups, liberals, radicals, conservatives, hard hats, are caught up in the problem of the police. The difference is only that of support or attack. None thinks of ignoring the police and looking elsewhere.

The struggle against the police, as representative of the naked strength of the State, as symbol of the State, may be viewed as a trap into which all types of groups have fallen, from the militants who blow up, or fire on, police stations to those liberal organizations that expend energy and money in trying to reform the police through civilian review of citizen complaints against the police.[19]

[19] A. Wildavsky has observed:
  The game begins with a publicity campaign focusing on fascist police, various atrocities, and other lurid events. The police and their friends counter with an equally illuminating defense: nothing is wrong that a little get-tough campaign would not cure. The game ends with a ballot in which white voters are asked to choose between their friendly neighbourhood policeman and the spector of black violence. The usual result is that the whites vote for the police and defeat the review board.
('Recipe for Violence', *New York* magazine, 20 May 1968, 28, cited in *Editorial Research Reports on Challenges for the 1970's* [New York 1970], 82).

A subsidiary — but most important — benefit to the mayor is to concentrate a good deal of reform effort on the police in lieu either of changing the basic structure of society or of holding the mayor and other governmental officials accountable for police actions. Much reform effort goes into trying to obtain civilian review boards, police race-relations programmes, etc. Since reform efforts suffer from a shortage of protagonists as well as of money, this diversion weakens the overall effort.

Accepting such an explanation of current city-police relations does not mean that one need think of this mechanism as a conspiracy. Rather, it represents a series of benefits and accommodations that constitute a repetitive pattern in police history.

THE USE OF THE POLICE as a target group began when the London police force was created in 1829 by Sir Robert Peel, the Tory Home Secretary. A year later, his government fell and the Whigs came to power. While out of power the Whigs had opposed the police, particularly as the police had been used repeatedly and successfully to quell riots against the Tory government, and had promised to abolish the organized police force.

But on taking office, they discovered that riots continued and the police were an effective means of controlling them. They learned as well that the discontent of the mob could be turned against the police. Throughout the early 1830s, the Whigs encouraged criticism of the police, as a way of deflecting criticism of the administration. Meetings were sponsored in which resolutions were passed demanding abolition of the police. Such petitions, however, met with no favourable action when forwarded to the ministers. Instead, the ministers vigorously objected to any reduction in the special taxes for the support of the police. An instance, in 1833, of Whig manipulation of the police is particularly blatant. The 'Ultra-Radicals' of the Chartist movement called a meeting of protest against Whig policies. On government orders, a notice was posted proclaiming the meeting illegal, the notice being signed, 'By order of the Secretary of State'. He gave the order orally, and refused to sign it when requested to do so by the police commissioners. After the meeting ended in a battle between the police and the protestors in which both sides suffered injuries, the police were subjected to criticism for breaking up the meeting. The Home Office denied giving the police any such order.

Only inquiry by a Royal Commission established the fact.[20]

This period is past when a government in a complex society may use the police to deflect blame from itself while simultaneously provoking the incident that results in the blame. Recent historical research, particularly the seminal essay of Alan Silver,[21] and the staff reports of the President's Commission on the Causes and Prevention of Violence,[22] have traced the evolution of the police-government relationship to its present degree of political sophistication.

These studies show a parallel development in England and the United States in the use of the police as instruments of social control. Before the time of professional police forces, police were drawn from the lowest ranks of society,[23] were poorly organized, were politically appointed, and were completely incapable of handling the recurrent riots that plagued the authorities.[24] Disturbances grew out of forces released by the demands of the nation-state,[25] and by the evolving industrialization that attracted masses of people to the cities.[26] Such riots became an accepted channel of political communication and negotiation between governing and governed at a time when other means of political expression were unavailable to lower economic groups.[27] Riots were suppressed by a militia, often consisting of local yeomanry (a mounted force drawn from the middle ranks of the agricultural classes),[28] who were occasionally the neighbours and employers of some of the mob.[29] This easy access of the lower classes to the

[20] This episode is recounted in C. Reith, *New Study of Police History* (London 1956), 157–65.

[21] 'The Demand for Order in Civil Society: A Review of Some Themes in the History of Urban Crime, Police and Riot', in Bordua (ed.), *The Police: Six Sociological Essays* (New York 1967).

[22] *Violence in America*, Historical and Comparative Perspectives, A Staff Report to the National Commission on the Causes and Prevention of Violence, Vols. I and II (New York 1969).

[23] Blackstone said of the 'constable': '. . . they are armed with very large powers . . . considering what manner of man are for the most part put into these offices, it is perhaps very well that they are generally kept in ignorance'. *Blackstone's Commentaries*, I, 11th ed. Dublin 1788, 356.

[24] *Violence in America*, op. cit., vol. I, 45–46, n. 25, 207.

[25] Ibid., 14–15.

[26] Ibid., 10.

[27] Ibid., 7, 14–15, 199–205.

[28] Ibid., 198, 202, 208.

[29] Silver, op. cit., 20, n. 21.

élite,[30] and the élite's direct participation in government, even in its martial defence, accentuated class conflict, and was very unsatisfactory for the governing class.[31] Moreover, '. . . industrialization and market economy required stability and did not lend itself to such a dialogue'.[32] As a consequence, in both England and the United States the organized police were created to replace the militia in controlling such uprisings and to intervene between the mob and the governors:[33] '. . . the newer sources of wealth turned toward a bureaucratic police system that insulated them from popular violence, drew attack and animosity upon itself, and seemed to separate the assertion of "constitutional" authority from that of social and economic dominance'.[34]

As cities continued to grow, as commerce became more complex, and as the interests pressing on the government proliferated, the 'governing class' gradually sank into obscurity. For the police, on the contrary, visibility at the scene of turbulence became its

[30] The townhouses and carriages of the great landowners, merchants, government officials, banks and other such institutions, at the 'urban seats of power' would come under direct attack by the mob. Both the Whigs and the Tories, at times, bargained for the mob's favour (*Violence in America*, op. cit., vol. I, 19–20, n. 22, 199–200.). For descriptions of mob actions during the American Revolution, see Morgan, *The Birth of the Republic* (London 1956) 20–21, 39–40, 55–56, 151; and L. Becker, *The History of Political Parties in the Province of New York, 1770–1776* (Madison, Wisconsin 1960), 31–35.

[31] In several instances where there was an effective resistance given to the rioters, we have been informed that the animosities created or increased and rendered permanent by arming master against servant, neighbour against neighbour, by triumph on one side and failure on the other, were even more deplorable than the outrages actually committed . . . The necessity for such painful and demoralizing conflicts between the connected persons should be avoided by providing a special trained and independent force for action in such emergencies.
(*The First Report of the Commissioner Appointed as to the Best Means of Establishing an Efficient Constabulary Force in the Counties of England and Wales* [London 1839], 205; cited in Silver, op. cit., 11, n. 21).

[32] Ibid., 20.

[33] In the United States, 'the modern urban police system was created in reaction to the riots of the 1830s, 1840s and 1850s, and the present National Guard system was developed in response to the uprisings of 1877'. (*Violence in America*, vol. I, 19, n. 22, 28, 41, 45, 209–10; and Lane, *Policing the City: Boston, 1822–1855* (1967), 30–38.

[34] Silver, op. cit., 11–12, n. 21. J. J. Tobias, in a letter to the author (5 January 1973) asks: 'Do we need a special explanation for the improvement of the policing of the growing towns, other than that there were improvements in *all* aspects of town government—drains, schools, streets, and a multitude of other things?

most prominent characteristic. The government dissociated itself from the police, which became 'independent' and dealt directly with the discontented, leaving the government blameless and without responsibility for consequences of police operations.

GROSS PARALLELS TO THIS exchange of visibility between élite groups (in recent times, élite businessmen) and the police, with the connivance of government, may be found in Chicago. In contrast to European and Eastern United States cities, Chicago's growth was so rapid that it had no 'families of long-established social standing' to supply a social élite.[35] Instead its 'first mayors were drawn from commercial leaders, regardless of family background, who were caught up in the growth and speculative investment of the community'.[36]

This group in turn declined upon the arrival of 'large industrial, trading and meat-packing firms'.[37]

> By the end of the 1860s they had lost their position of economic supremacy . . . The new leaders of business did not replace the old commercial élite in politics, however, partly because . . . the office of mayor became a less desirable sideline occupation for a businessman . . . and more energy and time were required to maintain a commanding position in the business community . . . In addition, businessmen found they could buy advantages from the developing ward bosses of the city council.[38]

Thus, in this early period there was already a separation of the business élite from those who did the actual governing. Law enforcement followed the same course. In 1818, Illinois was admitted to the Union; in 1831, legislative authority was given for the formation of the town of Chicago. By 1830, while Chicago was still a frontier town, 'respectable citizens, though comparatively few in number, banded together and maintained law and order among themselves'.[39] One of the first ordinances (1831) was a 'prohibition

[35] D. S. Bradley and M. N. Zald, *From Commercial Elite to Political Administrator: The Recruitment of the Mayors of Chicago*, 71; *Amer. J. Soc.*, 153, 166 (1965).
[36] Ibid.
[37] Ibid., 158.
[38] Ibid., 158–59. Most of the city's physical plant (sanitation, transit and water facilities) necessary for economic growth, had already been completed, and the office of mayor became a full-time job that could not be shared with economic enterprise.
[39] Forkosh, *History of Chicago Police Department*, 1820–1886 (1968), 3; an unpublished manuscript prepared for the Chicago Police Department Public Information Division, deposited in the Police Academy Library.

of riots and disorderly conduct'.[40] Military forces from nearby Fort Dearborn were frequently called to control mobs and crime. In 1833 the town was incorporated with a population of about 350. In the public meeting called to decide the question of incorporation, twelve persons voted for and one against the incorporation. Town trustees were elected and in 1835 they were empowered 'to establish night watches and to regulate the police of the town'. In 1837 the city council was authorized to appoint a police constable.

By 1851, the population had grown to 30,000. The mayor, aldermen, police justices, an elected marshal and constables elected from each ward with day and night watchmen, constituted the police of the city. The mayor, as 'head of the police department' was to superintend and direct the police generally.[41] In 1855, it could be said of the city and its law enforcement:

> Riotous conduct . . . and 'mob violence' were merely symbols of the general lawlessness prevailing. Street brawls were common-place among the criminals infesting the city. There was no law enforcement worthy of the name. The police force was composed of an elected city marshal and nine police constables, with one constable elected from each of the nine wards in the city. To provide more adequate police protection, ordinances were passed by the city council in April and June 1855 creating Chicago's first police department and providing for three police precinct stations.[42]

Local officials continued to participate in law enforcement. An ordinance of 1855 provided that aldermen be members of the police department with power of arrest, and they were used as part of the force by the police chief.[43] Mayors of the period entered fully and visibly into the law enforcement task.

[40] Ibid., 5.
[41] Ibid., 21. 'This force was completely political in character, insufficiently manned and poorly organized.' (Peterson, *Barbarians in Our Midst* [1952], 20). R. B. Fosdick, *American Police Systems* (New Jersey 1969 report, 1920 ed.) attributes the 'difficulties of the time' to 'the spoils system [which] had taken a firm grip on popular imagination . . . The police department was still a *ward* affair, used to satisfy the demands for district patronage, and the chief of police was a figurehead with no authority and little honor'.
[42] Peterson, op. cit., 20, n. 46. Forkosh, op. cit., 22, n. 43, observes that at the time at least half of the city's population was foreign-born.
[43] Ibid., 24. This power survives in state law. 'The mayor, aldermen . . . in municipalities, shall be conservators of the peace [and] shall have the power (1) to arrest . . . all persons who break the peace, or are found violating any municipal ordinance or any criminal law of the State . . .' *Ill. Rev. Stat.* (1973) Ch. 24, Sec. 3–9–4.

A district known as the Sands was probably the worst of many disreputable spots in Chicago. Located just north of the river and extending to Lake Michigan, the Sands was filled with gambling dens, houses of prostitution, and lodging houses of the most unsavory character. Men were lured into this area and robbed. Murders were frequent . . . April 20, 1857, Mayor Wentworth personally descended on the Sands with a raiding party of thirty police.[44]

The last quarter of the nineteenth century was a turbulent period in which there were many examples of mob action and use of the police to protect the new industrial élite. Thousands were unemployed following the panic of 1873. In 1876, as many as 15,000 unemployer workingmen marched on City Hall demanding 'work for all'.[45]

By 1877, mobs were commonplace on the streets of Chicago . . . Frequently, when the mobs came upon a warehouse or factory where non-union men were employed, they assaulted the men and destroyed the property . . . The situation finally assumed such grave proportions that . . . the Mayor called upon all law-abiding Chicagoans to form armed civilian groups to preserve the peace . . . Thousands of citizens answered the Mayor's request for aid and organized neighbourhood patrol corps . . . Employers were urged to organize and arm trusted employees . . . Local regiments and other military organizations such as the Veteran's groups were alerted for action, and mobilized in their armories . . . Even the members of the Board of Trade prepared to arm themselves and report for special service.[46]

Following the riots, police stations were supplied with muskets, and, in order to expand the force, $110,500 per year was added to the annual departmental appropriation.[47]

The dedication of the Board of Trade building in 1885 provided further reason for working-class protest.[48] In that same year, the strike of street-car conductors placed the police clearly on the side of the bosses. To protect non-striking drivers, police rode the street-cars. 'Stones, dirt and other missiles, plus . . . invective and abuse, were flung at policemen as well as at strike breakers.'[49] The police were strongly denounced at workers' meetings.[50]

[44] Peterson, op. cit., 23, n. 41. That summer, after directing a raid of a gambling den, Wentworth also 'supervised the booking of prisoners and made certain they were actually jailed. He warned city license holders that if they furnished bail for the arrested gamblers, he would revoke their license'. (Ibid.).
[45] Forkosh, op. cit., 90–91, n. 39.
[46] Ibid., 91–97.
[47] Ibid., 103.
[48] Ibid., 145–47.
[49] Ibid., 150.
[50] Ibid., 154.

Popular opinion was so strongly on the side of the strikers that nearly all the men arrested were discharged without punishment, and in response to the request of a Committee, Mayor Harrison released the man whom he had himself arrested . . . for attempting to tear up the track.[51]

The mayor reported that 'in mingling with the crowds he found that nine out of ten citizens were in sympathy with the strikers'.[52] Police Captain Bonifield, later a principal in the Haymarket disaster, told the men who were to go on strike duty: 'Whatever your private views or mine may be, property must be defended, the law must be upheld and you are its defenders'.[53]

Antagonism towards the police by the workers was raised to a fever pitch by the use of the police to protect strike-breakers in the McCormick Harvester Plant strike of 1886. Over one third of the entire force was assigned to such duty.[54] 'It was a common sight to see patrol-wagons filled with armed policemen dashing through the city. The force was busy dispersing gatherings of workingmen, regardless of their nature, and, on occasion, the workers retaliated, attacking patrol wagons or assaulting the police . . . '[55] It was this strike that gave rise to the protests that culminated in the Haymarket riot of 4 May 1886. That incident acted as a catalyst in crystallizing feelings of the middle class and better-off working classes about the police.

It came at a time when the new urban middle class seemed to be caught between the twin daggers of monopolistic capitalism and the increasing claims of the labouring man. Should one see oneself as part of the downtrodden masses being crushed under the heel of oppressing capitalists, or as one of those progressing with the nation, threatened by an assortment of foreign anarchists, communists and radical agitators, dangerous to the American way of life? Whichever way the emerging middle class—consisting of white-collar, professional, semi-professional and skilled workers

[51] J. J. Flinn, *History of the Chicago Police: From the Settlement of the Community to the Present Time* (New Jersey 1887).

[52] Ibid.

[53] Ibid., 241.

[54] Ibid., 162. Agitators among the crowd 'openly advised warfare against the McCormick factory, and the police in particular, and upon law-abiding people of Chicago—known as the privileged classes—in general. Flinn, op. cit., 289–90, n. 51.

[55] H. David, *The History of the Haymarket Affair* (New York 1958, 2nd. ed.), 186.

would choose, would affect the way they and the nation saw the police. It was into this vortex of forces that the Haymarket bomb was thrown.

> Chicago and the entire country were momentarily stunned. One policeman killed, almost seventy officers wounded—it was inconceivable . . . Public opinion quickly decided that the bomb was the work of the motley crew of socialists, anarchists and communists infesting Chicago . . . Beneath the rage which shook the city there ran a definite current of fear . . . they were readily convinced that they, their government, and the social and economic system under which they lived were in danger of immediate destruction . . . Because the 'anarchist' and socialist groups were composed largely of foreigners, aliens were indiscriminately damned . . . it was felt that 'respectable' workers had to make it clear that they had not been contaminated. . . . Throughout the country the conviction prevailed that the radical groups had been given excessive leeway. For the well-being of society they now had to be suppressed.[56]

The police, on the other hand, had become heroes and martyrs. Two weeks after the event, over $67,000 had been contributed to a fund for the victims of the bombing. 'The city at large was conscious of a genuine debt to the police force.'[57] When the death penalty was pronounced for all but one of the eight defendants, 'not a daily newspaper of standing in the entire country had a word to say in criticism of the conduct of the trial or the verdict'.[58] The governor, beseiged by petitions for and against the executions 'apparently said that if the business interests of Chicago were opposed to executing the men they should meet . . . and inform him of their decision'.[59] A meeting of business leaders was held but one of the most powerful opposed executive clemency. Others were afraid to act contrary to his views and no action was taken.[60] 'Behind this insistence upon reprisals lay the assumption that fundamentally the masses could understand only the bared fist, that without the authority of an indisputable force—always visible, always ready—chaos would reign.'[61]

One effect of the Haymarket Affair was that this élitist view was adopted by the urban middle class with the symbol of the bomb-

[56] Ibid., 206–17.
[57] Ibid., 226.
[58] Ibid., 323.
[59] Ibid., 433.
[60] Ibid., 435.
[61] R. H. Wiebe, *The Search for Order, 1877–1920* (New York 1967), 79.

carrying anarchist. The police became protectors against this ever-present threat.

Chicago, meanwhile, had been developing its social élite and from 1876 to 1930 most of its mayors came from this group.[62] Such men were 'party men' and were clearly dependent on the developing political machines. In effect, the machine bided its time until it was ready to present its own candidate, Anton Cermak, in 1931. At that time the social élite dropped out of the top echelons of Chicago government.[63]

Until the emergence of Anton Cermak in 1931 as *both* mayor and party leader Chicago had been characterized by 'ward feudalism'. Once Cermak had firm control, all the aldermen and ward committeemen 'retained in return for the privilege of delivering the vote was a limited amount of patronage, and their man . . . as czar of vice. City business in general was handled by the high command in the mayor's office'.[64]

> The driving force in community politics becomes the [democratic party] machine, and the style of the mayor becomes that of the political administrator. The machine and city politics had become a full-time career . . . The new men expand their support from ethnic organizations by becoming the leaders and initiators of programs of physical and social city renewal.[65]

All four mayors from 1931 to the present started near the bottom of the occupational hierarchy and three had only a high-school education. All but one slowly worked their way up through the party apparatus. But all had shown ability to organize large administrative structures.[66]

Both Cermak (1931–33) and Kelly (1933–47) continued to have one foot in the old foundation of machine politics; a union of ward politicians and vice interests with the police acting as sources of patronage, and, when necessary, restraining the unyielding. On coming to office, Cermak appointed James P. Allman police commissioner on the understanding that law enforcement policies regarding gambling would be dictated by the political leaders.[67] When Cermak was killed in 1933 by an assassin's bullet intended

[62] Bradley and Zald, op. cit., 166–67, n. 35.

[63] C. Banfield and Q. Wilson, *City Politics* (New York 1963), 79, 261–65.

[64] L. Wendt and H. Kogan, *Bosses in Lusty Chicago* (Bloomington, Indiana 1967), 35.

[65] Bradley and Zald, op. cit., 167, n. 35.

[66] Ibid., 164.

[67] Peterson, op. cit., 155, n. 41.

for President Roosevelt, the party boss, Patrick A. Nash, selected Edward J. Kelly as mayor.[68]

The Kelly–Nash machine used the police to accommodate and control ward committeemen:

> Police captains agreeable to the ward committeemen were assigned to the various police districts and took orders from the ward boss. Gambling was permitted to flourish unless the ward committeemen needed discipline. In this event, a police captain would be dispatched to the district with instructions to enforce the gambling laws. The ward boss usually made peace with the machine and gambling once more flourished in his district.[69]

A number of scandals rocked the last years of the Kelly administration so that by 1946 Kelly was under almost constant attack from the press. In 1941, a Cook County grand jury reported that 'shocking conditions' existed in Chicago and Cook County where 'protected syndicate gambling has openly and flagrantly operated for a long period of time without any real interference from the police whose duty it is to prevent this evil'.[70] The November 1941 grand jury 'recommended that the Morals Squad be disbanded. There was strong reason to believe that the principal function of the squad was the protection of gambling syndicates rather than the enforcement of the law'.[71] A 1943 Cook County grand jury indicted fourteen police officers, nine of whom were captains. The county clerk testified: 'Everyone knows how promotions are made in the police department. Most captains are appointed by the Mayor on recommendations of the Ward Committeemen. Every Ward Committeeman knows that Civil Service examinations for promotions are mostly a sham—it's all handled through the Mayor'.[72]

[68] F. Gosnell, *Machine Politics, Chicago Model* (London 1968, 2nd. ed.), 15.

[69] Peterson, op. cit., 165, n. 41. The 1931 Citizen Police Committee reported: The police force really consists of two distinct sets or hierarchies, the one official and the other political . . . Individual patrolmen and sergeants sometimes assume an importance out of proportion to their ranks. An occasional deputy commissioner will, to all intents and purposes, assume prerogatives of the commissioner, and captains will run their districts as though these were separate corporate entities, with the local political leaders playing the role of political mayors. (*Chicago Police Problems*, op. cit., 43, n. 2.

[70] Peterson, op. cit., 194, n. 41.

[71] Ibid., 196.

[72] Ibid., 207.

More important than such scandals, some of Kelly's own committeemen had lost confidence in his ability to win the 1947 mayoralty race. In the preceding election, the Republicans, for the first time in sixteen years, had recaptured the offices of sheriff, county treasurer, probate court judge, the president of the Cook County Board of Commissioners and others.[73]

Jacob M. Arvey, the Cook County Democratic Party chairman, persuaded Kelly to retire and proposed Martin H. Kennelly as the candidate. Kennelly (1947–55) took the nomination on the understanding that the party would not interfere in city affairs and he would not interfere in its affairs.[74] Kennelly was an outstanding businessman and civic leader of unimpeachable integrity, but his pledge meant that most department heads, including Kelly's police chief, were retained. Kennelly's changes in the police department were limited to the traffic division. He did, however, give the commissioner a 'freer hand . . . without regard to political considerations'. Gambling laws were enforced, reducing gambling to a 'sneak' operation.[75]

But Kennelly was not completely insensitive to politics. When in 1950 police maladministration seemed to affect the election returns, he appointed a new police chief, Timothy J. O'Connor. Until this point, Kennelly had stoutly defended the police commissioner and the police against all charges of corruption and inefficiency. The department's Captain Gilbert was the party's candidate for sheriff. One of his campaign promises was to 'drive all gambling places out of Cook County within six months'. But when, shortly before the election, he appeared before Senator Kefauver's committee investigating organized crime, his income-tax returns 'reflected yearly profits from gambling' amounting to thousands of dollars. Gilbert was overwhelmingly defeated, apparently because many Democratic voters cast Republican votes in protest. The Republicans captured a number of key county offices. A week later a new commissioner was appointed.[76]

Kennelly's conception of the police function is eloquently set forth in an excerpt from his 1949 'Joint Statement of Mayor Martin H. Kennelly and Commissioner John C. Prendergast concerning Police Organization':

[73] Ibid., 227.
[74] Banfield and Wilson, *City Politics* (New York 1963), 107.
[75] Peterson, op. cit., 228–29, n. 41.
[76] Ibid., 229, 252–70.

> The Police Department [represents] one of the largest phases of the business operation of our City's government. Sometimes we think of the Police Department as just having to do with crime. Actually, however, how it is run and how it is administered has a great effect on the economic and social welfare of the city. Its failure to perform its functions properly could have an effect on the entire city, *even to the point of depressing property values.* (Emphasis added.)

By 1955, the ward bosses had had enough of Kennelly.

> The result [of Kennelly's attempt to ignore the party machinery and to rule on the basis of the authority of his office together with such other support as he could attract] was a weak and ineffective administration. The mayor did not have enough power to run the city; important matters were decided by default or else by an informal coalition of councilmen—the Big Boys, they were called—whose authority and party-based influence made them independent of the mayor.[77]

Kennelly had served his purpose. The machine was still strong but continued separation of party and city leadership would weaken the party's control of patronage.[78] The committeemen, therefore, refused to restate Kennelly for the 1955 mayoralty race. When he nevertheless ran in the primary, they beat him with Richard J. Daley, the party chairman who had arranged to dump him.[79]

As one of the few independent Chicago aldermen said in summing up the result: 'Every fourth year since then, Chicago elected him and called him Mayor Daley, but his really important office is party chairman'.[80] Daley, mayor of Chicago since 1955, has consolidated his control to such an extent that the earlier decentralization of authority in Chicago has been reversed.

> The mayor of Chicago is a boss . . . He is a broker in the business (so to speak) of buying and selling political power. He performs an entrepreneurial function by overcoming the decentralization of authority that prevents anything from being done, and in this his role is very like that of the real estate broker who assembles land for a large development by buying up parcels here and there. Much of what the political broker gathers up is on speculation: He does not know exactly how it will be used, but he is confident that someone will need a large block of power.[81]

[77] Banfield and Wilson, op. cit., 107, n. 74.
[78] Ibid., 144–45.
[79] Peterson, 'The Chicago Police Scandals', *Atlantic Monthly* 58, 62 (October 1960).
[80] Despres, 'The Chicago the Delegates Won't See', *The Progressive* 24, 25, August 1968.
[81] Banfield and Wilson, op. cit., 104, n. 74.

Of the city's 50 wards, 38 have consistently been in the hands of Democrats voting with the mayor.[82] In addition, the mayor controls 'the school board, the park district, the library board, the housing authority, the transit authority, two-thirds of the county board, nearly all the county offices, many suburban governments, the state's attorney, the judiciary . . . a chunk of the state legislature, the Chicago Congressmen . . . '[83]

The patron-client relationship developed to the highest degree. By 1958, 'one-third of the Democratic legislators from Chicago and Cook County held city or county jobs (the minority leader of the House, for example, was a civil service examiner in City Hall), and almost all the others had relatives or henchmen on the public payroll.[84] Chicago became renowned as 'the patronage capital of the world'.[85]

Once the power was attained, it had to be used in such a way as to neutralize those forces that might object to such concentration.[86] Although the style of Daley is not the style of Kelly and Cermak, Daley until very recently counted on the votes from the 'delivery' wards, and had the means to deliver them. Such votes were, however, insufficient to carry the middle-class Republican suburbs and the state. To attract these, the mayor made some ostentatious gestures: minimizing his use of patronage, finding 'blue-ribbon' candidates for office and inaugurating civic projects.

> The mayor's program conspicuously neglected goals of militant Negroes, demands for the enforcement of the building code, and (until there was a dramatic exposé) *complaints about police efficiency and corruption*. These things were all controversial, and, perhaps most important, would have no immediate, visible result; either they would benefit those central-city voters whose loyalty could be counted upon anyway or else (*as in the case of police reform*) they threatened to hurt the machine in a vital spot.[87] (Emphasis added.)

[82] Rose and Canter, *Mayor Daley: Solvent But Worried*, The Nation 3 (1 September 1969).

[83] Despres, op. cit., 24, n. 80.

[84] Banfield and Wilson, op. cit., 93, n. 74.

[85] M. and S. Tolchin, *To the Victor* (New York 1972), 27.

[86] They know that as long as they do nothing they are probably safe, and, anyway, they want to allow time for public opinion to form. When a magazine writer suggested to Mayor Daley that the mayor had never in his whole life committed himself to anything whatsoever until he absolutely had to, the mayor laughed. 'That's a pretty good way to be, don't you think?' he said. 'Pretty good way to run any business.'
Banfield and Wilson, op. cit., 30.

[87] Banfield and Wilson, op. cit., 124, n. 74.

We have now come full circle. We began with the time when there was a clear delineation between the propertied governing class and the poorer class. With the maturation of the industrial revolution and the formation of the nation-state, the police were organized to take over from the propertied class the task of maintaining order. As the propertied class evolved into the business class, its members became too involved in the business world to hold government office, leaving actual administration of city affairs in the hands of the immigrants, particularly the Irish. Out of this development came an understanding between the machine politicians and the business élite: 'You leave us alone and we will leave you alone'.

The political machine distributed benefits to those who could influence its prosperity. As long as the neglected groups made no insistent demands for important concessions, the system worked fairly well. But when those demands became increasingly strident, and wards that were formerly secure began moving towards a political renaissance, conflicts arose, which under current strategy can only be resolved by calling on the police.[88]

Because such police action is likely in itself to cause reaction against the administration, and because it accommodates the police idea of professionalism, the notion evolved of a police independent of the city administration. Such an idea would not seem acceptable in a city such as Chicago where a strong mayor-party chief might be expected to take a hostile view of an independent agency within his political bailiwick. But at the same time, the mayor's political style puts him in the role of referee among competing groups. Where do the police fit? We have examined one instance in Chicago in which the mayor asserted police independence in order to avoid blame for their conduct. Is it a real or feigned independence?

THE CHICAGO POLICE DEPARTMENT'S almost unbroken record of corruption and political interference was strengthened in 1960 when a police scandal surfaced that could not be resolved by a change of commissioners. A burglar accused a number of policemen of having 'hired' him to steal merchandise. While he was so engaged, the officers cruised the area in patrol cars to warn him of approaching police not in on the scheme.[89]

[88] For instance, it has been suggested that the attack by the police on Chicago gangs is directed at their political organization of the black community rather than at their alleged criminal activities. (*Chicago Journalism Review* [June 1969], 12–13).

[89] Peterson, *A Report on Chicago Crime for 1960* (Chicago Crime Committee 1961), 3–7.

With the scandal breaking in an important state and in a national election year, it was inevitable that corruption in the Chicago Police Department would become a major political issue. Republican State's Attorney Benjamin S. Adamowski charged that the department was rotten to the core and fixed the responsibility on the Democratic machine, which controlled the police force. Republican Governor William G. Stratton called for an administrative reorganization of the Chicago Police Department and pointed out the urgent need for 'very drastic measures'. Former Democratic National Chairman Stephan A. Mitchell, who was campaigning against the organization candidate for governor in the impending primary, stated, 'Everywhere, I hear people discussing the police scandal . . .' Democratic Mayor Richard J. Daley pledged that the three remaining years of his term of office would be devoted to ridding the ranks of the police force of unfit officers and restoring the good name of the department and the city.[90]

After Police Commissioner Timothy J. O'Conner resigned under fire,[91] a professor of police administration, O. W. Wilson, was selected to replace him.[92]

Wilson's integrity has never been questioned. That characteristic and his reputation for administrative independence and competence were major factors in his appointment.[93] In order to induce him to take the post, Mayor Daley is said to have given him 'a guarantee of complete authority with no political interference'.[94]

According to one person interviewed, the mayor and Wilson soon developed a comfortable relationship. Wilson liked the mayor and voluntarily consulted him frequently about his plans for the department, making excursions to city hall about twice weekly. Estimates of the wonders accomplished during the Wilson administration vary, but it seems probable that neither Wilson nor Daley contemplated that it would last longer than was necessary to shore up the ship. Wilson's function for the machine was similar to that of Kennelly. At the time of his retirement in 1967, Wilson was content to 'recommend' for appointment a man as different as possible from himself in training and disposition—his deputy superintendent,

[90] Peterson, ibid., 61, n. 89.
[91] Ibid., 59, 61.
[92] Peterson, ibid., 9–11, n. 89.
[93] Ibid., 10. One of Wilson's first acts was to move his office out of City Hall, where it had always been, to police headquarters. (Ibid., 15). Such a move had long been resisted.
[94] B. Davidson, 'The Professional Policeman', 41 *Holiday Magazine* (March 1967), 13–17.

James Conlisk, Jr.[95] Although the police board went through the motions of searching for a replacement for Wilson, the Chicago newspapers did not take it too seriously. They reported that 'shortly *after* the April mayoral election, Wilson disclosed his plans to retire. At that time, it was widely believed that Wilson would not have picked Conlisk for the job unless he had been given tacit approval by Daley'. The same article quoted Daley as saying, 'After studying the recommendations of the police board and counselling with O. W. Wilson for many, many hours, I have concluded that the outstanding man to carry on his policies is the deputy superintendent, John Conlisk'. He called Conlisk 'a man who is aggressive, a man of integrity, a man with great administrative qualities, a man determined to continue the practices and policies of O. W. Wilson'. Wilson said of Conlisk, 'No man in or out of Chicago is as well qualified'.[96] For some time before his appointment, Conlisk had 'been meeting and dining with top religious, civic and political leaders'.[97]

At the beginning of his superintendency, Conlisk made sounds like Wilson;[98] left to his own devices he might have continued in that direction. Police restraint in the handling of the Martin Luther King disturbances of April 1968 even brought accolades from liberal leaders.[99] But counter-pressure apparently influenced the mayor to issue his famous 'shoot to kill' order in which he publicly criticized

[95] Conlisk's father had been a police officer for twenty years, and as police captain had been administrative assistant to three police commissioners, a neighbour and crony of Mayor Daley, and one who had developed important connections within the Democratic Party. He was among those quickly retired by Wilson (*Chicago Tribune*, 4 December 1968, 1, col. 3). The son maintained his father's connections and, even under Wilson, Conlisk, Jr. was said 'to take orders from the Mayor'. (O. Demaris, *Captive City* [New York 1969], 255.)

[96] *Chicago Sun-Times*, 23 June 1967.

[97] *Chicago Tribune*, 20 June 1967.

[98] Upon his appointment, he 'spoke with awe of his former boss, and said he wanted nothing more than to be another O. W. Wilson. In those early days he granted interviews and press conferences, and talked of the "social roots" of crime, and the need for police with college degrees who get along with people'. (*Chicago Daily News*, 4 December 1968, 6, col. 2).

[99] *Chicago Daily News*, 4 December 1969, 6, col. 1.

Conlisk for disregarding his order.[100] Without comment Conlisk relayed the command to his men.

A few days later, as protest mounted at the severity of the order, it was 'modified', the mayor claiming the original order had been misunderstood.[101] Various explanations have been given for the order besides that of putting the superintendent in his place. One city hall reporter thought the mayor was angered at seeing on television police officers standing around while looters carried off merchandise; there was also the fact that the man who might have intercepted such an order, the mayor's public relations chief, was out of town. Another interpretation was given by John Dreiske, a columnist who wrote that the first statement was 'what the insurance and business interests wanted to hear about cracking down on destruction of property'. By thereafter issuing a softer statement, 'The crackdown advocates had his first statement to keep them warm . . . and the non-violent Negro element and their white brethren were assured with his second act that he hadn't meant it at all . . . '[102]

If Daley's public rebuff of the superintendent—an almost unheard of move—was intended to tame the already placid Conlisk, it succeeded.

> Those who know both men say Conlisk's silence probably saved his job . . . Daley is a man who greatly respects loyalty—to family, church, party, friends. He also gives loyalty to those who give it to him. Conlisk, by meekly reacting like a good soldier to Daley's outburst, proved his loyalty to his chief. And, so his associates say, Daley now will stand by him.

[100] *Chicago Sun-Times*, 19 April 1968; *Chicago Daily News*, 4 December 1968, 6, col. 2. A 'partial transcript' of the mayor's press conference stated:

> I have conferred with the superintendent of police this morning and I gave him the full instructions, which I thought were instructions on the night of the 5th and were not carried out: I said to him very emphatically and very definitely that an order be issued by him immediately and under my signature to shoot to kill any arsonist or anyone with a Molotov cocktail in his hand in Chicago because they're potential murderers, and to issue a police order to shoot to maim or cripple anyone looting any stores in our city . . . I assumed the instructions were given, but the instructions to the policemen were to use their judgment. I assumed any superintendent would issue instructions to shoot arsonists on sight and to maim looters but I found out this morning this wasn't so and therefore gave [Conlisk] specific instructions.

(*Chicago Daily News*, 15 April 1968).

[101] *Chicago Sun-Times*, 18 April 1968, 1, col. 1.

[102] *Chicago Sun-Times*, 19 April 1968.

In every statement about police action since that day, Daley has been lavish with praise.[103]

That Conlisk now knew his place was made evident in December 1968, when the mayor and Conlisk were called upon to comment on the Walker Report which criticized Chicago police for their actions during the 1968 Chicago convention.[104] Conlisk issued a statement a few days later that he 'disagreed' with the summary of the report which condemned the police. But he nevertheless urged all to read its 345 pages in order to form their own conclusions. He also said that his department was acting against the few police who might have misbehaved. Strangely enough, Conlisk's statement was almost a word-for-word duplicate of the mayor's statement of a few days before.[105]

Retrospectively, it is apparent that the scandal turned out to be a windfall to an astute mayor who knew how to use reform to consolidate his power. Changes in the structure that would otherwise have been strongly resisted were accepted as necessary to preserve the party. At the time, Daley reigned over a feudal police and political structure in which the police captains were beholden to their ward committeeman as sponsor and protector. Power within the department was in the hands of a small clique of very senior captains, many of whom were well beyond the normal retirement age. The former commissioner (O'Connor) had had little effective control over these men.[106]

> By 1964 there were 226 new lieutenants and 94 captains. Soon the majority of men in each senior rank owed their promotion to the new superintendent. The effect of this was not only to alter completely the status system within the department but also to change radically the composition of the various protective associations.
>
> When Wilson left, these profits accrued to the mayor.

WHILE INDEPENDENCE OF THE police department in Chicago may be a sham, something akin to real independence can occur and assume serious political proportions. A staff report to the National Commission on the Causes and Prevention of Violence calls attention to recent politicization of the police. This was defined

---

[103] *Chicago Daily News*, 4 December 1968, 6, col. 2.

[104] D. Walker, *Rights in Conflict* (New York 1968).

[105] *Chicago Daily News*, 12 December 1968, 1, col. 2.

[106] James Q. Wilson, 'Police Morale, Reform, and Citizen Respect: The Chicago Case', in Bordua (ed.), *The Police: Six Sociological Essays* (New York 1967), 142.

as the police seeing themselves as an 'independent militant minority asserting itself in a political arena'.[107]

In a number of recent incidents, the police have acted with varying degrees of independence in opposition to the mayor of the city, their chief or both. Some of these incidents are spontaneous, individual reactions by policemen against a specific policy of a mayor.[108] Others represent efforts by organized groups, such as police fraternal associations, to block administration policy. Still others are aimed at 'enemies' outside the department, principally militant blacks or student or peace demonstrators.[109]

When the black mayor of Cleveland, in order to quiet a riot in a black ghetto, ordered all white police withdrawn for a night from the affected area, a number of police refused to answer calls and some cursed the mayor over their radios.[110] During the 1966 campaign for a civilian review board in New York City, police actively campaigned against it although the mayor vigorously supported it. Cars bearing anti-board literature were said to have been immune from receiving traffic tickets.[111] The prime organizing force in the review board issue was the Patrolmen's Benevolent Association. This organization, active in both New York City and Boston, is able to lobby successfully against laws affecting police.[112]

In August 1968, the president of the New York City PBA suggested that policemen disobey any superior officer who placed restraints on their enforcement of the law. He cited an order asking

[107] J. Skolnick, *The Politics of Protest, Violent Aspects of Protest and Confrontation, A Staff Report to the National Commission on the Causes and Prevention of Violence* (New York 1969; hereafter cited as *Violence Report*), 208.

[108] Such responses nevertheless are likely to represent only outward manifestations of profound and long-standing grievances.

[109] *Violence Report*, op. cit., 185, n. 123.

[110] Ibid., 206–7.

> For several weeks after the riot, posters with a picture of Mayor Stokes . . . under the words, 'Wanted for Murder' hung in district stations. Spokesmen for the police officers wives organization have berated the mayor; the Fraternal Order of Police has demanded the resignation of the safety director; and many have reportedly been privately purchasing high-powered rifles for use in future riots, despite official opposition by police commanders.

(Ibid., 207).

[111] Ibid., 209.

[112] Ibid., 211–13. In New York City, the PBA represents 99 per cent of the force. It has successfully lobbied against police cadets taking over traffic duties and broadening the statute on the use of deadly force. In Boston, the issue involved placing civilians in police jobs. In each case, the mayor was on the other side of the issue.

police to avoid shooting fleeing looters or making unnecessary arrests so as to avoid aggravating the situation in a riot-prone area. Police, he said, had been handcuffed. They were ready for a 'direct conflict' with City Hall.[113] When the mayor of New York City ordered flags to be flown at half mast to observe Vietnam Moratorium Day, the police union 'called on all precincts to refuse to lower the flag'.[114]

Chicago presents a clear contrast; there the chief executive is apparently in complete control of the police. This was not always so. Soon after O. W. Wilson took over his post, he set up the Internal Investigation Division, to look *actively* for police infractions.

> The Patrolmen's Benevolent Association called a mass meeting to demand Wilson's ouster, and several thousand officers cheered lustily as one speaker after another chided 'the Professor' and his naive theories. But if the PBA was counting on its customary political support, it was doomed to disappointment. Daley, who had passed the 'hands off' signal through the Democratic pipeline, backed his superintendent to the hilt and concurred that the department was justified in 'utilizing all investigative procedures and techniques which are legally available to it in ferreting out criminal violations of department regulations by its members.[115]

We have already described the successful restraining of the police superintendent through public issuance of a 'shoot to kill' order. Some commentators believe that the effect of this action and similar statements made by the mayor to the police were influential in provoking the police in the 1968 Democratic Convention disorders.[116]

Under the Daley administration police independence hardly seems a problem.[117] Whenever the police have been criticized, the

[113] Ibid., 207. The police commissioner responded to the challenge by 'promising disciplinary action against any officer who refused to obey orders'.
[114] *New York Times*, 15 October 1969, 16, col. 6.
[115] W. W. Turner, *Police Establishment* (New York, 1968) 109–10.
[116] *Violence Report*, 186–87, n. 123.
[117] At the 1968 Democratic Convention 'thousands of the "We Love Daley" signs were brought to the hall before the session. Outside, uniformed patrolmen were seen nailing them to the yellow police barricades'. (*Chicago Daily News*, 30 August 1968, 6). At the time of the issuance of the shoot to kill statement, Joseph J. LeFevour, president of the Chicago Chapter of the Fraternal Order of Police, sent a telegram to Daley saying 'You have our deepest respect and admiration for the stand you have taken with respect to putting down anarchy'. (*Chicago Daily News*, 16 April 1968, 5, col. 1).

mayor has given them vocal moral support.[118] Chicago now has the highest paid police in the country.[119] Daley has consistently taken 'get tough' law and order positions. His war on street gangs is an example.[120] Whether from personal belief or political acumen, the mayor has presented himself as a rallying point rather than as a focus of opposition to the right-wing police militants who have provoked the described incidents.

Thus, in comparing Chicago with cities in which the police showed opposition to the mayor's authority, we find that in Chicago there is a strong mayor heading the party apparatus, paired with a weak police chief, who has come up through the ranks, and who has a close tie with the mayor's political party. Where, however, as in most cities, there is not this control, and there is politicization of the police, the independence may be real and the mayor may find that the police department constitutes a constant potential of resistance to city law-enforcement policy, if such there be.

ASSUMING THE EXISTENCE of an independent police, how do we evaluate whether it is 'good' or 'bad'? A model system, and one more hierarchic than our own, might have the state legislature pass laws that set forth clear and concise policies. Even more utopian, the legislature might authorize the police department to establish procedures to set priorities for law enforcement. There could be periodic conferences of law-enforcement officials who would formulate objectives of law enforcement and priorities to be given to any law or set of laws. A clear set of do's and don'ts could be prescribed for the police. A strong mayor would both direct the police chief in the pursuance of these goals and accept responsibility for the failure of the department to achieve the defined objectives.

[118] After the convention disorders, Mayor Daley went all out in defending the police and thereby, of course, keeping the focus on them. A special report, *Strategy of Confrontation*, was issued by the city to explain its role and place blame elsewhere. The 9 September 1968 issue of the *Chicago Daily News* includes the complete report. In addition, a film defending police actions during the convention was prepared for television. 'The city team labored round the clock from Wednesday to Sunday morning, with Mayor Daley over-seeing the last few hours work.' (*Chicago Sun-Times*, 17 September 1968, 4). A federal jury which acquitted three Chicago policemen of beating up a *Chicago Daily News* reporter was praised by the mayor. (*Chicago Sun-Times*, 13 June 1969, 7, col. 2.).

[119] Present starting salaries represent almost a 100 per cent increase since 1960.

[120] *Chicago Journalism Review* (June 1969).

Desirable as such a rational hierarchy might initially appear to be, a system of law enforcement is only as good as the laws being enforced. More efficient enforcement of present laws on sexual offences, drug use, alcoholism, vagrancy and gambling—already totalling about 45 per cent of all arrests across the nation—would make the system more intolerable than it already is.[121] One test of the proper functioning of an institution is to ask whether, if it did its task more efficiently, society would be better off? If not, disorganization, decentralization or dispersal of power may be blessings in disguise.

Even the strong machine organization, as in Chicago, may, at times, be preferable to a weak mayor-police relationship where the police may run wildly independent pursuing police goals. As Banfield and Wilson have noted:

> The choice is never between the machine and some ideal alternative. If there is any choice at all—and in some instances there may not be— it is between it and some real—and therefore imperfect—alternative. It is at least conceivable that in some of the large cities the political indifferentism of the machine may be preferable to any likely alternative.[122]

Because of the decentralized nature of American law enforcement, which tends to build feudal units of power, such a hierarchical system of command and consulation is hardly likely to develop without considerable reworking of the entire governmental structure. Chicago, among the large cities, presents the nearest thing in the United States to a coherent government. Such concentration of power may present a more serious danger than the 'independence' that we have discussed. Particularly is this true in these days of the

---

[121] Legislation today often means making no policy at all: laws are framed in language so ambiguous that they essentially delegate legislative power to the police to make policy (for example, the disorderly conduct, gambling, vagrancy laws); that they may be enforced only by incursion on constitutional rights of privacy (for example, anti-contraceptive laws, consensual homosexuality and sexual 'perversion' laws); that they provoke illegal searches and the use of informers (narcotics and obscenity laws); that they provide overwhelming invitations to police corruption (prostitution, narcotics and gambling laws) and that they require police to operate in fields where they have no competence except as to detection and repression (for example, homosexuality, gang control and alcoholism).
See (C. D. Robinson, *Police and Prosecutor Attitudes Relating to Interrogations Revealed by Pre- and Post-Miranda Questionnaires: A Construct of Police Capacity to Comply*, 1968 Duke Law Journal 425, 496–506; J. Skolnick, *Justice without Trial* [London 1966] 112–63, 219–29).
[122] Banfield and Wilson, op. cit., 127, n. 69.

new machine.[123] Today's societal divisions offer the constant temptation of abandoning any concession to impartiality in favour of a reliance on the 'silent majority', meanwhile controlling the discontented by a police only too ready to assume such a role.

ALTHOUGH THE MAJOR PART of this paper has discussed the independence of the police department, there is something that rings false in speaking thus of the police. Independence implies not only a lack of substantial control by others but an ability to govern oneself, a relative self-sufficiency. It should also assume a stable consistency and a role that the agency itself is capable of defining and executing. Formally, the police department is an executive department of the city, with a civilian head, not an independent agency. Functionally, it is a 'service' unit, dependent on other parts of the government for its direction, both in the formation of goals and in supervision. The independence of the police that we have examined is a public image. A view of the internal structure of the department raises serious doubts about its capacity for independent, intelligent action in resolving anything but technical, police problems. Even where goals are generally formulated, the police may be incapable of implementing them satisfactorily on their own.[124]

Internally, a large city police department is a military hierarchy, characterized by strict subordination and a rigid chain of command.[125] Obedience and conformity have value. Innovation does not. The department has been structured and the men trained to accept commands, to use physical force—not to formulate policy.

We are thus presented with a string of contradictions. Because neither the legislature, the mayor nor the prosecutor have accepted or developed a policy-making role with respect to the police (while

[123] Whereas the spoils of office formerly went to 'the boys' in the delivery wards in the form of jobs and favors, they now go in the form of urban renewal projects, street cleaning, and better police protection to newspaper wards. Better police protection in white neighborhoods means greater police harassment in Negro ones. Appointment of white experts means non-appointment of Negro politicians.
(Banfield and Wilson, op. cit., 127, n. 69.).

[124] Robinson, op. cit., 495, n. 121. In the same article, the questions considered in this section are analysed in more detail. See especially 493–506.

[125] It has been argued that the analogy to a military force breaks down in practice because the military normally act in groups while police act individually or at most in pairs. (Reiss and Bordua, 'Environment and Organization: A Perspective on the Police', in Bordua (ed.), *The Police: Six Sociological Essays* [New York 1967], 30.)

at the same time using the police as a screen to hide this abdication), the department finds it necessary to formulate its own goals. The notion of independence implies the right, the duty and the capacity to do so. Yet the training, the personnel, the traditions and the internal structure of the police allows no place for innovation or elaboration of a policy which is an adequate response to the problems that society has swept under the police rug. Problems such as police control of ghetto residents, student protestors or other aggrieved groups become police problems because other parts of the system have allowed them to become so. By the time they manifest themselves, these problems have assumed proportions that almost no human agency, no matter what its resources, can adequately handle. The police department with its limited capability and obscure function, is among the poorest equipped to do so. Allowing the problem to reach such proportions that police action is necessary is one way of 'solving' the problem; all eyes have turned on the police so that the problem becomes the police and the police become the problem.

At the most, the police can and should perform a temporary holding operation until other institutions attack such problems with an array of resources. Any attempt to reform the police department so that it may perform tasks properly is the responsibility of other societal institutions and is not only unlikely to be successful, but the result can only be loss of crucial time and the exacerbation of an already grave problem.

SINCE THE ABOVE WAS WRITTEN, the Daley organization has been under siege. The 1972 election saw a reform anti-Daley Democrat take the governorship of Illinois, and a Republican elected state's attorney. More important, President Nixon appointed a young, crusading United States District Attorney. For most of the years of the Daley reign political patronage, trade-offs where Republicans were office-holders, and control of the electoral machinery, protected the organizational rear from effective attack. Investigations by independent groups with limited resources resulted in charges of corruption. Such charges were quickly denied by the mayor, labelled political and soon blurred by the levelling of other charges followed by further denials. Because all sources of prosecution were controlled by the mayor, trial of the charges could take place only in the newspapers. This lent credence to the mayor's claim that there was no substance to the complaints.

But beginning in 1973, the new district attorney obtained a series of indictments involving all aspects of the Daley machine, election workers charged with voting frauds, aldermen implicated in intricate land speculation deals, and finally scores of police engaged in shaking down tavern owners.

Another shock was the loss of the solid black vote. Until 1972, the black vote had been controlled by Daley workers. But that fall, the community split its vote, a mortal sin in the Daley catalogue of vice, voting for a reform anti-Daley Democrat for governor, and a Republican for state's attorney, bringing defeat to Daley's candidate. The incumbent state's attorney had defended a raid by his office that resulted in the death and wounding of a number of members of the Black Panthers, a black militant organization.

The raid was widely condemned in the black community. Black leaders within the Daley organization had to choose between the organization and the community. One such leader was a congressman, who had risen within the Daley organization. Nevertheless, he broke with Daley on the reslating of the aforementioned candidate for state's attorney and thereafter adopted the popular issue of police brutality to put distance between himself and his former ties to the organization.

In the fall of 1973, all of these factors coalesced. Combined with convictions of a police captain and eighteen others for the tavern shakedown, a series of studies showing a higher number of killings by Chicago police than by police in other cities, another establishing the ineffectiveness of the Police Board to take any policy-making stance although it had ample statutory powers, and finally recommendations by prestigious bar groups for an outside agency to investigate complaints against the police, calls came thick and heavy for the resignation of the superintendent of police, James B. Conlisk, Jr., and his replacement by an outsider, who would restructure the entire department.

In September, during the trial for the tavern shakedowns, which showed that such practices went back to 1966 under Wilson's tenure, Daley was asked why he didn't bring in a reform police superintendent. In a non-sequitur that demonstrated that the mayor still took the view that he and the department were separate entities, he replied, 'O. W. Wilson was running the department (then). I'm not a member of the department. Superintendent Conlisk is running it now'.

On October 6, the nineteen police officers were found guilty. Numerous others were under indictment. October 10, the mayor announced that Conlisk had resigned effective November 1 'for personal reasons' which had nothing to do with the scandal. Comment was in accord that there had never been a question of Conlisk's personal involvement in corruption (the same could be said for the mayor). What was involved was Conlisk's inability to do anything about it because of his twin loyalties to the mayor and the men in the department. His last act of loyalty was as sacrificial lamb.

For the reform forces, the issue now became how to take advantage of the momentum they had helped to gather. Could the mayor ride out the storm by merely changing one loyal police chief for another or would the mayor be forced to appoint a man from outside the department of such professional reputation that he would have the political independence to make the structural changes that reform forces felt necessary?

Various groups and individuals expressed the principle of search as follows: that a person should be selected of such a high reputation that he would be insulated from adverse political influence; that the mayor should give the superintendent a completely free hand; that it would be better to go outside the department so that restrictions on his ability to change the department would not be imposed by prior associations; that it was critical that he act independently of outside forces; that the candidate for the post have a five-year plan for the department and that he obtain from the mayor a commitment that he could implement it; that he be guaranteed reasonable decision-making powers and that he had the assurance that he could be removed only for serious cause after a public hearing by a disinterested body—echoes of Wickersham.

Mayor Daley called on the Police Board to recommend to him the three best men available inside or outside the department. On November 1, when Conlisk's resignation became effective, James Rocheford, deputy superintendent, a veteran of 26 years on the force, the son of a police officer who married the daughter of a police officer, replaced him. Rocheford stated that he hoped that his appointment would turn out to be permanent. This is an 'age of accountability', he said, and 'I pledge accountability to the public'.

Rocheford had been the man in charge of police handling of the 1968 Democratic Convention disturbances, and the compliments

313

the mayor paid him at the time he temporarily replaced Conlisk, told the Police Board that the mayor would not be disappointed if Rocheford just happened to be one of those recommended. Rocheford, a few days after his assumption of power, began to act as if he meant to stay. On November 9, he ordered 75 top commanders to take lie tests to prove their honesty. When questioned about this, Daley replied that the tests were Rocheford's idea and that he had a free hand to clean up the department. From another quarter came the voice of the Police Board which ordered the department to set up a new pyschological screening procedure for police officers. This is the first order ever issued by the Board. On December 3, the Board's president endorsed a report of a liberal group, proposing an expanded board representing the community, particularly minorities, and calling for the Board to use its statutory powers. The Board president endorsed the report and pledged that the Board would push to the limits its statutory authority.

No one was surprised in February when the Police Board made its required three recommendations to the mayor, followed in a few hours by the mayor's announcement of Rocheford's appointment as police superintendent.

The strategy of the mayor became clear. It was to maintain one of the faithful, Rocheford, as chief, but to allow him to reorganize the department and make changes that would both allow Rocheford to consolidate his own power (just as Wilson had done) and to satisfy or at least neutralize police attackers. Almost complete victory of the machine in the March primary indicates that Daley's political power is almost untouched by the scandals.

A more subtle strategy is that attached to the likely changes in the Police Board. If liberal groups get what they want, the Board will be expanded to include minority representation (blacks and Latins) and will exercise more power. Why should Daley allow this? In other words, how can such a change help rather than hinder him in his main objective to maintain political control? The mayor may very well have reasoned as follows: It is unlikely that problems such as police corruption and brutality will disappear. Once the Board is seen to represent minorities, the place to complain will be at Board meetings rather than at City Hall. Moreover, if the Board is augmented by members of community or minority groups, it is likely that there will be divisions among themselves about who should be represented and in what proportion, whether those on the Board are pressing the right reforms or are sufficiently militant. While these groups no doubt believe that by sharing control of the police they are sharing power, what, in reality, they will be sharing, if not incurring entirely, is responsibility. One may presume, consistent with this logic, that one reason the mayor created the Police Board was for it to act as a buffer between himself and responsibility for police behaviour in case the myth of independence should prove insufficient. Thus, the mayor can live very comfortably with an expanded Police Board.

It is very questionable, in fact, whether the police are any longer necessary or even useful to the Daley organization. At the beginning, the police were the enforcers that saw that recalcitrants stayed in line. But today, the organization depends not on the police but on patronage, diverse opportunities for special favours to the faithful, and an intricate series of accommodations to potential opposition groups. That the police are no longer of importance in this way is seen in the changed nature of corruption. While originally corruption of the police functioned to bring large amounts of money into the party treasury corruption today is largely unconnected with the needs of the party. The police are in business for themselves.

At this juncture, the political function of the police is to keep non-participating groups (minorities, radical students, the organized poor) from getting out of hand. This has been its historical role for the governing élite. Whether activities of the non-participating groups consist of unorganized crime, organized crime, or violent protest, it is understood by Daley and anti-Daley forces alike that the police are to control such unlawful action. If one non-participating group (those on the Police Board) can be manipulated to control another non-participating group, so much the better.

It was stated earlier that the mayor found it useful to evade reponsibility for police misconduct by the simple device of encouraging the idea that the police department is independent of his control, and that such lack of control is healthy for the body politic. The demands by liberal groups for a superintendent 'independent' from city hall show that both sides accept the same premise, forgetting the wise counsel of Bruce Smith, author of *Chicago Police Problems*:

> The mayor of Chicago, and he alone, can dictate the kind and quality of police administration which the city shall receive . . . the voters of the city are confronted not with a police problem alone, but with the even larger problem of civic control.[126]

[126] For the full quotation see p.

Police Professionalism and the War Against Crime in the United States, 1920s-30s

Nathan Douthit

Since the late 1960s a number of studies of policing in the United States have appeared investigating major dilemmas of police professionalism.[1] These studies have been largely the work of sociologists and political scientists. As a result they have explained the dilemmas of police professionalism almost entirely in terms of the interrelationships between police and other parts of the criminal justice system, sub-cultures within society, law and the police bureaucracy itself. They have given little or no attention to the historical roots of police professionalism.

In this paper I would like to examine some of the influences on police thought in the 1920s and 1930s which helped to define police professionalism as we know it today. Although it is impossible to discuss here the record of progress in police professionalism in the 1920s and 1930s, it was during this period that the character of police professionalism in the United States took shape. Therefore the influences on police thought from outside in these years were critically important. Despite the existence of currents of thought in policing concerned with prevention of crime and social conflict, these outside influences channelled police professionalism in the primary direction of crime control.

IN THE SPRING OF 1919, newspapers in many parts of the United States reported crime waves.[2] Two years later, conditions seemed

---

[1] Jerome H. Skolnick, *Justice Without Trial: Law Enforcement in Democratic Society* (New York 1966); David J. Bordua (ed.), *The Police: Six Sociological Essays* (New York 1967); Arthur Niederhoffer, *Behind the Shield: The Police in Urban Society* (Garden City, N.Y. 1967); James Q. Wilson, *Varieties of Police Behaviour: The Management of Law and Order in Eight Communities* (Cambridge, Mass. 1968); Albert J. Reiss, Jr., *The Police and the Public* (New Haven and London 1971).

[2] 'Crime, "Crime Waves," Criminals, and the Police', *Literary Digest* LX (8 March 1919), 62.

as bad if not worse. A major newspaper reported that 'in the centres of population no man walks with absolute safety by day or night'.[3] Other newspapers expressed similar fears. Even Raymond Fosdick, whose studies of European and American police systems made him a respected authority, agreed that the country seemed to be experiencing a series of post-war crime waves of serious proportions.[4] It made little difference that, as another writer noted, the crime wave was world-wide in scope; it made America's crime wave no less serious and no less demanding of forceful action.[5]

As a result of what appeared to be an increasing threat of crime, numerous crime commissions were established and crime surveys undertaken in the 1920s and 1930s. They investigated the entire field of criminal justice, looking into the performance and interrelationships of police, prosecution and courts, and correctional agencies and institutions. They influenced policing in three major ways. First, they encouraged a climate of attitudes and ideas emphasizing crime control as the primary function of police forces and giving rise to a 'war against crime'. Second, they encouraged the use of the concept of efficiency as the principal criterion for the evalution of police policies and practice, the same criterion by which other parts of the criminal justice system came to be evaluated. Third, they emphasized the need for state and national co-ordination and leadership in the struggle against crime.

Beginning with the Chicago Crime Commission in 1919 and continuing through the 1930s, crime commissions were established or crime surveys conducted in some twenty-four states.[6] In addition there were two national commissions: the National Crime Commission (1925) and the National Commission on Law Observance

[3] 'How to Fight the Forces of Crime', *Literary Digest* LXVIII (1 January 1921), 7.

[4] Raymond Fosdick, 'The Crime Wave in America', *New Republic* XXVI (6 April 1921), 150–52.

[5] Joseph Gollomb, 'Meeting the Crime Wave; A Comparison of Methods', *Nation* CXII (19 January 1921), 80–83.

[6] John Pfiffner, 'The Activities and Results of Crime Surveys', *American Political Science Review* XXIII (November 1929), 930–55; Virgil W. Peterson, *Crime Commissions in the United States* (Chicago 1945); Edwin H. Sutherland and C. E. Gehlke, 'Crime and Punishment', in President's Research Committee on Social Trends, *Recent Social Trends in the United States* (New York and London 1933), vol. II, 1147; Esther Conner, 'Crime Commissions and Criminal Procedure in the United States Since 1920; A Bibliography, January, 1920–June, 1927', *Journal of Criminal Law and Criminology* (hereafter referred to as *JCL&C*) XXI (May 1930), 129–44; A. F. Kuhlman, *Guide to Materials on Crime and Criminal Justice* (New York 1929).

and Enforcement (also called the Wickersham Commission, 1929). The importance of most of the commissions and surveys was limited to their respective states or municipalities.[7] However, the crime surveys in Cleveland, Ohio, Missouri and Illinois, and the reports of the New York Crime Commission, constituted major contributions to the growing body of knowledge about crime in American society.[8]

The concept of a 'war against crime' did not make its appearance in any major way until Mark O. Prentiss, a businessman with a background in journalism and social work, who played a major role in the formation of the National Crime Commission, wrote an article on the newly formed commission in 1925 entitled 'War on the Growing Menace of Crime'.[9] But the attitudes which the concept came to represent were held by the men who organized the first crime commission in Chicago in 1919; they were also present in the Committee on Law Enforcement of the American Bar Association's report of 1922, as well as in numerous articles on crime which appeared in the early 1920s.[10]

The Chicago Crime Commission grew out of a concern over a series of bank hold-ups and payroll robberies in 1917.[11] A Committee on Prevalence and Prevention of Crime, composed of leading citizens, was appointed by the Chicago Association of Commerce. This committee recommended the creation of a permanent crime commision, which finally began work in January 1919.[12] The commission consisted of over one hundred men in the fields of banking, business and the professions, mainly law.[13] The commission hired a staff of investigators, statisticians and office workers to support the work of the professional volunteers.[14]

The commission believed that crime could be reduced by increasing the chances of the criminal being caught and by swift and certain punishment following his apprehension.[15] The crimes that

[7] Pfiffner, op. cit.

[8] Ibid.

[9] Mark O. Prentiss, 'War on the Growing Menace of Crime', *Current Opinion* XXIII (October 1925), 1–8.

[10] See earlier footnotes on 'crime waves'.

[11] Henry Barrett Chamberlin, 'The Chicago Crime Commission—How The Businessmen of Chicago are Fighting Crime', *JCL&C* XI (November 1920), 386–97; Edwin W. Sims, 'Fighting Crime in Chicago', *JCL&C* XI (May 1920), 21–28; Peterson, *Crime Commissions in the United States*.

[12] Chamberlin, op. cit., 387.

[13] Ibid., 388.

[14] Ibid.

[15] Sims, op. cit., 27.

most concerned the commission were burglary, robbery and larceny. The commission estimated that crimes of this nature cost Chicago businesses in excess of $12 million each year. As a consequence, Chicago burglary insurance rates were the highest in the country.[16] As a first step toward their goal of reducing crime in these areas, the commission proposed legislation to create a State Bureau of Criminal Records. When this was defeated, the commission set up its own records file.[17] The records system was of major importance, because without it the commission could not keep check, with any accuracy, on the performance of the police. The commission sought to eliminate police arguments that they lacked a way to make positive identification of persons believed to have committed crimes.[18]

Behind the commission's insistence on the need to improve drastically the system by which criminals were apprehended, tried, convicted and punished lay a belief that the criminal enjoyed too many advantages. Edwin M. Simons, President of the commission, wrote in 1920:

> We have for years agitated for improving conditions in the jails. Suppose we pause and spend some time and energy in providing safety for the law-abiding citizen and the property he has acquired by honest toil. We have kept on providing for criminals flowers, libraries, athletics, and hot and cold running water, social visiting organizations, probation, paroles, pardons, and a lot of things, until what was previously intended as punishment is no longer punishment . . . If we are going to make Chicago a safe place to live in, one of the things we must do is to provide punishment that punishes, instead of giving criminals a vacation in institutions where they have a better living than if they were free.[19]

Simon's remark perhaps reflects a somewhat harder line towards criminal rehabilitation programmes than the commission actually took. The Operating Director of the Commission, Harry Barrett Chamberlin, for instance, commented in an article a few months later that one of the important accomplishments of the commission to date was its investigation of probation and parole which resulted in the finding that complaints of 'laxity' in probation and parole actually applied only to probation.[20]

However, rehabilitative innovations in the administration of

[16] Chamberlin, op. cit., 391.
[17] Ibid., 389.
[18] Ibid., 391.
[19] Sims, op. cit., 27–28.
[20] Chamberlin, op. cit., 395–96.

criminal justice came under strong attack in the 1920s.[21] In general, the crime commissions tried to limit the discretion of court and correctional personnel in the administration of indeterminate sentences, probation and parole.[22] Police officials at the annual meeting of the International Association of Chiefs of Police (IACP) in 1922 passed two resolutions against rehabilitational programmes. They recommended the adoption of uniform laws requiring determinate rather than indeterminate sentences and the consent of the prosecuting attorney and presiding judge of the court in which an offender had been convicted before the granting of parole.[23]

Although this attitude toward criminal rehabilitation emerged at a time of changing crime conditions, it also came after a period of expansion in rehabilitational programmes. In 1900, only six states had adopted probation as an administrative tool of criminal justice, whereas by 1915 some thirty-three states had.[24] Parole laws had been passed in twelve states before 1900; but by 1920 some forty states had them.[25] Similarly, in 1900 there were only five states with indeterminate sentence laws (allowing for administrative determination of a sentence by correctional authorities subject to certain minimum and maximum limits set by law). Twenty years later, thirty-seven states had indeterminate sentence laws.[26]

As the problem of robberies increased in the first part of the 1920s, bankers and businessmen in some Middle-Western states resorted to aggressive means of anti-crime action. The basis for concern was reflected in increased premiums for burglary insurance which rose from $1,377,000 in 1914 to $26,513,000 in 1924. Insurance losses increased from $508,000 in 1914 to $11,812,000 in 1924.[27] Iowa experienced fifty-six bank robberies in 1923, of which

[21] E. R. Cass, 'National Crime Commission Conference', *JCL&C* XVIII (February 1928), 497–513; Charles L. Chute, 'The Crime Wave and Probation *New Republic* XXVI (6 April 1921), 150–52: Robert D. Highfill, 'The Effects of News of Crime and Scandal upon Public Opinion', *American Law Review* LXII (January–February 1928), 13–93.

[22] See Pfiffner, op. cit.; and Sutherland and Gehlke, op. cit.

[23] International Association of Chiefs of Police (hereafter referred to as IACP) Proceedings, 1922, 53.

[24] Sutherland and Gehlke, 'Crime and Punishment', 1155–56.

[25] Ibid., 1157–58.

[26] Ibid., 1157.

[27] Frederick L. Hoffman, 'The Increase in Murder', *Annals of the American Academy of Political and Social Science* (hereafter referred to as *Annals*), CXXV (May 1926), 21.

twenty-six were successful; losses totalled $258,000.[28] Illinois had seventy-three bank hold-ups in 1924. In both states, vigilante committees organized under the direction of bankers' associations.[29] In Iowa, 4,200 men were deputized. A year later, the total number of bank robberies in Iowa had been reduced to eight, of which only three were successful.[30] Bankers' councils in Illinois deputized some 3,200 men and furnished them with 1,800 sawn-off shotguns, 1,400 rifles and plenty of ammunition.[31] The number of robberies was reduced from seventy-three in 1924 to fifteen in 1927, and losses from $347,945 to $15,000 in the same period.[32] The Federal Bureau of Investigation made its reputation in the 1930s tracking down some of the more daring of the bank robbers.[33] From the point of view of the banking interests in the Mid-West, the decrease in bank robberies resulting from such vigilante action demonstrated that in fact criminals could be deterred by fear.[34]

However, it would be mistaken to assume that all businessmen shared the same attitude towards crime. The Boston Chamber of Commerce, for instance, in a report to its Committee on Municipal and Metropolitan Affairs, 1 March 1926, expressed strong opposition to proposed legislation that would increase penalties for certain crimes, The Chamber's committee declared that 'improvement should be sought in better administration rather than additional and more rigid law'.[35]

The Committee on Law Enforcement of the American Bar Association in its report of 1922 also reflected impatience with what was considered to be lax treatment of criminals. The committee charged that 'the prevalence of the abnormal volume of crime in our larger cities is the result of years of molly coddling and sympathy by misinformed and ill-advised meddlers'.[36] The com-

[28] US National Crime Commision, *A Full Report of the Proceedings of the National Conference on the Reduction of Crime Called by the National Crime Commission* (23 November 1927), 21–24.

[29] Bruce Smith, 'Rural Police Protection', in Illinois Association for Criminal Justice, *The Illinois Crime Survey* (Chicago 1929), 342.

[30] US National Crime Commission, op. cit.

[31] Ibid.

[32] Smith, op. cit., 342.

[33] Jack Alexander, 'Profiles; The Director-I', *New Yorker* XIII (25 September 1937), 20–25.

[34] US National Crime Commission, op. cit.

[35] 'Facing the Problem of Crime; A Report of the Committee on Municipal and Metropolitan Affairs of the Boston Chamber of Commerce, March 1 1926', *Massachusetts Law Quarterly* XI (May 1926), 9.

[36] American Bar Association, Committee on Lawless Enforcement of Law, 'For a Better Enforcement of the Law', 589.

mittee made special note of the fact that Canada, with far lower crime rates, had more severe criminal penalties. 'In fact', the committee commented, 'the theory there seems to involve protection to the public, with only a secondary concern for the criminal'.[37] First on the committee's list of recommendations was restriction in the use of probation, parole and the indeterminate sentence.[38]

President Coolidge announced the appointment of a National Crime Commission in 1925. However weak the National Crime Commission—really little more than a committee of men with national reputations—its existence marked the beginning of a new interest in crime at the national level of government. A 'war on crime', as Mark O. Prentiss one of the organizers of the commission described the objective of the organization, meant that the 'crime problem' had now been recognized as a problem the federal government would act upon.[39] Of course, the federal government had always had criminal jurisdiction; and in recent years numerous federal agencies had taken on law enforcement functions.[40] But these law enforcement functions had been very specific, undertaken on the understanding that these were unarguably federal in nature (e.g. enforcement of customs laws) or that they were beyond the control of the state (e.g. 'white slave' traffic).[41] What were the implications of this new, and much broader commitment?

The National Crime Commission accomplished very little during its four years of existence. However, it did hold a National Crime Conference in 1927 which served to bring together representatives of state and municipal agencies throughout the country. A critic of the commission, John H. Wigmore, Dean of Northwestern University Law School, had questioned how much a national commission could do without working through the states.[42] He had also pointed to the striking absence on the commission of any representatives from such fields as sociology, psychiatry, social work, corrections, statistics and criminal justice administration.[43] The commission apparently took this line of criticism to heart.

[37] Ibid.
[38] Ibid., 591.
[39] Prentiss, op. cit.
[40] See J. Edgar Hoover, 'Some Legal Aspects of Interstate Crime', *Minnesota Law Review* XXI (February 1937), 229–62.
[41] Ibid.
[42] John H. Wigmore, 'The National Crime Commission: What Will It Achieve?' *JCL&C* XVI (November 1925), 314–15.
[43] Ibid., 313.

The 1927 conference was attended by representatives of some twenty-six crime commissions and over fifty other organizations in the crime field.[44] The commission explicitly stated that its aim was to encourage the organization of state and local crime commissions. Although many of the groups represented at the conference had existed prior to the commission, the commission no doubt stimulated their growth to some degree.[45]

The significance of the National Crime Commission, however, lies not so much in what it accomplished as in the federal sanction it gave to the anti-crime movement. The reports of state and municipal crime commissions presented at the conference, as described by E. R. Cass, President of the American Prison Association, stressed the need to increase penalties, tighten criminal court procedure, and discard probation, parole and the indeterminate sentence. Cass reported that 'these systems were frequently advanced as the "cause-all" of the crime situation'.[46] In general, Cass noted, 'a return to good, old-fashioned hard justice was something of a keynote'.[47] Although later sessions of the conference heard papers by experts in criminology and penology, the general tone of the conference was reflected in the attitudes of the crime commission representatives.

By the late 1930s, the attitudes toward crime which the members of the various state crime commissions brought to their task was reflected in a vast body of criminal legislation. A statement on legislation prepared for the National Crime Commission Conference reported that 2,761 amendments to penal codes had been introduced in forty-two states. Of these 587 had been passed.[48] The criminologist, E.H. Sutherland, commented in 1927 that 'within the last decade the development of policies of dealing with the problem of crime has to some extent been turned from the trend of the preceding years'.[49] Six years later, when he and C. E. Gehlke surveyed crime and punishment for the President's Research Committee on Recent Social Trends, they found that approximately 68.9 per cent of the criminal penalties altered since 1900 in the penal codes of eight states had been made more severe.[50] In general, they noted a

[44] Cass, op. cit., 497.
[45] Ibid., 497–98.
[46] Ibid., 498.
[47] Ibid., 499.
[48] Ibid., 498.
[49] E. H. Sutherland, 'Criminology, Public Opinion, and the Law', in *Proceedings of the National Conference of Social Work 1927*, 168–69.
[50] Sutherland and Gehlke, op. cit., 1159.

trend in the period from 1917 to 1927 towards more severe penalties, longer prison sentences, increased use of the death penalty, and more opposition to the trend towards humane treatment of the criminal (probation, parole, the indeterminate sentence, as well as improvements in the conditions of prison life).[51]

Although the National Crime Commission Conference of 1927 provided a forum for the punitive approach to crime represented by the conclusions of state crime commissions and state criminal legislation, it did not result in a very strong commitment by the federal government to the 'war against crime'. In 1929, President Herbert Hoover created the National Commission on Law Observance and Enforcement (also called the Wickersham Commission). This commission was appointed to investigate the enforcement of prohibition laws. To fulfil this responsibility it decided to conduct a broad-scale study of crime and criminal justice in America. To this end, the commission, with the help of staffs of experts in various fields, published fourteen separate reports.[52]

One important study of the Wickersham Commission, its *Report on Lawlessness in Law Enforcement,* actually constituted a major attack on the 'war against crime'.[53] It also provided the best evidence available of the consequences of 'war against crime' attitudes. The *Report on Lawlessness in Law Enforcement* was a survey of police illegality in the arrest, interrogation and detention of criminals. It represented the culmination of a revived interest in the 1920s in the so-called 'third degree'.

Despite the Wickersham Commission's report on lawlessness in law enforcement, however, the rhetoric of a 'war against crime' grew stronger in the 1930s. Justin Miller, professor of law and chairman of the American Bar Association's section on Criminal Law and Criminology, pointed out that contrary to the intention of the Wickersham Commission some people took its reports as evidence of the need for vigilante action.[54] In 1931, wide publicity was given to Major General Smedley Butler's plan for the organization of state police forces along strict military lines,

[51] Ibid.
[52] US National Commission on Law Observance and Enforcement, *Reports,* 14 vols (Washington, DC 1931).
[53] US National Commission on Law Observance and Enforcement, *Report on Lawlessness in Law Enforcement* (Washington, DC 1931).
[54] 'Chairman Miller Comments on Reports of Wickersham Commission', *American Bar Association Journal* XVII (November 1931), 754.

with four-year enlistments, an army table of organization and barracks life, for the purpose of hunting down criminals.[55] Butler told a New Jersey audience that he thought the best way to control crime was to shoot criminals on sight and make jails unbearable.[56] In early 1935, the recently elected mayor of New York City, Fiorello La Guardia, declared at the annual ball of the Patrolmen's Benevolent Association, 'Mr New Yorker and Mrs New Yorker, this is no time for sentimentality; this is no time for coddling crooks. I have been in office but one year, and since that time, together with Police Commissioner Valentine, I have attended funeral after funeral of our brave police officers, I say this: The war is on!'[57] Speeches by J. Edgar Hoover, director of the Federal Bureau of Investigation, warned Americans that they confronted an 'actual armed invasion of America'.[58]

To the extent that the 'war against crime' involved enforcement of Prohibition, however, the police and other law enforcement authorities encountered strong opposition. The Wickersham Commission in its report on enforcement of the Prohibition laws noted that public opinion in many parts of the country 'presents a serious obstacle to the observance and enforcement of the national Prohibition laws'.[59] A number of writers in the early 1930s commented on the fact that certain types of criminals had become popular heroes. One writer concerned with the attitudes of children declared that 'one can say with as much assurance as one quotes the multiplication table that gangsters are heroes to today's children'.[60]

By the mid-1930s, the tendency to romanticize daring acts of crime by single individuals or small gangs had become less evident. In 1936, O. W. Wilson reported in the *Municipal Year Book*:

[55] Smedley D. Butler, 'Making War on the Gangs: A Plan to Take the Police Out of Politics', *Forum* LXXXV (March 1931), 134–41.

[56] Hopkins, 'Glorifying the Police', *Forum* LXXXVII (March 1932), 154.

[57] '22,000 Attend P.B.A. Ball', *Spring 3100* V (February 1935), 9.

[58] J. Edgar Hoover, 'The Influence of Crime on the American Home', 11 March 1936 and 'Patriotism and the War Against Crime', 23 April 1936.

[59] US National Commission on Law Observance and Enforcement, *Enforcement of the Prohibition Laws*, 99; see also Hopkins, 'The Lawless Arm of the Law', *Atlantic* CXXXVIII (August 1926), 62–67.

[60] Zelda F. Popkin, 'Children of the Racketeer Age', *Harper's* CLXVI (February 1933), 368.

The Hauptmann trial [for kidnapping] marked the climax of the swing of public opinion in favour of law enforcement. This change in public opinion in this country has been so obvious as to be apparent to the most casual. It was induced in large measure by the action of public-spirited citizens who were conscious that the crime problem of this country could not be solved without the complete backing of the public. A committee of the International Association of Chiefs of Police appointed to confer with the Motion Picture Producers and Distributers of America brought about a definite change in the sentiment induced by the movies. Gangster pictures, with sentiment definitely in favour of the criminal, were replaced by 'G' men pictures which induced the public to applaud the efforts of the police. As a result, audiences which once applauded when a police officer was killed now applaud when the gangster is brought to justice.[61]

A CHANGE IN THE ROLE OF THE FEDERAL GOVERNMENT in the 'war against crime' from one of encouragement to one of active leadership came in 1934. President Roosevelt, who had been a charter member of the National Crime Commission, showed an interest in the problem of crime and law enforcement even at a time when economic problems of the nation were uppermost.[62] At a federal government sponsored conference on crime in December 1934 (known as the Attorney-General's Conference on Crime), Homer Cummings, the new attorney-general, remarked,

The whole movement against crime, in any national sense, has been sporadic, intermittent, disjointed, and totally lacking in correlation. With an amazing development in recent years of crimes and violence, perpetrated by criminals of a roving character who pass rapidly from the scene of their crime into other jurisdictions, there has been presented in a very acute form, the question of the duty of the Federal Government.[63]

Although federal legislation in the crime field preceded the Attorney-General's Conference on Crime, it was nevertheless of major importance, both in a practical and symbolic way, in launching a federal crime control programme.[64] The conference represented a serious effort to bring together representatives of diverse points of view on the crime problem. The attorney-general

[61] O. W. Wilson, 'Police Administration', in *Municipal Year Book, 1936*, 81–82.
[62] Franklin D. Roosevelt, 'An Address', in US Department of Justice, *Attorney-General's Conference on Crime*, 17–20.
[63] Cummings, 'Lesson of the Crime Conference', ibid., 457.
[64] Newman F. Baker, 'The Attorney-General's Conference on Crime', *JCL&C* XXV (January–February 1935), 692–94.

took special pains to request that the participants, despite their differences, approach the conference with an open mind.[65] The topics presented at the conference covered many areas of crime and criminal justice. President Roosevelt made a particularly balanced plea for action 'starting with crime prevention itself and carrying this common action all the way through to prosecution and punishment'.[66] But despite the recognition given to the idea that the crime problem has many aspects and that many approaches to the crime problem must be taken, the 'war against crime 'outlook received strong reinforcement.

In his forward to the published proceedings, Attorney-General Cummings explained that he was publishing the proceedings 'to the end that we may go forward together in the great war against crime which we have solemnly declared and which it is our settled purpose to present with vigor and determination'.[67] In discussing the crime problem at the conference, he emphasized the immediate crime situation in which 'officers of the law are forced to engage in drawn battles on public highways, in railroad stations, and elsewhere, armed with the desperate implements of modern warfare'.[68] He went on to compare law enforcement officers to 'the soldiers and sailors who represent us in time of war'.[69] The topics presented, too, although wide-ranging, emphasized enforcement of laws against crime more than crime prevention.[70]

Attorney-General Cummings in the years that followed encouraged crime prevention and rehabilitation of criminals at the federal level; this too was considered part of the 'war against crime'.[71] And in 1938, he explained to Americans in a nationwide radio broadcast that in the future penal systems had to be based on the idea that 'They all come out'.[72] But the major effect of Attorney-

[65] Cummings, 'Opening Address', in US Department of Justice, *Attorney-General's Conference on Crime*, 4–5.

[66] Roosevelt, 'An Address', ibid., 18.

[67] US Department of Justice, *Attorney-General's Conference on Crime*, III.

[68] Cummings, op. cit., 7.

[69] Ibid.

[70] 'Topical Classification of the Addresses Delivered at the Attorney-General's Conference on Crime', *Attorney General's Conference on Crime*, xv–xvii.

[71] Sanford Bates, 'Protecting Society from Crime', in *Year Book of the National Probation Association, 1934*, 1; Justin Miller, 'The Attorney General's Program for Crime Control', in *Year Book of the National Probation Association, 1935*, 225–26. Cummings recommended creation of a Federal Bureau of Crime Prevention within the Department of Justice in 1935.

[72] Sanford Bates, 'Next Steps in Crime Control', in *Year Book of the National Probation Association, 1938*, 5, 6–8.

General Cummings's remarks at the 1934 conference was to further encourage the 'war against crime' approach, with its emphasis on the apprehension of criminals and severe punishment following conviction.[73]

The federal government's concern with the crime problem in the New Deal period centred on the most immediate and visible challenges of crime to the law. Although organized crime became of increasing concern to various persons, organizations and legislative committees in the late 1920s and early 1930s,[74] the federal government concentrated its efforts against notorious bank robbers and kidnappers.[75]

Following the stock market crash in 1929, a number of small, highly mobile, criminal gangs appeared in the Mid-West and South-west, specializing in bank robberies.[76] A rash of kidnappings also occurred at the same time. In 1931, 279 kidnappings were reported in 501 cities by police; law enforcement authorities managed to obtain only sixty-nine convictions.[77] These bank robberies and kidnappings provided the sensational news stories of the day.

In an effort to control kidnapping, Congress passed the Federal Kidnapping Act in 1932.[78] The Federal Kidnapping Act was followed by a number of important acts of criminal legislation in 1934, proposed by the Department of Justice in a twelve-point programme to the 73rd Congress.[79]

[73] Max Radin, 'Enemies of Society', *JCL&C* XXVII (September–October 1936), 328–56; N. S. Timasheff, 'The Retributive Structure of Punishment', *JCL&C* XXVIII (September–October 1937), 396–405; Hans Von Hentig, 'The Limits of Deterrence', *JCL&C* XXIX (November–December 1938), 556–61.

[74] Illinois Association for Criminal Justice, *Illinois Crime Survey*, 18–19; Henry Barrett Chamberlin, 'Some Observations Concerning Organized Crime', *JCL&C* XXII (January 1932), 652–70; John H. Wigmore, 'The National Menace of Organized Predatory Crime: How to Combat It', *JCL&C* XXXIII (January–February 1933), 734–35; US Senate Committee on Commerce, Subcommittee on S. Res. 74, *Crime and Crime Control* (Washington, DC 1933), 1–5.

[75] 'The Marines Are Coming', *Fortune* X (August 1934), 56–63.

[76] Ibid. See Robert S. and Helen Merrell Lynd, *Middletown in Transition: A Study in Cultural Conflicts* (New York 1937), 348, for a description of the effect bank robberies had on policing in local communities. Middletown began a 'Modern War School for Our Police'.

[77] Horace L. Bomar, Jr., 'The Lindbergh Law', *Law and Contemporary Problems* I (October 1934), 435.

[78] Ibid., 435–37.

[79] On federal legislation see Bomar, Jr., 'The Lindbergh Law' and Hoover, 'Some Legal Aspects . . .'; see also Homer Cummings, 'Progress Toward A Modern Administration of Criminal Justice in the United States', An Address Delivered at the Annual Meeting of the North Carolina Conference for Social Service, 27 April 1936, 5–6.

The most notable feature of this legislation at the time was that it provided a legal basis for federal action against certain notorious forms of crime. But it also followed the pattern of state criminal legislation by establishing severe penalties as a deterrent to crime, which were in sharp conflict with the growth of individualized sentencing and correctional treatment.[80]

Thus, by late 1934, when the Attorney-General's Conference on Crime took place, the federal government had already taken action in 'the war against crime'. J. Edgar Hoover reported to the conference on progress in law enforcement:

> John Dillinger, the flagbearer of lawlessness, is dead, killed by Federal bullets. 'Pretty Boy' Floyd, who for years laughed at the law —lies in his grave, dead of gunshot wounds inflicted in open battle by our special agents. The career of 'Baby Face' Nelson is over; he died of seventeen bullet wounds while two of the finest men I ever knew gave their own clean lives that they might serve society by ending his filthy one. Wilbur Underhill no longer carries the name of the Tri-State Terror. He too, is gone, as well as such men as Homer Van Meter, Tommy Carroll, and others. That is progress.[81]

Although federal action in the area of criminal legislation had met some initial resistance growing out of the fear of federal government control,[82] and even though federal representatives still felt it necessary to insist that the federal government had no intention of usurping the rights of the states in the crime field,[83] there was little opposition to federal involvement by later 1934.[84] One participant in the Attorney-General's Conference commented on what an 'amazing thing' it was to see state and local officials turn to the federal government for support when three years before they had been so resistant.[85]

[80] See earlier discussion of legislation resulting from the crime commissions and crime surveys; also Jerome Hall, 'Committee on Survey of Crime, Criminal Law and Criminal Procedure', *JCL&C* XXIX (November–December 1935), 576–77.

[81] Hoover, 'Detection and Apprehension', in US Department of Justice, *Attorney General's Conference on Crime*, 25.

[82] Bomar, Jr., op. cit., 435–37.

[83] Joseph B. Keenan, 'The Federal Government and the Crime Problem', in US Department of Justice, *Attorney General's Conference on Crime*, 332–40.

[84] However, for opposition see 'The Marines Are Coming'; Herbert Wechsler, 'A Caveat on Crime Control', *JCL&C* XXVII (January–February 1937), 629–37; and William Seagle, 'The National Police', *Harper's* CLXIX (November 1934), 751–61. August Vollmer, 'Police Administration', in *Municipal Year Book, 1934*, 77–79, discusses co-operation of local police with the federal law enforcement programme.

[85] US Department of Justice, *Attorney-General's Conference on Crime*, 341–42.

The federal role in law enforcement increased greatly in the 1930s.[86] This growth was reflected in the expansion of the FBI. It had a total staff of 772 in 1934 with budgetary appropriations of $3,002,348. By January 1941, its total staff numbered 4,370 (before its wartime expansion to 7,910 by January 1942) and had budgetary appropriations of $8,775,000 in 1940.[87] The federal emphasis upon enforcement as distinct from crime prevention and rehabilitation is reflected in the fact that federal probation officers numbered only 63 in 1932 and increased to only 239 by 1941.[88] The total personnel of all federal law enforcement agencies (in the US Justice, Treasury, Labour and Post Office departments) rose from 4,393 in 1929 to 17,000 in 1936.[89]

J. Edgar Hoover, his men, and the agency he directed, came to symbolize the federal government's role in the 'war against crime'.[90] Hoover repeated the theme of a 'war against crime' in numerous speeches throughout the 1930s.[91] With the rhetoric of an evangelist, he tried to awaken Americans to the sense of national purpose that had propelled them into action during the last war, he reminded members of Kiwanis International in June 1936:

> The memories of all of us, I am sure, are long enough to recall the stirring days of 1917 when America was plunged into the necessity of defending national honour. That was a defense of the home and the community. There were marching men and bands, and waving flags, and a coalition of every effort toward victory. Today, however, we find ourselves in the midst of another war in which we are threatened by a foe which outnumbers our armed forces two to one. Yet, there is no allied effort, no concentration of defence and often nothing but sheer apathy against this most desperate menace.[92]

---

[86] See Arthur C. Millspaugh, *Crime Control by the National Government* (Washington, DC 1937); David Fellman, 'Some Consequences of Increased Federal Activity in the Law Enforcement', *JCL&C* XXXV (May-June 1944), 16–33.

[87] Fellman, op. cit., 18.

[88] Ibid., 17.

[89] Sutherland and Gehlke, op. cit., 1139–40; Millspaugh, *Crime Control by the National Government*, 42, 283.

[90] O. W. Wilson, op. cit.; see also Wechsler' op. cit., 629.

[91] J. Edgar Hoover, 'The Influence of Crime on the American Home', 11 March 1936; 'Crime and the Citizen', 24 June 1936; 'Patriotism and the War Against Crime', 23 April 1936; 'The Enemy on Our Soil', 4 October 1937; 'Crime's Challenge to Society', 9 November 1937.

[92] Hoover, 'Crime and the Citizen'.

In trying to arouse Americans to action, Hoover returned again and again to a few major themes; he usually began by pointing to the great increase in crime, and the imminent danger to every American from criminal activity. 'Crime has reached a pinnacle of appalling heights', he declared. 'It lives next door to us. It rubs elbows with us. Its blood-caked hands touch ours . . . No American home is free of this shadow. . . . The American home and every person in it is today in a state of siege.'[93] He described the danger in military terms: 'This army of crime is larger than any unified force in history. If this tremendous body of evil-doers could be welded into a unit of conquest, America would fall before it not in a month, not in a day, but in a few hours'.[94] Hoover feared that America was too sentimental, too 'peace loving'. 'Because we are a peace loving nation', Hoover explained, 'we should be a fighting nation, ever belligerent in the cause of happiness and contentment and security.'[95]

Despite his rhetoric, and his occasional measurement of 'progress' in terms of the number of criminals killed, Hoover noted in 1937 that the FBI had killed only nine men seeking to escape arrest in the last three years. During that same time, he pointed out, municipal police officers had killed 1,200.[96] But he directed his rhetoric to the police as well as the general public. In a speech before the IACP in 1935, he remarked, 'Here, at this meeting, a criminal is understood to be a criminal, with a gun in his hand and murder in his heart. It is not necessary here, in discussing what shall be done with that human rat, to persuade some altruistic soul that he is not a victim of environment or circumstances or inhibitions of malformed consciousness, to be reformed by a few kind words, a pat on the cheek, and freedom at the earliest possible moment'.[97]

J. Edgar Hoover, the evangelist against crime, was also a symbol of police professionalism. No police official was held in higher esteem by the newly emerging cadre of police professionals.[98] The Hoover who declared that he preferred to be considered a member

[93] Hoover, 'The Influence of Crime on the American Home', 1.
[94] Hoover, 'Patriotism and the War Against Crime', 2.
[95] Hoover, 'Problems in Modern Law Enforcement', 2.
[96] IACP, *Year Book, 1936–37*, 16.
[97] IACP, *Proceedings, 1935*, 65–74.
[98] See August Vollmer to J. Edgar Hoover, 24 August 1934, Vollmer MSS, Bancroft Library, University of California, Berkeley.

of the so-called 'machine-gun school of criminology', rather than the 'cream-puff school of criminology',[99] also insisted time and again on the need for police to be trained and equipped to fight crime in the most scientific manner. It was Hoover who proudly pointed to his agency's record of convictions without resort to the 'third-degree'.[100] Hoover's thought and action reflects the degree to which ideas of police professionalism became associated in the 1920s and 1930s with attitudes centered on the 'war against crime'.

[99] Hoover, 'Crime's Challenge to Society', 4.
[100] Hoover, 'Problems of Law Enforcement'.